PHILOSOPHICAL FAITH AND REVELATION

RELIGIOUS PERSPECTIVES

Planned and Edited by

RUTH NANDA ANSHEN

———

RELIGIOUS PERSPECTIVES · VOLUME EIGHTEEN

PHILOSOPHICAL FAITH AND REVELATION

by Karl Jaspers

Translated by E. B. Ashton

HARPER & ROW, PUBLISHERS

NEW YORK

Originally published by R. Piper & Co. Verlag, München under the title 'Der philosophische Glaube angesichts der Offenbarung', copyright © by R. Piper & Co. Verlag, 1962.

English translation by E. B. Ashton

LIBRARY OF CONGRESS CATALOG CARD NUMBER: 67-14944

CONTENTS

RELIGIOUS PERSPECTIVES

RELIGIOUS PERSPECTIVES

Its Meaning and Purpose

RELIGIOUS PERSPECTIVES represents a quest for the rediscovery of man. It constitutes an effort to define man's search for the essence of being in order that he may have a knowledge of goals. It is an endeavor to show that there is no possibility of achieving an understanding of man's total nature on the basis of phenomena known by the analytical method alone. It hopes to point to the false antinomy between revelation and reason, faith and knowledge, grace and nature, courage and anxiety. Mathematics, physics, philosophy, biology, and religion, in spite of their almost complete independence, have begun to sense their interrelatedness and to become aware of that mode of cognition which teaches that "the light is not without but within me, and I myself am the light."

Modern man is threatened by a world created by himself. He is faced with the conversion of mind to naturalism, a dogmatic secularism and an opposition to a belief in the transcendent. He begins to see, however, that the universe is given not as one existing and one perceived but as the unity of subject and object; that the barrier between them cannot be said to have been dissolved as the result of recent experience in the physical sciences, since this barrier has never existed. Confronted with the question of meaning, he is summoned to rediscover and scrutinize the immutable and the permanent which constitute the dynamic, unifying aspect of life as well as the principle of differentiation; to reconcile identity and diversity, immutability and unrest. He begins to recognize that just as every person descends by his particular path, so he is able to ascend, and this ascent aims at a return to the source of creation, an inward home from which he has become estranged.

It is the hope of RELIGIOUS PERSPECTIVES that the rediscovery of man will point the way to the rediscovery of God. To this end a rediscovery of first principles should constitute part of the quest. These principles, not to be superseded by new discoveries, are not those of historical worlds that come to be and perish. They are to be sought in the heart and spirit of man, and no interpretation of a merely historical or scientific universe can guide the search. RELIGIOUS PERSPECTIVES attempts not only to ask dispassionately what the nature of God is, but also to restore to human life at least the hypothesis of God and the symbols that relate to him. It endeavors to show that man is faced with the metaphysical question of the truth of religion while he encounters the empirical question of its effects on the life of humanity and its meaning for society. Religion is here distinguished from theology and its doctrinal forms and is intended to denote the feelings, aspirations, and acts of men, as they relate to total reality. For we are all in search of reality, of a reality which is there whether we know it or not; and the search is of our own making but reality is not.

RELIGIOUS PERSPECTIVES is nourished by the spiritual and intellectual energy of world thought, by those religious and ethical leaders who are not merely spectators but scholars deeply involved in the critical problems common to all religions. These thinkers recognize that human morality and human ideals thrive only when set in a context of a transcendent attitude toward religion and that by pointing to the ground of identity and the common nature of being in the religious experience of man, the essential nature of religion may be defined. Thus, they are committed to reevaluate the meaning of everlastingness, an experience which has been lost and which is the content of that *visio Dei* constituting the structure of all religions. It is the many absorbed everlastingly into the ultimate unity, a unity subsuming what Whitehead calls the fluency of God and the everlastingness of passing experience.

These volumes seek to show that the unity of which we speak consists in a certitude emanating from the nature of man who seeks God and the nature of God who seeks man. Such certitude bathes in an intuitive act of cognition, participating in the divine essence and is related to the natural spirituality of intelligence. This is not by any means to say that there is an equivalence of all faiths in the traditional religions of human history. It is, however, to emphasize the distinction between the spiritual and the temporal which all religions acknowledge. For duration of thought is composed of instants superior to time, and is an intuition of the permanence of existence and its metahistorical reality. In fact, the symbol[1] itself found on cover and jacket of each volume of RELIGIOUS PERSPECTIVES is the visible sign or representation of the essence, immediacy, and timelessness of religious experience; the one immutable center, which may be analogically related to Being in pure act, moving with centrifugal and ecumenical necessity outward into the manifold modes, yet simultaneously, with dynamic centripetal

[1] From the original design by Leo Katz.

power and with full intentional energy, returning to the source. Through the very diversity of its authors, the Series shows that the basic and poignant concern of every faith is to point to, and overcome, the crisis in our apocalyptic epoch—the crisis of man's separation from man and of man's separation from God—the failure of love. The authors endeavor, moreover, to illustrate the truth that the human heart is able, and even yearns, to go to the very lengths of God; that the darkness and cold, the frozen spiritual misery of recent time, are breaking, cracking, and beginning to move, yielding to efforts to overcome spiritual muteness and moral paralysis. In this way, it is hoped, the immediacy of pain and sorrow, the primacy of tragedy and suffering in human life, may be transmuted into a spiritual and moral triumph. For the uniqueness of man lies in his capacity for self-transcendence.

RELIGIOUS PERSPECTIVES is therefore an effort to explore the *meaning* of God, an exploration which constitutes an aspect of man's intrinsic nature, part of his ontological substance. The Series grows out of an abiding concern that in spite of the release of man's creative energy which science has in part accomplished, this very science has overturned the essential order of nature. Shrewd as man's calculations have become concerning his means, his choice of ends which was formerly correlated with belief in God, with absolute criteria of conduct, has become witless. God is not to be treated as an exception to metaphysical principles, invoked to prevent their collapse. He is rather their chief exemplification, the source of all potentiality. The personal reality of freedom and providence, of will and conscience, may demonstrate that "he who knows" commands a depth of consciousness inaccessible to the profane man, and is capable of that transfiguration which prevents the twisting of all good to ignominy. This religious content of experience is not within the province of science to bestow; it corrects the error of treating the scientific account as if it were itself metaphysical or religious; it challenges the tendency to make a religion of science—or a science of religion—a dogmatic act which destroys the moral dynamic of man. Indeed, many men of science are confronted with unexpected implications of their own thought and are beginning to accept, for instance, the trans-spatial and trans-temporal dimension in the nature of reality.

RELIGIOUS PERSPECTIVES attempts to show the fallacy of the apparent irrelevance of God in history. The Serious submits that no convincing image of man can arise, in spite of the many ways in which human thought has tried to reach it, without a philosophy of human nature and human freedom which does not exclude God. This image of *Homo cum Deo* implies the highest conceivable freedom, the freedom to step into the very fabric of the universe, a new formula for man's collaboration with the creative process and the only one which is able to protect man from the terror of existence. This image implies further that the mind and conscience are capable of making genuine discriminations and thereby may reconcile the serious tensions between the secular and religious, the profane and sacred. The idea of the sacred lies in what it *is,* timeless existence. By emphasizing timeless existence against reason as a reality, we are liberated, in our communion with the eternal, from the otherwise unbreakable rule of "before and after." Then we are able to admit that all forms, all symbols in religions, by their negation of error and their affirmation of the actuality of truth, make it possible to experience that *knowing* which is above knowledge, and that dynamic passage of the universe to unending unity.

God is here interpreted not as a heteronomous being issuing commandments but as the *Tatt-Twam-Asi:* "Do unto others as you would have others do unto you. For I am the Lord." This does not mean a commandment from on high but rather a self-realization through "the other", since the isolated individual is unthinkable and meaningless. Man becomes man by recognizing his true nature as a creature capable of will and decision. For then the divine and the sacred become manifest. And though he believes in choices, he is no Utopian expecting the "coming of the kingdom." Man, individually and collectively, is losing the chains which have bound him to the inexorable demands of nature. The constraints are diminishing and an infinity of choices becomes available to him. Thus man himself, from the sources of his ontological being, at last must decide what is the *bonum et malum.* And though the anonymous forces which in the past have set the constraints do indeed threaten him with total anarchy and with perhaps a worse tyranny than he experienced in past history, he nevertheless begins to see that preceding the moral issue is the cognitive problem: the perception of those conditions for life which permit mankind to fulfill itself and to accept the truth that beyond scientific, discursive knowledge there is nondiscursive, intuitive awareness. And, I suggest, this is not to secularize God but rather to gather him into the heart of the nature of matter and indeed of life itself.

The volumes in this Series seek to challenge the crisis which separates, to make reasonable a religion that binds, and to present the numinous reality within the experience of man. Insofar as the Series succeeds in this quest, it will direct mankind toward a reality that is eternal and away from a preoccupation with that which is illusory and ephemeral.

For man is now confronted with his burden and his greatness: "He calleth to me, Watchman, what of the night? Watchman, what of the night?"[2] Perhaps the anguish in the human soul may be assuaged by the answer, by the *assimilation* of the person in God: "The morning cometh, and also the night: if ye will inquire, inquire ye: return, come."[3]

RUTH NANDA ANSHEN

[2] Isaiah 21:11.
[3] Isaiah 21:12.

PREFACE

Today the faculty of faith lies hidden in innumerable human beings. We have no prophets any more, to put this faith into appropriate words; it manifests itself initially in individuals, but in anonymity. Philosophical thinking promotes it.

Our basic questions have become questions of mankind. Fewer and fewer people can satisfy their inmost needs in present forms of the ecclesiastically authorized faith in biblical revelation. These forms will never unite the globe, not even the West. For almost two thousand years the Christian, ecclesiastically fashioned faith in revelation has failed to realize the ethos of truth in ways of life and of thinking, in action and in personalities, so as to make it convincing for all.

Only in freedom can men come to be of one mind. Today we seek the ground on which men of every religious persuasion might meaningfully meet around the world, ready to recommit themselves to their own historic traditions, to purify them, to transform them, but not to abandon them. The only common ground for the diversity of faiths would be clear thinking, truthfulness, and a common basic knowledge. These are the premises of that limitless communication in which the serious origins of faith attract each other.

The present universal language of 'enlightened rationalism' does not unite. It makes narrow-minded, rather, and unfree. It furnishes the means of sophistical delusion which keep the world in its fraudulent state. To make us free, enlightenment must progress endlessly, must enter into every horizon, must never be complete.

We are told that modern science will unite us. It is indeed universally valid and rightly acknowledged everywhere, but it unites only our minds, not our selves. Its unanimous knowledge yields no common ground of life.

Scientific knowledge and technological skills are admirable things, fascinating and inescapable even to those who resist them. But their consequences and their obviousness are equivocal. They imperil man and his existence. Paradoxically, their light obscures the essence. Yet even from this obscurity, as from every past one, the philosophizing that makes man truly human can bring him back to his eternal source. It will support him when he has to start afresh in time, over and over with the birth of every individual, under constantly changing conditions. Today he is to master science and technology.

What I would like to do in this book is to speak from the source of philosophical faith, a faith that has lived as long as men have been thinking. I would like to show that loss of faith in revelation does not exclude a constant recommitment to the Bible's irreplaceable store of truth. Instead, the situation of our time makes a transformation of faith – of biblical religion for us Westerners, of other religions for their believers, of philosophy for all – almost palpably evident.

The title *Philosophical Faith and Revelation* is not supposed to imply a superior perspective. I do not pretend to a standpoint detached from both points of view; should they prove irreconcilable, I would be speaking from the first, although affected by the second. But if philosophical faith and faith in revelation can meet, without coinciding, I want to try whatever thoughts may help this chance along.

Basel, June 1962   *Karl Jaspers*

Introduction

A point of departure:
how do we find ourselves
in the world? where do we
come from? what are we?

1 To begin with, let us look at the results of objective observation of our genesis – first, from infancy, second, from history, and third, from the world. These ways of inquiry tell us interesting facts, but they do not answer the meaning of our question. They divert from it, rather, by leaving man an object of biology, psychology, history, or cosmology.

We observe the development of a new-born child. It shows us man as a creature among others, but we note a quality peculiarly his own. His very biological evolution depends upon his awakening in a human-historical environment, and in observing him biologically and psychologically we soon encounter facts we can grasp only by a shift in the manner of observation – facts indicating a shift in reality itself. For observation changes where man, as distinct from all other creatures, meets us in communication, in his specific humanity. The first faint rudiments of this show suddenly in the infant. Time and again there occurs this astonishing mystery, this break in mere observation, when a human being answers, speaks, and understands, untouchable in its own dignity, different from any animal. Communication is more than observation. With animals too there can be a kind of inter-course, of question and answer; we are touched by the intelligent look of eyes in which something impervious seems to find expression, and yet cannot find it. A dachshund, let alone a monkey, may seem uncanny. And yet, a gulf remains between behaviouristic studies – possible on man as well, if we ignore his humanity – and mutual communication in speech. I cannot even hint at the wealth of research results in animal and infant psychology. The crucial point is this: the course of human life is biologically and psychologically determined from beginning to end, most impressively during puberty; but within this determinacy there occurs something derived from another source, something unresolved by the continuity of biological and psychological processes. The form of knowing ourselves as objects of observation does not touch our essence.

1

Observation shows further that we come from a history which goes back to the unfathomable past. We get to know past human worlds, their creations, their transiency, their plunge into an oblivion from which mere fragments let us remember and visualize an infinitesimal part of what has been. Isolated links of cause and meaning may be progressively uncovered by historical research; yet we cannot grasp the historic process as a whole – not the first cause, nor any of the creative steps, nor a necessity governing the whole.

Men have often envisioned a total historic process. Believers in revelation have conceived it as the way from Adam's fall to the Last Judgment; empiricists, as progress in knowledge and skill, as technological and social change; a few philosophers, as the advancing consciousness and realization of freedom, often coupled with ideas of a perfect world or of the world's end. The course of history is then considered inevitable, an inescapable process determined without me, leaving me only the choice of co-operating with necessity or being discarded as chaff.

But history does not enable us to comprehend ourselves. If it were a necessary process, either spiritual or material, men would have no chance to intervene in it and to change it; at most, they would be able to speed it up or to retard it – a matter of no consequence. But these interventions, the great transforming, creative acts of the spirit, rest on human freedom. They are not products of history. They are products of freedom and become factors of history.

The human will, present and future, can never be known as a whole. We cannot stand outside the whole, or above it, knowing it. At best, total views of history are drafts of an idea of the whole, but no such idea will be the reality of history.

A total knowledge of history would permit total planning, and man would become material for man, to be shaped and transformed to suit his purposes. Humanity would be at man's disposal. Since this would presuppose a surrender of human freedom, such a will to 'make' man can only destroy him; its final consequence would be the end of man. For one cannot 'make' freedom. Only the conditions for it can come about or be planned, and they can make freedom possible or impossible. The conditions may exist, but they produce nothing. Freedom comes from a different source.[1]

Finally, observation shows that mankind must have originated among the creatures on earth, and, like them, from the nature of the world. But the world's own origin defies comprehension. Science penetrates the world into infinity, but it does not comprehend the world. To science, the world is unfathomable.

Human knowledge penetrates the universe as far as the remotest stellar

[1] For the concept of freedom as Karl Jaspers uses it in this book see pp. 235 ff. *Translator.*

nebulae, and as close by as the very spot in the brain to which our consciousness, our mind, and our freedom are tied in the world of space and time. A breath of the same mystery touches us from the outermost reaches of the cosmos and from the structure of cerebral matter under the microscope. In both cases something recedes, unilluminated by all this illumination.

This way never takes us within. Even if we knew each structural refinement of the grey matter, the step from this to the inwardness of sense perception and consciousness would always remain incomprehensible. We are sure of this inwardness; but of an inwardness of the world we have not the least intelligence, not the slightest sign.

The Cartesian doctrine of two substances, an external one of space and an inner one of consciousness (*extensio* and *cogitatio*) starts with a statement that is correct from this viewpoint of immediate experience. It says that – having realized the fact that our brain is a condition of our inwardness, our soul, or freedom in the world – we see externally, as matter, the minute brain particle facing the mass of the universe, while as inner reality the knowing consciousness encompasses this universe. This means, however, that the objective material world, far from being encompassed by a brain particle, is an object for something to which even this brain particle can become an object. Science penetrates the infinity of matter, of the universal matter of the atom and of the infinitesimally structured matter of the brain. There are no limits to its advance, but the ways of this advance never take it to inner reality either.

All philosophical total knowledge in objective metaphysics is bound to move in a circle. The quality of the circle makes up its content. In our case it is a material circle: an infinitesimal part of the world knows the whole world that produces it; the brain as matter harbours within itself the world from which it has sprung. Or is there another source at work, rather, materially presupposing this circle, but breaking through its materiality?

Infantile growth, history, and the universe were to let us observe our genesis – three cases of potential knowledge in which we find immensely attractive but invariably unsatisfying facts. Each time, we come up against a limit where research becomes clear only to lose its intended object, man himself.

What we are cannot be understood by objectifying a genesis. No discoverable genesis makes me comprehensible to myself. Objectively we always grasp our existence only on the side of discoverability, without a chance to complete this infinitely advancing research.

By the physiological-psychological process of life, by tradition, by history, we awaken in the world, so to speak, but the world does not help us to understand ourselves. What we are, who we are, how we find ourselves in the world – this we do not learn by observing something else, but by reflecting upon ourselves and the world.

2 In simple fashion, in brief sentences, this has been done through the ages, indicating an essentially human concern. Let us look at some examples.

a: A medieval verse reads as follows:

> *I come I know not whence,*
> *I am I know not who,*
> *I die I know not when,*
> *I go I know not where,*
> *I wonder why I am of good cheer.*

This is not a 'Christian' verse. For the faith in revelation provides answers to everything. It lives by marvellous pledges and would perhaps conclude its answer by saying, 'I wonder why I am sad.'

It was this question that prepared the Nordic race to follow Christian promises. The Venerable Bede tells of an Anglo-Saxon king who in A.D. 627 had to decide whether to accept Christianity or to reject it: 'My liege,' said one of his councillors, 'compared with the time unknown to us, men's present life on earth reminds me of your sitting at meat with your lords in winter. A blazing fire warms the hall, but outside a storm is raging. Then a sparrow flies in and swiftly flits through the hall, in one door and out the other. For the moment of being indoors it is safe from the wintry blasts; but after the quick passage through the short, pleasant span it disappears from sight and returns from winter to winter. So, too, this human life is but like one single instant. We do not know what has gone before, nor what will follow. Hence, if this new religion reassures us on that point, I deem it right to accept it.'

The deliberation of these men, why they should try the Christian religion, is without an impulse of faith, utterly rational, derived from concern about what might come after death. But the parable of the sparrow shows how serious our eerie existential situation seemed to them on reflection.

b: What the world in which we find ourselves is as a whole, whence it comes, where it goes – this we do not know, and never will know. But the mere question changes man's inner condition. Answers have been given and, from the earliest times on, have only intensified the question. In the Rig Veda, the oldest Hindu text, we find these lines:

There was not non-being, nor Being . . . there was neither death nor immortality. . . . Moved by no breeze, the One breathes. . . . Nothing was but this. . . . Yet who has been able to bring it to light, who has learned whence Creation comes? The gods do not reach that far. . . . Whence and when this Creation has come, whether it is created or uncreated, he alone knows, the All-seeing One in the highest heaven – or does he not know either?

The pure, unsurpassable basic thoughts may have occurred to men at all times. How secondary is the meaning of ages and history! Essentially we know no more than that Hindu sage of three thousand years ago knew about what concerned him, and what concerns us.

c: What we are is as mysterious as the world. If our knowledge of worldly realities has increased immeasurably over scores of centuries, notably in the past few, we still know as little as then what we ourselves really are. The basic question – which may arise even in early childhood, astounding and changing the individual – has at all times been put in various deeply moving forms, as in the Hindu Mahabharata: 'Man is ignorant, helpless before his own joy and grief, sent by God. . . .' Or by St Augustine: 'I am cast into the world. . . . I have become a question unto myself. . . .'

We are more than all our knowledge. What we know confronts an infinitely encompassing unknown. The world is a mystery, and each of us is a mystery to himself.

d: We might add to the historic instances; yet the issue is peculiar to the human being as such. Its particular forms differ vastly in the ways of their concern, their questing and answering. But what is immutable in all this historic diversity?

First: with such questioning views man has really awakened. Before, he was living in the world as behind a veil that served to conceal the essence. He has no inkling of the inscrutable as long as the shrouds remain un-questioned matters of course.

Second: with this questioning man takes a leap. Not until then does human life proper begin, with man aware of his humanity. Before the leap he is only potentially human; now he is really human. Once this ascertain-ment has begun, nothing remains a matter of course. Existence, previously unquestioned, has become an immediately boundless sum of questions, answered each time by an act, a creation, a love, a community, in an unceasing process.

Not until then does man set out on the conscious venture of his history. He wants to be shown what is. He wants it manifested. It cannot be nothing. I have not come into this existence in vain, for nothing. But what it signifies goes beyond all definite significance.

Third: the question is linked to a powerful impulse. Appearing together with awe is the will to move from boundless blights to endless blessings.

The urge to learn from the source of things what is, what can be, and what may come to be, has one sole goal that can be phrased in many ways. We long to be sure of the source, to return to it, to be sheltered in it, to find contentment in its being. We want the source to reveal the goal we seek in it, to find our way in its light. We want the attraction of Being to uplift us, to give us, amid the currents of change, a part in eternity.

There is an interrelation: the urge to know what really is means a will to selfhood; the consciousness of not really being oneself urges to Being. To come into being, selfhood seeks to exceed itself. This is the cause of man's infinite restlessness. He wants to think, to act, to live so that salvation will come to him. Its most remotely perceptible trace grants him a matchless tranquillity.

3 Two inseparable points are realized in abstract reflection: 'I think' and 'I am free'.

a: I think. Whatever exists exists for me as I think of it.

What is a being unknown to itself and knowable to none? It is like non-being.

Thus I grow conscious of being both the eye in the world, so to speak, and the light the eye sees by – and of being this jointly with others, with their eyes and with their light, which I encounter. With other human beings, I belong to the only known species that is this light in the world, and thereby differs infinitely from all other creatures.

My kinship with those others lies objectively in common biological reality, and subjectively in a possible indefinite sense of unity with all life – as with all worldly reality, even with the unorganic one. Yet this sense of unity cannot evolve into communication. Our way of intercourse with it lacks speech and thought illuminated by a common knowledge.

b: Aware of myself in thought, I am certain that *I am free.* To the extent of my freedom I come to be, and to bring about, what I can accomplish in the world around me.

But I do not accomplish my freedom. I did not make myself. I do not exist by my own means.

I am myself, and free, as I freely feel the source of my freedom, and as I think the source together with my freedom.

I can forfeit the chance of freedom and let myself be caught in bonds which I produce by its surrender. I cannot produce freedom, as by an absolute freedom that would be myself. Instead, in my freedom I encounter that which makes me free.

An imagined possession of absolute freedom, in licence, actually makes me unfree. For the substance of freedom is a pursuit of illumination, and it exists only as an advance into a darkness that grows brighter. Licence, as the form of random choice, is the advance into a darkness that keeps darkening. It ends in abandonment to the discernible processes of biological and psychological and sociological existence.

The sense of our different origin – an origin that lies before and beyond any world, but cannot turn into an object in the world – intensifies and illuminates the experience of our responsibility. We come to open our minds to the cause of this difference – which, in the sense of anything in the world, we cannot know.

The crucial consequence of this realization how we find ourselves in the world is that the world is not everything to us, but that there is no other, second world either. In ciphers which are forms of this world we grow aware of what speaks to us from our real origin, points to it, and links us with it.

The Phenomenality of Existence

To begin with an ancient philosophical insight, definitely clarified by Kant: the eye in the world, the light that we are and see by, signifies to us the way of being.

Whatever exists for us, whatever we think and perceive, exists for us in the forms in which we become conscious of it. It appears to our senses as present reality in the forms of space and time, to our minds as cognition in the forms of categories we can think in. Such phenomena are products of consciousness, but only in their forms, not in their existence. They are apparent, but not illusory. Their forms are fleshed out, complemented by something otherwise inaccessible. This makes for the reality of the appearance.

Consciousness at large, the source of the forms of phenomena, is the one thing identical with itself, all-encompassing, and general – the one thing shared more or less by everyone who comprehends reality.

The phenomenality of the world at large, of time and space and of all possible cognition, does not imply a distinction between this world, as merely apparent, from another real world. There is only one world. But this world is phenomenal; it is not absolute Being. To our cognition, 'Being in itself' is a boundary concept, not an object. The concept indicates nothing beyond our imprisonment in appearance.

Our freedom alone is directly related to Being – and therefore non-existent for our cognition of things, not an object that we might explore empirically.

This insight into the phenomenality of the world transforms the meaning of objective cognition. Against the prevailing view, against the ineradicable experience of knowing things themselves, all cognition relates only to objectified appearances. So do all basic thoughts, as mental images belong to the realm of appearance.

We ask, then, about the significance of finding ourselves in a phenomenal world. Are we, so to speak, cast from elsewhere into this real, rich, glorious, and terrible world – as into a jail that takes philosophical insight to be comprehended as imprisonment in forms of view and thought? Do we live as in a dream? Is the philosophical awareness of this dream life the rudiment of an awakening to our source? Or is it the other way round: is life in the phenomenal world our awakening from the night of immemorial unconsciousness – the only light there is?

We have to answer that for us human beings jointly there is no light other than that of our phenomenal world.

Revelation

1 We do not call on revelation to ascertain the situation we find ourselves in. Revelation comes from another source. No knowledge, no human ascertainment can say whether and what it is.

The explorable empirical phenomenon is not revelation, but the faith in revelation. Rather than with the reality and truth of the revelation, the inquiry deals only with the reality of the faith in it. Yet even faith can settle only the absolute validity of revelation for the believer and the community of believers, not its general validity for all. In none of its historic forms has the faith in revelation proved valid for more than limited segments of mankind. All claims of general validity raised in behalf of its one truth have been futile.

The questions posed in this book relate to the inconceivable that is before and above the world. How does it speak in the forms of mundane being, in the language of this world? Does it speak at all? Does it speak without revelation? Or does it speak through revelation only?

We have the experiences of freedom and selfhood, experiences which the world does not help us to comprehend. In the world we experience the boundary situations[1] – death, struggle, guilt, chance – which awaken us. All this happens without revelation.

And if people tell us that an invasion of the world – by the revelation they believe in – gives them answers to vital human questions, we are put out. This has always been the case, and it is the case today.

Thus the Hebrew prophets heard and spoke – Moses, the prophets of doom and salvation, and Jesus – and so, in different fashion, did Buddha. The human situation was ripped open, not so as to bare a knowable, explorable cause, but as the experience of an inconceivable reality that appears to man and uses him as its voice.

2 I do not believe in revelation; to my knowledge I have never believed in the possibility. Why, then, should that faith be taken seriously even by those to whom it is not given? Because of its great historic impact? Or because of the believers of moral and intellectual eminence? Considering the claim, those are superficial factors. The crux is that we cannot be indifferent to revelations which men proclaim they had, or to men in whom others believe as revelations, if the weight of what is believed to have been revealed makes it a matter of inescapable existential import to this day. The faith in revelation has brought forth contents, impulses, works, deeds, which are now true and humanly accessible without it.

Besides, there is the magnetism of incomprehension. A failure to understand this faith does not pacify us. Marvelling at the pronouncements, the thoughts, the acts it has spawned, we remain restless.

[1] For a definition of this frequently recurring concept see p. 210—*Translator.*

There is a tendency to make light of the faith in revelation. An 'enlighten-ment' that should not be confused with the great enlightenment proper of Plato and Kant would have us admit no reality which is not manifest to our senses and proved by operations of the intellect. To this merely intellectual consciousness, revelation and philosophy are two great historic fallacies of the kind that used to be treated under some such heading as 'delusive ideas in the life of nations'. Today the same language is used for a scientific superstition that makes men feel above 'delusions', a superstition that fails to distinguish what science knows and can know – what thus remains tied to method, criticism, and proof – from mere opinion, which in such pseudo-science prevails as if it were knowledge.

What science can know must not be evaded today by any truthful human being, whether philosopher or believer in revelation. Yet scientific judgment takes methodical experience, and this, for all our infinite progress, confers and confirms an awareness of the bounds of knowledge.

Contrary to the exposition of these bounds is an age-old diabolic method: showing man his limits by confusing him intellectually, leading him to bottomless scepticism, to despair of his ability to know, and then offering him an absolute salvation to be accepted unreasoningly and obeyed without question.

The faith in revelation which we take seriously has a different original character. It is not thoughtless, nor did it spring from any despair of thought. It was a thinking faith. The thinking of its great figures, of St Augustine, St Anselm, Thomas Aquinas, or Nicholas Cusanus, can match any other thinking in rank – that is to say, in substance, thoroughness, acuity, and method. Though entirely different, it is thinking just the same.

Science itself makes us aware of its limits, but this awareness does not clear the way for random possibilities, for a belief in miracles, for ecstatic fancies. Statements referring to things that can be experienced in the world – to resurrection of the flesh, for instance – are subject, rather, to the methods and the criticism of scientific research. Our thinking about things outside this area differs in character, method, and meaning. There is nothing arbitrary about it. It is more profoundly based than all things in the empirical world of time and space.

If this thinking springs from, and is defined by, a historically determined revelation we call it theology; if it springs from the source of essential humanity, we call it philosophy.

In philosophizing I adopt biblical truth in my own interpretation. It is not tied to authorities which represent the revelation and presume to have the only correct exegesis. To philosophy, revelation becomes a cipher. Philosophy resists theological dogmas.

3 I hear two opposing objections.

This philosophy, says the believer in revelation, knows no 'firm statement, and therefore loses all substance. If revelation is not reliable, it is nothing;

if everything is left in suspension, we lose everything. We lose the ground under our feet. Hence, we hold fast. We cling to revelation and promise; we are not to be parted from God. We believe, and faith alone gives us strength, an ethos, our salvation, our liberation.

I do not admit this alternative. Strength, the gift of selfhood, an ethos, liberation and freedom, unconditional seriousness – all this is possible even after discarding what the believer in revelation so stoutly affirms and upholds.

It might be the very challenge of our human condition – into which God, to speak in the cipher, has placed us while shrouding himself – that we shall not seek to escape by any kind of self-delusion or concealment. In concrete acts, in their conduct, in their own words the believers in revelation face the question of philosophy: To accept your statements, your doggedly held theses, must one perhaps delude himself at a crucial point? Are you asking the impossible? Could it be that truthfulness, which God demands of us, oppugns phenomena which men assert in the name of faith in revelation? To this question there can never be a final answer.

The other objection says that my philosophizing leads to a single conclusion: that revelation would be desirable if only it were believable. Philosophy is called a training course for revelation.

I should not mind that. For philosophy, unlike the faith in revelation, does not proselytize. It leaves every man to be himself, free to make his own choices. Philosophy does not preach, nor does it persuade. Free men meet in it, sharing a common fate.

Nothing is farther from me than to want my philosophizing to cause a belief in revelation. I myself cannot but hold with Kant that if revelation were a reality it would be calamitous for man's created freedom. And yet – however impossible it seems to me to believe it – I want no thinking that would ultimately bar a revelation. Philosophical faith is a source of its own, but it admits the possibility of revelation for others even though it cannot understand it. It wants honesty, not enmity; communication, not rupture; liberalism, not violence.

Summary

1 There are seven parts to this book.

Part One gleans facts, events, ideas, and forms of organization from religious and ecclesiastical history. As facts, these can be scientifically established and agreed upon by all, irrespective of faith. Our purpose is to clarify the circle of concepts that has taken shape around the faith in revelation.

In *Part Two* we show a set of facts whose clear perception seems of the greatest importance to all present thinking. Modern science, for the first time in history, has achieved a universal scientific approach, a consciousness of its methods, of its limitations, of its meaning. Science differs from both philosophy and theology. The old dividing line, between rational cognition and cognition by faith, no longer hits the mark; we can become more aware than ever of the independent source of philosophy.

In *Part Three* we draft a philosophical 'basic knowledge', showing philosophical insights in order to find therein a common ground for all men. This cannot be done where the substance of faith is at issue; nor is the basic knowledge generally valid like scientific discoveries – as shown by its failure thus far to be universally disseminated and unanimously accepted in any form. But it is a field in which we may think on the hopeful assumption that human beings as such can be of one mind. Their unanimity would be the medium of boundless communication for totally different states of faith and life. Never complete, in a permanent state of advancement like the sciences, it might possibly furnish a meeting-ground for all the ways of insight.

The heart of this book, the discussion of the realm of ciphers, is reached in *Part Four*. Faith understands itself in a language in which Transcendence speaks and is addressed. This language is manifold and equivocal. In history it has been definite or vague, but in principle it holds sway in one of two forms. Either an embodied Transcendence will stake its claim in the world – and being embodied, will use bodily, physical force for its protection – or else the language of the disembodied ciphers will touch the serious, ever-personal potential of the human soul. Either the claim will appear as a flat statement uncommunicatively confronting other statements, or else the ciphers will remain suspended, not generally valid, much less absolute, and take effect historically in their time.

If Part Four shows the nature of the realm of ciphers, *Part Five* takes up the struggle of ciphers in concrete forms, as a phenomenon of existential self-discoveries. In this part I see the essence of what this book is about.

The theme of *Part Six* is the intellectual situation of our time, the present situation in which all this thinking occurs. We ask: have our liberations carried us to freedom?

In *Part Seven* we conclude with the question whether philosophical faith and faith in revelation can meet without coinciding. If such a meeting is at all possible, it surely takes unbounded truthfulness toward oneself and others. No one is born with this truthfulness; everyone has to wrestle for it all his life, with himself and with others. But nothing else – no compromise, no tolerance and no intolerance, no considerate silence and no sudden judgment – can lead to the development of human unanimity in a ceaseless struggle of love.

2 Remarks on the structure of this book.

We shall pursue four ways of thought. *First*, we take our bearings in facts and concepts (Parts One and Two), thinking relatively superficially, as mere spectators. *Second*, we make sure of the basic philosophical knowledge that shows us how we find ourselves in the world and in the presence of encompassing[1] (Part Three). *Third*, we unfold the realm of ciphers, clarify their nature, demonstrate their substance, and transcend the ciphers themselves (Parts Four and Five). *Fourth*, we reflect on our present historic situation, asking what it is, what it may come to be, and what our tasks are (Parts Six and Seven).

Observing as spectators, making sure of philosophical premises, adopting ciphers, asking about freedom and faith in our time – these are four basic attitudes of active thinking. Even in separation they still belong to a single manner of thought: to the philosophical faith that follows the several paths in quest of determinable ways to understand its own, necessarily indeterminate essence. Each time, therefore, the separation of the ways will stress one and yet cut across the others, because all of them communicate the one philosophical manner of thought. What is now just mentioned by the way will elsewhere be the main topic. The one thing common throughout, which should be heard at all times, is neither subject nor object at any time.

Another way to look at the structure is this: the first three parts put us into a thinking condition; the fourth and fifth let us hear the ciphers; the last two, turning to the present, inquire into faith in liberation, into the relationship of philosophical faith and faith in revelation. They pose objectives that seem like impossibilities: an inner condition that is to lead to the existential liberty of all, and a relationship of philosophy and faith in revelation that will preserve the chance of their alliance.

The structure of the book is meant to be an organizing idea, essential in itself. It would be easy to dissolve the structure and substructure, turning the text into a loose sequence of essays, but then the reader would first have to start thinking about the order that governs them.

3 The manner of presentation.

a: A philosophical treatise combines two kinds of thought, separable in individual operations but not on the whole: the kind that is readily understood in conventional form of thought, and the new thought produced by an about-face in thinking.

The presentation should reduce both to the utmost simplicity. What can be known should be fitted into a concise pattern of points essential to our purpose, without getting lost in the maze of historic reality. That maze has to be entered in historical research, to know reality truthfully, but not for the purpose of this book. And then the result of the about-face should always be concentrated in the comprehensive movement of a single act of thought.

To proceed from particular thoughts to an insight into the overall way

[1] For a definition of this fundamental concept of Karl Jaspers' philosophy, see p.61— *Translator.*

of thinking, the reader will have to think along with the author. I should like, therefore, to make my thoughts as accessible as possible by technical means also. Subheadings, specific designation of steps, and other indications that may seem pedantic are intended to draw attention to the various positions, so each may be grasped in its parts as well as in context. *b:* The several themes of this book turn about one that must stay indefinable. Even so, I hope this pole will firmly guide our trains of thought – not by rational logic alone, but with its aid by existential logic.

When deduction and the conclusive arrangement of thought can work only in sectors and must fail in philosophizing as a whole, the philosophical task changes.

The task, then, will be to employ objective observation in order to preserve facts from an oblivion that would make the rest untrue.

It will be to save us, by way of ascertaining the never-finished, ever-advancing basic knowledge, from imprisonment in the objectively closing drafts of a total knowledge.

It will be to give us our historic footing, by way of ascertaining the truth we can be.

I admit that for long times on end I shall be speaking as an observer of things including faith in revelation and philosophical faith; that I shall carry out thinking operations in the guise of valid facts; that by my own experience I shall try to find the truth in statements about existential possibilities.

What is my goal? Certainly not an impossible and therefore non-existent philosophical knowledge that man might acquire without first being himself. Instead, the ever-provisional goal of philosophizing in books is to clarify premises, to unfold possibilities, to draft images, to construct thoughts – in short, a thinking that prepares the philosophical ground on which philosophy may be realized by individual self-realization, by man's taking courage to love, finding his community, fulfilling the mundane destiny he never knows, although it guides him; by his sensing his place in the sea of Being and experiencing his own unique historicity in the historicity of the appearance of all things. What really matters cannot be put into words; it can only be said indirectly. Despite their assertive phrasing, all theses outside the sphere of cogently correct and generally valid science are mere questions, addressed to self-being. Only when this, in both the listener and the speaker, answers in thought that turns into inner action will the presentation gain philosophical substance.

c: History will be cited, but not for the sake of historical knowledge. We shall see historic facts that are still effective; we shall see active forces we face. All of them exist in men, are tied to men, and thus spring from man's own source. We are part of them even if we fight them. Their view adds to our potential.

There are thoughts we meet· n history in an unsurpassed consistency and greatness. What men have thought shows us what we were ignorantly seeking. Its acceptance and rejection brings us to our own responsible thought.

d: These are assertions. They squarely call for agreement. As a form of language they are unavoidable, but a presentation based upon them as a simultaneous state of mind leads to flat statements and fixed positions. Those give a reader the satisfaction of gaining positions he can adopt in dogmatic movements of thought. He is handed something. He, as himself, need do nothing.

This procedure suits a student in areas of perfected, rational, objective cognition. It may also be found in structures of philosophical thought; but there a presentation exalted into a statement of absolute knowledge becomes deceptive, facilitating and restrictive at the same time.

It is different if we mean to present something which does not exist as an object. This presentation shows an original way of thinking that seeks to visualize its origin even though the crux of the matter cannot be objectified.

The very presentation must seek, then, to detach the thinker from his thought, the reader from what he is reading – a detachment achieved by making the act of thought simultaneously conscious in reflection. This is what we call methodological consciousness. It helps us to retain control of our thoughts. It frees us from the chains which all thought threatens to forge for us by turning absolute.

Methodological consciousness keeps our vision clear and prepares us for new horizons.

Yet it is fruitless to cultivate a methodological consciousness for its own sake, let alone to substitue a reflection on methods for cognition and philosophizing. This would extinguish thought and experience. The first prerequisites of substance are presence in encompassing, seizure of the historic situation, and the strength to draw cognition and speech from it. Methodological consciousness comes later, controlling, purging, clarifying the meanings and the limits of what has been thought.

In this book methodological consciousness finds expression in scattered remarks and extended passages, and it is meant to pervade the mood of the whole.

If, in the nature of communication by statements, I seem to speak peremptorily, the understanding reader will not be deceived. He will note the import of the way of thinking, shown in the sequence of parts. He will see it manifested in the continual appearance of seeming contradictions which have meaning nonetheless. He will find the contradictions resolved by referring to the one undefinable something expressed in so many ways, to the communicative way of thinking, to existential reason, to philosophical faith, to this one present form of Being.

Part One. Faith in revelation: concepts derived from religious and ecclesiastic history

From the reality of thirty centuries of biblical religion and almost twenty of Christianity I take some features vital to our purpose. It is all far more abundant, of course, and quite different from such a simplifying, standardizing sketch. For the documents, the critical analysis, the reference works, the accounts we are indebted to historical science; but not even this can ever show reality itself with its infinite facts and possible interpretations. Science also has to simplify, to standardize.

Ours is a modest task. By stressing well-known things we are to stake out a historic horizon that will embrace whatever we should know for our further discussions.

a. The Diverse Origins of the Concepts of Revelation

Seen from without, revelation takes several forms.
1 *Prophets* proclaimed what God told them, and commanded through them.
2 *Apostles* testified that God, in Christ, appeared on earth, was crucified, and rose again. They bore witness to the event of salvation.
3 *Churches* and *priests* declared texts as inspired, as God's word, essentially differentiated by their origin from all other writings.

The three types of revelation are matters of faith, and a critical view would like to elucidate them. Then the believer as well as the unbeliever can perceive the step to faith more clearly – for faith means something radically different from the possible leavings of critical doubt. This criticism differs in the three cases.

Ad 1. The prophets proclaimed that they had heard God's voice; others believed, and believe, that God had said what the prophets were saying. The prophets heard; the believers in their revelation believe their account of it. The prophets could not doubt their immediate experience; the rest, whether believing or doubting, heard it from them. Thus faith in prophetic revelation differs in kind from the revelation granted to the prophets themselves.

Indeed, the prophets make a deep impression even on a sceptic. They really felt overwhelmed by God. Many resisted the call; the burden was too great, the dread too shattering. They tried to escape but could not. Their experience still strikes us as a phenomenon that may have been possible, without dishonesty or madness, under the conditions of their time.

If they thought about it, the depth of their words – unmatched to this day, and at times of an eternal validity that no one can ignore – was probably beyond their comprehension. It could not be their invention, not the work of men. They bowed to something greater, something encompassing that made them feel like tools. And what would it have meant to people to hear the concerns of all presented as merely their, the prophets', views and insights and commands? As the work of mere men, what they had to say would have lost all its meaning. To reach human hearts, it had to come from God. Only by citing God could one dare say it.

The experience of such revelation may be interpreted as a cipher of the mystery how man can step from the shadow of his usual unconscious orders to the height of simple, essential moral law, to an insight into his existence and the world's, to resolution in concrete situations, to a knowledge of the need for all to change. There were Greek thinkers who took that step without the cipher of revelation, but with no less a sense of mystery.

Ad 2. The apostles' testimony was their faith, a faith created by telling. They did not mean to establish anything, to relate historic facts subject to proof; they meant to tell about what was to them the uncritical coincidence of historic and believed facts, of empirical history and the event of salvation. St Paul stated the case of homiletic witness: 'How then shall they call on him in whom they have not believed? and how shall they believe in him of whom they have not heard? and how shall they hear without a preacher? And how shall they preach, except they be sent? . . . So then faith cometh by hearing, and hearing by the word of God.'

Though analogous to the prophets, the apostles did not spread a revelation of God's will and word; instead, they told of the Risen, the incarnated God. They referred not to God but to Christ. Christ, to them, was the same as God. This was new and unheard of, 'unto the Jews a stumbling block, and unto the Greeks foolishness'.

The man Jesus stood in the line of prophets, proclaiming the heavenly kingdom, the end of the world, the ethos of the Sermon on the Mount, and a faith in God based on a human attitude less radically new than the apostles' proclamation.

In a time of critical historical research we tend to question an apostolic testimony in which the witness to faith is uncritically mingled with the witness to fact. Once we apply historical methods and investigative refinements to find out what is more or less likely to have been historic fact, we have abandoned what matters to the believer in revelation, what exists for him alone. Kierkegaard was the first to draw the conclusion that historical research is irrelevant to the believer. Its results do not matter to him; the occupation with them leads away from faith rather than toward it. What we should hear is not a historically questionable witness but the witness of faith; this is the mouthpiece of revelation.

Ad 3. Inspiration is an experience. Nietzsche has reported it in modern times:

You hear and do not see; you receive without asking about the donor; lightning-like a thought flashes, of necessity . . . To be completely beside yourself, and most distinctly aware of countless little shudders. . . . An abundance of light . . . instinctively rhythmic relations . . . a craving for widespread rhythms is virtually the measure of the force of inspiration. . . . Everything happens quite involuntarily, and yet with a cyclonic sense of freedom. . . . The involuntariness of the image, the parable, is the strangest part. You no longer know what is image, what is parable. Everything presents itself as the simplest, most apt, most proximate expression.

Such inspirational experience may be a clue to the belief in the inspiration of the Bible. It is altogether different, in any case, from the canonization process of the Scriptures chosen over generations from a large mass of writings. We ask about the principle of selection – is it due to long habit of majority evaluation, to the quality of writing, or to chance? Or do people believe in the very process, as in a divinely guided choice of what God has inspired?

There is always the basic difference between prophets, apostles, and priests on the one hand, and the rest of believers on the other. The rest believe on the ground of what witnesses tell; they do not believe at first hand. Any kind of faith in testimony requires the believer to be able to believe. This ability dumbfounds the spectator in quest of communication. He cannot understand it; it is the 'first-hand' experience of all believers. But it has to be questioned; to others, it is not unequivocal, fixed, untouchable, and identical everywhere.

b. Faith in Revelation, and Faith at Large

Historically there are many forms of both revealed and philosophical faith. We find faith in revelation in its biblical forms, also in Islam, Hinduism, Confucianism. Is faith the general concept covering both philosophical and revealed faith, and revealed faith the general concept covering Christianity among others?

1 Generically, we can define revelation as a direct manifestation of God by word, command, action, or event, at a definite time and place. God issues commandments, establishes a community, walks among men, founds a cult. All this happens by an objective invasion from without.

The substance of revelation is not identical everywhere, due to man's general religious nature. It varies in form, in images, commandments, rites, and sanctities, each considered immutable in its time.

'Generically' means that an outsider sees the revealed religions side by side in history, while the insider in each one conceives it not as a specimen, but as the one and only truth.

If revelation were a general concept, there would indeed be several, with the biblical a case among them. But to the faithful it is not a general abstraction; it is absolute historic reality.

2 The concept of faith at large can be defined as follows:

Faith is not a knowledge I have, but a certainty that guides me.

In faith I live by the source that speaks to me as I think what I believe. The faith that makes me believe is inseparable from its content, which I imagine. Subject and object of faith are one. To live in faith, I have to live as a believer in something.

If I believe, I want to think what I believe in. Yet if I try not just to think but to possess that content, in dogmas and creeds which I know no matter what I am, then I want my assurance as a certainty, without encountering the source of faith in myself. Therefore, failing before Transcendence and myself, unbelieving in my will to believe, fearful of being left to my own devices, I can join with others in 'believing' what we profess as the content of faith, upheld and insured by our community.

Faith cannot be forced by thought, nor can it be stated and communicated as mere content. Faith is the strength in which I am sure of myself, on grounds I can keep but not make.

Faith is the ground before any cognition. In cognition it shines more brightly, but is never proved.

3 Christianity, if it is to be so defined, turns against the generic concept of both faith and revelation. Christianity knows only one faith and only one revelation, the only one attested by Holy Writ and tradition. No historical view of various claims to revelation matters to this faith; it claims to be true outside any categories of religious history, philosophy, or psychology.

Revelation belongs to none of these. In a manner of speaking, it cuts across everything thinkable, comparable, and general, across everything that exists more than once. As an investigable reality, revelation does not exist. It can be heard in incomprehensible fashion, and then attested by the hearer in a fashion unlike any other testimony.

And yet, one no sooner talks of Christian revelation than he must inevitably do so in general categories. When its claim to be unique and exclusive is mentioned, it must be based on general ideas. This happens in the propaganda for the faith, addressed to those not yet aware of its uniqueness. The faithful do more than proclaim; they want to persuade, to show ways to the unique vista. Then they talk of the specific characteristics that set Christianity apart from all other religions.

a: They cite history: the word of God; his covenant with Israel, the godly people; his promises; his speaking through the prophets; the appearance of Christ, and the glad tidings. The Holy Scriptures and the reality of the church are pointed out. But all history is singular, including that of other revealed religions and of any reality. This singularity does not suffice to establish Christian revelation as unique and exclusive.

Moreover, the claim itself is revealed: it is a claim of God – and one may point out that none of the other so-called revealed religions ever made a comparable claim.

b: What sets Christianity apart is that God is to the believer a personal God the personified Absolute. As a person, God speaks, demands, frowns, and has mercy. All religions know personal gods, but in Christianity there is the one personal God, at once one and all, the ultimate, the untranscendable.

c: The original revealers in India and China saw Being by means of superior wisdom and a superhuman vision. Prophets and apostles, on the other hand, heard God's voice, were sent, feel they were instruments of his will. The Asian figures are largely mythical; the Western ones are flesh and blood.

d: Another distinction is cited for Christian revelation: no thought, no experience, no volition can make me believe it. Faith comes only to those upon whom God bestows the grace of being able to believe. Man cannot seek God; he cannot, so to say, touch God on his own. God alone touches his chosen.

Linked with this is a specifically Christian contradiction. God remains hidden even though he reveals himself. The individual's ability to believe in revelation depends on divine grace, and yet he is commanded to believe – and guilty of disobeying God's manifest will if he fails to believe. To everyone reached by the word, revelation becomes judgment. Divine grace becomes a divine command.

Whether citing these or other traits to characterize the uniqueness of biblical revealed religion, we always have to speak in general categories, and we may well ask whether the same general thoughts are not historically applicable elsewhere. Indeed, what is central here occurs elsewhere in passing. If we want observation and thought to convince us that Christianity is unique, we will never get beyond equating its singularity in history with the singularity of all other historic phenomena.

4 History shows that the faithful – all of whom refer to the Bible – are so much at odds that splits involving the denunciation and damnation of opponents as heretics have always been a cardinal feature of Christian reality. The question, 'Which Christianity?' becomes inevitable.

We distinguish three types of believers: first, those who believe they had a revelation of their own, a phenomenon which even now occurs all over the globe; second, believers in revelation confirmed and warranted by ecclesiastic authority – a revelation which then lies in the past; and a third type which, though grounded in the biblical tradition, does not believe in revelation of specific acts by a personal God, but adopts it in ciphers.

The first kind of faith is a universal psychological and historic phenomenon, not specifically Christian; together with institutional religions it dimly appears as an element of all ritualism and sacerdotalism. In the

second, church-based form, the Christian idea of revelation has been
developed and so sharply defined as exclusive that only Christian revelation
can exist for it. The third form, while it may find its historic base in the
Bible, requires no revelation.

Christianity comprises every Bible-based reality, in Eastern and in
Western churches and creeds, in undogmatic, charitable Quakers and in
Calvinist zealots, in Francis of Assisi and in the Inquisitors who tortured and
killed in God's name. The historic Christian space contains all of the West
and more.

We Westerners, formed in this space, animated, motivated, and determined by this background, filled with images and concepts derived from the
Bible, are all Christians. It would be better – as we realize if we immerse
ourselves for a while in the spiritual worlds of India and China, get some
distance, and then, from afar, see what this whole biblically-based world
has in common – to speak of 'biblical religion', including not only Christians
of every kind but Jews, and in a sense, though more distantly, even Muslims.

Within this world, however, any answer to the question, 'Which Christianity?' involves some special group claiming it for its own. Most of these
groups feel that they believe, disseminate, and represent the real, unadulter-
ated revelation.

For centuries, mankind has witnessed an indecisive struggle over true
Christianity, an often most 'un-Christian' struggle, pitting Christian
against Jew and Christian against Christian. Churches have vainly called
themselves catholic, whether Greek or Roman, and remained special
phenomena. Protestants vainly seceded to form the true, solely Bible-based
Christian community; they quickly split into a host of divergent denominations. There is no common trait of true Christianity, not even the belief in
Jesus as the incarnated God. Christianity exists only in special groups.

All this is so because the Bible – the literary residue of the unique religious
experience of a thousand years, concluded in the first or second century
after Christ with the definitive establishment of the canon – is as ambiguous
as life itself. It offers texts for any situation and position; opponents have
always been able to draw on it for equally strong support. The Bible
requires adoption, selection, rejection, visualization, transformation.
Rather than a fixed point of departure for thought, it is the force that will
bring man to existential seriousness. It takes him to a brink where everything
becomes questionable. It does not let him conceal any anguish. It leads the
honest to the abyss, and there awakens them to a chance of trust beyond
comprehension.

We Westerners may feel, therefore, that we are living by the biblical faith,
may allow our lives to take many forms and many ways, may admit many
principles – and yet may resist the possessive claims of any group and any
church whatever.

Theologians may say disdainfully that Bible-reading alone does not make one a Christian. I reply that no one knows who is a Christian. All of us are Christians in the sense of biblical faith, and whoever claims to be a Christian should be so considered. We need not let ourselves be thrown out of the house that has lodged our fathers for a thousand years. The point is how one reads the Bible, and what it makes of him.

A man like Kierkegaard may deny that any of his contemporaries are Christians, least of all the priests and theologians, and he may not even call himself one. Churches and theologians, on the other hand, may deny our Christianity while protesting their own. Both extremes should be allowed to stand, but if they will listen at all, the protagonists should not go un-contradicted. We ought to view the biblical religions with respect, in all their historic ambiguity and incertitude, to see their horrors and yet to grant their realities of boundless veracity, freedom, and strength of love – for these might be the common features, and then they would be the lifeblood of philosophy itself. We may deny only one thing: the claim of any authority to say who is a Christian. In the world, he who considers himself a Christian ought to be deemed one.

Since tradition is tied to organization, since biblical religion is passed on by churches, congregations, and sects, anyone who, being Western, feels tied to the source will belong to such an organization. It may be Roman Catholic, Jewish, Protestant, or whatever else. Its point is to foster tradition, and to preserve a place from which the *pneuma*, if it were to take effect again, might spread through the nations.

The creed becomes immaterial, only historically of some interest for our background. The link is the reason-pervaded biblical faith which no man has by himself. And across all creeds cuts the potentially deeper link that would shatter the inevitably stifling confines of any creed.

c. *Revelation and Thought*

a: The understanding of original revelation is what we call theology. Its premise is the reality of the revelation. Where do we find that?

One may think it lies in the reality of Jesus, discoverable in the synoptic Gospels by means of historical criticism. But the real Jesus was human, the historic one the last of the Hebrew prophets, a preacher, a spokesman of God's will, a predicter of doom and judgment, a caller for penance. He was neither a self-appointed Messiah nor a self-made sacrament – by instituting the Last Supper – nor the founder of a church.

Revelation is also believed to lie in the *kerygma*, the first preaching of the apostles, beginning with the conception of Jesus as the Christ, of his messianic significance based on the belief in his resurrection.

There we distinguish revelation from its understanding. Theology follows upon understanding of the *kerygma*, and this theological understanding

– beginning, in regard to revelation itself, in the New Testament – permits and demands criticism and a discussion of whether we understand correctly.

Since the *kerygma* is communicated in human terms, it amounts already to understanding and thus to theology, no matter how far back we go. We hear in human terms. We cannot draw a line between what calls for obedience and what calls for critical discussion, between revelation and its understanding. What calls here for obedience precedes the language of general intelligibility and lies hidden, from the outset, in the revelation of the *kerygma* as well. It is the point of reference meant in the language, though itself not communicable in this language.

No man who does not believe in revelation can get a clear concept of it. Definitions always say either too much or too little. But the indefinable still exists as human faith.

Neither revelation nor the faith in it are facts to be unequivocally established and operated with, like things in the world. Hence the effect of faith in revelation differs in essence from that of human orders, philosophies, or sciences.

b: A revelation we believe in is a manifestation or an act of God. We can ask no further; we have to obey. Yet if we believe in revelation, grow aware of this belief, and communicate our awareness, we are thinking.

We are certain that the thought of revelation rests upon the revelation itself. The revelation itself is the word, in the sense of the original *logos* Without thinking what is revealed to him, the thinker could neither be aware of the content of his faith nor communicate it. The thought, to him. is not additional; he has received it together with the revelation. Hence, though he cannot ask beyond it, he can address unlimited questions to the revelation. The final answer will always be the *logos*, what can be thought within reason. The possibility of all exegesis rests on this original logic.

This is not the sole answer. Thought cannot be accomplished without general concepts. But we regard revelation as absolutely historic, and thus to be neither attained nor exhausted by general thoughts. All our thinking of revelation revolves around what defies thinking, what will always defy thinking. This thinking is mutable, therefore, while we regard it as referring to the immutable.

c: Revelation exists in affirmation and commandment. The believer's reply is confession and obedience.

Asked whether reason (thought) or revelation takes precedence, the believer will say either that revelation takes precedence and reason has to submit; or he will say that both are one, each given within the other – that they cannot conflict, that profession is the same as cognition, obedience the same as freedom. Against these two, a third thesis gives precedence to reason, maintaining that a revelation in conflict with reason cannot be a revelation of God.

Thus, through all the ages of the faith in revelation, thought has indeed been active without ever resolving the difficulties other than by acts of intellectual violence – by saying either, 'I believe in the absurd, because it is revealed', or, the other way round, 'Being sure of reason as my only source of insight and good will, I deny revelation, not just for myself but altogether'. We shall see that we reject this alternative.

1 THE LITERAL SENSE OF THEOLOGY AND PHILOSOPHY, AND THE LINE BETWEEN REASON AND FAITH

Theology, as a word and in substance, is a creation of Greek thinkers. Aristotle gave the name 'theologians' to the old poets and cosmogonists who told of gods, to the Orphics in particular, and he referred to his own philosophy as theology wherever it dealt with the first, immobile moving spirit. To the Stoics, theology came to be the highest branch of physics. In Rome, since Panaitios, they distinguished realistically between poetic (mythical), political (practical), and physical (speculative) theology.

When the Christians made contact with Greek philosophy, sought recognition in the cultural world of Antiquity, and strove to clarify their faith in their own minds, they looked upon their message as the true philosophy and called it so. By theology they meant, at first, the pagan philosophical doctrines, and later on the Christian doctrine of God which took their place.

In the Western Church, the word theology had no specifically ecclesiastic meaning either to St Augustine or in the centuries that followed. A separation of theology and philosophy was never considered, because it was inconceivable. With cognition due to divine illumination, was not all knowledge founded in God? Like faith, its motive power, divinely illumined rational thought led to revealed truth. To St Anselm as to Augustine, thought as such aimed at the deity, which in turn led the way. A distinction would have stripped philosophy of content, and theology of reason. The one great unity lay in God's omnipresence, eternal truth in all high-minded thinking.

The twelfth century brought a change. Abelard occasionally called theology the *sacra eruditio*, dealing with Scripture, as distinct from the philosophical fields. Hugo of Saint Victor drew a line between *theologia mundana*, the highest branch of philosophy, and *theologia divina*, the understanding of God by the incarnation and the sacraments. Still, within the cognitive concept there was no conflict.

St Bonaventure may have grown more acutely aware of the methodical antithesis: his theology, as *sacra doctrina*, issued from God, while philosophy led to God. He also used the word differently, however, as 'speaking of God' – coincident with the Scriptures – or in tracing all sciences back to theology and arranging philosophy according to trinitarian principles.

Thus far, the Augustinian-Anselmian unity of thought and faith remained unquestioned. Difficulties had appeared to heretical thinkers, to Berengarius of Tours and others, but without leading to basic methodological reflections. It was Thomas Aquinas, following leads shown by Abelard, who simultaneously grasped the contradictions and their resolution in a form which governs Roman Catholic thinking to this day. The *sacra doctrina* of Aquinas is seldom called theology; but with him the antithesis of faith and knowledge, previously vague and in the background, turns into an antithesis of a revealed supra-rational science and a science of human reason. At the same time it is comfortably resolved: as the realm of nature to the realm of grace, philosophical cognition is subordinated to theological cognition. Ultimately, since both come from God, they can and must never conflict.

In principle, however, the line could only be drawn by abandoning the Augustinian concept of cognition. Thinking ceased to be the same as divine illumination; unlike Augustine, Aquinas considered it a natural activity of the mind. Thought lost its supernal splendour and became a creative realm of its own as man's proper, healthy, natural common sense. The price of theology's rescue from the contradictions of rebellious thinking was the degradation of that thinking to mere intellectual labour. It enabled the thinker to receive the Aristotelian world view, but in a mood of unphilosophical rationalism. The consequences of this degrading surrender were Aquinas's actual employment of philosophical methods in theology, and his treatment of the same objects – except for the mysteries of revelation and the sacraments – in theology and in philosophy, although now viewed in the light of higher principles obtained from revelation.

Aquinas established theology as an ecclesiastic science based on revelation, as opposed to philosophy as a human science based on sense perception and intellectual thought. Subsequently, theology came to be the general term for ecclesiastic science.

The seemingly so clear Thomist division and reunion of theology and philosophy proved deceptive. Unrest continued. Secular thought and cognition did not cease pounding and undermining the rock of ecclesiastic thought. A new rescue effort came with the doctrine of twofold truth: reason and faith, it said, are unrelated. Each is right in its own field; they may conflict, but this does not matter, since neither truth claims to be valid in the realm of the other. In practice, whether clearly stressed or dimly veiled, this doctrine played a great part in subsequent centuries.

The beautiful, harmonious Thomist order confirmed the world and its realms, conceived its measures and bounds, and let it radiate in the glory of God's creation. It left the world free in its every positive sense and kept it under the guidance of God who spoke through the Church, had made the world well, and had directly revealed himself in the bargain. Without seeming contradiction, God and the world, revelation and reason, could now be acknowledged in order of rank. The world in the diversity and autonomy of its realms, man in his humanity, civilization as the God-related sense of human structures and institutions – all were allowed to unfold, and were termed 'Christian'. This great harmony came to be possible despite the shadow cast by the consequences of the Fall of man. The Fall explained all physical and moral evil, and religious cognition could point to deliverance without a need to deny both the world and man on grounds of total corruption.

And yet, in New Testament thinking there were moments – stressed by Protestantism – which pointed elsewhere. The world was deemed free and autonomous as the realm of sin; for eternity, there was vindication by faith alone. We came to hear that in this world, wholly corrupted by the Fall, we must live subject to the qualities of worldly realms, sinning within them. This was the meaning of Luther's *pecca fortiter:* the hope which in this world sustains our spirit amidst unavoidable sin lay solely in the faith in redemption outside the world. The world was not an altogether hostile anti-principle; but in its present state of corruption due to the fall it scarcely differed in essence from that old Gnostic concept. History was a sequence of acts of human pride and obduracy. In the world there could be no guidance other than faith – a faith detached from the world, which allowed man a secular existence in the world but put his proper life elsewhere. Reason itself was corrupt, and the only truth lay in worldless isolation or in common prayer, both related to God's eternity.

Such irresponsibility toward the world, appearing in God's name, was intolerable. Hence the recurring attempts to affirm the world as such even in Protestantism; hence the lasting vitality of Aquinas; hence the continuing appeal of philosophical concepts of one divine principle encompassing the world, like the *nous* of Aristotle and the Stoic *logos.* The greatest harmonizing endeavours were those of Leibniz and Hegel, with Hegel's the more impressive for his vision and interpretive acceptance of all negativities and horrors. To Hegel, revelation, made transparent and comprehended by reason, dissolved in the spirit's rational passage through history. God was the spirit, the reason that underlay all things. This spirit was one; unfolding, it appeared in nature, man, and history. Faith also had its place in the scale of the moments of truth, all of which came to be transparently present in the one speculative thinking of philosophy. Everything was reconciled. Whatever existed had its place, its right, its limits, its negation. Reason was not corrupt thinking turned against God, not defiance to revelation, but the one all-encompassing source.

Of all the historic ways in which the relationship of reason and faith was first posed, then thought through, and eventually either solved or comprehended as insoluble, none can satisfy. Can we come to a better insight? The great achievement of theology tends to discourage us. It has developed an extraordinarily rich, spiritually intense, intellectually acute and systematic thinking, and as religious cognition has produced an admirable literature. Though compelled to adopt Greek philosophy and every later one that might serve its purpose, theology did create its own topics and ways of thought, ways whose meaning endures even where the faith in revelation has vanished.

In Part Two of this book, on theology, science, and philosophy, we shall try to show an element of better insight that has already been brought forth by history. The crucial event which past thinkers could not know – and the news of which, however odd this may sound, has not yet reached modern theologians and some philosophers – is the realization and consciousness of specifically modern science. An insight into the methods and limitations of this genuine science resolves a major portion of the troubles encountered in the struggle of faith and reason – although in another, more profound form they will reappear. A fundamental ambiguity in the centuries-old debate on reason and faith, philosophy and theology, can now be illuminated and made comprehensible for all.

2 CONCEPTS OF 'CHRISTIAN PHILOSOPHY'

a: If philosophy and faith in revelation are undivided in a thinker's mind – as in the cases of Augustine, Anselm, Cusanus – the historical observer may call such thinking Christian philosophy. To us, it is a philosophy that has absorbed Christian revelation as an essential source.

b: If philosophy and theology are separated on principle – as to most thinkers since Aquinas – some will still use the term Christian for the figures of so seemingly independent a philosophy as the modern Thomist one claims to have become. But such 'Christian philosophers' have ceased to be true philosophers. In their factual attitude they coincide with the 'scientific' philosophers of today. The only essential difference is that the Thomist thinkers' faith rests upon Church and revelation, while the modern 'scientific' philosopher, having lost the philosophical faith, relies on something alien to his own 'science'.

Today, Thomist and scientific philosophers are unwittingly allied against philosophy proper. Both have departed from the encompassing thought of reason and confined themselves to intellect and experience. They mean to prove theses by natural means, not only like scientists, but as scientists. They mean to explore 'facts' and 'phenomena' – but endlessly, at random, without guidance – and they meet on a common ground that is neither scientific nor philosophical, on the ground of a supposed philosophical craftsmanship, in joint opposition to philosophy itself.

Yet there remains a great difference between Christian, believing philosophy, and a merely scientific, unbelieving one. The Christian one is explicitly dependent. In principle, it never wants to oppose the ecclesiastically formulated faith; whenever there is a conflict it will submit, denying any intellectual dishonesty because philosophical truth and the truth of faith, being both derived from God, cannot contradict each other. The other, non-believing philosophy is existentially confused and proclaims its independence without noticing its accidental dependencies.

Christian Thomist philosophy is not serious as philosophy, because its seriousness lies in the ecclesiastic faith in revelation. It has a word for the great independent philosophy proper, the thinking of thirty centuries of philosophical faith: 'ersatz religion'.

In this confusion one might think of returning to the highroads of unified thinking as practised by Augustine, Anselm, and Cusanus. But in our present intellectual situation this is impossible, unless the thinker ignores its inescapable features – the meaning and reality of science in particular – and arrives at a romantically restricted thinking which would now seem bizarre.

c: Finally, philosophy may be called Christian philosophy because it is part of the Western world. If we look at it from the point of view of Greek philosophy, not to mention the Hindu or Chinese ones, we feel this pervasive atmosphere, noticeable even to our sceptics and materialists. This description of Christian philosophy has an indefinitely broad meaning and implies a historic localization.

Speaking of 'Christian philosophy' in these three ways makes sense. It makes no sense, however, if the term is to imply either a philosophical case for the faith in revelation – which is futile – or a case for philosophy deduced from the faith in revelation. This is just as impossible; the contrary impression left by the philosophically great thinking of Augustine, Anselm, and Cusanus is deceptive.

3 THE QUESTION OF TRUTH IN REVELATION

Reason cannot make a case for revelation. Reason, as philosophy, does indeed claim to be independent, to originate in itself; but vis-à-vis the 'point' and the 'reality' of revelation it has no authority to decide whether or not revelation exists. For revelation, like the origin of philosophy, precedes all reasoning. This originality is the premise of all reasoning.

No rational authority can deduce a priori that there can be revelation – that it fills a given place, so to speak, in our thinking. It is neither possible nor impossible. It comes from without, as something quite different from all thought and experience. If it had not happened, it could not occur to anyone that it might happen. No general concept enables us to predict an act of God as possible, or to comprehend it afterwards. The case for revelation lies solely in hearing it and accepting God's work.

From the beginning, however, the faithful have tried to make a case, and they have not yet ceased trying. To be sure, the truth of revelation is established only by revelation itself; but people keep pointing to resultant phenomena which make it effective in the world, as in the following arguments.

1 Revelation is said to be established by the testimony of the Holy Spirit, which I find in myself when the outside testimony reaches me. By this witness of the spirit, not by reason, is its truth seen and known. Reason is corrupt and may confuse the pure language of the spirit.

2 It is said to be established by the testimony of the congregation – whom Augustine can accordingly address as '*vestra sanctitas*'. This communal witness is not an experience which psychology or sociology can adequately grasp; it is the Holy Spirit working in and through the congregation. On grounds immemorial, borne by tradition, Scripture, and sacred custom, the congregation is seized by the revelation entrusted to it since the covenant with God. This reality lies before all thought, though it is instantly present in thought. It is no prejudice in the sense of a removable delusion or untenable premise, but a prejudgment in immemorial reality.

3 Revelation is said to be established historically, by God's covenant with the faithful. This covenant derives its claim from an act of their forebears, anticipating one of God: 'And they said unto Moses, Speak thou with us, and we will hear; but let not God speak with us, lest we die.' The line states expressly that the source of revelation is not the individual's or people's direct relationship with God, but an indirect relationship with God. This faith in revelation does not rest on a vision or mystical union, but on belief in the truth of the intercession. The believer believes by means of intercessors ranging from Moses through the prophets to the apostles. He does not found his faith directly on God, but on their testimony. This form of belief is belief at a distance. Truth is what the decision to believe acknowledges as intercession, as witness or tradition. Established in this manner, truth is understood by quoting Scripture.

Every historic example shows that revelation is established only by itself, not by anything else. It cannot be otherwise. Philosophical faith can cite no other ground either. Where man is truly in earnest, the choice of what he will live by and for is his to dare and to destine.

d. Revelation and Authority

1 AUTHORITY AT LARGE

One man alone cannot live. But if men live together there is always some cohesive authority which the individual heeds without feeling unfree. There are standards, acknowledged in fact without being clearly thought out. A feeling of substance, a common ground, establishes affinity and an order of existence.

a: This authority was a fact of life in China, in India, in Antiquity, and in the medieval West. The individual, from the time he awoke to consciousness, found it extant, enduring, sheltering. Its views, its symbols, its ways of action, its customs served to interpret and to justify all things. Unquestioning joint participation in common affairs was a matter of course. The landscape was sacred – the pious landscape of the Greeks, formed and strewn with private special shrines, as well as that of the Hellenistic-Roman world, of the Middle Ages (remnants of which still survive), and of China, though not that of colonized North America. The past, grown mythical, was present in customs, institutions, and ways of speech. Revolutions could occur and individual authorities could be menaced, but even this would happen within the lasting, unshakable authority of the world as a whole, which men felt to be immutable. The greatest horrors, the mercilessness of man and nature, wholesale cruelty and death – all this was natural, so to speak, cancelled out in the one entirety of mankind, and of mankind's world. Human life was lived within this multifarious, all-encompassing authority that was like the air breathed by all.

In part, and throughout history, this authority has consisted of religious acts, cults, and concepts adopted and formed, each in its historic way, by churches. They are not our subject, and I merely mention these potent realities in passing: the promulgation of the faith in liturgies, prayers, chants, and sermons; the sanctification of birth, marriage, and death in baptismal, nuptial, and funeral rites; the sanctification of the seasons, of Sundays and holidays; sacraments, dogmas, and the order of encompassing communities.

b: It was the age of technology, and this alone, which breached that world of authority. Not since the beginnings of humanity in the 'Promethean age' can we imagine so incisive a breach as the one we are involved in. Round about us, as all round the globe, remnants of the old authoritarian worlds still stand, strong but steadily weakening and of small moment to the course of events. The original technology that was essentially human and yet evoked awe and dread a few thousand years ago has yielded to a new, fundamentally different technology based on natural science, leaving nothing untouched, advancing ceaselessly, transforming restlessly. It is this technology with its domination of life that laid the breach into all previous authority.

The basic phenomenon remains: man needs an authoritarian vital sphere to guide him as a whole. Is this still possible in the world of technology? Does this new, conquering world differ from all past ones?

Freedom was part of the old authorities. If they grew weak, if injustice, tyranny, and personal corruption made the powers seem untrustworthy, they would protect themselves by violence and coercion; yet despite the corruptions, what was protected had substance and depth of its own.

The authority of our time, on the other hand, is the organization of technological labour. Its purely purposive collaboration of men in standardized performance tends to destroy all authoritarian substance, and thus the

personal appearance of authority. The world of technological labour knows
nothing but the obligation to perform. Fulfilling the norm is both living
condition and honour – if this word still has meaning. It is limited to the
realm of work, and to the living conditions that promote work. It fragments
the entirety of life into disciplined working hours and more or less
bewildered leisure hours governed, in analogy to the joint authority of the
past, by a living practice of wishing to act, to talk, to live, to show and
express oneself like everybody else. The past authority's scale of substantial
rank is replaced by the prestige of another scale, determined by the means
of consumption at the individual's disposal and by their display – by the
possession of cars, houses, appliances, clothes, etc. There is an etiquette
with commandments such as 'Keep smiling' and 'Don't be imposing'. The
point is to enjoy life by means of amusements and 'holidays', a word misused
now to describe social occasions without any sacred base. Motion and
change are pursued as ends in themselves. One needs the sense of being
with the mass and at the same time against it – and that too in the form of
being 'with it'. One is mass and *élite* at once. Yet in the process more and
more men lose their bearings. They yield to violence, to scientific superstitions. These people cease to seek a haven in the Church, to venture and
fulfil their humanity in lucid philosophizing; instead, they seek salvation
in such pseudosciences as psychoanalysis, with the place of existential
sacrifice taken by financial sacrifices brought to the analyst.

c: Today the age of technology appears in two diametrically opposed
variants – in the nations that produced the world of technology, and in
those which take it up suddenly as an alien achievement. To both, traditiona
authority has become untenable in this age; both are undergoing a human
crisis. But the relationship to past authority is altogether different in the
two cases.

The nations which produced the age of technology know from experience
how their whole condition changed in the process that began slowly in the
eighteenth century, accelerated gradually, and has now risen to breakneck
speed. Theirs is a world in which traditional authority is slowly crumbling
but by no means impotent as yet, and within this world they have not just
recognized the new at an early stage but realized that they are not necessarily doomed to dehumanization. They have taken practical, successful
steps against the culmination of the evil, against the new thraldom, the
loss of human dignity, the injustices, and the lies spread in justification.
They are committed to this continuing struggle. They have set themselves
the task of subjecting the world of technological labour to a political order,
of promoting freedom and justice. In the long run this endeavour can
succeed only if all take part in politics, in political thought and in political
responsibility. Changes in the world of technological labour require new
laws; what matters is to postulate a state of political affairs in which citizens
are trained for political judgment, so that through their representatives they

will find legal forms to guarantee the freedom to be human amidst technology. Men must live in order, but should not be subdued. Hence the lawful means to fight for their freedom to live, to venture, to realize the unpredictable forms of what makes men human.

The other nations are in quite a different case. The age of technology has come upon them suddenly, from without. It is alien to their past existence. They themselves might never have created the present, all-transforming science and technology. They received a finished product that has nothing to do with their own traditions, with their own authorities. In fact, the technological invasion promptly destroys those authorities.

The non-Westerners want this invasion because world power, prestige, and dominion are no longer possible without technology. They seize the means of the West so as to turn them against the West that used to rape and disdain them. They now have a chance to achieve world dominion in their turn, to subdue the West by the technological labour and equipment of their masses.

Catching up with the world of technology takes special methods, however. What the West did gradually must now be done all at once, and it is by force and coercion alone that people moulded in very different authoritarian traditions can be instantly transformed into the working men required by technology. Total rule seems the only way – certainly the only quick way – to break resistance to the technological organization of production. The West has ceased to do violence to those people; they are violating themselves. But in the process they learn to read and to write, acquire knowledge and skills, marvel and, in part, wax enthusiastic at the technological realities and possibilities.

Only in the West is the technological age part of history. The rest of mankind has been swept up in a spirit not its own, which it eagerly yields to. For Westerners this age is an end whose origin may indicate the forces of a new beginning; for the others it is a beginning that means a complete break with their own past.

The West alone has spawned and sometimes realized the idea of political freedom. To the rest of mankind the idea is originally foreign. The West has always seen its every rudiment of total rule opposed; to the rest, there is something natural and self-evident about total rule. Only in the West has the political struggle for truth, freedom, and justice been a recurring event for twenty-five centuries. Today mankind faces the question whether total rule will snuff out this Western flame or the constant striving will continue despite constant failures. Will the place of past living authorities be taken by the lifeless total authority which technology makes possible? Will the organized work of the world be directed by force and terror instead of securing freedom? Or will a new, substantial authority aiming at human dignity be set up on the continuity of pious moral and spiritual traditions? Will the West be more than the source of the technological age; will it accomplish the illumination of a humanity based on Transcendence – an illumination that would cause mankind to re-adopt and re-form all its great traditions?

The nations ruled by totalitarianism or vegetating in chaotic conditions suffer their fate in passivity or thoughtless activity. It is up to the free to fight for truth and veracity, for justice and freedom. They are to keep doing this even though the result will never do. Despite constant dissatisfaction with themselves, despite huge risks, they are to face the future with a confidence assured by their faith in reason.

How an authority including freedom will take effect in the world that is politically free, as a community of faith in the chances of an ordered human existence – this is the fateful question not only for the free world, but for mankind. The faith in revelation cannot be this authority, because it is truly held by only a fraction of Westerners, who in turn are but a small minority of mankind's billions.

d: Every authority has met with opposition. Historically this would emerge from the depths of the authority's own ground, breaking with it when it grew ossified and came to be upheld by mere force rather than by any living faith. At all times, however, the opposing force rose rationally against an authority that countered rather than included reason, hampered rather than advanced the growth of reason. Then the authority would make men coerce their own minds and sacrifice their intellectual integrity.

Original authority preserves freedom even in obedience as the individual experiences his will as one with the fullness of the encompassing whole. Subsequently, authority becomes solidified in its effective forms and narrowed by the exclusion of nonconformists. It resorts to coercion to protect itself from deviations and new vital forces. Its spirit withers.

This recurring process rests upon the need for change which freedom imposes on all human affairs. Conditions may founder on a failure to win relative stability as well as on petrifaction and violent falsehood. All conditions must end. They cannot be perfected in time. Either chaos or total order may put an end to a life that lasts as long as these two limits are faced without yielding to either. There are no lasting solutions; there is only the march through time in constant struggle for temporary solutions. Chaos pulls us toward a confusion in which nothing remains; total order pulls us toward a rigidity that is soon fractured. Both exclude the existential possibilities – for chaos permits no endurance, and a sole order, no truth. To exist, man must derive order from unity while finding truth in diversity.

This is why the freedom of intellectual struggle is of the human essence. It depends upon the self-control of the free, on their curbing their freedom from within, by true authority; it depends upon universally open minds, on truthfulness in speech, on the restraint of each will to power by its guiding idea, which must be fulfilled to justify freedom. This takes self-critical thinking and eradication of the sophistries that threaten our thinking. Without such inner controls there will be outward coercion.

We are now talking like observers of the course of history. But man cannot live as an observer. He thinks he knows how things are, and he is not entirely wrong; but what counts – and what an observationally phrased line like the following mis-states already – is that man must freely be himself as part of his original existential reality, which in turn includes its proper historic[1] authority.

Why is this line a mis-statement? Because the point it seeks to make is no possible object of meaning. The line seems to say that I might know and determine this historic character of mine, and that I should now stand by what I know, against other historic characters. In so doing I would violently segregate myself as an object of historic knowledge. An existential historicity calls for the opposite: for a communicative, universally open mind. It is precisely when I want to be something that I fail, existentially, to become this. If I make an effort to be a personality I become the impersonator of a personality. If I want to be original I become unoriginal. If I measure my thoughts and actions by the source, I lack the yardstick. In reflection I can illuminate my self-being, but I can neither know nor make myself. There is no escape from that restless inability to know the crux of the matter. It turns restful in moments that grant us the experience of unwarranted, unobjectifiable original certainty.

I return to observation. Freedom – as opposed to licence – exists only by authority. Substantial authority exists only by controlled freedom.

Can authority be founded on the realization of its necessity? An authority that is rationally planned, 'made' rather than historically grown, can only be coercive. It remains unsubstantial. Particular obedience, the heeding of specific directives that is justified and inevitable in purposeful joint undertakings, does not make men unfree; such obedience is limited, freely willed so as to reach a goal jointly desired. Total obedience makes unfree because it stops man from becoming himself, and any manufactured authority exacts this kind of obedience.

With the loss of historic authority, however, freedom is lost as well. For freedom does not spring from nothing. Dependent on nothing, it can find neither its substance nor itself. It remains licence, and this, in an objective psychological view, is subject to necessities that will not permit it to be free.

The unity of freedom and authority – originally envisioned as an ideal – cannot endure. The two will split up, will fight, will conquer each other as independent entities, although in fact they can be truthful only together. The will to authority, as coercion, destroys itself along with freedom. The will to freedom, as licence, destroys freedom as well.

The battle of divided freedom and authority is resumed again and again.

[1] For a discussion of the terms 'historic' and 'historicity' as employed by Karl Jaspers see pp. 105 f. – *Translator.*

Historically, their seemingly perfect union occurs in moments of culmination and transition.

2 REVELATION AND AUTHORITY

a: There are authorities, binding powers, without faith in revelation. From
those, the claim staked out by ecclesiastic authority differs in principle. The
revelation administered by the Church is not an authority like others, one
added to others – it is the only authority, the one revealed God's own. The
Church claims divine authority as interpreted by itself.

It makes the other authorities its own, but controls them as derivative.
They are not entitled to the name 'authority' (which means original,
initial, governing) if they claim independent validity; they are entitled to it
only in so far as the word of the only authority speaks through them.

The sole source of this authority is the word of God in Scripture and
tradition. Other religious authorities would cite 'old sayings' *(palaioi logoi),*
the exegesis of myths, or institution by some god, demigod, or founder.
They claimed no present jurisdiction over all men, but remained in a free
flow of interpretive adoption and transformation of the world of myths.
Only the exclusive revelation defined by the Church brought the new total
authority.

b: The rise of Christian authority to a point of being able to direct temporal
powers and command their strength to realize its own aims was a process of
centuries. It was accomplished by death-defying believers, preachers, and
confessors who were not yet fighting but suffering, who would reject
violence but accept martyrdom.

At first, the struggle was exclusively spiritual. The faithful pondered the
revelation and its consequences, evolved their theology, and adopted
philosophy for their ends while fighting it as a whole. They turned into a
community whose vital forces seemed inexhaustible. The spiritual energy
of their thinking and their practical energy in spreading the faith by all
means of propaganda were great enough to bring them into contact with
every creative age. Even in combat there could seem to be a solidarity
between faith in revelation and philosophical faith, the mutual echo of a
powerful unconditionality, as in a meeting of forces originally akin but not
interdependent. Despite their battle of centuries, despite their inability to
join in a common faith, it would seem that they might indeed see their
common task in listening to each other, in carrying on their fight so as to
purify them both.

In those first centuries the Church found itself constantly at the brink of
doom. It was competing with other mystery religions and Gnostic-cosmic
ways of thought, which it either received into its own magnificent structure
or branded as heresies. That in the process – to a great extent, at least – it
achieved the unity of catholicity gave revelation that absolute, universal

authority which for a long time dominated the West, despite constant tensions with the temporal powers. How, out of all the bewildering speculative fantasies, out of such mighty cults as that of Mithras, out of extremist sects such as Marcionites, Montanists, and Manicheans, the Church managed to adopt and conquer whatever could concern man as such, whatever created any essential language – this historic picture compels the observer's admiration.

c: That this authority originated as a martyr's religion is symptomatic of the militant nature it had from the start, both outwardly and inwardly. It is embarrassingly notable even among the apostles. As a result, this ecclesiastic religion no sooner won temporal power than it began in turn to exterminate heretics and unbelievers, making a great many more martyrs than had died for it in the time of its origin. Buddhism has no martyrs, Buddhists suffered persecution in China without raising up militant martyrs against their environment. Islam was a warrior religion, conquering and dominating from the outset; martyrdom is alien to it. But the Church saw itself as both the Church Militant, witnessed by its martyrs, and the Church Triumphant, which made martyrs. The measure of its pride is symbolically evident in the famous statues of Church and Synagogue on the cathedral of Strasbourg: in the figure of the Church, the radiant arrogance of the supposedly knowing who see God himself in Christ; in the Synagogue, the human destiny of failure in the 'blindness' of not knowing, of never seeing the invisible God. The Synagogue is carved so lovingly that one is tempted to ask whether the artist felt this, whether his secret heart beat for the truth of this Synagogue.

d: The idea of unity is thrilling. Its original truth inspires life, action, creation. Within the transcendent framework of historic diversity it is present in communication, but not identical for all. If it is transformed, however, into an anti-pluralistic unification of the world, it becomes rapine. It is then no longer that true, transcendent unity but a mundane, usurped one. Such unity may build impressive works, but it inevitably leads to the ruin of freedom and of its creative possibilities. Whatever grandeur may be displayed in these processes, there is an analogy between the Roman empire and the Catholic Church, and between its alliances with medieval feudalism, seventeenth-century absolutism, and the nineteenth-century bourgeoisie. The fight against all these was waged for freedom.

e: To enforce its authority, the Church had a unique weapon even before it came to temporal power. The weapon was exclusion from its community. To the faithful, belonging seemed like life itself; the threat of excommunication forced them to obey and enabled the Church to keep its institutions invincible throughout the Middle Ages. The Church stood on revelation, on its profound tradition, on the monopoly it then enjoyed in knowledge and thought, on the sacredness that was all over – and it ruled by the threats of excommunication and interdict of purgatory and hell.

Remnants of this indirect power still work on believing Catholics. Priests will practise incomprehensibly cruel encroachments on the human soul and its decisions.

f: Long after the Church became unshakable, its basis – the Christianity of the New Testament – remained at work. An unbridgeable gap yawned between ecclesiastic facts and original Christianity; so the early energies resurged in anti-Church movements borne by the same self-sacrificing courage and pervaded by the same spirit. In so far as the Church did not absorb these energies, their bearers and their writings are largely forgotten. We know only of a select few. Church power has accomplished this act of extinction. It is a prejudice of all victorious powers in the world that what they consigned to oblivion deserved oblivion; but our judgment tells us how much that was great in the world has thus been for ever lost to memory. The prejudice of the victors is inhuman, unbiblical, unchristian – it is ecclesiastic.

3 AUGUSTINIAN THOUGHTS ON AUTHORITY

Augustine based the need for authority on the weakness of the human mind. He held that the greatest mental giant, granted full leisure for speculative reflection, cannot find truth, and that the concerns of all must not depend upon him even if he could. It is by faith alone, therefore, not by any conclusions of thought, that all of us become sure of truth and salvation, and this faith is impossible except by divine authority.

Is there such an authority? And if there is, asks Augustine, how can we know it? Whom shall we believe? The sages? How can we tell a true sage from a false one? We cannot. Christ is the only true authority. For he alone, by his miracles, forced even dull eyes to recognize his authority. We can believe no one else.

Yet what is belief? Augustine calls it a flawed knowledge, dependent on authority. In our present state, in time, all we can do is believe; we can see only in eternity. Eternal life has been promised to us. We shall attain it by 'truth'. Our faith is as different from a direct grasp of truth as mortality is from eternity. Once we come to see, eternity will follow on mortality as unveiled truth follows on faith.

So truth is veiled, but it is manifest as authority, in Christ. Until eternity grants us the unveiled vision, there must 'be no discord between the mortal life of faith and the eternal life of unveiled truth'. Truth, which is eternal, has therefore had a beginning in the world, when the son of God came to earth and directed our faith to his person. In Christ, God assumed our mortality without losing his eternity. He had a beginning, as we have it, and remained eternal at the same time. 'We, having had a beginning, would not be able to enter the realm of eternity if an eternal one had not had our kind of beginning and thus a link with us, leading us to his etrenity.' That he had a beginning and died is what we know of ourselves; that he rose and went to heaven is our hope for the future, because we believe it happened to him.

Here in Christ lies not only the source of all hope, but the sole authority. Man cannot find truth by himself. For man, truth begins with authority.

The greater a man's mental powers, the more likely is he to deceive himself about his mental independence. By his example he hurts the less powerful thinker, and by lovelessness he deprives even himself of the divine light which he, like every human being, needs in sublime questions.

Authority – we may conclude from Augustine – can be neither achieved nor produced nor evaluated by reason. It is singular and encompassing, recognized in the original act of faith, in the obedience that precedes all thoughts and questions about it.

There is a contradiction in this Augustinian Christian thinking. On the one hand it is deemed essential to authority that invisible truth – always close to our mind's eye – became visible also to the eyes of the flesh, to mend our malady. To help man, the divine entered into temporality; in visible means of salvation it descended to our weakness. But against this stands an equally vital thought of Augustine's – philosophically, indeed, his only vital one: that even this temporal, bodily visibility is not a manifestation but a cipher. For our reason is incapable of seeing divine things, and in pressing toward them it is repulsed by the light of truth and thrust back into its familiar darkness. Then we take refuge in the dusk assigned to us by an ineffable wisdom; then we meet that darkness of authority which answers tenderly by miracles of things and words of Scripture, as by signs *(signis)* and shadows *(umbris)* of truth.

It is like a back and forth: God bodily visible, in time – and God invisible, close but not visible even to the mind's eye, only to be felt in signs and shadows. God in the flesh and in the spirit – temporal and eternal. Embodied, he is authority; disembodied, unseen, unknown but believed, he has no authority in the world.

To place authority on a more solid footing we need another basic thought.

e. The Church

1 AN AUGUSTINIAN LINE

'*Ego vero Evangelio non crederem nisi me catholicae Ecclesiae commoveret auctoritas,*' Augustine wrote, with magnificent simplicity. 'I would indeed not believe the Gospel if the authority of the Catholic church did not prompt me as well.' *a:* In other words, Christianity is churchdom. Pre-ecclesiastic and extra-ecclesiastic Christianity means individual interpretation and adoption, independent of the one true exegesis claimed by the Church; but as a historic reality the Christian faith in revelation is faith in the Church, just as the reality of theological dogmatics is ecclesiastic dogmatics. The reason for believing is revelation, but in the form known and guaranteed by the Church. The Protestant revolution, having first rejected the ecclesiastic tradition to give full sway to the Bible, quickly restored a watered-down ecclesiasticism and thus betrayed its own original point.

The present Church is more than formal tradition, administration, and dogma. It is the mystical body of Christ, a Christ not past but present. This incarnation of Christ in its body uniquely sanctifies the Church. One who does not so believe can scarcely understand this, but he can observe the consequences.

To the believer, the Church is in fact primary, his only way to the divine principle. Separation from the Church is accordingly felt to be a separation from God himself. Faith in God has no reality outside the faith in the Church, and freedom is placed within the pale of the Church, the sole arbiter of any conflicts with it.

That the Church exists to this day, despite all errors and crimes of its officials, is held to indicate its divine origin. As a human being the priest may be what he will – he can personally go to hell – but as a priest, thanks to his ordination, he has the indelible character of his office and 'magical' powers in administering the effects of grace. In view of the corruptions one was shocked to observe in the very first centuries, Origen conceived the Church as the house of Rahab, the harlot, which God spared at the destruction of Jericho; and there is talk of a solidarity of the faithful with the sins of the Church. It all goes to show that nothing, no nonsense, no crime in its field, can shake the faith in the Church. It remains the unchallengeable and invincible authority whose warrant prompted Augustine to believe the Gospel.

b: Not everything that we may call revelation is what the Church means by that word. Revelation is not the perception of something 'unearthly' – when an event, a thing, a place, an act fails to conform to the natural course and is experienced as a miracle, as vaguely uncanny, moving, inspiring awe, fear, or bliss. Nor is it the personal inspiration which some will cite to this day. Nor, finally, is it the experience – not to be explained by chance – of destiny in personal achievement, in escape from danger, in indissoluble fellowship, in a course of life which in retrospect seems fated or else steered from bad to worse by demons from hell.

The objective revelation meant to be valid for all is quite another matter. This alone is tied to Church and priesthood. It is a completed revelation, found in canonized books, and today only in the Church which has to pass on everything that might be revelational in character. In the exegesis of the sacred books the Church has full, final discretion. Revelation is the ecclesiastically certified sequence of divine acts in history, and of promised or threatened future occurrences here or in the beyond.

c: As the substance of revelation may not apply directly from Scripture to the individual but must be certified by present, common ecclesiastic authority, the Church becomes the unifying and controlling factor. This has happened in greatly changing ways. In the Middle Ages there was the rich life of Christendom; monastic orders kept springing up; serious thinkers about the faith were in constant revolt – the Church found itself amidst a flowing tide from which it drew whatever new blood it could absorb without jeopardizing its existence. Its very strength came from realizations and creations spawned not by itself but by the spontaneity of Christian life. Confirmed by the Church, those new movements came to prevail, enhanced in the world, though mostly enfeebled within. The greatness of the Church lay in dealing with all this life and thought it was continually offered. In those days, anything original began equivocally and was then either moulded into forms suitable for absorption or destroyed as heretical.

Today it seems to be the other way round. Everything must issue from the Church. People look to it for what they used to bring to it. Strenuous wooing of the forces at work in the nations, among the 'laity', permits it only to keep vegetating a while, tranquilly if circumstances are favourable. Christian churches are no longer deluged with an abundance they need but to administer; they are expected to produce what is beyond their capacity. They have had no more success than philosophy in forming a nucleus of earnest spirituality in the modern world. The changes in the state of the world, the ferment in individuals isolated and left to themselves, their reversals and resolutions, their true inner condition – all these crucial developments occur outside and alongside the churches, even in the ranks of denominational membership. They also occur outside philosophy – thus far a failure limited to supposedly factual occupations that have become hobbies. Both hardly bother with the new situation of mankind, with its unprecedented challenges. The rhetoric which is now common to philosophy and churches throughout the world, a rhetoric that sounds at times like the intoxicating drumbeat savages use to ward off evil spirits, is mere superimposed noise, idling alongside the momentum of world events and the individual potential. A ghostly abyss seems to separate this talk, this acting 'as if', from reality.

2 THE UNIFICATION OF CHRISTIAN BELIEF BY THE CHURCH

The Church is central to any historical inquiry into the Christian faith in revelation. In the Roman Church exclusiveness is a decisive tenet. Historically, the unity of belief has been a Church product; it is objectively false to call even Gospel Christianity a unit, although it was no accidental jumble of adopted concepts either. It remains idle, at any rate, to try to comprehend the unity, the point of reference of this faith, as an objective identity within its diverse expressions. We can comprehend it only as the unity of the evolving Church, and along with this it has evolved in history.

An almost total historical darkness shrouds the primitive community, the nascent form of Christian belief – which did not exist when Jesus preached, originating only when the apostles preached of him as Christ, the Risen. Myths and legends, stories that the resurrected Jesus Christ had appeared and ascended to heaven, document the content of this faith.

The crux is the statement that God had become human. Since this statement as such is incomprehensible, however – since it requires telling what it means, how the thing happened – it became the point of departure for a multifarious, richly phrased theology known as Christology. The dogmatic battles over this shook the Church until the rationally unequivocal formulae were eliminated as heretical and the mutually contradictory elements combined in one mystery. The initial unity of the faith is a fiction of the Church, which in fact produced this unity.

As the unification process cannot be understood as necessary, it is a miracle – analogous to such other great movements as the ones toward world empire, or the evolutions of art to classic peaks and turning-points, or the connected philosophical developments that have a beginning and an end. In part, the Christian Church can thus indeed be explained by the confluence of religious, philosophical, and political motives. It can be explained by the reception of almost everything that had human appeal, excluding only what would have destroyed its own existence. Yet in historical retrospect the whole seems like a plan – which no one had. The unconscious plan seems self-supported and self-restoring over long periods of time. We see a whole that no one put together, a structure of inner consistency and wisdom, the more marvellous and admirable the farther we penetrate it.

Historically the New Testament concludes the profound religious experiences of the Jewish soul. Jesus was the last of the Hebrew prophets. The Christian Church, a new beginning, rests on the whole Bible; efforts to base Christianity on the New Testament alone have failed. It was this growth in constant association with the whole Bible that helped the Church to exert its tremendous effect. A purely Gospel-based Christianity would long have vanished as an odd sect without worldly content, denounced, as by Tacitus, as *odium generis humani* – an offence to the human race. From the factual point of view, therefore, I prefer to speak of biblical rather than Christian religion.

Yet not even the Bible alone sufficed to make the Christian West possible. Greek philosophy, Roman law, government, and politics, and the Hellenistic, notably Stoic, arrangement of all human things in a pattern – all of these had to contribute, to unfold that 'catholicity' whose formative power derived from its universal interests.

Wherever anything particular in faith or living practice aspired to primacy – as monasticism, for example – the Church took action. The Church, being universal and absolute, is nothing particular, but everything particular owes its rights and meaning to the Church.

An irreversible tension prevails between primitive Christianity, which saw the end of the world impend directly for the living generation, and the need to adjust to a world that had to be shaped and institutionalized. The fact that this tension pervades the history of Christendom is the constant spur responsible for its luxuriance, but it also caused endless mendacities. Unity was never stabilized here either.

Marvelling at the overall picture of Christian history, we tend to liken it to such great analogous phenomena as Confucianism or the Egyptian religion which lasted for thousands of years. This shows, however, that longevity is not proof of truth. Confucianism and the Egyptian religion survived longer than Christianity has to date, and yet they are no more. Buddhism is five centuries older than Christianity; both still exist. But the question today, for both, is whether they are doomed or in the process of a new, radical transformation.

Both Buddhism and Christianity have undergone vast changes in the past. In the age of science and technology they cannot stay as they are. Their coming change will be more profound than any past one, or else they will perish. It will be like a rebirth when the real earnest breaks through the façade of religious conventions and national habits. The submergence of man, which we see today and shudder to foresee in future, might be halted and eventually surmounted by a new great form of humanity we can as yet not adequately imagine.

Coming back to the Church, let us take a glance at its unplanned principles, its intellectual and political methods – a glance confined to the Roman Catholic Church which brought the matter to a peak of perfection and stability. It originated in the first centuries A.D., and under Constantine it negotiated the great turn to dominion. The persecuted Church became triumphant. The masses flocked to it. Its entire rank and state of aggregation changed – and yet, after this turn the methods of belief in it continued.

3 THE INTELLECTUAL METHODS OF THE CHURCH

The premise: there is only one true faith, the Christian one. Being unique, it not only claims universal validity; it really is catholic, i.e. universal. Whatever else makes the same absolute claim is untrue, blind, wicked, and must be conquered by such intellectual methods as preaching, teaching, and persuasion, and ultimately by the political methods of coercive force.

a: Whatever truth appears in pre-Christian times, and later outside Christianity, bears some of this catholic character and is accordingly absorbed. There is a primal revelation preceding the biblical one; the human soul is naturally Christian everywhere – *anima naturaliter christiana*. The Catholic way is to be receptive to what seems alien at first, to be ready to enter interpretatively into pagan beliefs and to discover facets of the Christian faith in them.

b: The truth of any thought that appears in the Christian world depends on whether it leads to, or does at least not infringe upon, the necessity and essentiality of Church power, understood as the dispensation of God.

In the questions of free will and grace, for instance, the most profound thoughts were conceived in the West, by St Paul, by Augustine, by Luther All three arrived at the ideas of predestination and irresistible grace; yet the Church rejected this doctrine because it would render its sacraments and means of grace superfluous. Also rejected, however, was the Pelagian doctrine of the power of moral reason, which called for man's free will – for this too would allow man to do without grace by sacraments. One might say that ecclesiastic doctrine does not decide but distinguish and somehow adopt everything. The result – neither predestination nor freedom, but an adjustable semi-Pelagianism – was credited to Augustine, although his predestination ideas were never adopted.

Another example: the theory mentions the naturally Christian soul and assumes that a godly life will bring eternal salvation even if lived outside the Church or in ignorance of the Christian message. Against this, however, stand the words *Extra ecclesiam nulla salus* – outside the Church there is no salvation. The Church manages to combine the two theses.

In general one may say that, having been stirred by the great believing thinkers, ecclesiastic dogmatics will always receive the two opposite points of view so as to be able to take either one, depending on the situation. It can do this, first, by expounding a middle way from which both opposites can be rejected, and secondly, by positing the 'mystery', the secret that is thinkable – i.e., phenomenal – only in seeming contradictions. To cope with the contradictions, there are all the procedures known as *complexio oppositorum*, the fusion of opposites. The Church employs this principle of synthesis in theory and practice, but in reference to something unequivocal that can only be grasped as a mystery. We see both a principle of being unprincipled, ready for all possibilities, and an intangible point of absolute unity. A factual resoluteness is at work in the seemingly irresolute universal receptivity. Arguments are kept in flux until a concrete situation calls for a decision; this will be final – *Roma locuta, causa finita* – and yet the ecclesiastic method will seek to keep the minds in its vast structure as open as possible, for the unequivocal and rigid can no longer cope with every situation. Typically, a Catholic thinker takes up the alternatives, rises above them, rejects each position as one-sided while recognizing elements of truth in it, and makes distinctions previously overlooked, only to decide in the end by transcending all mere alternatives. Aquinas came to be the master of this method.

The method degenerates into countless distinctions resulting in endless discussions. Simple facts are befogged, and thought itself is voided by such thinking, both for the sake of the required charges or defences. Another side of it is the distraction by an apparent philological thoroughness that drowns you in quotations.

c: The objective bases of the truth of faith are the sacred books, followed with some qualification by the Fathers of the Church, the formulated creeds, and the binding decisions of Rome and the ecumenical councils. In case of doubt, the Church alone decides on the further interpretation of these sources.

The interpretation is guided by the Holy Ghost – subjectively put, by a *sensus catholicus*, an instinctive feeling for what will give truth the broadest possible scope while safeguarding the unity and power of the Church.

d: A factual, unexpressed preponderance belongs to some concepts without which the Church could not keep human souls in its power, because the fear they cause drives people into its arms.

There are the eternal punishments of hell: the Church relentlessly spurned the doctrine of Origen, who regarded the punishments of hell as limited in time by the restoration of all things (*apokatastasis panton*). It upheld the intermediate possibility of a limited purgatory and the aid of means of grace, but it never gave up the eternity of hell. Epicurus had already tried in vain to liberate men from the widespread concepts of eternal punishment; and Nietzsche pointed out that the Church seized them as 'the most fertile egg of its power', attracting 'the fearful, the strongest adherents of a new faith'.

There is the passionate condemnation of suicide, because this proves the independence of man. Eternal punishment threatens the suicide who has withdrawn from the ecclesiastic means of grace, providing a dangerous orientation for others.

Nowhere in the world have the methods of soul control been developed to such magnificent heights as in the confessional. Because the priest penetrates into the inmost soul – on the strength of his office, not as a mere mortal – he can put unheard-of pressure on the believer. Parents may be held liable and threatened with purgatory for failing to keep their grown children in the Church. To the hour of death the priest may bring comfort or torment; to this day Catholics who have ceased to believe are seen to turn back then, as if held by an inner chain and thinking, perhaps, 'Just in case'. Documents gathered by Groethuysen show the dismay with which priests in the seventeenth century discovered that men could go to their deaths without them. They felt the ground shake under their feet, for this evidence of the ability to die was the existential refutation of their method of coercing souls. Giordano Bruno spat at the crucifix which his priestly murderers held up to him at the stake, supposedly for his salvation.

e: The method combines rigour with indulgence. The rigour lies in the principle (e.g., the ban on divorce) and in the· enforcement of concrete administrative measures (e.g., the ban on the French worker priests). It lies in the eternal punishment of hell, in the insistence on believing the whole multitude of dogmas. It is convincingly manifested in degrees of true asceticism among monks and clergy.

At the same time there are kindly aspects: the Church knows the means of confession, penance, and cure. It relieves man of the burden of his bad conscience. It has a broad sense of the tolerable; it fits the average person. It knows how to let live, to acknowledge the natural splendour of creation. It permits men to enjoy this, provided they obey the Church. It shores up distraction, dissipation, indecision, without making excessive demands on man; it eases life, according to its motto, 'Dreadful to heretics, to sinners mild'.

Yet all this it can dare only by making sure that its relentless severity is not forgotten, by guarding the impassable frontiers that make the believer feel the absolute.

How wise – provided one does not believe in the potential of human freedom based upon Transcendence, in the honest, unlimited self-revelation of man! But how reprehensible if the result is to foster his self-shrouding seclusion to provide surrogates that will keep him from a lucid view of himself!

4 THE POLITICAL METHODS OF THE CHURCH

The most profound transformation of Christianity was its entrance into the political arena. For the Church as such this came early, when Constantine suddenly brought it to power in the state. For a time the medieval papacy could aspire to world domination, and in varying forms the political claim continues to this day.

Violence and coercion complemented and at times replaced preaching and the exemplary life of the faithful, although it was emphasized over and over that faith could and must not be forced. Augustine upheld this view for decades, until the Donatist controversy made him commandeer the state power for ecclesiastic ends: 'Coge intrare – compel them to enter the Church!' His irrational justification by an allegorically interpreted New Testament verse was a horrifying reversal of Gospel Christianity into its opposite. And this has remained the basic ecclesiastic attitude. In Protestant times it took the cynical form of the phrase Cuius regio eius religio – whatever creed a prince professed determined the creed of his subjects. Later, under the pressure of modern public opinion, this compulsory link between throne and altar was abandoned and gave way to milder forms.

Even today, however, the churches keep exerting political influence. One result, for instance, is political patronage for communicants, possibly in proportion to the membership strength of a country's denominations, to the detriment of non-practising Christians and at the risk of ruining a free spiritual life

The basic phenomenon is that the Church, a group of men, turns the call upon God into an instrument of worldly power. The human will to power is disguised as God's will. The demands of a secular struggle are falsely sanctified and made absolute as divine demands. As a result, ecclesiastic politics deals a death blow to communication, peace, and loyalty. There is no talking with religious warriors.

i. Authority, power, and force

True authority conquers inwardly. Once this inwardness ceases, external authority will dwindle too. In jeopardy, it will resort to force.

The substance of authority is more than any individual wants and knows. Authority encompasses; it is total, not particular. Its historic forms are definite at any time. It covers the man who commands and the one who obeys; both feel subject to it. It is binding on a kind of human action that responds in inner freedom.

Yet authority gains permanence in time by force, either by inward pressure on the soul or by external, physical force. Unallied with force, it would comprise none but the elect. To involve all in the continuity of its existence – not only in rare exalted moments – authority requires means of compulsion.

A stable authority, therefore, has a voluntary and a compulsory side. The voluntary side is an awareness of unwritten but inwardly binding laws, of awe-inspiring orders, offices, and forms. Compulsion controls, stands silently by, and enforces if need be. There is tension in authority, due to the freedom it implies; the concrete action freely heeds authority.

The union of authority and power is the vital problem of nations. They derive their rank from the content of authority, their permanence from power.

Authority has always grown historically. It cannot be produced; it can only be found and renewed from the depths of a tradition that will recognize its own changed form.

Authority alone, in a purely ideal sense, lends power to an individual without bringing him into the community of all; it comes to naught because his impotence makes its preservation an exercise in futility. Power alone is tyranny, which robs authority of its content and thus cannot have a stability borne by the state of men's minds. If authority and power part company, both will be lost.

ii. Extremes of compulsion

When it had the power, the Church punished heretics by death. According to ecclesiastic thinking they deserved to be excluded not just from the Church, by excommunication, but from the world by execution – *non solum ab Ecclesia per excommunicationem separari, sed etiam per mortem a mundo excludi,* as Aquinas put it. The procedure, after the Church had pronounced the excommunication, was to do the rest by a secular judgment – *iudicio saeculari* – for the Church, as the reality of Christian love, did not besmirch itself with blood.

Religious slaughter has marked human history from primeval times.

Several philosophers of Antiquity observed the phenomenon and its roots in superstition, in the will to power, in psychological drives, and the Christian ecclesiastic faith has succumbed to it for long periods. From the twelfth century to the seventeenth the Roman Church dressed up the process in the legal garb of the Inquisition, a long-continued display of the spirit of ecclesiastic compulsion, visible whenever social and political conditions gave it free rein. True, there were always great Christians speaking out against it, but the artful development of those methods has remained an unparalleled outrage against souls and nations. At the same time it gratified a mass delight in execution and torture, secrecy and terrorism – though now and then, when fear became too general, the enraged populace would kill some inquisitors.

The trial procedure was in line with this spirit. Denunciations, anonymous or otherwise, were solicited. The accused never knew his accusers. No one defended him. With sadistic inventiveness every degree of torture was used to compel self-incrimination; but as confessions were supposed to be voluntary, they required repetition after torture to be valid. In fact, whatever the accused said and did proved his guilt: he was guilty if he confessed, and if he endured heroically, if no tortures could wring a falsehood from him, he was guilty because this could only be due to the devil's aid. Suspicion was tantamount to conviction.

Besides heresy and schism, the charges extended to witchcraft, sorcery, and devil worship – i.e., besides opposition to the Church, to unreal acts whose very existence was an outgrowth of the ecclesiastically sanctioned superstitions.

The historian who cites the spirit of the times to explain such things, who exculpates them, so to speak, in the sense of a historical judgment he regards as superior, forgets that there were always others who did understand. We are betraying those, our allies, to the supposedly compelling spirit of the times. If this historical attitude is made absolute, it will produce the kind of inner spinelessness we have shudderingly come to know.

We know the instances of a churchdom that is supposed, after all, to be the vessel of the biblical faith: the Inquisition; the Crusades; the religious wars; the actions taken by the papal Church against the Albigenses and against Giordano Bruno, the great martyr of modern philosophy – a greater hero than any Christian martyr, since he had to hold out solely on the strength of philosophical faith, without either the assurance of revelation or the community of a church, but standing alone before God. We know Luther's inflammatory squibs against the peasants and his counsels against the Jews, which Hitler followed to the letter; we know of Calvin's ecclesiastic régime, his treatment of Servetus in particular; we know of Spinoza's excommunication and denunciation by the Jewish synagogue. These few examples of ecclesiasticism demonstrate that any church, as a power organization and a possible tool of fanaticism and superstition merits the utmost distrust, however indispensable it may be to tradition in the world.

iii. The difference between ecclesiastic and modern total rule

The Church rests upon sacred writings whose content will always offset the totalitarian trend and never allow human dignity, freedom, and justice to vanish altogether. The ecclesiastic horrors happened in an atmosphere of superstition, replete with mysterious meanings; the modern horrors happen in an atmosphere ruled by the superstitions of intellectual enlightenment. The totalitarian Church lacked the means of limitless power which the technological age puts at the disposal of the state, and nowhere does the state today serve as an arm of the Church as in times past.

Now that they no longer have a 'secular arm', the churches firmly reject the methods once developed by their own totalitarianism and now far more cunningly used in behalf of total rule. Yet even now the ecclesiastic faith, with characteristic totalitarian naïveté, regards itself as the sole, authorized infallible vessel of truth and inwardly denies the equal rights of the 'heathen', the infidel, the heretic.

iv. Specifically ecclesiastic political methods

The Church never had armies of its own. With the temporary exception of the small papal state – to whose interests, then, even the Catholic Church could bow – it lacked all the major implements of power and thus had to work by indirection. To enforce its demands it used the faith of individuals and nations.

For centuries the intellectual superiority of clergy and monks was such as to make them indispensable to administrative and political affairs. They alone developed the basic concepts and maxims of government, the warrants of action and the sanctions by the Church. They developed the canon law and provided a substructure in the Donation of Constantine and the collection of the Pseudo-Isidoran decretals. That these were forgeries is irrelevant. The whole matter was not a forgery, in the sense of fraud, but a far greater calamity: the transformation and falsification of original Christianity into the political Church.

The complex history of the Church is of the greatest interest to those who would understand ecclesiastic political thinking. The Church was unified by the papacy in such inner struggles as the conquest of intra-ecclesiastic democracy as represented by the conciliar movement, and once accomplished, unity was enforced by administrative and financial techniques. If threatened and weakened by schisms – as of the Oriental churches and of Protestantism – it was the more strictly reinforced within the narrowed sphere. Depending on the social, economic, and political structure of the West at large, the Church adjusted to feudalism, to absolutism, to bourgeois nationalism, to parliamentary democracy, to socialism.

The Church still stands. From the eighteenth century on it could seem as if it were swamped by the tides of an intellectually superior world, by freedom of thought and research, by the expansion of humanism, by the grandeur of Western literature and philosophy. But these tides receded, and like a rock the Church would reappear, unchanged in its intellectual-political structure.

It keeps employing its political methods, seeking as ever to work through the believing masses. Only, today it has reached a limit: if individual clerics may still be ready for martyrdom, populations are not. The Church must yield much and compromise extensively – as in the Nazi era, for example – lest the material interests of the faithful suffer too much damage. And it has reached another limit: in the global politics that count today its relatively small, tradition-bound structure seems to have lost the political vision and prudence to perform world-wide tasks. It has come to delude itself radically about realities, as in the case of its pact with Hitler in 1933.

Conclusion

Our historical observations, though transcended in anticipation here and there, have remained on the surface. They missed the main point, for any strictly historical view will lose sight of the essence. But in so far as we make use of history, to hear from it what concerns ourselves, it will put us in touch with its supra-historic side.

The objectivations of historical knowledge are the foreground. What takes place in them is motivated from the existential ground, and only there do we meet the other self and become involved in the struggle of powers. Staying in the foreground, we would lose sight of the timeless Existenz[1] of men, but a disappearance of the foreground would silence the ground itself. Without the objectivations of the foreground, the powers to which we as ourselves owe the assurance of our origin are voiceless. What does not come to appear is as if it were not.

We must not be content with the historic foreground, however. The risk of historical objectivation is that our knowledge may blind us to things that were serious and real – just as the themes of philosophical discussion will both advance and jeopardize what counts.

The satisfaction we feel in viewing an infinite historical variety is justified as a transition, but it may distract us existentially. The supra-historic is inaudible without a grasp of historic facts – and yet, grasped purely as such, the facts conceal it. We cannot do without a view of the phenomena that give us our bearings in reality; we must know the history and the human world we live in. But lingering to observe history, enjoying what is great and beautiful in it, abhorring the mean and the petty – this does not take us

[1] This crucial concept of Karl Jaspers' philosophy is analysed in detail on pp. 64–68 – *Translator.*

beneath the surface. All it shows us is a world of cultural humanism, a second world suspended in the real one. We welcome the humanistic contact as a freely observing game tied only to texts and monuments; we welcome the why and the how of tracking down facts, and the delight of understanding. But we sense danger in a state of mind that shrinks instinctively into itself before the abundance of grandeur and horror.

This state of mind, however awed by what seems great to it, does an injustice to men as human beings. It objectifies and assesses them on the pretence of being able to see and judge history.

But we are supposed to touch the essence. And we can do this only by penetrating the phenomena and achieving a supra-historical communication with a human earnest that works a change in us. The sound of that language transforms our association with historical phenomena. We grow indifferent then to mere history, and dispense with its endlessness; we know there are gods everywhere, but we know also that we lack the superhuman faculty of universal response. We cease to be spectators following their emotions; we heed the call to become ourselves in mind and in action. Each of us knows in his way how limited we are in our ability to do so, but there is no telling where an open mind will take us.

Our brief exposé aimed at judgments – for possible judgments are included in historical understanding. Their source, however, did not clearly emerge as yet. They remained on the surface.

Historical exposition is limited by a use of general concepts; being general, they are inadequate to historic reality. We were asking in concepts, aiming at something general, but so as to make us feel what is not general, not generally comprehensible, and for that reason not generally valid. Thus our inquiry into revelation took us to the general concepts of faith in revelation and faith at large, and our question how to think of revelation, to thinking at large; the question of the authority of revelation made us ask about the meaning of authority at large, and the question of the real authority of the Church, about the Church at large. What is real for an individual who is historically, existentially involved was bound to be lost in the process. But we did arrive at a language in which not even a man so involved can refuse to speak and to answer, unless he wants to do the truly anti-human thing and break off communication.

Part Two. The modern tripartition: science, philosophy, theology

a. *The Universal Scientific Approach*

The vast intellectual achievements of almost thirty centuries of philosophical and theological thought do more than excite our admiration. They contain truths to be reabsorbed and rescued from oblivion time and time again.

But in our whole state of mind, in the pattern and structure of our thought and cognition, a change has occurred that casts a new light on all things. It happened in recent centuries, due to a phenomenon which earlier, even among the Greeks, was only dimly foreshadowed: the phenomenon of modern science.

First, modern science is methodical cognition in which we are aware of the methods we use. Second, it is compelling: no one who understands it can deny it without intellectual dishonesty. Third, its general validity is not a mere claim as was made for all past cognition. It is a fact: scientific results alone will spread as comprehensible to everyone. And fourth, it is universal, affecting all that is real and conceivable.

The experience of modern science creates a state of mind which we call the scientific approach. In this approach there is no knowledge without knowing its limitations; there is no certainty without uncertainty; the scope and premises of every method are seen, and it is understood that this sort of cognition can always be achieved by restraint and renunciation only and will never reach the whole of Being.

The cogency of science makes it unavoidable as far as it goes. If we avoid it we become untruthful. While we have access to a large area of truth outside the sciences – in philosophy and theology – this also stops being truth when its theses conflict with scientific cognition.

The universal scientific approach has become possible in our time, and sometimes real, as a state of mind. Though on the way to realization in all sciences, it has not yet been generally and reliably adopted. Sometimes, scientists have it only in their own fields. In the thinking that prevails in public we see more of an uncritical 'enlightenment' than of this scientific attitude.

The universal scientific approach is not a universal science. For a long time philosophy used to appear as a universal science, and accordingly had a world outlook. Both have been destroyed by the modern approach. In a sense, it has changed the state of all truth ever handed down to us. Just as a single hormone transforms an entire organism without destroying it, the modern scientific approach transforms all traditional thinking. We need not give up this great, living, true thinking, the carrier of our humanity; without it we would lose ourselves. But the scientific approach exists. Adopted in pure form, it is by no means fatal; rejected, it will be fatal. In a dishonest atmosphere, in the confusion of pseudo-enlightenment, neither philosophy nor theology can keep the faith in a garb conflicting with science.

Both must adapt themselves and their views of themselves and their methods to the new situation created by the new approach. Philosophy has ceased to be a science; it is a source of its own, between science and the faith in revelation. By the truth of this line hangs the treatment of all our questions.

1 THE MODERN SCIENTIFIC EVOLUTION

Science came to stand on its own feet in recent centuries, most strikingly as mathematical natural science. Galileo personifies the development of this way to achieve knowledge by mathematical propositions, subsequently confirmed or refuted by experiment and observation. The new type of cognition had a profound impact; as a result it was absolutized as the only science or turned into a model for the rest.

From the start, however, modern science had a more far-reaching significance. It is the idea of compelling, generally valid cognition proceeding by specific methods, progressing infinitely but always particularly, aimed at things in the world, at whatever occurs to us in reality as objective and conceivable. What came thus to be known as correct would in fact – unlike most previous assertions of truth – prevail everywhere. Not mathematical natural science alone but biology, history, the whole assortment of sciences that cannot be conclusively arranged in any system, moved in this direction.

Everywhere, then, tension arose between the immediate pleasure in observation, contemplation, and expression of present reality, and the scientific exactitude of searching inquiry and intelligent, causal cognition in constant interaction of propositions and their confirmation or refutation by real phenomena. The first kind of seeing is completed in the present; in the second kind of searching, the grander our achievements and the more lucid our awareness of them, the more we keep feeling en route, viewing the most impressive results as mere steps, as mere beginnings for the most conscious of scientists. What mattered to a scientist was the pure elaboration of the scientifically possible.

This tension, which continues to this day, rests on a basic fact of all research activity. Each modern science has grown in a space filled with a peculiar philosophical substance. The motivations of natural science grew in the mundane piety of nature lovers, chemistry in the profound natural philosophy of alchemists, biology in the observers of universal life, the philological and historical sciences in the humanists' cultural urge to absorb the classics. It was always a joy in realities that spawned the will to know them precisely. But then, abandoning the tension, science can detach itself from this ground and become bustle, technique, and consumption of philological data. It can lose its meaning in increased methodical acribia. Where science keeps its meaning, a scientist will pursue it on grounds that are not scientific but philosophical, grounds which he conquers by transforming rather than destroying them.

The tension leads to peculiar problems in every cognitive field. The historical sciences, for instance, move on two levels. Philology, criticism, the substantiation of historic realities, editing technique, linguistics, antiquarianism – all this grew along with philosophical humanism and provided an indispensable, scientifically lucid infrastructure. On the second level, of comprehending meanings in their full scope and depth, the road from humanist erudition to science was more difficult. Dependent on congeniality and phraseological skill, extraordinary hermeneutical achievements were registered by Hegel and the Romanticists, for example. The procedure was supposed to become scientific in the 'Historical School'. But the methods of checking comprehension for accuracy were still deficient and frequently lacking altogether, and so was a sense of the diverse ways to understand; as a result, cognition remained entangled in arbitrary opinions. A vital step within the modern scientific approach is the basing of the philosophical sciences on a factual and theoretical clarification of the methods of understanding – methods which until then were ingeniously applied, but scientifically inexact. One representative of this step was Max Weber.

The outcome of the past few centuries is that great scientists have striven for an independent, autonomous, accurate scientific cognition in all fields – i.e., universally – and have achieved it in many, though by no means in all.

At the same time, however, it became evident that science itself could not answer the question of its meaning – why it ought to be, and what makes men pursue it. To call science an end in itself did not avail against the charges of superfluity, of knowing things not worth knowing, of turning thought into paths detrimental to life, undermining the human substance, and finally threatening to abolish mankind. Indeed, the talk of science as an end in itself indicated that its basis is one of faith and lies in philosophy.

2 THE NEW EXPERIENCE OF PHILOSOPHICAL INDEPENDENCE

The self-criticism of the sciences showed them their limits, but in a new way it also showed the independence of philosophy. Philosophy is not a science like the modern sciences; what belongs to them departs from it, rather. Left to philosophy is its substance of old: a kind of cognition which, if not generally valid for every intellect, is a movement of thought, the illumination of philosophical faith.

Historically, until the more recent centuries, philosophy used to include science as if both were the same. As long as their practice of 'natural reason' was considered as one, the question of philosophy's independence and the distinction between science and philosophy did not arise.

Now that an insight into the wholly different origins of their truth has separated them and their cognitive methods, they are indeed inseparably linked. The *raison d'être* of science; the seriousness and the danger of wanting to know, the '*sapere aude*' of Horace; the unqualified commitment – these things can be illuminated only philosophically and spring from faith.

Philosophy as an independent source has existed for thousands of years, since the first Greek philosophers. The thinkers of the faith in revelation took it up, only to deny that a faith of its own could come from it. Philosophy has its own great tradition based on writings virtually analogous to the sacred books, and despite revelation a philosophical current continues from its own source without revelational thinking.

The trend is to have philosophy overshadowed, whether by the exact, cogent sciences proper or by religious knowledge and obedience to faith. Against this, philosophizing individuals draw upon their own insight for the support of this great tradition of theirs, which has fed almost all theological thought as well.

The criteria for the truth of thought differ in science and philosophy. In science they lie entirely in the object, in the content of thought, in judgment. In philosophy they lie in outer and inner action, in the state of the soul, in decision.

In science the proof depends on objective researches, inquiries, tests; in philosophy it depends on existential reality.

3 WHERE SCIENCE AND PHILOSOPHY BREAK
WITH THEOLOGICAL COGNITION

The new independence of philosophy made a difference in the opposition to the faith in revelation.

If theologians make statements about facts subject to empirical, generally valid determination, they can never be right against methodically cogent science. Wherever science differs and a scientifically thinking person adopting its method must admit its result, the only alternative to being guided by science is intellectual dishonesty – the *sacrificium intellectus*. While such a sacrifice is unbearable to any rational being, an acceptance of scientific cognition is by no means the end of the faith in revelation. For this faith is beyond scientific cognition and untouched by it. It is neither cognoscible nor combatable if it gives up the aberrations it has kept falling into, due to misconceptions of itself. Whenever scientific knowledge belies a thesis of faith, faith has lost out; but in that case it had already engaged in a type of thought not its own.

The self-defence of philosophy against its negation by religious faith is another matter. There the confrontation is not between knowledge and faith, but between faith and faith. Yet this philosophical opposition, while refusing to bow and obey, does not negate. Only a dogmatic theology and a dogmatic philosophy, both fatally insistent on the absoluteness of their supposedly known faiths, exclude each other. The two faiths as such, in revelation and in reason, are poles which affect each other, cannot wholly understand each other, but do not stop trying. The individual can acknowledge in another, as the other's faith, what he rejects in and for himself.

4 THE WIDESPREAD MISCONCEPTIONS OF PHILOSOPHY TODAY

In principle, cognition has today been purified on scientific terms, in response to philosophical impulses. But this purification is not yet a reality in the broad strata of educated modern mankind – not in all scientists, not in all philosophy professors, not in the thinking of nations. What has been surmounted in principle, therefore, continues in fact to be a prevailing opinion.

Today theology, academic philosophy, and conventional public opinion put philosophy into the false position of a science. It is classified as a department of a faculty, treated as a branch of objective research using rational means for the generally valid cognition of its objects. Like other sciences it is expected to be making progress, to have always reached its latest and accordingly highest state. It is asked for results. It is supposed to be utilized. Or it is disdained because no such progress takes place, because philosophy 'knows' nothing. One does not say so, out of traditional respect, but one ignores the obsolete business.

Many of philosophy's own representatives have gone along with this image. It was made possible by self-forgetfulness, by the view that man and all his thoughts and actions are based purely on the intellect, that this foundation as a whole is philosophy, and that opposed to it, outside the intellect, are 'feelings' that do not concern the philosophical science. There has been talk of an unmentionable 'private metaphysics'. Or the mystery of faith was called incomprehensible – to be swallowed, as Hobbes said, like pills that are good for you but must never be chewed, lest the vile taste make you vomit.

The truth is that philosophy rests on ascertainment by thinking – on things which reason, utilizing the intellect, enables men to see – and that this does not happen in a void.

Philosophy has been lost sight of. Why? Because today, oblivious of itself, it fails in its function. It no longer illuminates what men live by; it lapses into the mere realism of a supposed knowledge of objects, into the vacuity of endless disputations. Its thinking loses the vigour of subsequent inner action. The philosophizer no longer thinks out of total involvement. His thinking becomes noncommittal, existentially lax in spite of acute logic and literary brilliance. It ceases to be philosophy.

It was like that once before, in late Antiquity, in the age of St Augustine. Despite his respect for the philosophically serious neo-Platonist speculation, the philosophy of those days with its comfortable rationalistic conventions, its interminable dogmatic and sceptical repetition of thoughts, its proclivity for the mere phrasing of academic doctrines and subjects, could not satisfy the serious Augustine. He restored philosophical thinking to its full earnest. His new, original philosophy absorbed the contents of biblical thought and revelation from the entire horizon of scriptural texts. It was like a blood transfusion, administered to philosophy by the still young, still vital Christian faith.

A thinker such as this did not make the later distinction between philosophy and theology, or even between nature and the supernatural. Philosophy and theology were one to Augustine – and then, in other ways, to Scotus Erigena, to Anselm, to Cusanus. Was revelation itself not natural? Was nature itself not supernatural? Was natural insight, the *lumen naturale* not supernaturally based?

When the line between natural and revelational cognition was finally drawn, philosophy seemed lost at first, to have become mere intellectual cognition on the one side, and a mystery on the other.

It had to recall itself and its source anew. Intellectual cognition – i.e., science – is identically valid for all men, theologians and philosophers included. But philosophy, detached from revelation and theology and from their basis in the Holy Spirit, knows the inner witness of its own spirit, of reason, of the human potential. For individuals this can be the source of insight and decision, the ultimate authority. With the faith in revelation finally dogmatized, philosophy was forced to realize that there could be no more fusions of the kind that had been possible once, in the stage of religious growth.

b. The Philosophical Concept of Faith in Revelation

Science has nothing to do with faith in revelation, philosophy a great deal. In Part One of this book we have seen that belief in revelation is a fact of this world, although only believers understand what revelation is. Yet philosophy, from Socrates on, enables men to tell the things they understand from the things they do not understand. Not to understand a thing is no reason to deny it, or to ignore it as irrelevant.

Does philosophical thinking allow us at least to recognize – from the outside, as it were – what defies understanding? Can an unbeliever, on his part, circumscribe and question revelation as a thing which men believe but believers alone understand? If so, its reality will look to him about as follows:

Revelation is a direct communication or act of God in space and time, definitely placed in history. It is regarded as a reality that has a profanely historic side but is essentially sacred history, seen only by the believer. To the believer, sacred and profane history coincide, so he wants to find out from historical tradition how the thing happened. He means the reality – but at the same time he means in it something quite different, which remains real and certain even if history grows uncertain and dim. Hence the believer's lively concern with historic facts supposedly related to the revelation, and his simultaneous indifference to these facts when the issue is the revelation itself. For this is believed, not known by historical evidence.

If the divine communication were an existing reality like a communication between humans, it could be more or less surely established by documentary evidence, as other historic facts. Since it exists for faith alone, however, the direct divine communication must, from the outset, differ fundamentally from direct human communication. It exists with so little certainty that belief in it is the believer's 'merit' – though his ability to believe is not free but granted, in an act of grace, by the self-revealing God. On the other hand, the revelation has so much reality that failure to believe it makes man 'guilty' – even though this failure is due to God's withholding of the grace that confers the ability to believe.

This general definition of revelation – as a direct (but unique, and thus not really direct) divine communication or act, localized in space and time – is by no means sufficient, however.

First, the Christian faith does not permit us to subsume its revelation with others under a generic concept. Christian revelation is unique. It shatters the generic concept. Only this one revelation is true.

Second, the revelation is believed within a church. The faith in it cements a community of worship in which God is present here and now, and in acts performed by the priest and by the congregation. This, to be sure, is a fundamental trait of all religions; no faith in revelation can do without joint worship. But the Christian one is characterized by definite sacraments, by definite preaching of the word, by a formulated creed.

Third, and paradoxically, the Christian Church is both temporal and supra-temporal by virtue of its establishment on the one unique, definite revelation. The Church is temporal because it was founded at a definite time, spread all over the inhabited globe, and organized in ever new communities; it has a history, a tradition to which it refers, and it derives the specific authority of its official representatives from the original call of the apostles. But this Christian Church is simultaneously supra-temporal, for its eschatological consciousness anticipates the end of time and history and makes the believer at home in an eternal kingdom that is not of this world. It will come on doomsday, on Judgment Day. But it is already here in the tangible reality of congregations, preachments, temples, and sacred acts.

In philosophizing we must be careful not to create a premature false harmony by diluting the concept of revelation. The concept which believers communicate to us must not be brought near and made accessible in pseudo-comprehension. We dilute and flatten Christian revelation if we equate it with things 'revealed' in insight, in poetic or artistic creation, or if we equate it with the great strides of the human spirit in history, this unpredictable and even retrospectively incomprehensible resurgence of basic human attitudes.

It is another dilution to equate revelation in the religious sense with essentially human experiences. In my freedom, for instance, I may be granted the 'miracle' of the gift of self. When, having sounded out, thought out, argued out a situation, I come to a resolution that is rationally not quite explicable even then, something happens which I cannot bring to pass. My thinking will be preceded by an incomprehensible assurance which thought serves only to brighten, an assurance which even scientific research needs to be meaningful. Our way of saying, 'It came as a revelation to me', or, 'It was like a revelation', is bad usage in so far as it recalls the Christian revelation. It is a self-deception and in bad taste to speak of revelation or grace without meaning the specific character of faith in revelation.

The dilution tends to confuse. This is a case of either-or: to be truthful, I have to admit that I do not believe in revelation. True, my admission is qualified by the never-finished process of genuine enlightenment, but the root cause is the reality of God himself. We know how this can be experienced; the Bible – itself the work of men, and thus full of fallacies – has made us aware of it, as have Plato, Spinoza, and Kant. If I go by this yardstick, especially by the substance of the Bible, I feel no impulse to believe in revelation, no urge to experience its reality in any of the forms offered, and then to confess that I believe. But I do feel impelled to keep seeing the amazing phenomenon of a belief in revelation, to keep questioning it, and to try – in vain – to understand it.

For one who distinguishes what he does and does not understand, the crux is that a thing he does not understand is far from nothing. It upsets him – especially when, like the faith in revelation, it has for thousands of years been real and consequential in men he esteems and deems worth loving.

To be truthful in philosophizing, we must let the faith in revelation stand as it is, acutely incomprehensible. To rational thinking its statements are contradictory, its actions and existence incompatible. Yet these very contradictions and incongruities become elements of the faith which they enhance and make conscious, from Tertullian's *credo quia absurdum*' to Kierke-gaard's paradoxon. Revelation reveals by concealment.

Tension has prevailed from the beginning between the faith in revelation and that which believers call 'natural reason'. But our problem is obscured by the matter-of-course way to speak of natural reason as if scientific cognition and philosophical insight were one and the same.

c. *What is Natural Reason?*

Is the faith in revelation, or the revelation it is so sure of, unnatural, anti-natural, supernatural? The antithesis makes sense only if we know what we mean by 'natural reason', and what we mean by the 'revelation' that is not natural.

1 THE CONCEPT FROM THE STANDPOINT OF REVEALED RELIGION

First, we conceive the distinction from the standpoint of the faith in revel-ation. Theologians characterize their opponents – i.e., those who refuse to submit to the revelation interpreted by the theologians – as men who confine themselves to the natural: to thought as such, to the intellect, to cognition of the world and to speculation about Being. This is what they call natural theology, maintaining, however, that all this naturalness, if it would be self-sufficient, is perdition – that salvation lies in the supernatural that is given in revelation and taken in faith. This alone, they say, invests the natural realm as a whole with relative meaning, whereas the faithful submit obediently to God, who speaks supernaturally through the historically unique prophets and Apostles, and through a traditional authority claimed by men whom the Church empowers to do so.

2 THE CONCEPT FROM ITS OWN STANDPOINT

Yet what is 'nature', what is 'natural thinking', conceived from its own point of view? The ambiguous concept comes from Stoic philosophy. It comprises whatever lies in man and in the world, 'is-ness' and 'ought-ness', necessity and freedom, the *logos* that is one with the deity, pervades the world as *pneuma*, and becomes accessible to man as such in thought and practice, by what he is as part and parcel of the divine nature. This concept of nature was all-encompassing. It left out nothing, knew no other pos-sibility. The Christian antithesis of natural and supernatural also lay in this one 'nature'. Religious cults, gods, magic, divination – all were 'naturally' comprehended by the Stoics.

From this Stoic interpretation of Being comes the current concept of nature, so indistinct as to include all opposites within itself. We adopt only one of its theses: philosophizing has access to whatever is accessible to human beings at large throughout the world, because as humans they are open to the world, to all Being, and to themselves.

Against this, the supernatural, anti-natural, or unnatural as conceived by revelational theologians does not lie in man as such. Revelation comes from without, as God manifests himself somewhere in space and time. Man cannot find him on his own, being 'by nature' not open to God. God never shows himself to men except at those particular places and times, and to particular humans who have existed historically and borne witness to him. By the divine intrusion man is changed in a peculiar, unique way: he is converted. He cannot accomplish this change himself, as in philosophizing; he becomes a new man. To the rest of mankind, revelation and conversion remain either unknown – because the testimony has not reached that far – or merely outwardly known in marvelling at a conversion process that defies understanding.

Psychological analysis does not extend beyond the multitude of aberrations or deceptive surrogates. The event which takes place, or has taken place, at the core – an undeniable event, in view of its extraordinary and comprehensible real consequences over thousands of years – remains alien to us. We may be inclined now and then to analyse it psychologically as a historic illusion; but we soon feel our failure even though we are right about much that is called Christian, and about many professed believers in revelation.

3 WHAT THE THEOLOGICAL USE OF PHILOSOPHY INDICATES

In fact, the core we fail to understand is always limited to people organized in ecclesiastic groups. They claim a specific holiness for the content of their faith, and for their religious acts in connection with it, as distinct from the merely natural.

Now a strange thing happens: philosophy – which they call 'natural' – furnishes the believing theologians with most of the forms of thought and many of the existential impulses they use in building up their cognition by faith. They appropriate what this natural philosophical thought calls Transcendence, deity, encompassing, and reality; they take whatever has been touched upon in sublime thinking operations since the birth of Greek, Hindu, and Chinese philosophy. But then, having borrowed their methods and contents of thought, the theologians tend to disparage their opponents as entangled in half-truths and, at the salient point, devoid of truth. All through the centuries of Christianity we find the same pattern of euchring an opponent out of his own. Even today theologians judge philosophy in the harshest terms, to the point of total rejection.

And yet the two move in a common sphere of thought. Do they, perhaps, share a peculiar kind of thinking, the philosophically speculative kind? Or is the thinking of the faith in revelation a specific one, which believers alone can accomplish? If so, we unbelievers would find it unintelligible. But we know the forms of thought in which it is communicated, and we feel, therefore, that we must understand. We would do so in a common speculative sphere inaccessible to the mere intellect (though this is used there too, at every step). But history shows that such understanding will not satisfy believers in revelation.

4 PHILOSOPHY NOT LIMITED TO A SPECIFIC 'NATURALNESS'

Philosophers object to hearing themselves and their cause called 'natural' by theologians – for such 'naturalness', as distinct from another reality would put philosophy in need of supplementation. Theologians would like that. They admit philosophy as a preliminary step, a means, but in so doing they deprive it of its essence and degrade it to a science. In philosophizing we should not unthinkingly submit to the categories of theologians who pretend to survey our work from a higher vantage point and restrictively characterize it as mere 'nature' or 'natural reason'. Philosophy must not wither in the confinement of a differentiated naturalness.

The 'nature' of man is more than he is as an object of physiological and psychological studies. 'Natural' reason is more than the mere intellect, the point where consciousness at large is capable of correct, compelling cognition. Rather, human nature is the human essence, man's existential vision of the world as he is given to himself, his insight into what is, his response to the ciphers, his resolve. We live by the relation to Transcendence. In this relation we know ourselves on the way, or we search for it and gain an indefinable confidence. What 'natural' man is remains open. There is no mere naturalness apart from the supernatural.

It is man's experience in philosophizing that the reality of a revelation which issues from God and still needs men to interpret it does not conform to the idea of God.

A refusal to believe in revelation is not due to godlessness; it is due to the faith of the soul created free by Transcendence.

Mindful of the truth it has access to, and of the remoteness of a Transcendence that is hidden yet inclined toward all men, philosophical faith must give up the reality of revelation in favour of the ambiguous movement of ciphers. This faith, which appears in many forms, becomes neither authority nor dogma; it remains dependent on communication among men who must necessarily talk with each other, but do not necessarily have to pray with each other.

Part Three. A basic philosophical knowledge (philosophy of the modes of encompassing)

In our tripartition – theology, science, philosophy (or faith in revelation, rational cognition, and philosophical faith) – we were operating as with fixed points. This pattern is not false in the sense we meant it, but it needs a background of basic philosophical ideas, an awareness of how we find ourselves in the world. I have tried to develop this several times in my writings – chiefly in Von der Wahrheit. The following is a brief summary.

a. The Modes of Encompassing

1 THE SUBJECT-OBJECT DICHOTOMY

Consciousness is the basic phenomenon of the split into subject and object: we are conscious of objects we mean. It is a unique dichotomy, comparable to no relationship between objects.

What does not enter into this dichotomy is for us like non-being. We can conceive of nothing without this dichotomy. Whatever we speak of has come into the dichotomy as we speak of it.

Reality becomes phenomenal to our consciousness. Even the unconscious is deduced from phenomena in consciousness; it can have reality for us only in so far as it affects consciousness, as it appears to our consciousness.

The subject-object dichotomy is our stage for the appearance of all that is and can be. In realizing the stage, we simultaneously become aware of the phenomenality of whatever appears on it.

We can illuminate the principles governing the stage: what phenomena there are, and in what sense, and from which originally different dimensions they come into the light of this stage – and thus, for us, come to be.

2 THE MODES OF ENCOMPASSING

We have a word for that which, split into subject and object, becomes appearance. We call it 'encompassing'.

When we bring this to mind, we think of it either as though – contrary to its reality – it could become an object; or we think of it as though it were the subject, visualized as an object. We have no other alternative.

If we pursue this inescapable way of thought, we find ourselves either conceiving the encompassing under its subjective aspect – then it is the being we are, the being in which all ways of being occur to us: our existence; consciousness at large; the mind. Or we conceive the encompassing under its objective aspect – then it is the being in and by which we are: the world.

This entire unclosed, and therefore inconclusive, being is called immanent being. It takes a further step to arrive where the encompassing is subjectively the self-being of Existenz, and objectively Transcendence.

Let us now bring these modes of encompassing to mind: on the subject side lie consciousness at large, existence, the mind, Existenz; on the object side lie the world and Transcendence.

3 CONSCIOUSNESS AT LARGE

Consciousness at large is what in our individually varied consciousness of experience and reality we call the consciousness common to all. It is not an accidental subjectivity of many; it is the one subjectivity which objectively grasps what is general and generally valid. Consciousness at large is the point where each can substitute for any other, a point conceived as unique and more or less shared by all. Whatever is conceivable and becomes cognoscible appears at this point, in its peculiar forms of conceivability, in its own structures and categories.

In the individual consciousness of our living existence, in the narrowness of individualization, we are encompassing only as the consciousness of this particular existence. Consciousness at large, on the other hand, lets us take part in something unreal but valid, in the generally valid accuracy of cognition – and thus, in principle, makes us potentially encompassing without limit.

In consciousness at large we are not encompassing in the multiple, similar, generically varied consciousness of life, but in the one that is identical with itself, means the same things, knows exactly, and is common to all finite intelligence.

Consciousness at large is not a reality. We construe it as the perfect consciousness, the knowledge that is one and contains all. No man has it, but all of us share in it.

Our own reality is existence, in which consciousness occurs in infinite variety. Though in this existence it is merely real, consciousness is at the same time valid in so far as it becomes consciousness at large. Existing consciousness is always simultaneously restricted, disturbed, and perverted.

Only in the one consciousness at large do we perceive the diversity of empirical consciousness. We know it as a psychological reality whose infinite variety we penetrate.

We distinguish consciousness by the stages of its illumination. Thus we know an inner consciousness in the experience of life that we share with the animals; it might almost be called unconsciousness, since it is not a thinking aimed at objects and aware of itself. Such unconsciousness goes back by imperceptible stages to the very beginnings of life.

In apes, for instance, we see for moments how close this inwardness can come to aimed consciousness, only to be promptly submerged again. In the animal's eye we see the act of invention together with the look of intelligence.

Human consciousness originated simultaneously with language, and is tied to language. It is the one place in the world where the line is drawn between all other types of consciousness – as really not adequately visualizable ways of inner experience – from our own consciousness of aimed thought.

4 EXISTENCE

Existence is our being in the environment we react to, and act upon. Existence as such brings forth no meaningful ways of objective thinking; but once such ways of thinking have begun in us, as consciousness at large, we subordinate them to existence and make them serve its interests.

We find existence as the unreflecting experience of life in our world. It is immediate and unquestioning, the reality which everything must enter so as to be real for us – just as, to be thought, everything must enter into consciousness at large.

We may try to outline how existence looks as we conceive it, provided we are more than mere existence. Then we may perhaps call existence 'a whole of inner world and outside world' (von Üxküll) – relatively self-contained in either case, but open in so far as each is possible only by way of, and in relation to, other existence. Existence comes to be and passes away; it has a beginning and an end in objective time, but it also has its own time and space, to move and fulfil itself in, though unable to transcend either. It is urge, drive, desire, the search for happiness, the experience of fleeting perfection and mortal agony. It lies in the restless struggle for self-preservation and aggrandizement, in the pursuit of that intangible happiness. It is always a singular, individual existence that we gaze into as we awaken to consciousness, as into an unfathomable, dark infinity. It might as well not be, and it makes us aware of the mysterious accident of existing as such.

We instinctively relate existence to narrowed concepts, to the living body, to inner experience, to the subjective perception of something without by something within, to finding and shaping an environment. But we never get over the awe of this 'I exist'. In reflection we ought not to veil this mystery, nor to leave it untouched.

5 THE MIND

The mind is the encompassing in which we draft images and realize the forms of a meaningful world in works. It differs from the intellectual calculation and production of tools and machines by consciousness at large. Unlike the irrational darkness of existence, however, the mind promotes illumination in rapport, in the movement of understanding and being understood.

Intellectual rapport touches on the meaning of the thoughts of consciousness at large; psychological rapport bares the motivations of existence; mental rapport finds valid meaning in the contents of creative invention.

To make these contents communicable, our mind employs the media of what can be objectively known, sensorily perceived, or purposefully done.

The subject of the mind is imagination. It plays in its inventions. It creates their meaning. It makes them tangible in symbols, and it finds words for all that can be. This subject is not the thinking 'I' of consciousness at large, but the individual sense of personal seizure by an impersonal and objective force.

In creative invention, the object is not really created but found. This objective side of the mind is the force of a cohesive whole that acts by order, measure, and definition.

Our imagination is chaotic if merely subjective, but as an objective one it conquers the reality of our existence, the endlessness of thought, and its own profusion. It does so by transforming everything into a temporarily closed system. Its encompassing reality understands, adopts, incorporates everything, eliminating what is alien at the moment.

Thus the mind as a whole realizes a world it has temporarily pervaded – in works of art, in poetry (infinity grown self-contained), in the professions, in the constitution of the state, in science (open to unending progress).

The whole is called idea. Self-contained, it is the Hegelian idea of the spirit; open, it is the Kantian idea of reason. The first is perfection and perfectibility, infinite but closed; the second is infinite challenge, never to be fully met, driving into the open by the anticipatory presence of its content.

6 EXISTENZ

Existing life, the *cogito* of consciousness at large, and creative imagination cannot be deduced from one another, and yet they belong together. There is no mind without a thinking consciousness at large, or without living existence. Existence alone seems able – in the life of animals, not of men – to dispense with the other two encompassing forms of our being, for the objective imagination of living forms is analogous to that of the conscious mind.

And yet, these three origins do not make us what we can be. Something, we feel, is lacking.

Existence is life trickling away, from nothingness to nothingness. After the joyous moment of perfection, after weakness and pain, it falls prey to repetitive boredom and to the frightening knowledge of harbouring within itself the germ of doom.

Consciousness at large will endlessly think trivia too. After the satisfaction of cogent validity it yields to the desolation of mere correctness.

The mind may see its creative magic turn into the splendour of soap bubbles. Imaginative abundance, the completion of harmony, may see perfection founder on reality. The charm of accumulated entireties may pall; the freedom of beautiful play may become trifling.

With our three modes of encompassing we are not yet ourselves. They leave us without direction, without a solid ground. Or are they all there is? Am I not myself anywhere? Is the void of nothingness the only limit to existence, to consciousness at large, to imagination – is this the abyss that engulfs us? Are we nothing but the ruthless egotism of our living existence, nothing but interchangeable points of correct thought, nothing but a deceptively beautiful bloom of the mind?

The cause of self-being, the hiding from which I come to myself, my freedom to make myself as my own free gift – all this disappears in those three modes of encompassing, unless they amount to more. But this cause, this freedom, this faculty of being myself, of coming to myself in communication with other selves – this is what we call possible Existenz.

Existenz as such is not to be observed in any manifestation. Existence lies in the reality of biological phenomena; consciousness at large is shown in demonstrable categories and methods of thought by the work of science; the mind appears in its creations. But Existenz has no tangible object side of its own. It must depend on the three modes of encompassing for its medium of appearance. Existenz cannot be objectified, so there can be no science of it, as of life, thought, or imagination.

In those three modes there is unequivocal communicability, but Existenz is only indirectly communicable in the three media. Its communication may be limited and unintelligible. One form of existential communication is involuntary silence, the fulfilled silence that is indeed the most trustworthy communication. Betrayals also can be committed in it by evasion and intentional silence, betrayals that are not subject to proof and never justify reproach – for I no sooner want to accuse my partner than I commit a betrayal of my own by closing my mind, ceasing to be receptive, finalizing a situation in time. Quite different from this intentional silence, this intentionally false, indirect communication, is the mute, helpless longing, the silent inability to communicate either with oneself or with others. This kind of silence may convey a depth that cannot and need not be confirmed by direct communication. It is confined to intimates, for all appearance in the world at large is limited to the communicable, to that which words can express. The rest amounts to nothing in the world; it remains outside the world even if its intimate communication has extraordinary, though not demonstrable, results. What occurs in indirect communication can be denied in objective discussion. It must not be expected. It cannot prove anything.

Existence, consciousness at large, and imagination appear by themselves in them we need to make sure only of what we are. The realization of possible Existenz, however, is part of a phenomenon of change, of having become different. We need not change to realize the first three modes, but Existenz is not so compellingly manifest. Existenz may default, may fail to appear, though a searching unrest will bear witness to it even then.

We realize each mode of encompassing as something we are, but Existenz as something we can be. The possibility must lie awake in us as we try, in words, to circumscribe what Existenz may be.

1 Existenz is not a kind of being; it is potential being. That is to say, I am not Existenz but possible Existenz. I do not have myself; I come to myself.

To be or not to be, that is the choice which Existenz keeps facing all the time. I am myself only if I will it. I do not merely exist, am not merely a point of consciousness at large or a place of mental creativity – in all these I can either be lost or be myself.

2 Consciousness at large already has three elements: the *subject* thinks of *objects* while being aware of, and thus relating to, *itself*.

Existentially, this construction contains a deeper one: Existenz is *the self that works on itself in cognizance of its relation to its constituent power* (Kierkegaard).

Existenz is freedom – not the licence of existence, not assent to the accuracy of consciousness at large, not the creative order of mental images, but freedom of an inconceivable sort: a freedom not of its own making, which may fail to appear. Existenz is freedom only as the gift of Transcendence, knowing its donor.

The place of Transcendence, or Transcendence itself, is the All-Encompassing – hidden as such, real for Existenz and Existenz alone, experienced in freedom. There is no Existenz without Transcendence. This is the structure of Existenz, so to speak, however Transcendence may be conceived and imagined in the areas of the mind and consciousness at large.

3 Existenz is the ever-individual self, irreplaceable and never interchangeable.

In the categories 'general and individual', Existenz would seem to be definable as individual. In the categories 'essence and reality' (*essentia* and *exsistentia*) it would seem to be definable as reality. But these categories will have to be extended so as to cover its uniqueness and irreplaceability.

We are not extending the categories if we regard the general and the essence as primary, as lasting, as the proper being, and the individual as an infinitesimal case. But if we reverse this approach – if we call Existenz primary, preceding the general and the essence – we go wrong again, since the individual needs the general to be himself.

As soon as we take Existenz for the empirical object of individual reality, of the individual things found in the world, it is no longer the Existenz of self-being. Instead, the brute fact that there are individuals in the world is falsely glorified, then, as Existenz. The fact does not amount to 'Existenz'.

Individuum est ineffabile is a statement that applies to both; but 'Existenz' is not an individual thing of infinite objective reality. It is a reality infinite as its own challenge. Existenz does not just happen in the world; it is an origin from elsewhere, come to be phenomenal in the world.

Nor should Existenz be regarded as the encompassing of each individual encompassing existence. This view is more profound than the mere observation of objectively occurring facts; but existence does not amount to Existenz, either. Being there, finding myself as life in the world, does not assure me of myself.

It is when I notice my faculty of decision – not as the simple ability to make random choices in existence, but as the chance of willing what I must, to be myself – that I see beneath this faculty my possible Existenz: what I am, I come to be by my decisions. If I see the freedom of Existenz in mere licence, or in the mere affirmation of correct thought, I have missed my existential freedom. If Existenz can choose to be or not to be, this being really means being in view of Transcendence. A self-creation out of the void of licence or general accuracy would be a fantasy.

For if we take the being that Existenz can choose for absolute Being (as if it could choose to come into being, into its particular being, out of nothing), we ignore the fundamental historic experience: that Existenz is potential being willed out of the gift of self – not out of nothing, but in the sight of Transcendence.

Within the categories of essence—reality and general—individual, therefore, it is a false categorial simplification to bracket Existenz with existence, with licence, with assent to general validity. To do so means to plunge its essence into the void. Existenz is more than can be measured in categories· What the words 'I am' mean as a statement of possible Existenz rather than. mere existence, and what its relation to Transcendence signifies, has been expressed by Dante, in a line about the angels – who are no longer 'possible' but altogether real Existenz (to us, a mere parable). 'In them,' says the poet, 'the splendour of God can resplendently say, "I am" *(subsisto)*.' The verse does not refer to unrelated, self-sufficient existence; rather, this *subsisto*, this 'I am' related to Transcendence, expresses what we, since Kierkegaard, have come to call 'Existenz'.

4 Existenz is historic.[1] Existence and the mind are also historic; they are objectively historic as mere multiplicities of the endlessly particular unfolding through causalities and comprehensibilities explorable *ad*

[1] Cf. pp. 105 f. – *Translator.*

infinitum, and subjectively historic as derived from the precedence of tradition in each particular situation. The historicity of Existenz, however, is the reception of its particular forms of existence, of the mind, of consciousness at large. Existenz pervades accidental existence, this peculiarity of mine which I can objectify and simultaneously come to know *ad infinitum*. But if I enter existentially into the temporality of existence, I have transcended it at the same time. Unlike the objective and subjective historicity of mind and existence, the temporal realization of Existenz is a historicity in which temporality and eternity coincide. Unlike history as mere transience, a continuity and rupture of traditions, Existenz is the identification of the self in time, a present manifestation of the eternal.

5 Existenz requires communication. Self-isolated, living for myself alone, I can no longer be myself. I come to myself only in communication with another, when the other comes to himself. This is why one element of Existenz is the loving struggle in which man abandons mere self-preservation, recovers from all anger, restrains injured pride. For no self-isolating truth can remain true.

6 I cannot really be Existenz and know it. If I want to know it, I fade out as Existenz. Whatever has been said, done, unfolded in regard to Existenz stays indirect. This indirectness is not my doing; it remains insurmountable even before myself. Nothing but the unreserved will to be as direct as possible, to eliminate every indirection, will turn the indirectness into truth.

This is why men will come to feel time and again that the main point remains unsaid, the essential thing undone – not due to any omission, but because even in the impossible case that everything were said and done it would not suffice.

7 At bottom – knowing that it is a gift – Existenz remains hidden. Why do I love? Why do I believe? Why am I determined?

These questions are unanswerable, no matter how many premises, conditions, motivations may be set forth for what appears in the world. Each answer makes us realize the radical unanswerability.

There is no reason why we should not ask; but experience shows that for our cognition the reality of Existenz is bottomless.

To us, anything so unfathomable is an origin rather than a visible, determinable object.

If we hear that reflection ought not to touch the unfathomable, that to scrutinize it might destroy its reality, we may reply that the contrary is true: if our thinking is philosophical, not abstract or rationalistic, it will only cause a more decisive manifestation of the hidden essence. If the crux of a matter is timeless, nothing can touch it, and thought – inner action – makes it only more effective. The immediately transient may disintegrate under scrutiny and reflection, but anything original will only gain in reality of appearance by revealing itself in thought.

7 WORLD AND TRANSCENDENCE

The encompassing of Being itself – encompassed by the encompassing that we are – is called world and Transcendence.

For natural conduct these are primary. We did not create them. They are not mere objects of our interpretation. It is they that produce us, whether as minute, infinitesimally fleeting particles of the world or as Existenz, of which we know that it is not self-made but derived from Transcendence.

We have no way to objectify the encompassing of Being. In the world we go in all directions, finding the things we can know, *ad infinitum*. The world as a whole is neither comprehensible nor adequately conceivable; it is not an object for our knowledge, only an idea challenging our research.

As for Transcendence, we do not explore this at all. We are touched by it, metaphorically speaking, and we touch it in turn – as the Other, the Encompassing of all encompassing.

b. Reflection on this Basic Knowledge

1 RECAPITULATION

Let us review the basic experiences of finding ourselves in the world:

I exist in my environment, among temporal and spatial forces, in success and failure.

I am a thinking person. I have thoughts of compelling validity in consciousness at large.

A world of the mind is both discovered and produced by me: *I have imagination.*

The objective entirety arising from these three origins is the *world*. Yet it does not fully answer the question how I find myself in the world, for I am aware of my freedom that lets me come to myself as possible *Existenz*. In this awareness I come to be sure of *Transcendence*, the power from which I receive the gift of self, in my freedom. I am not self-made. I did not create myself.

We see the step from immanence to Transcendence: on the one side lie existence, consciousness at large, the mind, the world; on the other, Existenz and Transcendence.

2 THE INDEPENDENCE OF THE ORIGINS

The point is to realize the originality of our basic experiences. In each mode of encompassing we ascertain an origin that cannot be deduced from any-hing else.

To clarify our consciousness of self and of being – the two are inseparable – we must feel each mode, yield to it, awaken it in ourselves.

Any perception and circumscription of phenomena presupposes these basic experiences, which are in turn enhanced by such illumination. But the basic knowledge fits only the forms of the basic experiences. To become real, they have to be lived.

3 THE PECULIAR MEANING OF TRUTH IN EACH MODE OF ENCOMPASSING

In consciousness at large, truth means cogent general validity for every thinking person. In existence it means the fulfilment of life; it means success, happiness, and self-realization for each individual existence. In the mind it means the flow of comprehension – the understanding of meanings (in the original discovery and creative interpretation of mental images) and the understanding of what has been understood (in interpreting the interpretations). In Existenz it means identification with the source, the unconditional historic resolve out of the infinitely deepened repetition of love and reason.

In communicating truth we come to agree, or to disagree. In consciousness at large we achieve the accord of compelling cognition between interchangeable points. In existence, the interests of self-preservation and self-aggrandizement will coincide or exclude each other. The mind unites us in the free, spontaneous joy of playing with images, movements, conceptions, with gestures and demeanour; Existenz unites us in the communicative loving struggle of individuals who are not interchangeable, each existing as himself and linked with one another in eternity.

A different truth decides in each mode of encompassing. Do they have a common base? If so, it lies in Transcendence, the Encompassing of all encompassing.

4 THE MEANING OF BASIC KNOWLEDGE

In the basic knowledge of our orientation in the world we renounce a 'total knowledge', which does not exist.

Such basic knowledge does not, therefore, serve as a starting-point for a deduction of all things. Instead, it serves as a tool for differentiating in each particular situation, whether of theoretical study or of living practice.

The basic knowledge cannot serve its ends by a method we might learn, only by the vigour of asking, which must always lead us to new particular findings. It teaches us to avoid mistakes and confusions in the very originality that we are and can be. By critical distinctions, the basic knowledge illuminates areas not reached by any adequately defined concepts. It clarifies our lives. It loosens our consciousness and promotes candour.

5 THE INAPPROPRIATE BUT UNAVOIDABLE OBJECTIVATION

Whatever becomes an object lies in the encompassing which is itself not an object. The encompassing comprises subject and object and is accordingly neither. Yet when we speak of it, it turns into an object of our thought. As we think of the encompassing we cannot help making an object of it for a moment, because we cannot get out of the subject–object dichotomy. The very thought puts us back into it.

We can speak only in objectivities. There is no non-objective speech or thinking. Yet in each object, as well as in the subject, there are supra-objective and supra-subjective overtones. If we cling to objectivity as such, our thoughts will soon follow meaningless paths without end or content.

So it is with the idea of reversing this objectivation that we think of an encompassing. We mean to make sure of it by a process that falsifies but cannot be avoided. The thought we pursue in an effort to visualize the encompassing that we are but cannot make an object of cognition – although for us, who encompass everything, it also occurs in the medium of objectivity – is a kind of thought that constantly takes away what it seems to be giving. We think of something; we cannot help thinking of it as an object; but as an object it disappears.

This is the paradox: that in thinking – i.e., in the dichotomy – we must conceive an encompassing as something it can never be. It is the only possible way in which, aware of the line that cannot be crossed in thought, we can try, despite this line, to bring to mind what is without being an object – what manifests itself, rather, as always object and subject at the same time.

If we persist in objectifying an encompassing, the philosophical meaning of the thought has vanished. The illumination of Existenz, for instance, may be objectified into a knowledge of Existenz. Then concepts evolved from an appeal to the faculty of freedom will be perverted into existential yardsticks for categorizing human beings, their actions and thoughts. Then a fool will want to know whether or not he is real Existenz. Then inner action, the form and purpose of the philosophizing that illuminates Existenz, will cease and be replaced by an alleged – albeit fantastical – knowledge that turns philosophy into a sort of psychology.

6 THE PARADOXES OF MUTUAL ENCOMPASSING

Thus the visualization of encompassing will promptly put us back into the subject–object dichotomy. But that is not all. The dichotomy also comes to guide us in organizing the idea of encompassing. The encompassing that we are confronts the encompassing that is Being itself: the one encompassing encompasses the other. The being that we are is encompassed by encompassing Being, and Being is encompassed by the encompassing that we are.

This mutual encompassing has also been couched in magnificently simple terms by Dante: envisioning God's relationship to the surrounding choirs of angels, he speaks of the deity which 'seemed engirt by what it girdeth'.

c. Reason

The modes of encompassing are many. Only the formula of the Encompassing of all encompassing would fit a unity, though not achieving it either.

1 DIVERSITY AND INCONCLUSIVENESS

Each mode of encompassing shows in itself another diversity. Mind and existence lie in the vast individualization of endless numbers. Consciousness at large, while conceived as one, is tied in appearance to the countless thinking points that share in it. Existenz lies in the concord and discord of many souls. The world is split into the infinite variety of aspects, fields of study, spheres of objects. The one Transcendence speaks, to those that hear and see it, in the diversity of historic ciphers and is inaccessible as the real One.

For us, the modes of encompassing do not make up one entire closed organism. We do not see in them any harmonious completion. Bringing them to mind is a mere tool for orientation in the being we find ourselves in – an orientation by the ways of its presence.

We comprehend in these ways that the whole is inconclusive, that the problem of the one whole is insoluble for our cognition.

We see the radical contradictions. We may scrutinize them by all dialectical means – by a dialectics that opens in the clash of paradoxes, by one that closes in a full circle, or by one that moves in dispute; the radical tensions will stay. Eventually we reach the limit of each mode of encompassing.

The tool extends our consciousness to every possible dimension of meaning, but as a tool it remains inconclusive.

2 THE WILL TO UNITY

Yet as we say this, we still feel the indelible urge of unity – a will to go where everything is related and connected, nothing futile and superfluous, nothing left out, nothing forgotten.

An attainment of this goal is for us unthinkable and unimaginable. Any anticipatory assertion will destroy it.

That we draft the dream of unity and fail, however, does not alter the fact that we dream it – that we feel its weight as if the object were real, as if the dream were true. Since its truth is still only a dream, we have in us something else: our reason, which keeps urging us to find the connection, and which inspires us to realize it both in the smallest circle of our existence and in the broadest horizon of whatever we can think, and thus promote, as possible.

If Transcendence is the Encompassing of all encompassing, if Existenz is the fundament, reason is the bond that materializes in time. It resists disintegration. Whatever we meet separately and divide in thought, whatever seems mutually exclusive and radically irreconcilable, is to be related to each other. We see our task, the task of philosophy, in reaching the path of union, of communication. All the modes of encompassing, encompassed by Transcendence in Being itself, are encompassed in us by the bond between these modes, by reason.

3 WHAT IS REASON?

By itself, reason is nothing. Yet in philosophy it ranks supreme.

Disruptive forces arise in each mode of encompassing, as if there were fetters needing to be torn to reveal truth; but in reason we have an encompassing vinculum for whatever tends to be sundered. Reason shows us the way of constructive realization. It permits no absolute severance, no final disjunction, no irrevocable break. It will not stand for anything to drop out of Being, to be submerged in the unfathomable, and to disappear.

4 REASON IS NOT A SYSTEM

And yet, this vinculum for every breach is not a given order, nothing we might know as fixed for all time. An edifice, however found, would invite demolition; a system, however construed, would need transcending; but reason is neither. For us, in time, in all the modes of encompassing, reason is always in evolution – but so that we expect to find it in an existing eternity.

All real and possible standpoints, the irrational and anti-rational included, are assigned their places, so to speak, in the realm of reason – which itself is more than a standpoint.

5 REASON KNOWS NO SUBJECT-OBJECT DICHOTOMY

What, then, is the subject-object relationship in the encompassing of reason? What is its subject, and what its object? We can answer only that here the structure differs fundamentally from all the modes of encompassing. Reason enters into all the ways of the subject-object split; but in itself it does not know the split. It is like nothing, therefore, unless it achieves reality in the media of the other modes of encompassing. It is not a new subject encountering a new and different objectivity.

Reason works in league with Existenz, to which it owes its earnest. It is motion in the world, gravitating toward the One that transcends everything thinkable and unites all directions.

6 REASON AND INTELLECT

Intellect is not the same as reason. Our common usage, in which we scarcely distinguish between intellectual and rational, makes it harder to put into philosophical terms what true humanity does – or can do, at least – while thinking.

The intellect determines, defines, delimits, and thus clarifies things for us. Reason opens doors, provides impulses, and forbids us to rest on what we know.

Yet reason never takes a step without the intellect. Ceaselessly it seeks to broaden consciousness at large. Nowhere is the intellect abandoned; to despise it is to despise reason. Spurred by reason, the intellect can transcend itself on its own, can reach the limits where, though neither abandoned nor forgotten, it comes to be more than intellect – where it becomes reason.

7 REASON IS PHILOSOPHIZING

This sounds extraordinary. Is reason a figment of our imagination, perhaps, like many a philosopher's dream? Are we asking the intangible to do the impossible? Having brought the modes of encompassing to mind in immanence and Transcendence, having discussed what is and what we are, are we proceeding to talk of a bond where in fact there is nothing? It takes our breath away to find not even a subject facing its object any more – as the thinker is confronted with his thought, existence with its environment, imagination with the mental image, or Existenz with Transcendence.

And here, in this instability, philosophizing is to have its fixed point – here, where nothing has a handle to it, where all is flux without a substrate, where the incomprehensible shall be all-comprehending?

Yes, it is here in this encompassing that the motion occurs into which philosophizing is supposed to put us. But the task cannot be accomplished in a vacuum, only by entering into all the modes of encompassing. Their contents will never be clear and pure unless we search on all sides for the unifying bond.

d. Characterization of this Philosophy

1 ESTABLISHING APPEARANCE

This philosophy is neither idealistic nor realistic, neither metaphysical nor ontological. About the things we would like to know – whether and what God is; what the world rests on; what may be the basic process, or eternal Being – about these it tells us nothing.

It is just an attempt to establish how and where we find ourselves. It shows the ways of appearance for us, and the ways of our own appearance.

To be, for us, whatever is must reach that point, must manifest itself upon that stage.

Thomas Hobbes wrote: 'Of all the phenomena or appearances which are near to us, the most admirable is apparition itself, τό φαίνεσθαι; namely, that some natural bodies (i.e., human beings) have in themselves the almost of all things, and others none at all.' Hobbes, a man who rarely used such terms, called appearance 'admirable'. It is our point of departure, and our point of return. Nothing else will let us understand it.

The basic fact that something becomes phenomenal – or else: that it appears, reveals itself, exists, finds expression in words – is as much an overall mystery as a clear and present reality.

2 ILLUMINATING THE WAY TO THE MYSTERY

The mystery clears up as we become aware of appearance as such – of the way it happens, of its manifold forms, of its peculiar basic features.

We may think we can save ourselves the effort of this cerebration by simply yielding to the direct impact of our senses and of intellectual thought, of corporeality, of myths – to the unquestionable truth and abundance of all that exists for us in technically usable objective cognition, in poetry and art, in religious ritual. All of this, we are told, is merely befogged and indeed put in doubt by reflection.

Such attitudes balk at the human road. They are tempting, for they seem to save us. But even truth, as unquestioned immediacy, can be deceptive. It can confuse us. And if it stays pure, for once, despite a lack of reflection, it will be defenceless against perversions from outside. It requires testing by thought, in the basic knowledge of our self-orientation.

If we take the direct impact with us into the width of all the modes of encompassing, the mirage of blind self-preservation in existence will vanish along with the mere magic of the mind, the mere assertiveness of intellectual argument, the proprietary pride in the truth of a religion.

The false mysteries grow transparent to the extent to which thinking manifests the true, great, all-encompassing mystery.

3 PERIECHONTOLOGY, NOT ONTOLOGY

When we bring the modes of encompassing to mind we are not looking for steps in categories of objective data, as in the metaphysical scales taught ever since Aristotle. We look for the realms of encompassing. That is to say: we do not want to find layers of Being, but origins of the subject – object relationship. Ours is not an ontological search for a world of objective definitions, but a periechontological one for the source of subject and object, for their relations and interrelations.

4 RELATIONS OF DIFFERENT ORIGINS

The series of modes of encompassing shown in our brief summary is not an aggregation on one level. They do not stand side by side. A gulf divides the ones in mundane reality (consciousness at large, existence, and the mind, all facing the world) from the ones in the reality that transcends the world (Existenz facing Transcendence). The interrelations of all these, their forms of pervading each other, are too manifold to be detailed here. At the end, of course, we find the one Encompassing of all encompassing, Transcendence; we address it as such and relate to it directly, in so far as we are possible Existenz. But we realize it in the many modes which complement each other, are not self-contained, and not conclusive.

We cannot deduce them from Transcendence, however, nor is our thinking adequate to a conception of Transcendence itself.

The modes of encompassing are our basic realities. Their tensions are our facts of life.

e. *The Turnabout*

1 ORIENTATION IN THE WORLD AND IN OURSELVES

We take our bearings in the world, coming to know reality, conquering and forming nature. We destroy fictions in order to grasp reality, including ourselves as psychological creatures occurring in the world. The road is endless, steadily extending our knowledge and increasing our skills.

There are boundary concepts: that space flight will turn the universe into the field and habitat of rational creatures thus far occupying the earth alone (today a physically and biologically utopian concept, all satellites notwithstanding); that life on earth will be wiped out (which now seems possible) or that the globe itself will vanish in a nuclear chain reaction (not yet in the realm of the possible); that human nature, in accord with human plans, will undergo a psycho-physical transformation by breeding and by the creation of new living conditions. Though important to our existence, these anticipatory orientations do not fundamentally change our sense of existence, or of Existenz.

On the other hand there is the very different orientation within ourselves. We are the stage on which everything that is and can be for us assumes the forms of its appearance. This orientation, which we call visualizing the encompassing, tells us both about the stage with its receptive organs, and about what is received there – in as many different ways as there are modes of encompassing, which are the organs of comprehension and the thing comprehended at once.

2 THE BASIC PHILOSOPHICAL OPERATION

This second, philosophical orientation takes objectiveness to realize the non-objective. It is a two-sided kind of thinking: first, it elaborates the various realities that serve to bring the modes of encompassing to mind, and, secondly, it retrieves us from these objectivities, to sense the encompassing. The turnabout requires the objectivities – without which we cannot be conscious of anything – but it needs the retrieval at the same time.

Or, put another way: we turn about by putting the encompassing into objective terms, only to discard them. Or, in a third way: the turnabout, for its own illumination, produces what it must extinguish as soon as it succeeds – a success that we feel in the increasing vigour of the modes of encompassing.

What we do when we think so as to take our bearings in the world from the modes of encompassing is called the basic philosophical operation. From the subject-object split, in which we aim at objects and are tied to them, this operation turns us about into an encompassing that is neither subject nor object, comprising both. And when our thinking makes the inevitable object of the encompassing, our philosophical sense instantly compels it to turn back to non-objectiveness.

To be made clear, the turnabout requires the very means of objective thought which threatens to void it. The basic operation, stated as such, would tempt us with statements of a knowledge if its underlying sense of non-objectiveness did not constantly control our speech and thinking.

We face an antinomy: though the encompassing comprises both subject and object, we deal with it in thought – i.e., we must make it an object for a subject. Our only help in this antinomy is the constantly repeated basic operation.

The philosophical challenge is this: instead of seeing things in themselves in an objective knowledge, instead of taking a definitive view of the world and of man, instead of conceiving a system of Being, we must get our bearings in the world by doing all that while comprehending it as imprisonment in objectivity.

The basic operation strikes off the chains that tie us to the object and lifts us out of our confinement in the subject.

3 THE TURNABOUT AS AN ELEMENT OF CHANGE

The turnabout, which the basic philosophical operation achieves and makes us realize at the same time, is a factor in the change that lets us become truly human.

When we sense that the world is bottomless, that our origin is unfathomable, that humanity, this eye and light in the dark universe, this voice in an otherwise silent world, is unique – when we doubt ourselves in our freedom that is not self-made but a gift from elsewhere – then the basic philosophical operation gives us room, so to speak, to find a place and a point for everything.

4 CONSCIOUSNESS AFTER THE TURNABOUT

Once the turnabout has clarified our basic knowledge, all that is Being for us may come to strike us as a disguise of Being. It may seem like the hiding-place of true reality.

As a result, we may come to experience life as if it were a dream. Or conversely, because we comprehend the dream as a dream, we awaken in the consciousness of the encompassing that lets us transcend all Being.

But the ambiguity of the objectified non-objectiveness returns in a new form: does the awakening free us from the subject-object dichotomy, to realize the encompassing – or do we wake up in the dichotomy, rather, to perceive what in the silent darkness of the unsplit encompassing would be as though non-existent? Awakening is both in one: a ceaseless entering into the subject-object split, our one font of clarity, and a constant recollection of the encompassing, our one source of substance for whatever is and happens in the dichotomy. We are asleep in the sham glow of mere objectivity and subjectivity, forsaken by the encompassing; we are also asleep in the darkness of the still, motionless encompassing.

5 PERVERTED THINKING IN THE TURNABOUT

A self-limiting perversion of philosophizing, contrary to the liberating turnabout, occurs when the language of illuminating our basic situation turns into ontological statements.

Then the basic question 'What is Being?' is no longer answered by making sure of the stage on which Being appears; instead, by objectifying that appearance into theses on Being, the answer is transformed into an ontology.

Matters of fact indispensable to the course of Western philosophizing have emerged throughout its history. They either turned into objects of research, acquiring their own base independent of philosophy, or they were ciphers denoting an indeterminate and evanescent language of Transcendence rather than a cognition of Being.

But if the result is neither science nor a persuasive cipher, we get the petrifacts, the so-called school pieces. We deal with them as with things that can be learned. A spark may smoulder in the embers; but the intellectual toil of stirring them, so to speak, of putting these extinct conceptualities through their paces in endless mutations, has something painful and depressing about it – with the lost philosophy so near, but as a corpse.

So there is original, imperishable truth in the great pattern of world, man, God, and Being, as dealt with in the philosophical disciplines of cosmology, anthropology, theology, and ontology. But in the logically construed pseudo-knowledge of complete objectivation the contents have been abandoned to a lifeless conceptuality.

In general it may be said of philosophizing that its factual objectiveness, unlike the mere consciousness at large of science, is tied to the Existenz of the thinker and to his experience in all the modes of encompassing.

f. Subjectivism and Objectivism

Ever since the days of German idealistic philosophy, critics of philosophical and theological thought have accused it of subjectivism. Here we are not yet concerned with the underlying impulses of this criticism, only with the premises of any meaningful discussion of the forces expressed in it.

1 TRANSCENDING THE SUBJECT-OBJECT DICHOTOMY

Once we realize phenomena as products of the subject-object split, we begin to feel imprisoned in this one place that will let us see what is. The split alone provides whatever clarity is possible for us, but we want to get out of it just the same. We want to transcend the dichotomy, to get beneath it, to get to the bottom of things and of ourselves. Two possible ways seem to lead out of this prison.

The first is the mystical experience. The mystical union of subject and object makes all forms of the I disappear together with all things. Language ceases along with the split, and so, with language, does communication and what might enter into communication. Seen from our world of appearance in the dichotomy, there is nothing at all in that state – nothing but odd experiences that can be psychologically described but have no common meaning. For the condition – described as infinite bliss, the perfect clarity of pure light – is to each his own. Individuality is erased, but not replaced by communion.

The second way to transcend the split is to realize encompassing as such. If this transcending, this basic philosophical operation, occurs in the thinker's state of mind rather than in abstract directives, it has wrought a turnabout in human self-awareness. We remain in the subject-object split, but our realization of it takes us to limits where the sense of our condition in encompassing effects a change in us. It does not free us now, in time, from the reality of our jail, but it does liberate by reflection on an unknown whence and whither felt as our destiny. The phenomena in the dichotomy grow brighter. We sense the encompassing in them. The prison walls are not toppled, as by the mystical union that makes us inaccessible; but if we know the prison, if we see it from outside as well, so to speak, the walls become transparent. The unfoldment of phenomena in time, in the light of encompassing, makes the jail less and less of a jail.

2 PLAYING SUBJECTIVITY AND OBJECTIVITY AGAINST EACH OTHER

Frequently one disputant will chide the other for submerging objectivity in subjectivity, or for submerging himself in his alleged objectivity.

Once, for example, I had written: 'Fanatics fail to hear the ambiguity in every experience of God's voice. He who knows for sure what God says and wants makes God a being in the world, a thing at his disposal, and is thus on the road to superstition.' I meant, first, that if I know what God says and wants, if I cite this to justify demands which I make on others, I have turned God into an object comparable to the objects of cognition in consciousness at large. To make God an object in this sense means to make an idol of God. This is what we call superstition. Secondly, to state divine commandments as known and generally valid is to justify human demands by something that makes them absolute, that removes them from further examination. This is what we call fanaticism. A theologian criticized my thesis that any faith laid down in a definite creed is thus transformed into objective knowledge, not a pure faith any more. In this view, he wrote, 'we face the strange fact that truth, understood entirely as conviction, lacks its objective correlative. I am not convinced of a truth that has its own validity, but my conviction itself is the truth. Jaspers likes to refer to Kierkegaard's dictum: "Subjectivity is truth" '.

With such critics, I think, understanding is not impossible if one will just look at the specific subject-object relationship. Truth is not a merely subjective 'conviction', but the conviction together with its object. In consciousness at large, which rightly or wrongly knows about objects, the subject is the general, interchangeable point of this consciousness; but the subject of faith in God is possible Existenz. The cipher language of Transcendence is a rustle of dry leaves unless the seriousness of a historic Existenz corresponds to it. If we talk of ciphers as of knowable or revealed objects even when there is no subject present as Existenz – then, to be sure we are left with superstition and fanaticism. Kierkegaard's line, 'Subjectivity is truth', was deliberately written so as to provoke the merely 'lecturing' philosophers, theologians, and pastors. It was this very Kierkegaard who upheld the object in existential subjectivity, by demonstrating that here it differs in kind.

The phenomena that occur to us in the dichotomy have utterly different ways of manifesting their objectivity to the corresponding, utterly different ways of subjectivity.

The realization of the modes of encompassing enables us to keep subject and object, subjectivity and objectivity, from being played against each other. First, it is wrong to regard subject and object in the same manner. Secondly, it is wrong to charge subjectivism to anyone who points out the subjectivity that goes with a specific objectivity, or to take an allegedly non-subjective objectivity for truth. Each time, instead, we have to ask: which subject, and which object? Both always belong together and are nothing by themselves.

In each mode of encompassing the split of subject and object is a peculiar one, and so is their interrelation. In consciousness at large it is the direction at the objects we mean. In existence it is the relation of inner world and environment. In the mind it is the relation of imagination and image. In Existenz it is my free self in its relation to Transcendence, by which I am.

The rule applies to all phenomena:t here is no subject without an object, and no object without a subject. For the encompassing which appears in the split will always confront a mode of subjective being with one of objective being – as existence with our environment, consciousness at large with the objects we mean as we think, our mind with its images. Analogously, after the step from this immanence, Existenz confronts Transcendence. There is no Existenz unrelated to Transcendence.

g. The Step from Immanence to Transcendence

For our cognition the world is no complete whole, no harmonious total process, no consistently purposive web of unequivocal causations. It is not logically comprehensible. If the world were such a single totality, it would be Being itself, and there would be nothing besides.

To scientific cognition the world is unfathomable. It takes this insight to give our thinking room for the freedom of Existenz, and to make Existenz aware of its ability to step from the world to Transcendence.

This step has extraordinary consequences. First, we become free for the world. It is only when the world is not a closed totality that each world view, each world shell that would like to capture us and limit the world, will be penetrated in our advance toward unlimited cognition of what we meet in the world.

At the same time we become free for ourselves in the world. Although our reality as existence is fully derived from the world, we have a source outside the world as possible Existenz. It is from this source that we affect the world.

Lastly, we become free for ourselves in relation to Transcendence. When we hang in suspense, so to speak, in all mundane being, we touch ground in Transcendence. Here is our refuge. Returning from there to the world, we take up the tasks that fall to us in the situations of our way through the world.

The world, then, no longer weighs on us as Being in itself. We see through all total concepts, whether mechanism, biologism, or the world process of material dialectics; we recognize their fallacy and view them henceforth as aspects in certain perspectives. Our insight dismisses every dominant total theory, while many theories remain fruitful within limits, for empirical cognition in the world. Our minds are open to every reality in the world. We are free from preconceptions of the whole, ready for each new experience.

If the object in each subject – object dichotomy is called 'transcendent' in relation to the subject, the concept of Transcendence is levelled to the point of indifference. But if Transcendence relates only to Existenz – if it is the object side of the encompassing whose subject side we call Existenz – then this Transcendence is neither valid for consciousness at large nor a real object in existence.

When I experience Transcendence as a reality, I am real as myself, as Existenz. But when I assert the reality of Transcendence in existence, in consciousness at large, in the mind, it will in fact, in the sense of the realities belonging to those modes of encompassing, be a fiction. In that sense it will be superfluous or illusory.

h. Perversions into One Truth

1 THE POINT OF PERIECHONTOLOGY IN PHILOSOPHICAL FAITH

The attempt to visualize how and where we find ourselves is not tantamount to philosophy. It does not lead us to substantial truth, only to the forms and directions in which truth appears to us. But it is an essential element of philosophy, for the unreserved will to this orientation harbour a germ of faith: the readiness to keep an infinitely open mind.

Philosophical faith is unlike the faithful obedience that accepts the incomprehensible in forms of finite phenomena and submits to them as to the deity itself. Even in our preparatory attempt to visualize the modes of encompassing, philosophical faith is the will to convince ourselves. Because we experience limits and understand them in forms that may give way, depending upon our thinking capacity, we never allow them to turn into objectivities that would call for obedience.

Even in principle, this visualization is never complete, never finally determinable. Not only the notion of having accomplished it is highly dubious, since it may strike anyone; the most reflective effort must, as a whole, remain subject to questioning, unfixed, provisional. Like science, it must keep moving. Once it grows dogmatic, it has lost its truth.

The attempt is an attack on our tendency to think no farther, an attack that needs to be repeated time and again. It aims at the fear of finding something dangerous if we keep thinking, something to jeopardize our accustomed security or to make demands we cannot fulfil – the fear that leads to the cry, 'Not too much reflection! Thinking makes sick!'

2 PERVERSION INTO ONE TRUTH

The statement that there is only one truth seems self-evident.

It does apply to the thinking of consciousness at large. What we think is true or false.

It applies also to the idea of one truth in reason – an idea that is approached in an infinity from which it illuminates the present motion, without permitting us to anticipate it.

The statement applies to the truth of Existenz in so far as it is individual, and as such not knowable. The community of all possible selves can give an impulse to reason only in the idea of boundless communication among a substantial diversity.

Truth is missed, however, if one asserts it as a philosophy, in a single form, or considers it attainable by advances in philosophy. Truth gets lost, then, in a philosophical dogmatism.

Nor do we find the one truth where it is viewed as revealed, and salvation as impossible without it. This truth is valid for the believing groups it unites, not for all men. Truth gets lost, then, in a theological dogmatism

We can interpret the dogmatic perversions as attempts to have the truth of one encompassing in the form of the truth of another: philosophical and theological truth in the form of generally valid consciousness at large. The confusion or intermingling of the sense of truth peculiar to several modes of encompassing destroys the truth.

3 THE FALLACY OF ONE SOLE TRUTH DUE TO HYPOSTATIZING ONE MODE OF ENCOMPASSING

It is only in the totality of the modes that truth could be one and perfect We can actually chart the phenomena in which detachment and isolation of one encompassing lead to specific forms of the false single truth.

Existence is made absolute in so-called pragmatism, biologism, psychologism, and sociologism; consciousness at large in rationalism; the mind in 'erudition'; Existenz in existentialism (which becomes nihilism); the world in materialism, naturalism, idealism, and pantheism; Transcendence in a-cosmism.

Reason alone is not to be made absolute. By itself it is nothing; in its flow through all the modes of encompassing it cannot be exaggerated. There can never be enough of it. There is no transcending it either. The further it goes, the more truth will be in it. It has no objectivation and subjectivation of its own.

i. Scepticism?

A sceptic in philosophy is one who admits no conviction that has been systematically developed and laid down in sacrosanct – because supposedly definitively proven – theses; in revealed religion, he is one who will not confess and uphold the one true faith in a creed. Scepticism is a bad word, then. It casts doubt on a man. A sceptic is untrustworthy. He lives a lost life. He is dangerous and subversive. A few words about scepsis and scepticism seem indicated.

1 TO MAKE SURE OF ENCOMPASSING IS TO MAKE SURE OF FAITH

Thinking about the modes of encompassing – and thus about the appearance we find ourselves in – dispels the security of our natural sense of being, the sense of having tangible, definitive reality before our eyes. The accustomed ground is pulled from under our feet.

Yet the aim of such thinking is not scepticism but ascertainment of faith. We are, so to speak, allowed to free ourselves from imprisonment in the subject-object dichotomy by making it conscious. We are released from our entanglement in objectivations, by comprehending each one in its peculiarity. We are detached from the I, by realizing that no concept of 'I' is our real self. The realization of the dichotomy lifts us above it even while we stay in it.

It is this detachment that puts us into the state of philosophizing – a state of suspense, in which the ground from which we have detached ourselves will give us our bearings toward truth itself.

Fulfilment by the encompassing in which both object and subject are present as one – this is what we call faith in the broadest sense. To make sure of it is to make sure of faith. Faith in an enhanced sense, a faith that goes beyond immanence, is found in ascertaining Existenz and Transcendence, while the ascertainment of reason as the *sine qua non* of philosophizing illuminates rational faith, the concomitant and innate force of philosophical faith.

2 DISJUNCTION AND UNITY

In several modes of encompassing unity is shattered. They are not to be deduced from one principle. The world is disjoint for the sciences, and encompassing Being for self-ascertainment. If the diversity were final, truth would be lost too, along with unity.

The realization of diversity is not indifference to unity, however, but a will to true unity. In any such premature unity as we are often seductively offered, truth itself is not attained. Disjunction, because it is an unbearable experience, keeps us in search of a unity that no question can shake. We want the one true unity, since nothing else will give us peace.

3 'LIFE AS AN EXPERIMENT' LEAVES THE SCEPTICISM OF AN EMPTY EGO

In the uncertainty we find ourselves in, life has a character often misstated in the line, 'It is an experiment'. The man who conducts it would be both the experimenter and the experiment. But if a man deserts his serious way in the world by regarding his decisions as wholly tentative and himself as a detached background figure, he becomes incapable of any faithful engagement in historic continuity. He loses his self-being. As a mere experimenter he exists neither for others nor for himself. For in refusing to venture into Existenz, in treating everything as a foreground for its experiments, that supposedly aloof ego is a mere point, a non-being really, that preserves nothing. A 'substantial' sceptic might perhaps accomplish this, though to us it seems incomprehensible. Philosophical faith wants to immerse itself in existence, rather, so as there, historically, to come to itself with other Existenz.

To let life happen as if I had nothing to do with it means not only to quit the world for an 'unworldly', point-like ego; it seems, in fact, to mean a renunciation of Existenz. There are then no more decisive practical alternatives, no unqualified decisions. A 'decision' to choose a possibility that makes the world and our being in it matters of indifference would, even if carried out, no longer be an existential decision.

For a decision that is not decisive and effective in the reality of the world seems to come from something other than Existenz, from something odd and incommunicable, from the non-being of an ego that cannot be trusted in any encompassing. It seems like a scepticism that has become nihilism.

And yet, here we hesitate again. For while this apparent non-being, this waiver of claims in the world, lies outside the horizon of our attempted ascertainment of the modes of encompassing, its possibility – like that of revelation – remains an unanswerable question.

4 SCEPTICISM AS A MODE OF PHILOSOPHY

Scepsis is an indispensable way of philosophizing. Real philosophy is bound, therefore, to strike a philosophical doctrinaire as scepticism.

It is a sceptical approach rather than scepticism if we apply methodical criticism in science, so as to achieve the maximum accuracy open to us at a time. It is also a sceptical approach rather than scepticism if, in philosophy, statements claiming to be scientific insights without qualifying as methodical, generally valid science are repudiated as objective cognition.

It is scepticism, however, to deny all sense to such statements. That they are not science does not mean they ought to be rejected altogether as tomfoolery. They should be reversed in form, but examined in substance.

5 SCEPSIS AS A MODE OF FAITH IN REVELATION

Even for the believer in revelation, scepsis may be an indispensable way of faith. A man who does not 'confess' need not be a sceptic. His very faith may bar the formulated creed. Confessing a creed, as a statement of absolute truth worded in human language, seems to be a fatal act, for it divides people and opens the chasm of uncommunicativeness if accompanied by the demand that others join in it, as in the language of absolute truth.

Opposition to confessing in words – rather than in actions and in the way of life – is not scepticism. It is faith itself that may keep a sceptical eye on its own statements.

6 INDECISIVE SCEPTICISM

Philosophizing is diluted by the indecisive sceptic who does not want to be one, though proceeding in sceptical fashion. Unable to distinguish between the modes of encompassing, the average educated person cannot adequately express what is philosophical faith in him. His language tends to vacillate between scepticism and dogmatism. Lines from Cicero and from the so-called New Academics may serve as examples. 'It is quite possible,' said Cicero after citing Stoic, Epicurean, and Academic theories about the gods, 'that not one of these views is true, but it is impossible for more than one to be true.' Philosophically, this ranks with a lecture on immortality I heard in my youth, marvelling at the lecturer's unconscious self-demolition: after subtle disquisitions in the style of scientific reasoning from logic and experience, he came to the result that about seventy per cent of the argument was in favour of immortality, and thirty per cent against it.

Cicero agrees with the Academics: 'We are not people who will admit no truth; we say only that every truth has an admixture of falsehood too similar to it to find any sure criterion of judgment and assent. This has led to the thesis that there is probably much that cannot be fully understood, and yet, because of a certain clear and lucid appearance, will serve to guide a philosopher's life.' Such is the unwitting un-philosophy of indecisive scepticism.

Scepticism becomes practical reality in so far as individual modes of encompassing wither – above all, by the diminishing presence of the Encompassing of all encompassing.

j. Historic Diversity of the Original Basic Knowledge

The structures of how, where, and as what we find ourselves have been conceived in historic ways so different that one wonders what they might have to do with one another. The mere definition of the common element in this diversity is questionable. If we call it understanding of self, and understanding of the world, these very terms rest already on definite categories.

We live always in a basic knowledge that may be more or less clear. In great historic communities it is present at every step, from vague feelings to images and on to a systematic unfoldment in philosophy. Each time it is like one great matter of course.

But when all modes of the basic knowledge are made conscious in mutual contact and historic knowledge, nothing remains self-evident. No one truth remains certain. This leaves two possibilities:

Either the diversity goes on and we seem able to take part in all modes of the basic knowledge. We know them, pick up figures of speech from them talk their language for a moment. The whole condition is distracted, disconnected, discontinuous.

Or, for all my interest, the information about the historic basic knowledge and its intelligent penetration is distinguished, as mere information, from the seat of my own encompassing consciousness.

All past ways of the basic knowledge were linked with a knowledge of Being. They were ontologies. Our modern basic knowledge can make no such claim; its character is different, periechontological rather than ontological. It does not mean a knowledge of Being, but an ascertainment of encompassing.

If we call the great historic forms of ontological consciousness a basic knowledge, each one amounted to more than our periechontological attempt. For each of them, already filled with the whole substance, was self-sufficient, complete, life-supporting, sheltering the thinker.

Yet each of them, being limited, was also less than the modern attempt to bring to mind all of the modes of encompassing. For us, in our time, to obtain mastery over these modes is not, to be sure, a gain in truth content – at first, the new expanse may even mean a loss – but the reflection on the forms of the modes, on their origins, dimensions, and conditions, provides the scope without which each definite content grows questionable for us. Besides, as form of all the modes of encompassing, the basic knowledge is itself a vital content. It awakens the sources and widens the space, so to speak, where any content that fills us will find a place and conscious, critical control.

Thus the form of the basic knowledge is always simultaneously a state of mind of the man who thinks it and lives in it.

The basic knowledge of the modes of encompassing also corresponds to a state of mind – but to one that merely broadens the space, points out the sources, and must be complemented by filling the space.

The great historic forms of the basic knowledge were fulfilment in themselves; the modern form is not.

k. The Idea of the Universal Basic Knowledge

1 THE IDEA

We can hold different beliefs and still understand each other in the fact that we believe, just as in preserving our existence we can understand the self-preservation of others.

In visualizing the modes of encompassing we illuminate the common ground of humankind – where we tell each other what we mean, want, and realize. We seek what we can jointly understand and do.

The idea is that once we know the encompassing as our common meeting ground, we can leave each other free to live by our separate and vastly different sources.

According to the situation into which we are born today, the idea is to do what remains for those who know: to keep expanding the knowledge of all possibilities already realized in history, but not necessarily to constitute a new way of these historic forms. Wrenched out of all past religious matters of course, man can neither restore any of these – an artificial restoration would be a futile attempt to preserve traditions grown false – nor can he make a new one according to plan. Something else may arise, though. Aware of his traditional origins and spiritual realizations, understanding and absorbing this tradition, capable of infinite reflection, man will have to find a new form of seriousness and may seek its premise in the universal vinculum of a communicable, formal, basic knowledge.

There is not, thus far, one valid, generally acknowledged basic structure of our orientation in Being. Each of the great historic forms seems to have its own structure, incommensurate with any other.

Historical analysis shows each one to be marked by a definite limitation, a blindness to anything different, an absoluteness that can assimilate others but cannot let them stand.

It may seem utopian to search for a basic structure such as we are drafting here, in the modes of encompassing; but the point of such a draft is no self-understood faith and no description of historic data. Nor is it to abstract the general from the common content of all religious realities, in a dilution supposed to be acceptable all round. Our draft is suspended and fleeting, solidifying only for the moment it is told, but it also adopts long-stated basic experiences. It is not a plan to bring order into the historically given possibilities of faith. It is a means of communication.

The draft requires listening to what believers throughout mankind have to say, and not just so as to react to every serious encounter. We want to lose no dimension of the original, common formal possibilities. We want to broaden our minds, which are still not sufficiently open.

The question is whether all men on this globe might ultimately find a common ground in universal reason, which is essentially our concept of the unifying form as such. Is there a chance of a common framework so broadly based that historically heterogeneous faiths could communicate in it without abandoning themselves – that they could transform themselves by their own depth, rather, into the new foundations that human seriousness needs under the conditions of the coming age?

The self-understanding of the great religious forms of mankind thus far rested on metaphysical, ontological, revealed premises either indifferent or fiercely hostile to each other, but never understanding one another. They could achieve a full understanding of themselves and each other only in mutuality, if they were linked by a communicable framework in which no historic source of faith would be lost or forced to surrender.

2 BASIC KNOWLEDGE AND SCIENCE

Unlike science, the unfolding basic knowledge does not lead to any cogent, generally valid cognition. Even so it does not mean to state a faith. It lies on the borderline of scientific cognition and existential philosophy.

Like science, this basic knowledge is never complete. It takes no final form. In making it conscious we continue to test it.

In the basic knowledge we work out the forms in which, for ourselves, we are in the world – comparable to the categories or forms of appearance of whatever is thinkable for consciousness at large. Now these categories, which determine the whole thinkable world, turn into a specific group within consciousness at large and are encompassed. Objective thinking comes to be included among the modes of encompassing; though our visualization of these modes does draw them into the realm of thinkability, they do not fit in there. Compared with the objectivity of cognoscible things, this visualization moves by means of objectivities toward the non-objective, the encompassingly present. Moving along the boundaries where all objective knowledge ends, it cannot become compelling science.

Thus our elaboration of the modes of encompassing does not mean that we could now get to the bottom of things. We are drafting a pattern that must always be provisional, allowing for change, for widening, for deepening; our draft results from no principle and guarantees no completeness. It becomes no closed system although, as a pattern, it must take this form for a time.

The insight into the modes of encompassing remains in suspension and brings us into a state of suspension.

3 BASIC KNOWLEDGE AND EXISTENZ

Nor does our ascertainment of encompassing make us encompassing. The differentiation of conceptual draft and reality shows that the act of expression makes all things relative; we cannot tell if we are in what we say. The relativity of stated thoughts about encompassing corresponds to the seriousness of Existenz.

There is, therefore, no statement of an encompassing that might suffice us to know as truth. Knowing words must not replace a real decision.

Yet reflection on encompassing moves our consciousness closer to our real will which we cannot express directly.

For reality itself is purely historic, not general. Resolution cannot be derived from anything general, although it spurs us toward general illumination, toward an awakening by general principles.

If our draft of encompassing is criticized as indecisive, we can answer that decision does not lie in thought; indeed, the thought as such turns it into a mere possibility. Decision lies in the historic Existenz alone. Thinking is no more than orientation and illumination. It is a tool. Hence, philosophy does not manifest itself in the stringent unfoldment of thoughts but in the life of the thinker.

4 THE ARGUMENT AGAINST THE IDEA OF ONE BASIC KNOWLEDGE

The argument goes like this:

Each basic knowledge is in fact one statement of faith among others. The one sought here is not the only one either. But as each source of faith regards itself as the only true one, so does the source of this basic knowledge. It is a self-delusion that a general basic knowledge might be gained, so to speak, before and beyond all faith; this philosophical attempt that claims to be neither faith nor science, that purports to throw off the bonds of faith in order to pretend to a general, uniting truth, merely hides an abstract faith – as shown also by the lack of general acceptability for any such basic knowledge.

We answer:

This argument itself is abstract, for it does not deal with our concrete attempt to draft a basic knowledge. But the argument is not unfounded – for this is not a matter of compelling science. Only the conclusion is unfounded: that because it is not a matter of science, it must, like all philosophy, be a matter of faith.

At bottom it is indeed a matter of faith. But this faith has no religious content that would exclude others; it is solely the faith in the possibility of unlimited mutual understanding. It is the faith that says: Truth is what unites us.

In the modes of encompassing we visualize our human situation – to the end that in spite of a clear view of our divisions, in spite of knowing the roots of our mortal struggles, we may find ways to limit and transform these struggles.

The end requires that our minds be open all round, and that each be aware of the scope of his potential. It does not require a definite content of faith, or an absoluteness of the basic knowledge. In drafting this modern form we announce no lasting insights; we hold out our hands. We ask that this basic knowledge, this condition of general understanding, be developed in the understanding.

To be sure, no merely intellectual effort can accomplish this. It takes the guidance that is not of our making. In philosophizing as in the way of life we presuppose human beings, not intellectual machines, functionaries, exponents, or robots.

In the thinking person there is a power at work that is not he and yet is in himself, urging self-understanding and communicability. We must call it by a name, yet none will fit; if we call it reason, this is essential but insufficient. The thinking person cannot see through this other power, but he feels its presence in his motives. It will grant him no rest. It reacts to events and situations. To be experienced only in its flow through the phenomena, it indicates the permanent and timeless, the point of reference for the manifestation of the truth content in concrete historic forms.

Part Four. On ciphers

Introduction

1 Ciphers light the roots of things. They are not cognition; what is conceived in them is vision and interpretation. They cannot be experienced and verified as generally valid. Their truth is linked with Existenz. The magnetism of Transcendence for Existenz is voiced in ciphers. They open areas of Being. They illuminate my decisions. They enhance or dampen my awareness of being, and of myself.

2 In consciousness at large we think of objects which inquiry, as a point of general thinking, allows us to know as realities in the world. They can be grasped in unequivocal concepts, independently of ourselves.

As Existenz we think in the direction of Transcendence, in objects we call ciphers. This thinking takes place in the medium of conscio usness at large which is the premise of all lucidity since we can perceive, conceive, and think only in objectivities. Whatever is and happens, whatever we are whatever Transcendence is – all that appears reflected in the mirror of consciousness at large. It is in this medium that, thinking in ciphers, we think in the direction of Transcendence and hear its language, intensely but never entirely, in the clarity of coming to ourselves.

Ciphers have a venerable character. Their historic forms used to impress men as true reality, to guide them, to illuminate their lives. They were modes – vastly different modes – of man's inner condition, his unquestioned matters of course.

3 When we say 'ciphers', we expressly do not mean to refer to things, matters, facts, realities, although it seems that the cipher contents have mostly been viewed as realities, like physical realities in space and time. People lived under their pressure as under the pressure of physical threats. It was as such that they conquered nations and ages.

The great step in which man transforms himself occurs when the supposed corporeality of Transcendence is given up as deceptive and the ambiguous cipher language is heard instead – when the contents that have been conceived and visualized are stripped of objective reality. Instead of tangibles there remain ciphers open to infinitely varied interpretation.

Previously the cipher contents themselves were the final authority; now a higher one must decide whether or not truth speaks through the ciphers at a certain moment, within certain limits. The higher authority lies in philosophizing and in the living practice of Existenz.

4 Today we can know all the ciphers that appeared in history – unlike past nations, which were inclosed within limited circles of ciphers and ignorant of those abroad. Today we belong to none of the cipher worlds and submit to none. Does this mean we are bereft of all ciphers? We know them as objects of aesthetic pleasure, or as objects of historical curiosity, or as objects of a psychology that will pour those traditional glories into its banal categories, for use as stimulants.

Yet what does it mean to 'know' ciphers? We know them from collections of mythologies and revelations. This outward knowledge becomes inwardly, however, if the ciphers touch our own Existenz. In the first case we have them at hand, like endless data; in the second, they arrange themselves according to depth, rank, and possible interpretation.

Today the ciphers speak to us on the premise that we keep them suspended while comprehending them in the depths to which we have access. If we refrain from treating their contents as reality or cogent knowledge they will light our area of Being, and in moments of decision their glow will bear the message of Transcendence.

The inadequacy of all ciphers shows in the fact that I can only heed them as images or guidelines at the existential moment, not hold on to them as to an assuring reality. I always depend on the gift of myself from elsewhere – in the faculty of love, in reason, in a trust without warrant.

5 The purity of any ciphers we make our own depends on truthfulness. We must be truthful enough not to mistake them for embodied realities, nor for perversions of speculative thought into objective cognition.

Once in the suspension of ciphers, having overcome the postures of aesthetic pleasure and historical curiosity, we move in possibilities that say something to us. They are still noncommittal, however. It is as commitment grows for Existenz that the ciphers get to be a serious matter – that we experience their infinite, existentially effective abundance in great poetry and art, in speculative philosophy, in myths and revelations.

Here we feel the freedom of the mind – which is the power to create language – as well as the ambiguity of this creation. Like the techniques of the intellect, the productivity of the mind may be used for good and for evil. Ciphers may uplift us existentially or express Godless defiance or induce a Luciferian plunge into nonentity.

Man lives in ciphers from the day he starts to think, but not until discrimination brightens his world and his knowledge does he feel called upon to purify this realm of language. Now he seeks truth and veracity. He wants to draw a strict line between reality and ciphers, and the basic perversion seems to be that of transforming the suspended cipher language into embodied reality. Ciphers are never the reality of Transcendence itself, only its possible language. Faith seeks purity. It does not want confusions to obscure it.

In this Part Four we shall discuss the nature of ciphers and the meaning of their interpretation. The content of individual ciphers will be dealt with in Part Five.

a. Existenz and Transcendence
lack specific phenomenality

1 PHENOMENA, SIGNS, AND CIPHERS

If we class phenomena according to the modes of encompassing, our truth consciousness requires us both to separate and to combine them. The main point is that we become aware of Existenz only in immanent phenomena, while Transcendence itself does not become phenomenal at all. The cipher language takes the place of its appearance.

When man, as possible Existenz, thinks of Transcendence he will necessarily do this too in phenomena – in objects he thinks or imagines – in the medium of the subject-object split of consciousness at large. Without the dichotomy he becomes unconscious and stops thinking.

The objects in which we think of the non-objective, of Existenz and Transcendence, are called signs of Existenz and ciphers of Transcendence Thus I distinguish (a) phenomena of reality, (b) signs of Existenz, and (c) ciphers of Transcendence.

a: Phenomena of reality as varied as those in nature, psychology, society, and history can be described as generally valid. The premise is an impersonat faculty of understanding in the faculty of sense perception. Once shown, I will be convinced, because I see like everybody else. I can recognize and correct subjective deviations.

b: One sign of Existenz is freedom. Where there is freedom, any cogen showing ends; for any showing of freedom – a process that can be called 'showing' only by way of a vague analogy – involves Existenz itself. What I am shown affects my Existenz at the same time. In the signs I am shown I recognize my own positive and negative experiences of being myself or not being myself. Here my 'seeing' is not just the answer of a perceiving and thinking creature at large, but an inner action that engages both me and my possible self.

In the act of thinking I will unavoidably objectify here too, as in such further signs as decision, choice, communication, self-will, seclusion, self-revelation, and change. There is always a guideline: some objective phenomenon, a psychological actuality that can be understood, a definite, i.e., definable, conceptuality. But along with these objectivations I sense something which in such thinking will vanish as soon as I take the guideline for what I really mean. The terms of this objectifying guideline are called signs of Existenz, as opposed to the categories of whatever we can think and state objectively.

c: Transcendence is for Existenz what objects are for our thinking consciousness. The concepts, images, ideas in the medium of consciousness at large in which I, as possible Existenz, hear a transcendent language are called ciphers of Transcendence.

Appearance is described and thought in concepts. Signs convey what I am and can be as myself. Transcendent reality, to be experienced by Existenz alone, is manifested in ciphers.[1]

Since we cannot step out of the world – except in the incommunicable mystical experiences that will cause subject and object, man and the world, and phenomena at large to disappear – we need the mundane signs and ciphers to become conscious of the essential and efficacious that we can be, and by which we are.

The sequence of the three – phenomena, signs, ciphers – makes the understanding of each subsequent one depend on the one before. In speaking, therefore, we must use the guidelines without which no cipher language becomes real: phenomena for signs and ciphers, and the signs which illuminate Existenz for our relations to Transcendence. But even in their intermingling, the separate meanings of the three must not be forgotten, lest we get into an existential confusion of knowledge (of phenomena) with the illumination of Existenz (by signs) and our appeal to Transcendence (in ciphers).

2 FREEDOM

We live in a world of ambiguous, changeable meanings that never reach perfection. Every phenomenon may turn into a cipher. But in the phenomenon we search beyond the phenomenon, in the cipher beyond the cipher. We have an experience altogether different from the objective one – the experience of our freedom. This never appears as such, though its consequences do appear. In a demonstrable, explorable sense the freedom of Existenz does not exist, but it manifests its presence in a certainty that transcends all worldly phenomena. Its experience is not an experience of something which, having experienced it, I would know. But in a different sense it is the basic experience of responsible self-being.

With the realization of this freedom, however, we realize too that it is not self-made but granted. The false assurance of being free by virtue of freedom alone, of a baseless, absolute freedom, is shattered by the experience that it may default. The more decisive our certainty of our freedom, the greater our certainty of the Transcendence we owe it to.

[1] 'Cipher', a word I prefer to the word 'symbol', denotes language, the language of a reality that can be heard and addressed only thus and in no other way – while a symbol stands for something else, even though this may not exist outside the symbol. What we mean by a symbol is the other thing, which thus becomes objective and comes to be present in the symbol. Yet symbols may turn into elements of the cipher language.

As neither the freedom of Existenz nor Transcendence have a specific phenomenality, we might speak of analogues to phenomena. These are manifestations that invade the phenomena without becoming knowable phenomena themselves. We might speak of an analogous 'appearance' of existential freedom in human reality, and of the corresponding analogous 'appearance' of Transcendence in the cipher language. For what signs tell of freedom is not intelligible to any intellect, only to the self-being of an Existenz that sees its reflection in them. What speaks in ciphers is not heard by any intellect seeking sense experience and proof, only by the freedom of Existenz, with which Transcendence communicates in that language.

3 NATURE

Is existential freedom our only 'experience' in which Transcendence shows itself? Or may experiences of Transcendence lie in the moods, the forms, the events of nature and of our own nature – in being carried away and overwhelmed by elemental forces? Are these not more manifest, more fulfilling, more impelling than all nature that is merely explored, and cannot even the explorable become an intensifying factor of that directly experienced breakthrough?

How we answer these questions is a matter of great weight and greater consequences. At this point of our discussions an insight into the nature of ciphers already involves a decision on the content of the cipher world. The historic phenomenon of the prophetic idea of God battling the cults of nature, of Jehovah battling Baal, recurs time and again. A battle of faith is waged in the cipher language – a battle, not of creeds, but of realizations of life; a battle waged not just between religious communities but in each individual Existenz; a battle that may long hang in the balance. The one Transcendence and the daemonic powers, the drift to Transcendence and the drift away from it – these are problems to be decided existentially, not rationally, and concretely for the moment, not in generally valid terms. The following reflections may serve to prepare for this decision.

We are not yet referring to mystical illuminations, but to 'living experiences' of the encompassing fundament of 'nature'. An engulfing darkness is experienced as if it were reality itself.

This is not the darkness which natural science penetrates *ad infinitum*, objectifying, exploring, facing new darknesses whenever one has been dispelled. Instead, it is the encompassing of the existence we are. By plunging into it, we illuminate it in a fundamentally different fashion. The existence of nature stops being a natural reality we can objectify; it comes to be one with our own existence.

We investigate our nature biologically and psychologically. Sex, for instance, is a biological reality, and so – though not clearly definable to this day – is race. Psychologically we speak of our 'drives' – of the urge to live and of the urge to die, to destroy and to be destroyed, to inflict pain and to suffer it – in short, of the joy of life and of the death wish. These are biological and psychological phenomena. As far as I know them, they will fit into the things I can master and make. We may think of breeding sex and race by means of technology and science, of transforming man for our purposes as we transform all living and lifeless matter. Yet who is the man who will change man? Who is the maker who will use science to make what he himself is, what he himself can be? Today the robot concept dominates our views, leading men to conclude that there is no point to anything, because machines, chemicals, operations, or injections permit us, or will some day permit us, to make everything.

We are confusing things if we think so. For the appearance that exists for science – the appearance we call reality – is not the reality we are. We have in our minds a technical intellect of extraordinary capacity regarding all phenomena that are accessible to research, in any definable area of research. This includes the biological and psychological phenomena of our existence. Yet there is more to us than this cognition, this know-how, this productivity; and there is more to phenomenality than the phenomena that can be manipulated in a technical – biotechnical or psychotechnical – sense. However, since our modern, public, common intellect seems to be all but hermetically sealed against the reality of Existenz and Transcendence, since its exclusive pursuit enslaves us to the things we can explore, it can never take us to the things we discuss in philosophizing.

Fantastic nonsense has been produced by a science turned superstition; but there is another and, from the standpoint of that realistic knowledge, equally fantastic sort of nonsense. There the phenomenal world is invaded by an immediate experience of nature in blood-warm proximity. Sex and race and all of those psychological drives remain explorable, of course, but now they can be phenomena of something unexplorable, something not to be expressed in scientific terms. It is a kind of incarnation. Words come to have two meanings. Nature, sex, race, drives, etc., are facts; but the same words are now used differently, indefinably, as indices. 'Nature', then, becomes encompassing, unobjectifiable existence. Sex, within its biological phenomenality, becomes an all-pervasive element of life, encompassing from the depths of nature. Race becomes the appearance of a particular existence out of the same depths of nature. Concepts that fit only the phenomenal world come to serve as signs of a bottom ground of this world – a ground that can apparently not be unearthed as underlying, but can be existentially experienced as it breaks through the phenomena. This is what comes now to be reality itself, beyond all phenomena.

Yet how does this natural darkness that engulfs us in breaking through phenomena, through intellectual cognoscibility, through rational truth – how does this infinitely and ambiguously satisfying darkness relate to Transcendence? Can Transcendence join in, and speak through, whatever the depths of nature tell us in this plunge through natural phenomena? Who would dare answer? There are no definitive statements about Transcendence. We must resign ourselves to this fact, even though we feel unable to relate to Transcendence by any way other than reason, love, lucidity, and existential decision. We see the other way. Veracity compels us to perceive it, however fearfully, in its relentless radicality, to hear the fitting or unfitting ciphers in which these experiences are expressed.

Why do we speak of the unspeakable, of things which the language of the phenomenal world is bound to falsify? Because experiences of our existence ought to be communicable. These are not 'empirical' experiences in any general sense; if they exist – if there are such curious escapes from the phenomenal world in the garb of tangible phenomena – their evanescence is as swift as their presence can be overwhelming. They must not be confused with the phenomena known to biology and psychology. If we yield to the temptation to identify essentially personal experiences of our dark nature with known or knowable scientific facts, we are retreating from the reality that transcends real phenomena, from the reality embodied in them, to a supposed knowledge which in practice leads to blind brutality.

The question, to sum up, is whether the total experience of our natural being can come under what is knowable about us – or whether it contains something compelling, something that may be overwhelmingly present though as a knowable fact it would be lost. Empirical research knows no bounds, but the experience of being in nature precedes and transcends research and cannot be its object.

The crux is our starting-point: freedom alone relates to Transcendence. If our natural being is experienced in such an escape from the phenomenal world, and if the experience is to be more than a mere unfree, self-deluding surrender to nature, it must be capable of being freely seized and thus identified with ourselves.

It is not till freedom makes them ciphers that these tangible experiences have lost their crushing weight, their power to draw us into absolute darkness. Not until then can the light of reason make them subject to the law of day.

4 AMBIGUITY OF BASIC TERMS

In such discussions, signs and ciphers come to be ambiguous. Phenomenality has a double meaning: it means objectivity for our knowledge, and it means a non-objective presence. Whatever breaks through the knowable phenomenality must still be phenomenal as present experience; so the question why one cannot describe and explore it like all phenomena will have to be answered by pointing out these two meanings of the word.

This ambiguity applies to freedom also. It is an object in so far as we objectify it psychologically as licence, sociologically as political freedom, psychopathologically as the free determination which the will may be deprived of. It is not an object in the world, however – not even for psychology – if we mean the undefinable freedom proper of Existenz.

Yet both – freedom as well as that freely seized breakthrough in phenomenality – come to appear in realities that are more than realities: in communicability.

5 INDISPENSABILITY OF APPEARANCE

Though Existenz and Transcendence have no specific phenomenality, they still require phenomena to become real for us. What is not made communicable by appearing in the world is to others like non-being. Supposing it were vital to one aloof individual, the question still would be whether this is really and truly possible. Again we must withhold judgment, for we do not know all the things than can be, though incomprehensible to us. But we may question the appearances presented in the world by one who, living in the world, withdraws into his incommunicable essence; and we may question his way of dealing with us.

Personally, while withholding judgment on this possibility, I still think that being human carries with it the temptation I have wished to resist in a lifetime of philosophizing: the temptation to act as if we could live 'metaphysically', in monadic isolation; as if deep in our hearts we might remain aloof and tacitly refuse communication; as if we could bulwark ourselves in a solitude that would grant us the pride of untouchable suffering; as if, while aiming at the openhearted faculty of love, we might live without risking surrender; as if we need not fear the consequences of deluding ourselves about the secret despair of self-caused loneliness; as if we could desert from the world we exist in.

We realize ourselves only in so far as we enter into the phenomenal world, in which there is no truth without communicability. Even what comes to us only in indirect communication and in self-comprehension has thus become appearance in the world.

Just as, metaphorically speaking, the grandiose theoretical speculation of modern physics is a nullity until proved in the world of classical physics by the realities of observation and experiment, any experience of transcending the phenomenal world can be realized in that world alone, by being made communicable and being tested in communication.

Our task is to bring everything to appearance, while understanding the brightness of the appearance philosophically, as a kind of imprisonment. This paradox governs our Existenz and achieves the clarity granted us in hearing the ciphers.

b. Cipher and Embodiment

1 THE BASIC CONFUSION

Ciphers are spiritual realities in our language, in philosophy and poetry and works of art; they are not embodied Transcendence. Embodying the cipher contents is the basic confusion in our dealings with Transcendence. If the reality of Transcendence is thus captured for our own reality, we have lost Transcendence.

2 REVELATION AND INCARNATION INCONCEIVABLE IN OUR FRAME OF REFERENCE

The most effective form of that confusion seems to be revelation. Revelation has no place in our ascertainment of the modes of encompassing; in this framework of ours it is neither thinkable nor imaginable for Transcendence to find a specific incarnation as a divine reality, distinct from any other, in the world of time and space. This means only that we who live in those modes, in their separation, reunion, and tension, cannot conceive of such an incarnation.

We can do something else, however. Aware of the phenomenality of all that we know, we can visualize the presence of something altogether different, something underlying ourselves and all that we know.

The basic knowledge of encompassing, in which we search for the broadest horizons granted to us, has meaning even for believers in revelation. It allows them to feel the entire strangeness of revelation, its rational absurdity as a concept. The believer is made aware of doing something extraordinary, something beyond the power of the others he finds living in the world of men. Then the conventional faith in revelation, the comfortable matter of course, will be all but unrecognizable.

The believer sees Transcendence invading the world for purposes of direct communication, by means of a material reality that is now fixed as to time and place. For once, and for ever, this is to be the reality of God. The claim of absolute truth demands obedience and submission even in case of a failure to understand. Though in the world this claim is always made by men only, they maintain it comes from God.

3 SACRAMENTALISM

'Sacramentalism' is a common feature of all creeds and revealed religions. The holy, the unearthly, the sensory-supersensory, the powerful, the magical – all these appear in rich variations. The question is whether the sacramental acts and magical operations, whether sacrifice, prayer, devotion, and the homiletic proclamation of the word depend upon a corporeality of God, or of divine powers. Is it not part of the basic condition of man that he will turn there in cults, rites, and prayers? Are not all our holidays, our seasonal feasts, the acts of confirmation in the course of our individual lives from birth to death – are these not already sacramental? Do they not always imply a divine presence? Does the divine not bodily pass through the room where the community partakes of it? If we deny embodiment of the divine, are we not sloughing off everything sacramental?

The powerful, endlessly varied reality of sacramentalism dominates human history. Dare we deny it? May we treat it as obsolete? We note the constant recurrence of the 'ritual need'; we see it practically recognized even in atheistic societies, by such productions as 'youth festivals', ritualized party congresses, and the like. Would the seriousness, the dignity, the abundance of life not cease without celebrating its enhancement?

Equally real in the West, however, is the dwindling participation in ecclesiastic practice. Most of us, to be sure, will marry in church, be baptized, and receive religious burial; but the urban rate of regular practitioners of their religion is now estimated at five per cent, give or take a few. Unquestionably this apostasy is often a mere thoughtless plunge into the rationalism of the performance cult and its supplement, the pleasure cult – a plunge into obliviousness of ourselves and of the cause of all things. The ecclesiastic forms can be waived unpunished only by one strong enough for philosophical meditation. Daily reflection, with its outcome permeating the course of the day and its experiences; a state of mind in which the encompassing is present again and again – these are the premises of an 'existential existence'. Neither embodiment nor sacramentalism are essential to that, although philosophical reflection justifies a sacramental trend as long as it does not lure us into those embodying traps. Ritualism and sacramentalism are possible in a life with ciphers.

4 REVELATION AND NIRVANA

The ascertainment of the encompassing in which we find ourselves is breached not only by revelation but also by the Buddhist and Hindu Nirvana. However incomparable they may seem, revelation and Nirvana have much in common: all there is – the world, the conceivable, the cognoscible – is transcended as inadequate; the goal of transcending, or the power that seizes us, is a present experience; and those who experience it stay in the world after their fashion. They stay, first, because they are here, and because suicide misses the goal in the Hindu view and is forbidden on pain of eternal punishment by the Christian faith – but also, and above all, they stay because they mean to save others by teaching and preaching, and by the moral effect of their example.

Nirvana turns everything – the world, the gods, God, and all the ways of encompassing, including the relation of Existenz to Transcendence – into something that is not reality but delusion, magic, the 'veil of Maya'. In the world, seen from the world, Nirvana seems utter monotony, like nothingness. Revelation, on the other hand, is first diverse among Jews, Christians, and Muslims, and secondly it acts upon the world, promising and demanding. It becomes a factor of the utmost vitality and tension in a mundane existence that is not a matter of indifference, not an illusion, but the site of eternal decisions.

Nirvana cancels all embodiment. The road to it is marked by ciphers only. Revelation is embodied in the incarnate God and does not permit itself to be turned into a cipher.

5 THE CRUX: TEMPORAL AND SPATIAL EMBODIMENT OF REVELATION

We distinguish between two kinds of reality: the immanent reality of phenom na and the reality of Existenz and Transcendence. Because it is immutable, the reality of Transcendence ranks above the changing and vanishing realities in space and time.

Our life as natural beings is solely and inherently corporeal, an unbelieving existence in space and time, in the objects of empirical cognition, in the world. A life with ciphers is the believing life of Existenz. Thinking in ciphers, Existenz relates to a reality that is not of this world.

Without corporeality I lose existence in time; without ciphers, I obscure my possible Existenz.

The crux is this: to philosophical faith, all the modes of encompassing – particularly Existenz in its relation to Transcendence – are possible and real without revelation. A theologian will argue that such thinking makes it impossible to reckon with concrete divine approaches to the world and man as meaningful realities – and these precisely are of overriding importance to the faith in revelation. As ciphers, we are told, these real words and appearances of God would lose their meaning. To regard the story of revelation as a cipher would be the end of what the theological believer has in mind, and no philosophical uplift to Transcendence can substitute for it.

I would reply that this is not a matter of substitutes. We might as well say that the faith in revelation cannot substitute for philosophical faith. We might say that man cannot bear his situation; that as a creature of his senses he seeks embodiment, therefore, even where it will pervert what matters; that he seeks a substitute for the great faith which the hidden Transcendence demands, so to speak, in his situation, and that revelation is this facilitating substitute. To me, however, this retort would seem as wrong as the derogatory *ersatz* theory offered by theologians who are too sure of themselves.

I would reply, moreover, that it is unthinkable for the reality of Transcendence to become worldly reality in this fashion – for it to act on the world as a corporeal God, localized in time and space and distinct from all other realities, none of which are God or acts of God. Should the unthinkable be believed as a reality? But reality is not believed; it is experienced by finite sensory creatures. Theologians have rightly pointed out that by thought, by understanding, by logical conviction man will indeed never get to the reality of revelation. It is the other way round, rather, and the act of God comes first; this they call the fact which creates faith. God, by his grace, grants the condition for the faculty of faith. Since God has revealed himself in fact, they say, it is up to man to be obedient in faith.

What shall we do? Try to believe what we cannot believe? If God does not grant us this grace, we cannot believe without being dishonest; and if we feel that our first and foremost obligation is truthfulness, we must not believe. We cannot understand the believer who claims to be the recipient of such grace. His every statement tells us that God is corporeal – but for us, corporeality is limited to phenomena in space and time. For us, the insight into the phenomenality of all spatial and temporal things excludes the specific reality of God in a definite appearance.

6 WITHOUT EMBODIMENT, DO CIPHERS WEAKEN OR STRENGTHEN US?

The great question is whether anything stripped of corporeality can remain effective as a mere cipher. Is the cipher strong enough to awaken, to guide, to show up the roots of things – is it as strong as embodiment, or stronger still?

The eternal punishments of hell, for instance, used to have great terrifying and controlling power. Does the cipher retain its impact if at decisive moments we are not menaced with a future hell but impressed with the inconceivable eternity of our decision? Or will it then, perhaps, be even more manifest that human actions bear eternal weight – will the cipher reveal more clearly than the crushing fear of punishment that man's own self is his to win or lose? Instead of experiencing guilt and punishment as separated in time – the sin now, and hell in the future – will he perhaps come to feel them united in his act as a manifestation of instant eternity, of the irrevocability that we conceive in the cipher of infernal punishment?

The step goes from bondage to corporeal concepts and sensory fears to freedom in the realm of ciphers. This is where the existential, original decisions for eternity are made.

What was true in embodiment will be doubly true in ciphers. Resolution will no longer be due to a fear of something, but to the very different fear of the free for their freedom and for eternity. Whatever has discarded embodiment and become pure cipher can come true in the realm where Existenz reveals itself in action.

Have all the things that used to be goblins or soporifics not become fairy tales? They are not believed as they were once upon a time, in the beginning. It is indeed the great question of our existential destiny whether today we might not believe more purely, freely, seriously, communicatively than ever – even if we do not so believe as yet.

In the past ciphers mattered. Their energies moved the faithful, who in turn produced the ciphers by their faith. Embodiment was for the masses, and not a subject of inquiry for the thinking believers, the philosophers. The question might arise now and then, but in the intellectual situation of past ages it was not compulsory. The cipher language was the public language. It was the air you breathed. Today it seems different: the cipher language is no longer tied to embodiment. Embodiment cannot be maintained unchanged in a world illuminated by scientific realism.

Today an embodied reality of Transcendence would interfere with the human course of things, while ciphers give it wings and make it a course of love and reason.

Though embodiment may strengthen our psycho-physical vital forces, it weakens veracity, and thus our existential forces. Embodiment is capable of holding even one who really does not believe; but the disembodied ciphers cleanse the faith of free Existenz.

The unbeliever and the believer in embodiment are content with sensorily present energy as such; free Existenz requires the cipher language. As rational creatures of the senses we cannot do without language, and language needs the sensory prop of speech. Therefore, to illuminate our transcending Existenz, we need to imagine ciphers and to think in ciphers. What is indispensable to us, as sensory creatures, belongs to the world and to time; in eternity, in the truth of transcendent reality, it will vanish. But it does let us realize what, by the form of such realization, exists for us alone, not in itself.

That today the cipher language withers along with embodiment is a calamity of our time. The air we breathe is not only diluted but polluted by concepts of scientific superstition. An insight into the nature of ciphers is the premise of their chance to regain their old existential vigour and wealth of language.

c. Historicity, Cipher, and Revelation

The believer in revelation cites historic revelation. He calls historicity – and thus, singularity – the essence of truth. Similarly we who think in ciphers say they have power as a historic language, not as a general one.

Making it clear what 'historic' means can keep a philosophically 'natural' historicity from seeming to bring revelation closer, and thus veiling its essence.

1 MEANINGS OF HISTORICITY

The word 'historic' has vastly different meanings. It denotes, first, the infinite and inexhaustible individual concretion of all things at all times – what we mean by the words *individuum est ineffabile*.

Second, it means the diversity and infinite variety of events. It is objective history, seen and presented in recollection and documentation, and thus present. It is endless. No memory retains all that was and all that happened, everyone who lived, and all that everyone has done. Historical recollection is limited by the accidental preservation, rediscovery, or excavation of remnants. But these remnants themselves are endless and impossible to store in one remembering brain. Comprehending and presenting what is left depends on our perceptiveness, on categories of thought, on the concerns of him who remembers.

Third, we define history as those very concerns – as whatever knowledge of their origins is vital to individuals, groups, nations, and some day perhaps to mankind. It extends from the history of an individual or a family to the 'stage of world history'. What is objectively explored and related there has its import in the group's inner struggle for itself, within its external struggle for worldly self-preservation. It is because we today are motivated by the past, by what has been and by what has been done, that this history must not be forgotten. The choice of our future course depends on it. We hear the lofty demands of our acknowledged ancestors; they become part of our lives. We perceive and admit the reality of past guilt, of reprehensible actions, conditions, motivations, and decisions of the past, so that in eschewing the unforgotten we may find the way of truth. Changed views of our past come from a will to make the right decisions now, in a new situation. Mere presentation of history turns into responsible historic consciousness, the manifestation of a will to be either noble or mean, truthful or specious.

Fourth, we speak of existential historicity, of the individual's identity with himself in the sequence of time – but cutting across time. Objectively we cannot grasp this historicity. It appears as the course of an individual's life and identifies him as the historic form of something eternal.

Fifth, we become aware of the total historicity of all existence, of the universe, and of mankind when we compare it with immutable eternity. We objectify the singular in the reality of natural phenomena that cannot be deduced from general laws of nature – of phenomena ranging from an individual, singular landscape or tree to meteorological ones, and on to the order of the cosmos.

The historicity of revelation is an altogether different matter. Its singularity is that of 'God's history in time' – of the eternal that has become temporal by revelation. We get a 'sacred history'. Unlike all other historic phenomena, this cannot be attested as reality. Its witnesses can only say,

'We believed . . .'. The claim put forth in its behalf differs from any other. This charismatic history is claimed to be uniquely, exclusively absolute.

2 CONSCIOUSNESS AT LARGE AND HISTORICITY

As consciousness at large we always think in concepts. Historicity is the limit of thinking in general concepts; it eludes preservation in concepts. This shows in our way of dealing with others as well as with ourselves.

With others we claim to be dealing in a generally valid language. And indeed, when we communicate objectivities as generally valid – most perfectly in conveying scientific insights – the pure and impersonal contemplation of the matter requires that we efface our subjective self. Except as a dependable will to be objective, our self no longer exists. But if this posture, contrary to its meaning, dissolves all things into a sham factuality and objectivity – if hiding ourselves, living in masks of conventionally desired types that we finally mistake for ourselves, becomes the thing to do – then our existence will not come to be Existenz. We will hang back rather than put ourselves forward. Our dealings will not lead into the depths of possible historicity.

In dealing with myself, in my situation, the generality of intelligent planning is indispensable if I want to find and to fulfil my way in life. But my historic self remains unreal until I listen to whatever pertains to me, to chance disclosures and to the opportunities or obstacles presented by new situations. In adolescence especially this waiting and seizing, venturing and withdrawing in a mysterious world lends wings to us. 'No telling what may come' is both a disquieting and a confident thought. No accident is merely accidental; it may be an accident for our knowledge, but not for the consciousness of our own singular historicity, which no planning can wholly anticipate. Only our own immersion in reality unveils it.

The Stoics defined philosophical wisdom as harmony with the Providence of cosmic reason. The faith in revelation looks upon this Providence as the guidance of the God who has revealed himself.

The philosophizing individual experiences his historicity in dealing with chance occurrences; in the conjunction of spontaneity and given facts, of his audacity and his limitations, he achieves a relation to Transcendence which ciphers ambiguously illuminate. A believer in revelation experiences in the same things the dispensation of the one revealed God. Historicity provides another instance of the gulf between philosophical faith and the faith in revelation.

3 HISTORICITY OF CIPHERS

Ciphers are historic. As general ciphers they grow unsubstantial, though without some general structure they cannot last. They speak to us in the concrete form of their historic approach, not in abstractions. Described in types, I perceive them only in a fading and standardized state; talked about, they remain only distantly audible as possibilities of their historic nature. Compilation blocks the way of singularity, and a herbarium conveys only shadows of the appearance of plant life. Ciphers come to mind historically, whether in lingering calm or sudden seizure. They vanish as we rush through their massed conglomerations and endless classifications. Then, with the onset of fatigue and emptiness, the ciphers lose their voice.

4 RELATION OF EMBODIMENT AND HISTORICITY

As an object of our senses, every embodiment has a general character and is accordingly replaceable. Embodiment acquires distinction when it is taken into historic consciousness and thus becomes unique and irreplaceable.

Whatever is historic is corporeal. The faith in revelation rests upon an absolutely unique historic embodiment, not comparable to any other. The revealed God was not only embodied once upon a time; he remains presently embodied at each subsequent moment. This corporeality of God began in time. But the cipher that speaks in the revealed God as 'the Eternal', this powerful, challenging, sheltering, conquering cipher, is not tied to the corporeality of revelation.

The ciphers too are historic, but their only embodiment is in their language, in this ambiguous, historically animated language that is not spoken and is only metaphorically called a language.

5 THE TRUTH OF THE CIPHER IS THE HISTORIC REALITY OF EXISTENZ

The truth of the cipher – which at the moment illuminates existential decisions without compelling them – depends on whether that moment's decision will be for ever acknowledged and accepted as my own, whether I identify with it and renew it in repetition. Whatever is just understandingly experienced, and thus noncommittally done, carries no weight until it is received into a continuous Existenz.

But I remain *en route* and am not in possession. Instead of identifying with myself, I may come to part with myself. Then I do not want to be what I was in my action, in my way of life. I must accept it, to be sure, but I part with it by changing myself. If I am in earnest about this, I still have to live with something I can never get rid of. I am not the man I used to be; but in my changed life I must accept what was mine, though it is now alien to me. The change is true if its import is realized by a new vision, a new power of judgment. Despite this rebirth I accept the past; I do not reject it as if it had never been. I am not absolutely liberated – neither my own decision nor grace can do that – but I bear the consequences of my life and my actions. I cannot shift these consequences; I can only see, form, and transform them to the best of my ability. This existential process is illuminated in ciphers derived from the boundary situation of unavoidable guilt – a situation we need to come to ourselves as Existenz, which is always open to question.

No cognition and no insight attests the truth of the ciphers, only their illuminating power in the existential history of the individual.

d. *The Struggle for Purity in the Realm of Ciphers*

1 CIPHER OF TRANSCENDENCE OR OF REVELATION?

'Revelation of God's Word is divine sign language,' says Karl Barth.[1] I would ask how the signs of this language differ from those we call ciphers. They are supposed to be signs of a hidden act of revelation, and the ciphers, signs of hidden Transcendence. The veil covers God's act of revelation and Transcendence alike. Yet I am to take the signs of revelation for signs of a reality, which I cannot do with ciphers of Transcendence. The first are unequivocal signs of a temporally real divine act; in the second, Transcendence manifests itself in ambiguous ciphers. But if the signs refer unequivocally to the real revelation, they are means of unveiling. They are unique signs, divine reality. What is called sign and reality in this fashion is neither – not in the sense in which these words are generally understood.

Let us not be evasive. Either revelation is the spatially and temporally fixed act of God which the believer says it is – then it is not cipher but reality. Or it is a cipher among other ciphers and no longer real revelation. If revelation speaks in signs, it is no specific reality as long as these signs themselves do not differ fundamentally from all other signs of Transcendence. Only the reality of God – God's existence in the temporally fixed act of revelation, and in its signs – would distinguish revelation from the ciphers of Transcendence, the possible language of all things and the free work of men.

I ask myself whether the theologian's signs may perhaps be our ciphers. Is revelation a temporally real act of God to him, or does he conceive it as a cipher? I am sure he does not – but what then?

2 THE INTERPOSITION

Only the spatially and temporally localized reality of God could be revelation; yet this revealed reality would, so to speak, be interposed between the

---

[1] *Zwischen den Zeiten*, Vol. 7 (1929), p. 432. The theologian may forgive me for rapping on some of his theses in a way that must strike him as foolish – since to him, I presume, my theses can express only incomprehension and deplorable unbelief.

hidden God and human Existenz. It would bridge the abyss between God and man, like the divine 'mediator' revealed in Christ. But is this mediator not just as hidden as God – is he not an extraordinary, luminous, and true cipher of a man, Jesus, rather than God's own reality? And would this not turn our so-called 'mediation' into a superfluous interposition, a mere cover-up for the fact that the deity, defined as a reality beyond our reach, is now to exist for us as a reality, after all?

All over the world men hear and see and think in the suspended, ambiguous ciphers of Transcendence – ciphers which are just a language, never God himself. If the revealed reality too were manifested to man by signs only, it would remain as hidden from him as Transcendence. Instead of referring to Transcendence, the signs would refer to the interposed reality in time and space. The interposition is God, then; Jesus is human and, as Christ, divine at the same time. As Spinoza put it, this is just as understandable or as nonsensical as to call the circle square – and Spinoza may have been one of the strongest, most stubborn believers in God in recent centuries.

Signs are to give us access to that interposed revealed reality. Yet these signs no longer refer to the hidden deity but to a specified divine reality in the world, to God's entrance into the world at one distinctive place. They mark a fictitious point in the world where the reality of Transcendence and spatial-temporal reality are to coincide. By speaking in signs of the temporal reality of the revelatory act, instead of Transcendence, the theologian himself expresses the impossibility of such coincidence.

Something localized in the world and real – although removed from all other reality witnessed in history and literature – is still to be represented by signs. Then the interposition is superfluous, for this sort of revelation leaves Transcendence hidden. And it seems an impossible object of faith, for either revelation is the reality of God in the flesh or it is no revelation.

If the revealed reality manifests itself by signs alone, we have two Transcendences of the same description: both exist not as themselves, but in signs; both are 'revealed in concealment.'

Either the revealed reality exists, tangible for our senses as for Thomas, the doubter who thus became a believer, or it is hidden like Transcendence itself – a mere cipher, no longer revealed reality. Then it is humanly perceptible only by a new, different, and humanly incomprehensible faith which divine grace, according to dogmatic theory, grants only to a few, not to all men.

3 CONFIRMATION OF REVEALED REALITY BY WITNESSES

'To us,' says Karl Barth, 'it suffices to know that the Christ of St Paul and the Synoptics has in fact instituted the sacraments' of baptism and communion. In fact? The only 'fact' here is that Paul and the Synoptics mention the institution and quote its words (with some variations). Does this actual document prove that Jesus performed the act? No; historical analysis even makes it seem quite unlikely. But this does not matter to believers in revelation. Nor does Jesus matter to them. 'The Christ instituting the sacrament is the Christ of the prophets and apostles, not a historical Jesus abstracted from this testimony. This immaterial construct is theologically irrelevant, here as elsewhere. The founder of the sacraments is the Lord we know, not in the flesh, but in the spirit through the testimony of the men he called.' Thus Karl Barth, following Kierkegaard, who spurned all history and said that nothing counts but the one line that God became human.

But if it does not matter whether or not Jesus instituted the sacraments – if it is deemed a 'fact', rather, what the apostles understood and testified, not about Jesus, but about Christ (even Paul did not see Jesus himself, only the Christ who appeared to him on the road to Damascus) – why, then, is this witnessing process limited in time? Why can it not be continued, by testimony to the institution of more sacraments, for instance? Obviously because an authority in this world acknowledges those first witnesses but declares the process closed, the canon settled.

What matters to the theologian is a qualitative distinction. These signs or ciphers, these words, these writings differ from all other ciphers, words, or writings. They alone contain divine reality; everything else is the work of man or nature.

This means, however, that God is no longer hidden. I have not only his image, which the biblical God already enjoined – I have himself. The faith in revelation is indeed no longer a faith in the hidden God who gives me to myself in biblical and philosophical faith – immediately, not by some kind of mediation that is claimed to be God himself.

Obedience counts here, not the freedom of suspended ciphers. As Barth puts it, 'We must, the church must abide by the signs commanded to it.'

4 CULT, SACRAMENT, CHURCH

No kind of thinking helps us approach the reality which believers experience in the embodiment of God. Barth recalls that as late as the fifth century men were not taught about the sacrament until they had received it (much as the Greek mysteries, according to Aristotle, were *dromena* rather than *legomena*, shows of action, not means of instruction). St Ambrose called previous instruction a betrayal, and talk a hindrance to the illumination of the ignorant. 'To let something happen first, human talk has to cease.'

The realities in the world are cults and churches. Revelation and the word of God are not to be received in private. Their reality comes from the presence of divinity in an institution.

Thus the word is not 'God's Word' until there is authority to preach it, and the ecclesiastic act alone, the repetition of the instituting biblical formula, makes the sacrament a reality. Both, to be sure, are completed in the ever new and present divine revelation experienced by those who hear the word or take the sacrament – but woe to him who does so without making this experience! According to Barth, the truth of the sacrament 'depends at each time, and for each individual, on God himself. It can become God's judgment for the individual; the witness of the Holy Ghost can cast him out and make him obdurate. Grace would not be grace if we stood before God any other way.'

In any cult, places, times, meanings are obviously singled out from the rest of the world, to be holy thereafter. We see this in all religions. But the faith in revelation wants to differ. It calls the sacraments signs, but signs chosen over all other signs. They are not like other ciphers of Transcendence; they are chosen as acts of God. Barth, therefore turns upon those who, like Wycliffe, *exult in telling Christendom that all things round us, rightly understood, are sacraments, visible signs of the invisible God. . . . It is well-meant mischief to present and tout the sacrament as fitting so well and so plausibly into a whole line of symbols found in nature or wrought by civilization. . . . Let me say with all bluntness: in a row with other symbols, even the most venerable and profound, and treated as a 'meaningful' thing among others, the sacrament is not a sacrament any more – just as Jesus Christ in a line of religious personalities is not Jesus Christ any more. What has our cognition of all sorts of meanings to do with a sign God gave us?*

Hence the rich and glorious symbolism of water plays no part at all in the interpretation of baptism – only God's use of natural things for signs of quite another language. The effect of God's word on Karl Barth was *that things of this world, created, perishable things, were not and did not do what they are and do by nature. Instead, within their nature and yet beyond it, they were letters formed into a word which God had spoken to me so that I could hear it; and my human eye, this owl's eye fit for darkness only, found the gift to read them as letters and words. And so it was in the light befitting my darkness, in the parable of Creation, that God's Word condescended to me, and I listened.*

Yet at the same time the theologian will interpret his signs. 'The submersion in the water of baptism signifies our death and resurrection with Christ,' he says, and 'the eating and drinking of bread and wine in communion signifies our preservation by his sacrifice, by his appeal to the Father'. Such allegorical exegesis would kill any true symbol as a cipher, degrading it to a mere superfluous sign. But this is just what Barth does not mean. He means the reality in the symbol, 'nature's silent and yet so eloquent way to rise against all the mental and oral corrosion of truth, and to throw us back on the beginning' – not, however, as the reader might think, on the beginning of nature, but 'on that great recognition before all cognition'. This is to be the sacrament. This will protect the divine mystery and reveal it at the same time.

The pursuit of such theses plunges me from one amazement into the next, without bringing understanding a step closer. And for my instruction there are the general statements on obduracy, judgment, and being cast out.

What my own experience and observation has shown as cult and preach-ment looks quite different. To me the point always seemed to be whether a cult, in action, prayer, meditation, is approached as a cipher or looked upon as the reality of God's presence. Where worship was regarded as a cipher it seemed it could be solemn and serious in freedom, weighty in suspension, without loss of vigour. Where the experience was regarded as divine reality, however, it struck me as a case of magic – that is to say, as a causality without causality, a reality without reality. The impression this makes on obedient believers is overwhelming, of course; but in the world it has no consequences other than those in the soul of the believer who will live, act, and think differently and thus bear witness to the meaning of his experience, whether of suspended ciphers or of magical reality.

e. Ciphers and Dialectics

1 DIALECTICS IN GENERAL

Wherever thinking shows us contradictions we want to resolve them. We cannot bear to think of them. And if we cannot resolve them by favouring one alternative over the other, as true over false, we deal with them in a manner we call dialectic. The idea is to maintain and surmount the conflict at the same time, either by finding a synthesis that will 'reconcile' it or by exacerbating the contradiction into a paradox, so as to find truth and reality in absurdity.

In all thinking, whether philosophical or theological, we engage in dialectics from the outset, with or without methodological awareness. But dialectical thinking cannot only produce deep insights but may easily become specific sophistry.

As a way of dealing with existing contradictions, as their resolution by maintaining both sides rather than finding one true and the other false, dialectics is still an uncharted sea of thought movements. The great task remains unsolved: to show the diverse origins of dialectical constructions and to examine their evidential force, thus limiting their significance in every case and cleansing their application. Hegel, the developer of the most abundant dialectic fields, was the very man who failed to illuminate and clarify the method, practising it indiscriminately, rather, from profound movements to laughable tricks. Marx and Kierkegaard fed and trained on Hegel's thinking; but both of them transformed it into something different, fertile, and oddly enthralling.

Today, in Marxism and in theology, dialectics functions like a magic wand. It is treated as the absolute method, the sovereign remedy. Thinking people nowadays seem unable to withstand it, because the method is methodo-logically opaque. It is posited as a known, self-evident premise.

Yet each individual case brings up the question of the definite, limited sense in which a way of evidentiality applies. Could the dialectical manner of speaking be a means to admit contradictions as trivial, to evade them, in fact, so as to protect a quite undialectical and untenable embodiment of God's specific being? Or so as to cast a veil of seeming profundity over a presently desired unequivocal claim, by interpreting it as an impulse to perfection? For this dialectics lets us call for thought to cease, for obedience to be shown to God – a God who is an object of faith and, for mankind at large, only one phenomenon among others. Likewise, a brutal and capricious party line can be justified by a dialectics understood as the material dialectics of events – as the monocausality, the one, all-governing causality that perverts the freedom of man into his submission to the dictates of a necessity known at each moment to the party chiefs.

2 DIALECTICAL EXPRESSION OF REVEALED REALITY

Dialectics seems to solve the problems of the faith in revelation. The contradiction that revealed reality does and does not exist, that it is both affirmed and denied, is deemed necessary to the divinity of revelation. There is talk of 'revelation in concealment', of 'unveiling by veiling'. Theology is full of phrasings such as *simul iustus, simul peccator*, or 'voluntary obedience'.

'The mystery (a term the ancient church applied to the sacraments) is the paradoxical concept of the hidden truth that is so very manifest, . . . of truth speaking for itself alone,' writes Karl Barth, the modern theologian. 'Its revelation lies solely in concealment and indirect communication, in its unveiling to faith. God's word in signs can mean no unveiling of God save one that is also, and especially, a veiling. . . . The great Christian mystery or sacrament is the incarnation of the Word in Jesus Christ.'

This definitely marks an original reality that lies before all thought and can be experienced without thinking. Here lies Barth's 'fixed point where God is revealed to me, whence I must obediently dare to consider myself in a state of grace . . .'. And this point 'must, on principle, be a sign', as here in the sacrament and elsewhere in the word.

3 DIALECTICS IN THE CIPHER, AND UNDIALECTICAL CORPOREALITY

The philosopher – about whose paradoxicalities we shall hear in detail in Part Five – seems to think in the same fashion. The hidden God speaks in ciphers, but in such a way that the cipher never turns into an unequivocally direct word in time. At no point will its reality surpass the suspended ambiguity of other ciphers. The dialectical way of thinking is a form of communicating ciphers of Transcendence, ciphers which ambiguously appeal to man without making him their slave.

The direct statement of God's will – as in the institution of the sacraments, in the commandment to preach, in the promise of salvation, etc. – is quite another matter. This language, as a reality in time, calls unequivocally for obedience. There is no possible synthesis of the suspended cipher language and this reality of direct divine communication. An abyss divides their meanings.

The faith in revelation knows it rests on tangible reality. It admits of no doubt, because this reality is so certain, so overpowering, that the world fades and grows unsubstantial beside it. But the worldly threat comes not only from outside. The believer, carried away by the realization of revelation, is beset by doubts at the same time. He would like to hold his ground and at the same time to defend it from the charge of objectifying a cipher into a tangible God. Dialectics looks like the best way to do the impossible.

Now the question arises whether dialectics, as a form of stating theological thoughts, may perhaps be misused in order to save the 'fixed point', the quite undialectical corporeality. The point, after all, is reality, not an ambiguous cipher. If the theologian, on the strength of honest thinking, becomes aware of this possible abuse, there remains to him the magnificent clarifying attempt to counter the abuse with his own candour. He can declare the content, language, and exegesis of revelation as paradoxical, even absurd, and go on to define this very absurdity as the appropriate way of stating these matters. This is what Kierkegaard did.

But the conclusions of that great dialectician are intolerable to the human soul, and if they are not drawn and their practical consequences are not taken either, dialectics will be abused. For it is deceptive to apply the method to an utterly undialectical reality that rests on testimony and asks unequivocal obedience, and to expect dialectics to make this acceptable or comprehensible. Contradiction is then supposed to be the mark of revealed reality. Methodologically, dialectics makes sense as bringing to mind what I live by but cannot refer to. The misuse comes in when an objective reality, an objective claim, is fixed, allowed to call for blind obedience, and then supposed to be justified by dialectics.

4 SUMMARY

Ciphers, which can be interpreted and reinterpreted *ad infinitum*, are as such concrete and definite, but their objective embodiment is a perversion.

Dialectics as a movement of thought in the process of understanding illuminates our consciousness; but it becomes a tool of obscurantism if it lets us founder on factualities in space and time, calls these absolute and God, and requires us quite undialectically to submit to them.

If I do not believe in this revealed reality I fail to understand it. According to theologians, this will happen when the grace of God is not bestowed on the poor infidel I am, in their view; as for me, I am left with plain wonderment. Whether they talk of 'concealing revelation' or in the many other dialectic terms, I have no way to make the experience. The label 'dialectic' is of no more help than the label 'existential' in philosophizing.

Failing to understand, I wonder. I should like to understand; I follow their movements of thought – but in vain.

f. The Circle in Philosophy and Theology

1 THE CIRCLE IN THE FAITH IN REVELATION

Revelation exists only for the believer. His faculty of faith is conferred on him by the grace of the self-revealing God – *'ut credamus, Deus dedit,'* says Augustine. But that gift too exists only for the believer.

We hear from theologians that the sacraments were 'in fact' instituted by Christ. But what is a 'fact' if it is not demonstrable reality, only a revelation attested by believers?

Failing to understand, I confront a closed ring that repels the man who does not enter, whether as a poor, lost heathen, an infidel, or a heretic. The logical circle of understanding revelation is internally closed as well: when the believer enters it – through the faith which, he is aware, was given to him by the grace of God – he makes his exit from the rest of mankind.

2 THE CIRCLE IN PHILOSOPHY

Yet does the same circle not occur throughout philosophy? Every cipher that speaks of the bottom of things, of Being as a whole, is bound to lead to a circle. Whatever is to be 'the ultimate', to have nothing before or beside it, can always be only its own cause, not the result of any other. Hence Spinoza's formula: *causa sui.* This is the circle in its simplest form. We differentiate circles by their content; but whether it is Spinoza's divine substance, Hegel's 'spirit', or matter producing the mind that knows the matter – at the crucial point we always face a circle. It is universal throughout philosophy.

3 THE CIRCLE AND CIPHERS

The circle is inherent also in the cipher concept. Language, this sensory, acoustical and, in writing, optical phenomenon, is self-evident to us at every moment as the carrier of meanings, and yet it is the comprehensive mystery of our thinking existence. As creatures of the senses we need language; its meanings enable us to use its sensory form to grasp spiritual contents, and each time we speak we demonstrate that we are not mere creatures of the senses. Yet we call ciphers a mere language. This is a metaphor; in fact, ciphers are a new mystery, beyond that of language. As language is the handle by which we grasp the spiritual as such, ciphers are our way to circumscribe Transcendence.

The cipher language has no other reality than the language we hear and see. But it has no real speaker, nor even a real relation between cipher and meaning. Ciphers are a language, but not one that anyone speaks.

Thus the essence of what a cipher is can be stated only in another cipher. If we tried to define the cipher, we would have to call it 'the being of a transcendent meaning which is this alone, not a meaning of anything else'. Calling the ciphers a language is simply the cipher of what ciphers are. It is when they are heard and assimilated, when Existenz hears them and thus comes to itself, that we ascend to reality. What is meant cannot be comprehended in a definition, but it can be experienced in the use of communication. In definitions we move in circles, from circles to circles. There is no end to this rotation in circles. To the intellect it seems ridiculous.

The ever-renewed circles reveal that the merely thinkable is unfathomable as long as no Existenz responds from its source. Or – reversing this final circle – we reach the source in plunging into the unfathomable, catching ourselves as something incomprehensibly catches us.

4 THE DIFFERENCE BETWEEN PHILOSOPHICAL AND THEOLOGICAL CIRCLES

Circles in philosophy and in the faith in revelation have different meanings. Every circle, once become conscious, must be breached again. We breach philosophical circles by entering into new ones, until the thinkable is experienced as bottomless; the circle of the faith in revelation ends on tangible ground. The philosophical circles release steam and lead us back to the seriousness of Existenz here and now, to the unrest of being answerable for ourselves without conclusively knowing whence and whither. The circle of the faith in revelation is self-satisfied and secludes itself in its salvation, on the ground of its reality.

The different meanings of the two kinds of circles demonstrate a difference that seems to go to the root of Existenz.

The believer in revelation puts his Existenz into this circle and shuts himself up. Then the faith in revelation is an 'impregnable fortress'. It breaks off communication with others – and yet these believers are human beings like ourselves, and we would like to talk to them about the innermost that can be put into words. The impregnable fortress means much more, however. It not only shuts itself up when the occupants realize their impotence in the world; it also harbours forces that aim to conquer the world for their faith.

In philosophizing we need the circles as inevitable means of thinking, to bring the unthinkable to mind and to make room for our existential experience. They illuminate the unknowable, by voiding but not annihilating each other as circles – for with the disappearance of all objectivities the movement of thought brings to mind what will make possible Existenz real. In philosophizing, circles are there to be breached. Philosophizing does not seclude itself, neither in the edifices of its thinking nor in its existential reality. It remains infinitely open, without any final shelter except in its Transcendence-related freedom that defies conclusion. It does not know itself as an 'impregnable fortress'.

g. Interpreting Ciphers

1 RELIGIOUS AND MYTHOLOGICAL HISTORY

We have a wealth of material in the history of religions and myths, in the descriptive arrangement of myths and symbols, in the conception of their psychological motivations and sociological conditions. An endless world presents itself to the neutral observer who puts everything in place and traces the same general phenomena through widespread parallels. The ciphers lose their existential impact in the generality of concepts; but a breath of their original life remains even there. We can no more dispense with this kind of information than with osteology in studying the human body.

Yet if all this is to be no mere collection of age-old and lasting illusions, how do we judge the truth found in such phenomena? Surely not by neutral observation, but by present impact. The step from observation to adoption goes from knowing this cipher world to living in it.

In both cases we speak of interpreting ciphers. We aim either at a merely rational, psychological, sociological exegesis of given ciphers, or at personal experience and continued thinking in them. Both ways can be distinguished in principle but not separated in the actual interpretation. What begins as objective research in myths and symbols can in fact become a form of adoption.

2 PSYCHOANALYSIS

This is the case in the modern psychological conception. Ever since Romanticism, since Eduard von Hartmann, since Freud, we have been interpreting from 'the unconscious'.

The unconscious is a negative concept, defined as that which is not conscious. We conclude what it is, and we draw up hypotheses about its structure and about what happens in it. Their usefulness to psychological cognition cannot be established in general, only for specific investigations.

If the unconscious is made a positive substance, however, it absorbs everything. A whole world – eventually seen as the true reality – will be discovered in the unconscious. The conception 'psychefies' reality; it is metaphysics from the outset. If the unconscious is reality, whatever happens really and effectively must happen there. Consciousness, then, is just a surface phenomenon, the foam on the deep sea of the unconscious, a sign or symptom of what happens down there; it has no power of its own except, perhaps, that of disturbing the irresistible process. Psychologists, we hear, understand this and can teach us how to think and to act so that our conscious individual existence may find happiness in harmony with the unconscious.

Dreams, daydreams, works of poetry and art, the myths of nations and the hallucinations of the insane – all of these can mutually interpret each other by means of their construction as parallel phenomena on the one ground of the unconscious.

While it would be senseless to deny the unconscious – it is the concept of all that has the common trait of not being consciousness – it does make sense not to be deceived by the reversal of a negative into a positive, least of all by the divers constructions of events, steps, thresholds, and contents of the unconscious.

The interpretation of myths and symbols that has sprung up with psychoanalysis is actually their reconstitution in scientific garb. In the nature of things it cannot be scientific. It serves to soothe the lost feeling of many modern souls, and its influence on mythologists, archaeologists, religious and literary historians leads to thought processes wavering ambiguously between science and Gnosticism. This whole way of thinking is like revival of the thinking and the demeanour of the sorcerers, prophets, and founders of sects in late Antiquity. We meet an odd farrago: a mass of material knowledge, a little true science, then a scientific manner, but above all an overwhelming sense of depths, of being swept away by them, and finally a superior consciousness of lucid insights into the nature of things. A vague basic dogmatism exudes intellectual and practical perplexity disguised as sapient calm, extreme sensitivity, angry disdain, and a universal aggressiveness that remains negative because it has nothing to defend.

This is an aspect of modern opposition to philosophy, a pseudo-philosophy unconscious of itself and in need of rescuing. In part, its interpretations may be scientifically fruitful, but only after a laborious critical cleansing process; in general, this way of adopting ciphers leads to their existential extinction. One can neither see nor take hold of this opposition. What its renowned exponent, C. G. Jung, is as himself no man can tell; what appears in his doctrine and judgments cannot be taken in hand. The entire world of myths, symbols, and speculations seems to turn into a swamp when 'organisms' of archetypes are presented as world powers, when Gnostic world dramas are sketched out and the Jehovah of the Old Testament is psychoanalysed. Jehovah is unmasked like a neurotic on the analytical couch. And instead of the creative power in the visions of the old Gnostics and their successors down to Jacob Boehme, Schelling, even Ludwig Klages, we see the rationalistic mannerisms of psychoanalytical manipulation with emphasis on 'the irrational'. Scientific psychiatry is lost as utterly as philosophy. The existential consequences of such interpretation are frightening, for a metaphysics that regards life as a disease to be cured by analysis will permit ruinous satisfactions and justifications. To understand existence as a sick nervous system is both scientifically incorrect and existentially untrue.

3 THE CORRESPONDENCE OF EXISTENZ AND CIPHERS

Ciphers have their weight in an ascending series. First, they are manifested in noncommittal aestheticism as a vast sphere of meanings; then we feel their impact and partake of them; finally they illuminate our Existenz in real situations.

To interpret ciphers means to testify to our own experience with them. There is no objective, neutral understanding of ciphers. The interpreter does not come close to them until he lives them. Ciphers exist only for possible Existenz.

The cipher realm that speaks to the individual may be poor and meagre, or rich and vigorous. Anyone who thinks he has left it behind is only fooling himself. He is not aware of what remains cipher in him even though his world consists of supposedly knowable reality and dully serious performance.

4 ORIGINAL THINKING

To be true, an interpretation of ciphers must originate in the interpreter. He himself must be akin to the source they have come from, or are heard in. The source as such cannot be directly grasped; to designate it, we use many different concepts as signs of Existenz: the mind; the moving idea; the mood; absolute consciousness; decision; choice; real action; love. In so far as these terms mean phenomena we can describe and explore as empirical psychological realities, they miss what they are to indicate as signs of Existenz; and if we mean by them the existential source, the start of existential motion, the encompassing, they defy psychological description. Their outcome is what we experience as becoming ourselves. Consciousness needs to control it, but in a subordinate rather than in a dominant role. The original process is confirmed in renewal and repetition.

We ask: where does the knowledge of our faith come from? How does our faith come to think in ciphers? Where does the test of its truth arise? And the answers always point to something which lights up only in the thought movement, something we hear only there, never directly. We speak of inner illumination, of *pneuma*, of being changed, of intuitive decision, of sudden certainty.

There is an analogy between philosophical faith and the faith in revelation. Both know the source which no reasons can prove or refute, a source that can only be unfolded. The cause of truth cannot be caused once again. But there is a difference, for in philosophical faith I expose each definite statement of mine to questioning without limit – though my existential decision, arguable in its appearance, carries me as an unshakable certainty, as my identity with myself. The faith in revelation, on the other hand, rests on hearing the words and the message of Scripture and has its firm, objective content of reality in God himself. It is that, not his own decision and freedom to dare, that makes the believer unwavering.

Neither in philosophical faith nor in faith in revelation is there any analogy to objective cognition. This rests on premises which can be determined, and which cognition makes conscious. It thus makes its results relative to these premises or 'hypotheses', as the Greeks called the same thing. The premises can change. They can be differently posited each time. By definition they are never tenets of faith, and the results achieved are compellingly valid – on these premises. The 'premise' of philosophical and revealed faith, on the other hand, is the experience of the source. This cannot become a premise to be formulated, one from which the rest could be rationally deduced. The thinking of faith leaves everything determinable in suspension, but faith itself is unconditional and undeterminable. Faith always appears simultaneously in thought and living practice, in thinking the 'matter' and in the personality that thinks it.

What precedes the thinking of faith has been characterized in Tertullian's essay 'On the Testimony of the Soul' as the proprium of man as such. The soul comes from nature; its authority can be evaluated by the majesty of nature; but everything, including nature, has come from God. The soul is the student, nature the teacher, and God the teacher's teacher. The cause of the testimony of the soul precedes all things. 'In any case, the soul was there before writing, and language before the book, and man as such before the poet and philosopher.' This first testimony is true: 'Trust the soul. So you will come to trust yourself as well.'

5 SOURCE AND CONCEPTION

It seems clear and simple: the source should speak, and what covers it ought to be shed. But the original exists for itself only if it becomes conscious. Once conscious, it will express itself, and when it expresses itself it cannot help doing so in a way of conception. Originality always exists only in a form of thought or of speech. We deceive ourselves if we try to approach it directly; before we know it, we stop speaking clearly and start mumbling.

But original speech is subject to critical questioning. If it comes from the source, the way of conception will remain original in content; if it is empty, we keep speaking without saying anything. What used to be a reasoned concept, a consummated reflection, an effective figure of thought, may turn into unvisual, unmotivated, unexistential rationalism. It is to these empty conceptual movements that we must address our critical inquiries, spurred by our sense of shortcoming and testing mere thoughts not merely with other thoughts but with the experience of existential thinking.

The movement goes like this: originality is realized by consciousness, and consciousness by thinking; but the thinking consciousness awakens the originality, which then carries me beyond what I have been conscious of. Again and again, in this movement, I am required to pull myself back from lapsing into vacuous manners of speech. The ascent to brightness and fulfilment, in the unity of origin and thought, is my self-retrieval from a plunge. This retrieval alone will give real meaning to my interpretation of ciphers.

6 ADOPTIVE INTERPRETATION

An interpretation that involves adoption brings one origin in touch with the other. Taking part in the origin lends truth to our appraisal of ciphers, but it already implies a change in us. The result is original thinking, aroused by someone else's original thinking.

In such interpretation we distinguish between the real experience of others and the impact on the interpreter. I cannot in conscience entrust myself to what I cannot originally make my own.

This is the standpoint for questioning the philosophical and theological activities around us. Though indispensable as a premise, this factually perceptive burrowing through the heritage of a great past can become a superfluous hobby, for if I yield to toying with poetic and artistic beauties and speculative thoughts, if I feel the excitement of dramatic and complex historic events and am content, instead of doing and preparing something else with it, my furious activity results in existential distraction. The view of whatever we do not responsibly share tempts us to devious meditations which depart from present reality and thus are not serious.

Let no one misunderstand me: scholarly interpretation, conducted with the rigour of a purely scientific approach, is indispensable. We are indebted to it for our unobscured access to sources of tradition. It teaches us how to uncover demonstrable historic reality and the meaning of works in their time. It does what only professionals can do, and it is not an end in itself – for as long as demonstrable history is not ignored, it leaves the way open for the transforming adoption that cuts deeper than is possible for scientific interpretation. The ways of understanding in the contact of origins are unpredictable. Augustine could not read Greek, but in translations he may have understood Plato and Plotinus better than all his contemporaries. The scholarly interpreter can make the sources accessible not only as an editor and commentator, but as a translator. In the simplest form he can make audible and visible what he has understood. This research is significant in so far as teaching, and the interpreter's own example, will make the demands of our spiritual forebears credible in the mass of the population, in so far as it prepares for an adoption as living practice in our present world, in the age of technology, rather than for a historical understanding without existential grounds. Then and then only will a tradition be more than mere observation, and historical understanding will serve present tasks rather than estrange us from them.

7 MYTHOLOGICAL THINKING, SPECULATION, AND DOGMATIC KNOWLEDGE

The common feature of mythological (visual) and speculative (conceptual) ciphers is constant mutability. From the beginning, man has been thinking in myths, in primordial images, divine events and actions, in creations of the world and of mankind – all reflected and newly realized in present thought and action. These views, handed down from a mythical primal age, from times out of memory, were adopted in bright consciousness, transformed, and deepened by the authors of Greek tragedy, for instance. In the same way and at the same time, the Greek philosophers threw light on the foundations of the world, the gods, and human things. Their pure, speculative thinking climbed heights we cannot envision. To them the very concepts were ciphers. They acquired the same mobility in adoptive and transforming interpretation. Their figures of thought are analogous to mythological views, governed by an inner logic but suspended as a whole, like the ciphers of mythology.

The intellectual situation changes when myths and speculations congeal in dogmatic knowledge, as has happened from the beginning. Existential vigour and original thinking in ciphers will flag, then, and freedom will vanish. There was freedom even in the intellectual despotism of some of the oldest philosophers, who claimed absolute truth for the insights that each had won first and, for himself, definitively. One would hit the other in the face, so to speak; but the overall situation was one of living in the most untrammelled originality. Subsequently, comprehensive philosophical systems arose and absorbed all past thinking whose rational figures could be detached from the source. These systems too remained mobile in part – as Stoic thinking, for instance – but the basic mood was now altogether different. The ciphers lost their purity. As in embodiment, ciphers go down in the guise of an absolute scientific knowledge of facts, of entireties and details, of the general and the particular. What is true for Existenz alone could now be learned. Reasons were now to make compelling, as cognition, what is serious only in suspension and for freedom.

8 THE MODES OF CIPHERS

The realm of ciphers is not a series of signs standing side by side. There are modes of ciphers. Their only common quality is to be more than signs – for signs denote something which can be said, seen, or known directly as well. Ciphers mean a language that is heard in ciphers alone, that does not refer to something else, and whose speaking subject is unknown, unknowable, untraceable. They can be interpreted, but only so as to leave their meaning inexhaustible. At bottom, they will have to be interpreted in other ciphers.

What can be a cipher? Anything there is, and anything men can make, be it real or a product of thought or imagination. They are found in mythological, ritual, sacramental, poetic, and artistic tradition as well as in philosophy.

Here I should like to say only a few words on art and poetry, the wellsprings of the purest and most glorious cipher language. They lift us out of barbarism and make us human. The great poets – Aeschylus, Dante, Shakespeare – transcend the question of realization. Their ciphers touch us to the quick because they mean no such embodiment as a dogmatically fixed cult does in its object of faith.

Like all human activity, poetry and art involve a danger. Plato's attack on the poets – begun by Hesiod, continued all the way from Augustine to Kierkegaard and Nietzsche, and found analogously in Confucianism – will be true for ever. It never denies poetry, but demands that it be guided. Why?

First, because of the temptation to heed evil impulses which some types of poetry and music arouse and intensify; because falsehood may take root in the soul of the viewer; because the fascination lies in viewing as such.

Secondly, because poetry lures us into 'aestheticism' – that is to say, into a noncommittal view of things, a delight in the way they are, in forms and figures. It leads us to enjoy a lack of commitment and the appearance of all possibilities of life, the good as well as the evil.

This lack of commitment is merely the degeneration of the unique freedom which art and poetry grant in the game of 'disinterested' seeing. Without it, man remains darkly serious, locked in the dull purposiveness of his naturally closed mind.

The game of seeing is true in so far as the sight – which means all kinds, the ugliness and weirdness of nature and man, criminals for Dostoevsky, prostitutes for Toulouse-Lautrec – becomes a true cipher. The game is untrue in so far as it portrays the mere self-understanding of decay, the insolence of vulgarity, the chaos of desperate pleasure. We talk about 'quality' in poetry and art; but this ambiguous term covers everything, because it lets mere technical skill coincide with the transparency of figures created as ciphers.

For moments, now and then, modern aestheticism infects even theologians. A young divine may call the creeds of the Reformation period 'burnished word figures' and hear the 'music frozen in its formulas'. The next step would be a similar delight in the tests of biblical revelation. It is the same perversion as the pleasure cult of word figures and poetry developed by modern snobs.

Peculiar phenomena, misunderstood or misleading and rarely seen in their true greatness, are such poets and artists as Hölderlin and Van Gogh. What they, in the early years of mental illness, created at the borderline of human faculties is a cipher world that moves us differently from the worlds of others, but no less deeply. Themselves touching, fear-inspiring ciphers throughout their existence, these men exert a singular magnetism by their achievements on the ground of insanity, though not due to insanity alone. Uncannily and credibly, their voices ring out of depths where the unspeakable, through them, becomes speakable. One would have to be humanly blind to see such wondrous beauties without horror; but the reality of our Existenz does not join these rare artists and poets if it gives them room at the borderline.

Philosophy can adopt all kinds of ciphers. Its own speculation will produce ciphers. But no true philosophy could speak as though empowered, like a faith in revelation.

9 THE ORDER OF CIPHERS

There is no appropriate order to put ciphers in. A draft of their world would become an inconclusive compendium of historic data viewed from outside, in neutrality. It would fade into irrealities. It would be a lifeless herbarium.

We may perceive ciphers in their effective historic appearance, as we do in scientific mythology, presenting specific groups that affect us and translating them into the language of our time. We may untangle their diversity, distinguish their ranks and dimensions, and show them in all the particular forms of their historic mutations.

Thus we obtain a wealth of images. But from these arrangements of ciphers we must take the step to their reality, which nothing short of personal involvement will reveal. Then the ciphers will appear as an infinite network or a multi-dimensional space. From self-chosen points of departure our thinking enters these unfolding spaces that penetrate, complement, and answer each other.

Any fixation would extinguish them. To stay alive, they must remain suspended. Talking in ciphers, we are philosophically truthful only as long as we keep them in this suspension.

10 LANGUAGE AND SILENCE

The end of language is the limit of interpretation. It is completed in silence. But the limit itself exists by language alone; it is the course of spoken communication that makes of silence a manner of speech. This kind of silence is no suppression of something I know and could say. For those who think with me, for myself, and for Transcendence it is a fulfilled silence at the limits of what men can say. It is not the dumb speechlessness that says nothing and is thus not silent either.

This is the way of the ciphers. We hear them, so to speak, from various orbits placed about Transcendence, or we speak in them about Transcendence. But ciphers are never what we seek or sense or experience in them. Hence our effort to transcend them, to plumb the depths or to ascend to the heights where the cipher language also comes to an end, where in knowing that we do not know – that is to say, in fulfilled silence – we touch Transcendence.

One way of approaching the thought of Transcendence is to think the infinite. We succeed in forming concepts of the infinite and operating with them, but beyond the concepts lies always the infinite itself. Our thinking fails us when we want to think the infinite – and in this failure, in this contradiction and circle, it indirectly shows the infinite.

What we cannot say, because we cannot think it, exists for us as we speak and think in what Augustine called 'I know not what struggle of words' – *nescio quae pugna verborum*. And this struggle of words is better guarded by silence than silenced by talk. The interpretation of ciphers will keep this limit constantly in our minds.

Yet the silence at the limit of cipher thinking is realized, not by refraining from thought and speech, but by carrying them to the extremes where they revert to silence. In time, they will shortly make us speak again.

h. The Twofold Struggle

The inner struggle is waged, first, for the purity of ciphers against their realization in myths and revelations, and secondly, in the ciphers' own realm, by cipher against cipher.

1 THE STRUGGLE FOR PURITY IN THE WORLD OF CIPHERS

The first struggle concerns the cipher world as such. It is fought for its preservation, against its confusion. It is by no means the struggle of some enlightenment against the reality of Transcendence; on the contrary, it is a struggle for the reality of Transcendence against its distortion and restriction.

Both philosophical faith and the faith in revelation speak of God. In philosophical faith we do not know about God; we hear only the language of ciphers. To this faith, God himself is a cipher. The believer in revelation thinks he knows what God did when he revealed himself for the salvation of men – when God, in other words, took particular actions in the world, tying himself to time and place. The biblical commandment 'Thou shalt not make unto thee any image or likeness' is taken seriously in philosophical faith, and when we fail to comply with it as we hear and unfold ciphers, we know what we are doing.

Embodying the image means to go a step farther. As finite and sensory rational creatures we constantly must overcome a tendency that will not vanish even after it has been understood: the tendency to objectify not just pictorially but corporeally.

Must a belief in revelation necessarily pervert the cipher language into reality? We are bound to think so, at first; yet though this insight may seem inescapable to us, we hesitate to look upon it as definitive. We cannot take another view, but philosophical faith keeps urging us to question the utterances, the phenomena, the consequences of the faith in revelation, to question them time and again with open eyes. There too, above all, it shows us truth in ciphers that were effective as such even in corporeal guise.

If charges of atheism, nihilism, and other categories of ecclesiastic-theological invective are flung at us, it would be a mistake to hurl them back with the thesis that God himself is violated by the faith in revelation. I reject this faith for myself; to me it does seem like a violation of the deity; but God is untouchable and inviolable. It is only in my own possible relation to Transcendence that I would be guilty if I adopted a faith in revelation that remains incomprehensible to me.

2 THE STRUGGLE IN THE WORLD OF CIPHERS

The second struggle is waged in ciphers, by ciphers against other ciphers, and does not clearly emerge until the first, for the purity of the cipher world, has been won.

It begins when ciphers evoke an existential response, when they are not merely ambiguous. They correspond to existential possibilities whose sources vary, as do their ranks of proximity to Transcendence. Some will illuminate our path in life; others will be spurned as speaking a dark, strange, seductive language. Ciphers that thrill one man revolt the next, while others leave both of them cold. Ciphers that are not just non-committally noted are either repudiated or made our own. This is the struggle in their realm, and the stakes for any present Existenz are truth or untruth of individual ciphers, their import, their closeness to the ground of Transcendence.

3 THE CORE OF THE EMBATTLED CIPHER WORLDS

The silent battles in our souls occur unspokenly, perhaps unconsciously, in our way of living with the ciphers we meet everywhere. We may experience them casually or remain deeply impressed, or we may push them aside – the crux is always the fight for the adoption of what pervades and guides all ciphers appearing in a particular cipher world. This core determines our attitudes toward them all, and our association with them. We cannot, for instance, equally assimilate the worlds of Greek tragedy, of Dante, Calderon, and Shakespeare. A pure literary historian in his legitimate universal detachment may do it; so may an aesthete in his illegitimate noncommittal posture. But a man who is in earnest as possible Existenz may somehow relate to all ciphers, may in some fashion feel the impact of all, but the core of each will either find him outside, in dissent, or inside it, sharing its life.

What is this core, this pervading 'principle'? We may try in each case to express it, but we shall fail – for we cannot survey the battle of powers around us. We have no fixed point where all things are comprehensible, where everything in its place is wholly true and real. Only the deity could occupy such a point, not any human being. The greatest receptiveness of a poet reflecting these forces will not suffice, nor will the broadest philosophical understanding. However grand a universe of ciphers the few greatest minds have produced, it is a universe in encompassing, not an encompassing universe.

Part Five. The struggle in the realm of ciphers

Introduction

1 THE SITUATION

The cipher world is not a harmonious realm, an unequivocal manifestation of the abundance of Being.

Some ciphers promise peace, but knowing their world as a whole brings anything but peace. Ciphers contradict each other. Listening to some, I deny others. If we delve into specific ones, their background remains this entire embattled realm.

But what kind of battle is this? It is not fought for existence, not for power, but for original truth. It can, so to speak, incarnate itself in struggles for existence, and they can take their banners from the cipher world. Then the pure meaning of ciphers, their motion relative to Transcendence, will fade or spoil or vanish.

The fight does not cease until the world of the cipher language – and thus the world at large – is transcended in the silence of the ineffable. But then we have lost the world.

Or, if no ciphers are taken seriously, if all of them are seen on the non-committal level of fantasy and stimulation, the fight will end before it has begun. Then, in relinquishing our questing consciousness, our concern with the cause of things, we shall have lost Transcendence.

2 THE OBJECTIVATION OF POWERS

The cipher struggle relates to Transcendence. The individual feels that Transcendence itself is not directly with him, nor with him alone – for it underlies all things, him and his worst enemy, him as Existenz, and him as nature that both bears and destroys him. What rages in the ciphers is a battle of truthfulness encountering a diversity of forces that we try to grasp in vain. Standing in their midst, we cannot survey them.

We objectify the diversity as a struggle of powers encountering each other in the ciphers. This very objectivation is either a sign – indicating how our Existenz appears in existence and becomes the battleground – or it is a cipher of something rooted in Transcendence. The struggle occurs as we, each individual Existenz, choose ciphers to heed, as we stand by our choice, as we come to depend on special ciphers as absolute ones, or keep moving freely within them.

3 EXAMPLES

One unreflective but magnificently visual objectivation of the struggle of powers has always been polytheism. The Greeks knew, and we still believe we know with them, what it meant to worship Apollo or Dionysus or Hermes, Aphrodite or love-hating Artemis, Hera, guardian of marriage, or Athena, the goddess above sex, not born but sprung from the forehead of Zeus – sage, militant, rational, uniquely Greek Athena who was comparable to no other goddess in the world and may have been polytheism's most moving figure in her natural, never extravagant appeal to the pure, artless nobility in man. Those were incompatible devotions, but they would open and justify all human possibilities. The gods had different domains, made mutually exclusive demands, walked side by side or battled with one another. In serving one, man could offend the other. Whatever form the powers assumed, the Greeks, without logical reasoning, would marvellously clarify and sanctify them in personal gods.

Polytheism harbours a lasting truth which not even the monotheistic churches have been able to ignore in practice. This truth continues to this day, though not called polytheism.

A very different matter is the modern effort – without reference to myths, in rational objectivation – not to conjure forces, but to construct concepts. There we aim at a conceptual understanding of the situation of the battling forces. They do not become ciphers; they are figures of thought on the borderline of science and philosophy. Of these too I cite only a few examples. *a:* The weightiest attempt of the kind, to my mind, is the thinking laid down by Max Weber in his 'intermediate reflection' on 'steps and directions of religious rejection of the world' (*Gesammelte Aufsätze zur Religionssoziologie*, V. I, pp. 536–73). Taking a scientific attitude, Weber claims only 'to provide a means of orientation in ideal types, not to teach a special philosophy'. His theme is the rejection of the world. He shows its directions in the economic, political, aesthetic, erotic, and intellectual spheres, to make meaningfully clear how and where inner conflicts between orders of life are possible and adequate. He will not say 'that there is no standpoint from which they might be regarded as "void" '. In his construction Weber constantly recalls historic phenomena, thus indicating the historic character of what he presents as an aspect of the struggle of powers.

Each time, this construction of meaningful concepts in the reality of human conduct will lead the thinker to ultimate premises. It will teach the embattled how to reach these premises in thought, and how to make them conscious. Its aim is to answer questions about the historic realization – consistent or inconsistent – of the premises.

b: The basic knowledge that we draft as a theory of the modes of encompassing shows, first, a struggle within those modes by the diversity of phenomena appearing in them, and secondly, a struggle of the modes against each other. We construct the idea that the modes coexist in order and subordination, but will break up if individual ones – the intellect, the mind, existence, etc. – are made absolute and claim the right to lead the rest (cf. Part Three of this book).

c: In the horizons in which we think at a time, we may arrive at alternatives which initially defy transcending – alternatives such as boundless or conditional and limited communication, openness or exclusiveness, reason or catholicity (cf. my book, *Von der Wahrheit*, pp. 832–68).

4 OBJECTIVATION AND INVOLVEMENT

The mere thought of those powers will involve us in their struggle. Their tentative objectivation in patterns, from a point of view, does not mean that we might overlook the whole from outside, like a battlefield we keep aloof from. However hard we try to act as mere observers, we are bound to become involved as exponents. We cannot direct the powers speculatively, without participating, as a conductor directs the instrumentalists of his orchestra.

The situation is this, rather: in seeking to objectify the struggle, as though surveying it from afar, we simultaneously jump into the fray. We are always in it and out of it at once, existing and observing at the same time. We can, of course, strive for a maximum of detachment – and thus of freedom – from ourselves; but by the very act of conceiving such battlefields we are forging weapons for the battle. Any image of powers will serve powers. We cannot help that. Only a union of the freedom of detachment with the freedom of joining the fray will give us our whole possible freedom.

Throughout, the battle is not waged on one level, between clearly marked enemies. The fronts become confused. Not one power is definitely, substantially comprehensible. The struggle is such as to keep their cores, their substances or subjects, in the background; it may look like a foreground action that can be objectified in significant connections. Could there be, perhaps, one universal vinculum beneath the battle?

5 COMBAT AND COMMUNICATION IN CIPHERS

If philosophy gets into a struggle of powers that it cannot adequately overlook from outside, the fight will involve not just rejection but communication.

There is no truth without struggle, and the sharpest is the struggle for truth itself. In pure and profound form it occurs in existence without violence and coercion. When it deteriorates into the brutal struggle for existence, the guiding forces cease, and then the ciphers, like all structures of the mind, keep serving only for self-preservation and aggrandizement, as slogans interchangeable at will. We are no longer in a fight for truth.

This struggle is waged in leading the way to limits, in learning to see and to hear, in rational thought, in approaching Transcendence through ciphers, in interpreting ciphers. It is carried on in provocative communication. It takes talking about what is, until silence will take over as fulfilled language. The struggle depends on plain speaking, on saying all that I can say to myself, on holding nothing back. But even in success there remains the indirectness in which self meets self.

Wherever we hear ciphers we are involved. And once involved, we follow thoughts not just in logic, but as what we are.

The cipher struggle happens every time, even if we are not conscious of it or ignore it as trivial. Sometimes we seem to forget it. Often it makes us self-conscious. It takes all our freedom – our simultaneous detachment from the struggle and involvement in it – to keep our minds open, to urge communication, to remove the bars to our understanding and to base it on the historic reality of Existenz.

Mutual understanding in ciphers means communication in contact with Transcendence. It permits the closest ties and the oddest antagonisms. Men who agree are still obliged to wrestle for the purity and import of the ciphers; men to whom ciphers show an abyss between them will spurn one another's ciphers and yet seek to understand each other, driven by a desire to reach unanimity, not in this or that language but in the whole motion of the cipher world. The fight in concepts hides what may, despite all evidence to the contrary, serve to hold the exponents of warring powers together. Inexorable choices may seem like fateful play, merely provisional, if not indeed like affinities within a whole conceived in other ciphers – which in turn will always break up again in the phenomenality of time.

In history the great spiritual cipher groups have mostly been organizationally linked with social and political realities – as in Antiquity, in China and India, in medieval Christendom – though some, like Hesiod's, were purely mental philosophical constructions. In the polytheistic orders each god had his domain, and their struggle goes on in the sequence of divine generations. The universal systems of later days, finally climaxed in Hegel, seemed to depict all Being in a grandiose harmony coordinating the most radical conflicts.

In these structures we see the objective, factual, impersonal pursuit of one whole truth that is some day expected to unite mankind. But such totalities of human vision and conception will always prove to be limited. They founder on experiences made in the never-ending, never perfectible struggling communication that is dynamite for all systems – experiences needed to bring us to the full scope of our possibilities in the doom of time. Here, from insight, from the experience of insight, we draw the will to join in our motivation for the struggle, but not to enclose or close the struggle itself in a harmony of ciphers, however grandiose.

In the cipher struggle we can find no progress as in the sciences. We can see the great historic leaps as new ciphers appear. We see evolutions into particular circles of ciphers. We see, above all, changes in their vigour and veracity.

If the strife of theologians, therefore, is supposed to make one basic fact ('Nobody can lay a groundwork other than that laid in the beginning') better known and understood in faith by progressive insight, there can still be no talk of progress. There is only the ceaseless strife of religious cognition. Pitted against each other are forces we cannot survey, forces to which this cognition of faith – if it is no mere intellectual squabbling – will give a clearer comprehension of themselves as they institute their creeds and symbols.

6 LIBERALISM AND DOGMATISM

In the battle of ciphers, whether it appears as theology or as philosophy, we speak of liberalism and humanism as opposed to the dogmatic, orthodox, illiberal, and inhumane. It is the difference between an ingenuous, loving battle for truth and a disingenuous, loveless one. In the loveless battle the sole truth has already been established by revelation, by a church, a master, a school, a system, and the battler bows to it as to a recognized authority with power in the world, or as to a still powerless authority that he believes in.

Liberalism is tolerant. This tolerance is not indifference to things we secretly despise, things that happen to exist and cannot be exterminated; it means, rather, to take seriously what is alien, to listen to it, to make it our concern. Tolerance will not let us apply the same brush to all things which in time can result only from contention and boundless communication. Yet tolerance too must be questioned. Does it not take for the essence of freedom what simply expresses one power among others? After all, the sense of being *en route*, not in possession of one sole truth, is incompatible with a sense of obedience, of irrevocable submission to objectively warranted truth. Tolerance and intolerance cannot be reconciled. Hence the saying: Tolerance is intolerance of intolerance. And there we make a distinction. If, in existence, the intolerant resort to coercive violence, the tolerant must be – and have regrettably not always been – utterly intolerant of this perversion; but in the struggle of minds they will never give up hope that they can reason with others, open their minds in communication, and reach the kind of questioning accord that may link men who differ not only about some ciphers but in their basic attitude toward the cipher world.

Such an accord exists when adversaries mutually grant each other the unlimited right to their faiths, their insights, their convictions. It is possible when they permit each other to speak without reserve, to lift the veil that otherwise, throughout the world, facilitates social life and undermines it at the same time – for conventionality stifles communication. In that accord, opponents will not restrict the freedom of public communication, will not directly or indirectly keep others from stating facts and stating or preaching ideas. They will not just outwardly safeguard but inwardly affirm each other's right to bear witness to their Existenz. But the accord means also to be concerned with one another's inmost being.

We live together on a battleground filled with ciphers, in a spiritual living space always rent anew by seemingly irreconcilable conflicts. No man is everything. No truth we can grasp is the whole truth. Nothing tangible is absolute. From the viewpoint of this freedom all the firm stands that men take, the creeds they confess, the definitive truth they claim for ciphers, sound like claims voiced in captivity.

The illiberal will charge that our refusal to confess, to make firm statements, demonstrates our unseriousness. With our attitude, they say, we cannot find truth anywhere in the variety of possibilities, nor tell true ciphers from false ones. There will be no end to the struggle.

We answer that as long as we live in time there can indeed be no end to the struggle. Why not? Because unconditional truth, which is solely due to the historic decision of Existenz, must be distinguished from general truth expressed in tenets of faith.

Historic existential truth lies in the decision of the moment, and in its ever-original repetition. This unconditional truth cannot be generally stated. Though ciphers and general reasoning may illuminate it, they will miss its core. There is no reason for Existenz, no reason for love – we have lost sight of them if we look for their reasons. There is no way to prove existential reality, although without it we cannot seriously reason together.

Creeds and assertions, on the other hand, seem to give solid support. It makes us feel strong to find evidence in tradition for tenets based either on revelation or on a dogmatic philosophy.

This distinction leads to two further theses. The struggle always ends in the historic Existenz that has moved, by its decision, from possibility to reality and found the basis of its life. The struggle does not end in statements, judgments, or ciphers.

Here the discussion grows entangled. One side says, 'Your confessions and statements are ways to evade true seriousness, to free yourselves from your freedom.' The other says, 'You are evading truth by claiming a subjective, unobjectifiable truth for your Existenz.'

In these terms, each side will feel completely misunderstood by the other. But is the antithesis not merely superficial? Does it apply to deviations only? We cannot break through it to a thinking form of faith that would unite us; therefore, along with readiness to communicate, there is wonder on both sides.

The conflict will seem irreconcilable only when it is couched in general terms. But human reality does not fit into any scheme of alternative concepts, and however unreservedly a man seems to profess some formulated principle, there is always more to him than that.

7 PLAY AND NON-COMMITMENT

The ambiguity and mobility of ciphers leads to noncommittal aestheticism. To be serious, our thought movements require existential guidance. It may be said that the freedom of moving in ciphers, without an absolute, objective criterium of truth, demonstrates such aesthetic non-commitment.

We reply that in rejecting an aesthetic, noncommittal living posture we do not mean to reject the play that is indispensable. If I do not venture into the infinite world of noncommittal experience I shall never come to any serious commitment.

The seriousness of the great poets and artists derived from Transcendence, and they translated it into free forms, voiding dogmatism and coercion, speaking indirectly, but with an immediacy that overwhelms us still. We understand them only if we understand how much they were in earnest. They direct us toward the truth of Transcendence; but they leave us free. In play, they let us experience all possibilities. They enable us to experience them as though we, in ourselves, were acting out the drama of infinite metamorphoses. We become, potentially, what actually we neither are nor want to be. A whole world of views fills and individually expands us into the immeasurable possibilities of being human. Here lies a vital source of liberalism and humanism, for a seriousness without the free breathing space wrought by the arts will be a dull seriousness without breadth or humanity.

8 TRANSCENDING THE CIPHERS

Ciphers point beyond themselves, at the roots of things. They point to what we call 'Being' or 'Nothingness', or 'Above-Being' or 'before all Being' or 'beyond all Being' – concepts that have been touched upon in philosophizing for scores of centuries.

We ask: does the ban on images of Transcendence not void all ciphers? Does the sole truth not lie beyond all ciphers?

No cipher is more than a signpost or a light. No cipher is the last, the one and only.

Each cipher is a phenomenon as well, a foreground, a language. Each requires us to realize its limitations, to feel what lies beyond it. We also need the struggle of ciphers to keep from making any one of them absolute.

Thus we should like to transcend all ciphers, to reach the point where they will disappear. But even for this transcending we are dependent on a cipher language – on one that includes this disappearance.

We may think we have transcended the ciphers, but while we live we keep returning to the phenomenality of our temporal existence. Though existential thinking may for instants take us consciously to the adytum of the unthinkable, inconceivable, unspeakable, we always fall back promptly into the world in which ciphers are our language.

The struggle of ciphers will not let us come to rest. No cipher suffices; each holds out the lure of premature peace; but peace in a cipher is simply another cipher. It is not perfect peace. We know the wonderful peace of moments, but as a permanent state in time it is existentially impossible.

We long for peace; we always tend to find it in thoughtlessness, oblivion, or inertia. But the will to truth is stronger. It shatters every sham peace. It makes us realize that in giving up restlessness we lose the truth of Existenz.

The peace that is truly given to man must be anchored beyond all ciphers, where no human anchor seems to hold. It is from there that our ciphers get their light, and their shadows.

9 OUR PRESENTATION

We shall take up historic forms of ciphers. In making them our own we simplify them, in the sense of historical knowledge, for historic reality is far more complex, both more magnificent and more obscure.

It may be asked what we have to do with ciphers that were alive so long ago, with strange speculations, images, and stories. Have they not all become curiosities? Do they not give offence? We say no – for we live and think in the experience that the ciphers, though transformed, are as alive and true as ever.

From the outset, our presentation is an 'interested' one. We should like to get in touch with the truth of ciphers. We are not looking for the immense realm of facts from mythological or religious or philosophical history, nor do we follow psychological or sociological lines of questioning. What concerns us is the question of truth as such – more specifically, the question of the truth of ciphers that cannot be known, that can only be experienced existentially. In the historic forms of ciphers we look for their appeal as possible truth. Thus we are not acting objectively – that is to say, not scientifically, not historically, psychologically, or sociologically – but neither are we following subjective tastes and inclinations. Instead, we yield to the impacts that turn thinking into inner action wherever we are engaged.

Our ciphers are based on the Bible, on the Greek poets and philosophers, on their forms of adopting and transforming ciphers through the ages. In addition, there has for thousands of years been an inestimable influx of Asian ideas. Ciphers are forgotten and may reappear.

Our presentation cannot be arranged as a straight picture of the embattled powers, focusing on a series of them as fighting it out, through ciphers, in the human soul. This would mean to hypostatize one cipher – that of the powers. It would mean that one basic experience was fixed, aligned in clear battle fronts; but I cannot know those fronts, though I keep experiencing the battle. Fronts that impress me powerfully at one moment will seem to shift and change in the next. Constructing alignments of 'power subjects' in this impervious mêlée would simply produce another cipher, and that one might, by its premature absolutes, tend to cripple communication. The construction could never be a survey; it could always show only aspects of fronts that appear to one thinker aligned in them – one who will experience the powers, will yield to them or reject them, but can never stand aside.

We need some guideline, though, for the arrangement of our presentation. In the first section we shall speak of ciphers, in the second of what lies beyond all ciphers. In the first, we shall discuss the ciphers in three ways – first, the ones referring directly to Transcendence (God); second, those in which an immanent concept as such comes to refer to Transcendence (the universe, history, the *logos*); and third, we proceed from existential situations illuminated in ciphers (physical and moral evil).

Section One: The Ciphers

I CIPHERS OF TRANSCENDENCE

Let me repeat: Transcendence is present when we experience and conceive the world as a transition rather than as what exists on its own, what is in itself. This Transcendence is the point of reference for human freedom. Our freedom is our self-illumination at the source, a point beyond the world, beyond natural existence – the source of what we can be independently of the world, through our ties to the reality of Transcendence. And in receiving the gift of ourselves in our freedom we are made aware of our radical dependence at the same time.

This awareness – experience and thought in one – is by no means a matter of course. It has appeared historically, has never been shared by all men, and to this day is rejected by a good many. To deny Transcendence is not to deny God, or gods. Gods are seen, understood, believed in, as beings in the world. Even the world as a whole has been conceived as God.

But the rule of Transcendence is, 'Thou shalt not make unto thee any image or likeness'. This biblical commandment is ascribed to God but springs as well from philosophical insight. A 'negative theology' will cleanse the place where man – approaching the thought of God by way of a 'not' – can incomprehensibly experience the divine reality in his historic Existenz

And yet, without surrendering that radical commandment, the Bible teems with God-oriented ciphers. Likewise, despite that inexorable command, the finite, rational, sensory nature of man drives him to move in ciphers as he 'transcends' toward the deity. The ciphers, futile if seeking Transcendence itself, still guide man's way, each in its fashion. Our only access to the incomprehensible, the inconceivable, the all-encompassing, is by the ever-inadequate, endlessly variable ciphers.

a. The Basic Ciphers of the Deity

1 THE ONE GOD

i. Polytheism testifies to a belief that we are torn into mutually exclusive possibilities, doing and thinking the irreconcilable. Or, speaking in ciphers: there are many powers battling with each other in ourselves, and through ourselves. Against this stands – not equally clear throughout history, and seldom in great and exemplary form – the will to unity.

ii. The strength of unity brings me from distraction to myself. I want to be one with myself. The binding forces of my life grow in the same measure as my links with the source of unity.

Unity, for me, is the one Transcendence as well as myself, the one guide to my historic realization. This infinitesimal, variable, temporal Existenz becomes the cipher of that unhistoric, immutable, eternal One – which is another cipher. In so far as it is realized, the existential unit reflects the infinite one, so to speak, as any one of the innumerable drops of water reflects the one sun.

'The One' draws away into infinity if I try to grasp it, and close by it lets me be myself. Infinitely distant when I seek in it the ground of Being, it is quite close when I receive myself in my freedom.

iii. The one Transcendence is fulfilled eternity. It excludes nothing, since there is nothing beside it, and all things are due to it.

Nothing threatens it. There is no need for humans to fight for this One. We must fight for ourselves, however, so as to hear and reflect it, and to turn into its cipher.

iv. To me, unity is realized only in the historic form that makes possible, and calls for, an endless variety of other historic forms.

At work in my absolute historic immersion in unity is the distant God, who encompasses all ways of historicity and is encompassed by none.

Corresponding to the absoluteness of the individual historic Existenz is the relativity of each historic appearance, form, action, and utterance.

The more strictly singular Transcendence, the more receptive will the soul that is oriented toward it be to other souls, the more resolute its quest of the ever-inadequate communication from soul to soul. The One, while directly inaccessible, becomes communicable; our only way of access to it is an indirect one, by the vigour it lends to the boundless will to communicate. The One will not propagandize for a cause, but it will establish communication.

And where the struggle for existence grows inevitable, the unity that links all, even the battlers, makes the battle 'chivalrous'. Those doomed to this fate will fight with a sense of shortcoming, in horizons they know to be inconceivable, with the pliancy due to the incomprehensible. In grim self-preservation and in failure, fighters will be made to love each other by the unifying One.

Is this an idle dream? It is rare, but real. In the Middle Ages it was a lofty idea. There were rudiments in Antiquity. Today there are scattered individuals who ask and keep striving for this kind of combat. Though they fail, it is they who maintain the inner bond as human affairs trickle away in universal distraction and brittle conventions, only to be externally unified by violence.

v. The cipher of 'the One' aims beyond all other ciphers. It aims beyond the diversity of ciphers at their common ground, beyond their ambivalence at unquestioned unity.

This One – the great theme of philosophy ever since Plato – is not the One facing the Other, not one whole among other possible units, not the number One. Such ways of unity serve as guidelines for our conception of the cipher; but the transcendent One fades out if we identify it with them.

As the number One, in particular, the cipher is not adequately conceived. It means a qualitative, not a quantitative, unity; in the external character of the mere number the cipher fades out. The numeral is ambiguous: it conveys the meaning of the cipher, the luminary that kindles the glow of the one Transcendence in the numerical One – and it may lead astray and then, in the name of merely numerical unity, spread ruinous fanaticism through the world.

The meaning of the one love between the sexes may serve as an example.

The one love appears as a gift of Transcendence. It is not subject to our will, though we may prepare for it, perhaps, by willing the possibility. No one knows whether his is this metaphysically grounded love. No one knows it of the other. The illuminating philosophical thought can only confirm the possibility of something we experience without knowing why, of a certainty that we can neither determine nor lose.

The one marriage – monogamy – rests on the decision of fidelity through a joint life in time. This unity is willed and thus known, and it is objectively, numerically determinable. Society makes it legal.

Sexual love, the magic and abundance of erotic varieties, is naturally polygamous, without obligations other than those of beauty and art.

The idea of 'the One' transforms each of these three elements. Mono-gamous marriage will no longer exist on its own, but as a result of the metaphysical unity – 'marriages are made in heaven'. The magic of eroti-cism is enhanced, shorn of its polygamous character, by historic singularity. The very nature of sexuality may be transformed if the radiation of meta-physical love turns it into a cipher.

What we know – physiologically of sexuality, psychologically of eroticism, legally of marriage – concerns realities. The idea of unity turns these realities into special cases. As absolutes they would do violence to man by the power of sexuality and eroticism, by the enervation of marriage, by the abstractness of a 'Platonic' metaphysical love; but 'the One' turns the realized unity of these elements into their own cipher.

Here the number proves nothing. We cannot help speaking of 'the One' by the guideline of the word's numerical meaning; yet for all its unique significance and controlling influence on reason and communication, on love and loyalty, on the concentration of our Existenz, on proper self-being, it will fade out in the comprehensibility of a number.

Numerically understood, the one metaphysical love would lead to illiberal judgments which undeserving donees and supposed possessors would propound as general laws for all sexual relations. It would pervert illumination into knowledge: the number would result in violence of judgment.

Or, the ever-singular metaphysical love may suddenly break through the diversity of eroticism. Then the new source will change everything. No one knows whether this happens, and no one can find out – for as a psycho-logical reality it does not exist.

Such reflections on the metaphysically based 'one love' as an example of the cipher One – and on the meaning of the number One in it – show the futility of all attempts to let us 'visualize' the invisible One of Trans-cendence.

vi. The true One remains at its proper distance, speaking in ciphers as in mirror images, one for all, a magnet for every individual, and no one's possession.

By this One hangs whatever gains Existenz; it delivers us from the swamp of pure existence in which all of us are trapped; it is salvation on our path. But it becomes ruinous if anticipated in false forms, claimed as 'One' against 'the Other', commandeered by individuals and groups of men, and used as a battle flag. Unity, then, no longer reflects the unity of Transcen-dence but becomes the unity of a self-hallowing self-will.

The empty number One acquires substance by being linked with the uniquely particular, such as the sole truth, the chosen people, the one church – with some historic absolute that seeks to coerce others in the struggle for existence.

The One, then, becomes the one God as my God, a fighting God who fights through me and helps me against the others. The one God turns zealous and exclusive.

The one God means exclusive rule, the justification of rule in the world by an organized group of men.

The abstract number One as such turns negative but stays alluring, because behind it, despite its mundane perversion, there is still the majesty of 'the One'.

The lapse into finite, merely numerical unity, into uncommunicative exclusiveness and the poor abstraction of an empty oneness, leads to fanaticism.

By false rationalization, even the sublime can degenerate into vulgarity and give it a false sheen to boot. Abstract unity becomes numerical unity, claiming the right to be intolerant in the world. The transcendent One becomes finite, worldly, and a vindication of despotism. The phenomenon runs all the way through history, from the god-kings of early civilizations to the Roman empire and the one Catholic Church. Hardly comparable any more – and yet analogous in form, with 'the One' now stripped of all Transcendence – is the consummately inhuman phenomenon we have experienced in the loathsome bluster that keeps ringing in our ears: 'One folk, one Reich, one Führer!'

Thus mendacious distortion turns the one-time source of freedom, the strength and support of Existenz, into destructive savagery.

vii. Will the one God vanish unless identified with the One of some worldly reality?

It has been said that men cannot believe unless they realize the object of their faith – that if God is not One, in the sense of bodily reality, he will seem to them non-existent.

This argument denies the faculty of faith. A man who believes will precisely not realize God as some worldly oneness. This is what distinguishes his faith from superstition.

Unless it remains an infinite, suspended, evanescent language, the objectivation of Transcendence will be superstition. That is what superstition is: making an object of Transcendence.

The same point is made in other words when the distant One is called an abstraction, a void, a negation – when the negative uniqueness is said to make the one God rigid, lifeless, unsubstantial.

But only our intellect and our sensory nature speak this way. Totally tied to existence, they want to know objectively, to possess tangibly, what grounds our freedom and guides our Existenz. The self-hypostatizing intellect mistakes the thinking that will utilize it only to transcend it, to ascertain what really counts: Existenz and Transcendence.

2 THE PERSONAL GOD

i. The Old Testament has both the commandment to make no image or likeness, and a wealth of images and likenesses of the personal God. We must make a distinction: the commandment refers to Transcendence, while the images and likenesses – including the idea of God itself – are ciphers of Transcendence.

The cipher of the personal God is the only confrontation of the human and the divine as 'I' and 'Thou'. Our thinking, entangled in circles, tempts us to equate the personal God with Transcendence, but no personality, no Thou, can be one with Transcendence.

How we, as Existenz, can really relate to Transcendence is a thought repeated here time and again by circumscription, never unequivocally. The 'I-Thou' relationship is one effective form of doing it in the cipher world. Let us first see what happens in the cipher.

The personal God protects and commands, is mild and severe, merciful and angry. He loves man and is just. Man approaches him trustingly and fearfully.

In prayer, man feels personally addressed by God and addresses God in turn. He cries out his need, thanks God, and bows to God's inscrutable will. He asks questions and wrestles with God. He expects answers and feels forsaken if he does not hear them. Believing to hear God's directives, he goes his way in that assurance; feeling called on, he replies in thought and action. Leagued with God, man wants to make his way to purity in the world, to know that in fighting injustice, in the active love of his neighbour, God will be with him even in the hour of doom.

Prayer cleanses of selfishness, of magic, of the will to force God's hand. Renunciation of the prayer from person to person serves only to resurrect it in another form – as philosophical meditation. In this analogy to prayer, as in prayer itself, truth lies not in the conventions of form and formula, only in the historic singularity of an earnest shown in the creative power of the thought.

ii. If man as existence comes into the light of conscious thinking, he will experience his free Existenz as a gift of Transcendence. Existenz and Transcendence will seem like a single basic reality.

Existenz is the self-being of personality. Given to himself he knows not whence, man feels the urge to let Transcendence appear to him as a person. He finds a cipher for it: 'God'. But the cipher is inadequate, for even as the best that man knows in the world, as personality, Transcendence is still debased, so to speak, into his own kind of being. What is more than a person – what is indeed the source of human personality – and surely not less than a person, is pointed out to man by what he is as a person.

The personal God has been termed a creation of man, who produces the concepts he needs. The term does not fit, for transcendent reality is not to be grasped by taking human creative reality for the one and absolute one. We would put it this way: transcendent reality is the encompassing which in self-illumination shows us simultaneously the objectivity of the cipher 'personal God' and the subjectivity of our personal self-being. The encompassing itself, the transcendent ground, stays hidden.

Historically, we can see that ciphers of gods and God go with ways of being human. 'When gods were more human,' Schiller wrote of the Greek pantheon, 'men were more divine.' The unique and exclusive one personal God of the Bible let men of the greatest personal independence arise to wrestle with him. As the divine personalities grew more definite, so did the characters of human ones. In the fluid figures of Asian divinity we seem to see the fluidity of Asian people. The ciphers of God and gods are not random concepts; they are encompassing truth for true Existenz. Even the powerful, baffled rage at the devilry of events, at human folly, at the senselessness of chance, is clarified in associating the ground of things with the ciphers that lend the ambiguous voice of curses to the burdened dumb.

iii. Everything men do is done by persons. The fact may be concealed – whether in prehistoric times or throughout history, in the present technological bustle or in the seeming somnolence of the self-oblivious – but it is always individuals who are awakened and made aware of themselves, their freedom, and their responsibility and that by ciphers of Transcendence.

This contradicts the view that whatever happens is caused by anonymous forces and powers, by social orders and political conditions, by chance or by the laws of history. These, says that view, produce human forms of existence, ways of life, and states of mind; men are exponents of those impersonal events, or tools of a world spirit, of Providence, of history, of universal dialectics. From individuals they will eventually be transformed into functions of the machines they make or have made, from the technological apparatus to the political one. They will end up as the very types whose mass existence and interchangeability that anonymous process envisions.

The somnolence and self-obliviousness of man would be complete. That this remains impossible is due to the encompassing which unpredictably, in ways that can be witnessed but not proved in the world, will time and again bring forth what external powers – today the ones of totalitarianism and technology – seem always to have destroyed. Can man really cease to be human?

If he comes to live his thinking life with hidden, silent Transcendence, this association will mould him. And if the cipher 'God' shapes the association, its fear and trembling – soon forgotten otherwise – will extend to the depths of man, as question, defiance, submission, surrender: 'Thy will be done.' There will be a ceaseless movement from despair to fulfilment, to pacification, to renewed despair.

iv. Man cannot deal directly with hidden Transcendence. If it does not suffice him to accept the gift of selfhood and the responsibility of freedom while meeting silence with silence, he will deal with Transcendence in the cipher world – in this case, with the personal God. But the cipher God does not exist by our comprehending something general in the concept of the divine person, nor by our inventing personal figures of God, but historically by the tradition of ciphers of past and continuing appeal. It is in those that man feels the earnest, the intensity, the power; it is to them that he turns even in despair, unless he finds in himself a mute, non-objective, and incomprehensible trust in Transcendence.

Rather than a concept of divinity, the personal God is historic in many forms. In these forms we may perhaps understand and imagine the personal gods of India and China as ciphers; although they are true and acknowledged in their historicity, they leave us largely untouched. For us in the West, even if we deny it, the heart of our cipher language is the biblical God.

His many images, signs, appearances, and actions are his language – and he in turn is a cipher of the Transcendence which silently permits the incomprehensible to be voiced by the cipher of the personal God. It is this God who manifests his being in such lines as 'I am that I am', and his will by giving laws, entering into a covenant, fathering a son, and making history.

Throughout the Old Testament we find the tension between Transcendence – which is real without image or likeness – and Jehovah, who reveals himself bodily and concretely. This God is both: silent, incomprehensible Transcendence and the one God who speaks. Thus we tend to the mistaken usage of the word God as a synonym for Transcendence. We take the right to do so from the uniformity of our relation to Transcendence; the mistake lies in the effect of the identification, which erases the difference between corporeality and cipher.

Besides the line just cited – which Kant called 'the most profound word of the Bible' – there are numerous phenomena that make us feel the unity of personal God and Transcendence, the force of Jehovah's concrete action and language along with an overpowering intangibility. The people ask Moses to go up on Mount Sinai because they know that no man shall see God and live. Moses sees only God's back parts, Isaiah only his feet. God appears in the burning bush, in the whisper of the wind in the trees.

Its origin and essence require that the cipher of the one personal God be discussed historically, not just in general concepts. A famous phrase in Pascal's *Mémorial* – 'The God of Abraham, Isaac, and Jacob, not the philosophers' God' – says it perfectly, if understood to mean that the abstract idea of God is sapless and historic ciphers are vital. (That Pascal was thinking along quite different lines does not concern us here.)

The abstract idea of the one formless God has not been effective since Xenophanes and Aristotle first proclaimed it – except in so far as it was received into the biblical idea. First, the philosophical one lacks a cult;

second, it has no original ties to the common consciousness of any people; third, it is unhistoric, timeless, unrelated to any temporal decision of men. Furnishing no living, moving link of human Existenz with the one God, it cannot do without the cipher language either.

What used to happen historically may change as the encompassing, philosophical idea joins with the historic ciphers. Philosophy needs ciphers, as Plato demonstrates; and then they will complement and fulfil the indispensable force of the abstract idea.

v. The cipher of the personal God had tremendous effect as a corporeal personal God who comes and goes and resides somewhere, on Mount Sinai or in heaven. Can the reality of Transcendence be felt if the personal God is 'just a cipher'?

In childhood, for instance, while the personal God was our unquestioned companion, we had a naively, wonderfully sheltered feeling that we perceive only in retrospect. Once we began to ask questions about the personal God we were immediately doubting Transcendence itself: how is it possible to be calm, to live, if there is no God?

If the personal God does not exist, and thus does not speak either – if the silence is not one that might also be broken – have we lost all source of meaning? I do not think so. To do without the corporeal personal God does not mean to do without the ciphers of Transcendence. These are not lost if their object ceases to be corporeal, like things in the world. Language, radiance, appearance – images all – will remain.

Only in man do we know personality. To be a person is a singular, exclusively human reality in the world, distinguished from all other worldly being. But it is possible only by limitation; it takes another person. I am a person only with another person. By myself I cannot come to myself.

Transcendence, however, is the source of personality, more than personality, not limited like personality. Captured, so to speak, as a personality it is no longer the Encompassing of all encompassing.

Mystics – Master Eckhart, above all – distinguish between God and Godhead, *deus* and *deitas*. God is the form in which the suprapersonal, incomprehensible Godhead turns to man.

The personal gods and the conceptions of the one God vary in form; the Godhead, Transcendence, is indeterminate, indeterminable, and formless. Thinking in ciphers, we say that, because it is more than personal, it alone is eternal and immutable. It is the source of time, but it is timeless. It is the source of personal destiny and history, but it has no destiny or history.

The Godhead means more than God, not less. Trying to think it is futile, for it lies beyond all thinkability, as beyond all form. And yet it is the true reality of Transcendence.

As for us, we must live in the tension of wanting to touch this true reality and yet, in our thought and imaginings, always finding ciphers only. An example is the varied meaning of God's love of man. Spinoza, whose philosophizing was one single act of love of God, said that no one who loves God may ask that God love him back. In the biblical religions, on the other hand, God loves man; it is God's love of man, in fact, that makes man love God. Do the two theses conflict? I do not think so – for Spinoza's pure love of God is for the Godhead, for Transcendence itself, while the wish to be loved by God clings to the cipher. There is more than love in the Godhead, and we may trust to that inconceivable 'more'. And if our trust is conscious, we state it in ciphers and call it faith in Providence or *amor fati*.

3 THE INCARNATED GOD

The mighty cipher of the One seems indispensable to Existenz, provided we can see through its distortions. The cipher of the personal God is historically most effective, but not necessary. The incarnated God Christ is a philosophical impossibility, while Jesus can be heard as a unique cipher.

Let me elaborate. That the deity may become flesh and incarnate itself in a human being was believed among Hindus and Greeks as well as Christians The incarnation of God in Jesus seems to be a case of this type, but it differs essentially from all other cases. This is not just any incarnation. It is the only one, of the one God, and all other so-called incarnations are false. It is specifically Christian to believe that the one God incarnated himself only this once, and to make his one incarnation the focal point of all views of God, the world, and man. Christians believe, above all, that God is now really, corporeally present in personal form, at once wholly human and wholly divine. The conception of the divine personality has become a physically real human personality, which is God.

Man's longing for embodiment has never been more fully satisfied. The reality of God is guaranteed to believers by the corporeality of a human being.

That God himself became flesh, was crucified, rose in the flesh, and then showed himself alive to the living disciples and talked to them – this was the belief of the apostles, laid down in the New Testament. Belief in the truth of their testimony is the foundation of the Christian faith.

Here the primary event is not the promulgation of doctrine, the giving of law, the furnishing of guidance. Primarily and essentially, what happened is the revelation of God's being by his act of becoming human, of entering into the world so as to show himself in the lowliest form, in extreme suffering. His human experience is to be completely abandoned, left to die alone by his disciples, and on the cross forsaken even by God. But the end is the resurrection in the flesh, the miracle that voids all suffering, all boundless and horrible anguish.

To believers, this act of God is historic reality. The original congregation saw the risen Christ and – interpreting backward – God himself in the living man, Jesus.

God as a real man, human and yet not human, appealed strongly and deeply to believers. To others he seemed, and still seems, offensive and foolish. Believing Jews, moved by God alone, resented a thesis that was bound to strike them as blasphemous; philosophizing Greeks, untouched by such faith, considered it a curiosity not worth discussing.

Can we or can we not take Christ for a cipher? In Christ, Transcendence is no longer hidden in the diversity of divine ciphers; it is revealed as a monstrosity – the tangible reality of God! As a man like others, Jesus can affect everyone as a cipher, but it is not as a cipher that Christians believe in the tangibly divine Christ. In him they have achieved the maximum of divine corporeality, and there is no concealing this in honest thought. We have to choose between the cipher Jesus and the tangible God, Jesus Christ.

The cipher takes on extraordinary weight in Luther's distinction of *theologia crucis* and *theologia gloriae*. Venting his peculiar wrath on the Thomist *theologia gloriae*, Luther stressed the cross as the one road to God, of whom there can be no direct knowledge. Concentrating on his glory is easy and fantastical, a foolish distraction; and God as himself, abysmally wrathful at sinners, would merely deject men and leave them hopeless. Hence, God gave man the Mediator – a ladder, so to speak, by which to reach him – in his crucified Son. Salvation depends on finding ways to take up the cross. This is a hard and real task, but it saves us from despair. We are delivered by our faith in cross and resurrection, and in God's atonement by proxy, through his incarnated Son, for our sins. The assurance of this faith brings peace and felicity. Thus Martin Luther.

Not being a theologian, I take the cipher of the cross to mean that Jesus' suffering and mortal agony – epitomized in his last word, 'My God, my God, why hast thou forsaken me?' – was the result and the proof of his unprecedented, revolutionary spiritual truthfulness. As successor to the great line of Hebrew prophets he insisted on acknowledging the ills of man. He would not ignore them, would not gloss them over in mitigating interpretations; with unmatched ruthlessness he bared them and let the world bare itself. But he did this on the strength of his love, out of an overwhelming faith in God, being already in God's kingdom. He assailed the contentment of the favoured and successful, of the proper, of the happy. In the Sermon on the Mount – impossible to realize in the world – he showed how men from God's kingdom would act in the world. Like Socrates, he was killed because such uncompromising truth is not to be borne. Jesus was unbearable for the rulers because he unmasked their frightful wrongs, and he was unbearable for the masses, because he would not bring about better conditions and happiness on earth as a worldly king, by political action – which is why they preferred the criminal Barabbas to benefit by the Roman amnesty. The reality of the human Jesus is a unique, incomparable cipher of man's capacity before his God.

What the apostles' religious creation and the establishment of the Church have made of it is something else again. The Church wants to talk and to live past this human reality, to deny this cipher of infinite suffering of the truth, and because of the truth. What a man who can follow Jesus' faith in God, who can live with such utter lack of self-consciousness and reserve, is capable of – this extreme was sidetracked by the Church, promoted to a one-time sacrifice which God made to save man for eternity while relieving him of the need for similar sacrifices. If he will only believe in the creeds of the Church and obey it, man may live in peace.

This is the touching part of Luther's indignation at the *theologia gloriae*. But the various possible ways to follow Jesus in reality, the ways pursued by men who were serious about it, are unacceptable to the Church. It would receive and utilize these ways as far as they could be blunted, drained of their essence, and thus fitted into the Church's otherwise magnificent system of thought and life. Neither the multitude of sacrifices made in obeying the Church nor the admirable acts of renunciation or the continual emergence of valiant churchmen can disguise the fact that – all horrors of churchdom aside – there is a different obedience at work here, a courage narrowed by clinging to the Church as mediatrix of the deity, a spirit that leaves us uncertain whether its faith in the Church is not stronger than its faith in God.

Karl Barth took up Luther's idea: 'Ninety-nine per cent of what we hear today as "Gospel" even from Reformed pulpits,' he wrote, 'is in some way and on some pretext *theologia gloriae*.' He may be right – I would not know – but in another sense even his one per cent looks doubtful. Now and then, at least, the *theologia crucis* would seem to be preached in a style so glorifying redemption, in a tone so satisfied with grace, that it came to look like another *theologia gloriae* – as in Luther's own case, for instance.

On the *theologia crucis* I have nothing to say. I do not justify it, but it cannot blind us for the glories of the world and of the spirit that lie before the Godhead, are not the Godhead, but inspire us for the Godhead. The Godhead itself, hidden yet real, is above all conflicts, including that of the two theologies. It is quite another matter to trust and submit to the wholly unknown – 'The Lord hath given and the Lord hath taken away; praised be the name of the Lord!' – and to be thankful. This is the limit of philosophical faith.

To conclude: what a man comes to be depends on whatever God he envisions in his faith. This thesis seems to subjectivize the forms of the divine, to turn them into a matter of psychology. When we are serious about the cipher God, however, objectivity can be no more subjective to us than our subjectivity can lack for its objective.

To Isaiah God appeared in a vision, disclosing and concealing himself at the same time. Aristotle found in the delights of speculative philosophy an imperfect image of the inner bliss of divine thinking. To Spinoza, God's being was present in the pervasive radiance of pure, unconceptual thought.

To any person who remains one in the subject–object dichotomy, aiming at both, distinguishing one from the other, speaking always in transition – to him we say: whatever God a man sees will create his humanity. Or, to put it differently, man creates the cipher of the idea of God that will serve to guide and illuminate his possible Existenz. But in such talk we always keep our distance. Speaking merely provides us with methods of circumscription and comprehension. It is in speaking that we penetrate things, adopt them, or reject them.

b. Speculation in These Ciphers

The one God, the personal God, the incarnated God – these three fundamental ciphers of the Godhead are inaudible without thinking. We cannot bring them to mind except by thinking. But this thinking continues. The 'cognition of faith' – whether philosophical or theological – seeks to unfold what is inaccessible to objective cognition. By questioning further, in the ramification of ciphers, the resulting thought comes upon answers in new ciphers. This speculation will keep slipping into empty conceptualities, but wherever it sticks to the essence it hears new ciphers. It uncovers the wealth of ciphers, the manifestation of their hidden contents, their powerful existential effect as they contend with each other.

We always think in categories such as being, reality, substance, matter essence, and so forth *ad infinitum*. Speculation turns the very categorie into ciphers. They always have an objective meaning, but we use them to transcend', to pass beyond them into non-objectiveness – as lately with the categories of the One. Speculatively we bring to mind what we can only, and inadequately, refer to by categories or names, as being, ground, origin Transcendence, God. This is how the Stoics spoke of Necessity and Providence, Plato of 'beyond Being', Plotinus of 'the One', Spinoza of the sole substance, Hegel of the absolute spirit.

In his *Logic*, Hegel set forth the entirety of categories in a fashion that is still unsurpassed. He showed how at some time in the history of philosophy they were absolute in every group – and which of them, in the several groups, were not. But then, believing that he had now the complete system of categories, Hegel did not propose to let us use them merely as tools for conscious thinking. Instead, he proceeded to a thought that destroys Transcendence for us: the thought that we might, that indeed we must, conceive the entirety of categories as the Absolute – as God's thoughts before the Creation.

For scores of centuries men have been playing with the categories, rearranging their combinations, thinking the old thoughts afresh in endless possible variations. The Hegelian systematization liberates our consciousness in speculative thought. Yet this liberation promptly puts us into the new chains of Hegel's basic idea: taking the totality of categories for an adequate knowledge of God. His orderly insight saves us from the threat of entrapment in statements about God that sound like creeds and philosophical cognitions combined; but he then lures us into the supposed cognition of a God whose total knowledge may not be beyond the 'courage of truth'.

1 DUALISM

An example of universal significance may show the compulsory nature of our forms of thought.

We may, for instance, think of God and the world, of God and the devil, of Transcendence and Existenz, and we hear the charge that this is dualism, while only a monism can be true.

i. The thought form

If I think at all, I cannot but distinguish myself, the thinker, from the object I am thinking – and one object from the other. I can think nothing without distinguishing it; in other words, I cannot think anything without thinking something else. Thinking means thinking two. Without thinking two, I cannot think one. In all kinds of thought, therefore, we always find unity, duality, multiplicity – the One, the Two, the Many. That is to say: no monism can be stated without a dualism, and *vice versa*. Dualism is inescapable in thinking.

ii. Two powers

Transcendence is one, but in the medium of ciphers we instantly think of two. For our thought, then, there is a duality at the root of things. The distinctions of true and false, good and bad, good and evil, are not only conceived as valid meanings but objectified in ciphers into two real, original, embattled powers – mainly God and the devil, as by Zarathustra and by Gnostics, Manicheans, and Christians. This dualism makes objective powers of the alternatives that determine the deepest existential decisions of man.

Our imprisonment in the formal necessities of thinking shows in the fact that whoever denies this dualism – as in maintaining the unity of the one Almighty – must explain the origin of the Two. However this is managed, we always find the Two merged with the One as a possibility – as the primal source of nature in God who is already two in one, for example, or by positing a second origin in a free spiritual being to which God gave independence, and which then turned against God. Even if God keeps his power over this adversary, the possibility itself can to our mind only be due to something else in God.

The only way out of the maze of arguments that have sprung up here is to recollect the formal necessities of thought, and thus indirectly to sift the grains of truth from the motivations of objectively untenable statements.

iii. Mundane and transcendent reality

The reality of the world is visually, tangibly experienced. It is from the thinking perception of objects in the world that the sciences evolve *ad infinitum*.

God is not to be found anywhere in the world. He is beyond tangibility and visuality. His reality is no reality in time and space. There is no proof of his existence. If he exists, his reality must be radically different in kind from all worldly reality. The idea of God does not lead to a science aiming at the generally valid cognition of God and capable of researching the object 'God'. For there is no God for our knowledge.

But the relationship of the world and God, of the worldly and heavenly kingdoms, is conceived as the relationship of two worlds – we speak of a 'two worlds theory' – and thus misconceived at the outset. The cipher 'God' does not mean that a thinker standing outside and looking at God and the world in this utopian perspective might see two kinds of being. There are no two worlds, but there is a relation of things differing in essence – though the words 'relation' and 'relationship' already take us back to categories that objectify. When we think in ciphers of the point of reference for the awareness of our freedom, we promptly enmesh that extra-mundane, pre-mundane point in the alternative web of mundane logic.

If we see through these inevitable speculative chains, they will not deceive us but can make us aware of our inner struggle.

iv. Duality conditions all our thinking

The thinking of Existenz wants either to surmount duality to achieve unity, or else to show that unity is unattainable. This thought movement is called dialectics. It takes two forms:

Either all the dualities will round themselves into the one form of a circle. This sort of dialectics develops thought forms of unity in contradiction, the polarized unity of conclusive antitheses. It offers views of such totalities in reality and logically demands that we conceive contradictions as voided in the One.

Or the split will be carried to the extreme, to the un-form of disunion, to the irreconcilable alternatives – the disjoint world, the incomprehensibility of a Transcendence expressed in the category of 'absolute otherness', the either-or of ultimate choices in self-being.

The first form is completed in a harmony of all being; the second – the un-form – shows us the abyss as our thinking fails. Duality in distinction, in contrariety, in contradiction, is essential to thinking and will of necessity involve our every thought. There can be no end to this struggle as long as thinking and cognition illuminate our existence; the struggle itself is part of the unceasing movement of our life in time. It takes place in the phenomenal world.

v. Formulas of unity **and duality**

There is a familiar terminology. In pantheism the world as a whole is God; everything is God, and God is everything. In theism the personal God confronts, guides, and intervenes in the world he made. In deism God stands outside the world; he made it but does not bother with it any more. In panentheism God, though outside the world, is effective and manifest in all worldly being, at once without and within, as 'immanent Transcendence'.

Such distinctions are formulas for stating conceptual patterns rather than expressions of existential states of faith. We use them for objectivations and carry them into judgments – as when pantheists will call their point of view monistic and thus preferable to the dualism of a split between God and the world. Whereupon theistic dualists will score dialectical points to prove themselves better monists, and the panentheists will offer a simplistic synthesis of monism and dualism.

It becomes an empty rattling of words and definitions – empty, although it might set the spirits against each other in fanatical movements. The being of ciphers fades in such disputes. When we truly talk of the One, we do so as a cipher, not as a mere number. When we cannot help thinking of Two, we do not mean two objects; what we express in the cipher of duality is the non-objective relationship of Existenz and Transcendence. The thought becomes absurd if two, God and the world, are conceived side by side and we are then given the logical alternative of either one or two, of monism or dualism, and a synthesis on top of it. There is no longer any methodical consciousness of the speculative thought forms used. Their original contents are lost in such collapse into rigid categories of merely external, intellectual thinking.

We are going to take up other fragments of such speculation, but as we do so we must not forget the circle involved in all cipher thinking, nor the inevitability of objectivations that will lead to a perversion into seeming knowledge, nor our task: to proceed – through the failure of speculation in the embattled ciphers – from the emptiness of not knowing to the fulfilment of not knowing.

2 SPECULATIONS ON PERSONALITY

i. The personal God

The cipher of God's personality, the 'Thou' that man confronts in prayer, is a much-varied concept. Once we really think about it, the font quickly runs dry, leaving only speculations.

a: The qualities of God. The personally conceived God has emotions: anger, mercy, love. He is just and kind and knowing and incomprehensibly despotic. He is seen in the pattern of man.

Even Kant repeated this divine enhancement of known human qualities, justifying it as analogous thinking. According to Kant, the Existenz of rational beings under moral laws requires the idea of God, without which that Existenz would become senseless. God is to be conceived, then, not only as the giver of causal natural laws, but as lawgiving head in a moral realm of ends. Therefore, God is to be conceived as omniscient, so man's heart of hearts shall be no secret to him. He is to be conceived as omnipotent, able to fit all nature to the supreme moral purpose. He is to be conceived as both all-merciful and just; the two traits make up his wisdom. And God's eternity and omnipresence are to be presumed in regard to the ultimate end of all things. What used to be the substance of praise to God comes thus to be thought as analogously meaningful in a 'moral teleology'.

b: *The objection of anthropomorphism*. 'Man made God in his image,' as Feuerbach put it. Speculation to justify this has centred in the argument that God can be seen in man's image because man was made in God's – that having been created theomorphous, we may view God as anthropomorphous.

But personality can only be conceivable as finite. To be a person, I have to meet other persons; without others, persons cannot be themselves. The idea that for God these others are men led a great mystic, Angelus Silesius, to conclude, 'I know that without me God cannot live a trice'.

The inadequacy of the contrary concept – of God as the one and only self-sufficient personality – shows up time and again. Every statement endowing God with personality traits makes him finite. Hence the impulse to conceive God in the personal cipher, but as supra-personal at the same time.

c: *Picturing the divine personality*. One of the most curious efforts of speculative philosophy is trying to picture the personality of God, telling what it is in and for itself, how it lives and grows, and what its history has been. Schelling was the last to draft such Gnostic fancies.

He posed this question: either the first cause is immutably extant, without life and a personal nature, or it is both eternal Being and eternal Becoming, live, real, and personal. If the latter, it must be conceived in analogy to a human person. God, then, has a consciousness emerging from unconsciousness, has inner conflicts, has a nature, and so forth.

In ciphers the alternative does not apply. The idea of God's immutability, one of the great life-supporting ciphers, does not mean something immutably extant. In the category of immutability, the cipher turns our mind toward a reality that is neither temporal nor timeless, an eternal reality, but not a personal God.

The concept of the personality has two meanings. First, if the idea of personality is understood in its restrictive cipher character, it will let us break through it to supra-personal Transcendence. Secondly, what we think through in the personality of God is actually the personality of man. The thought enhances our consciousness of personality in the image of the divine personality that we conceive. The test of the image, the extent to which it will be illuminating, inspiring, fatal, or enhancing for man, is neither logical not epistemological but existential. Schelling's thought shows that the ambiguity may be fatal; it sounds as if he as much as his God were the object of his noncommittal poeticizing.

ii. God's omnipotence

a: The question of omnipotence has been alive in speculation ever since Christian Antiquity. St Jerome said God could absolve a fallen maid, but not restore her lost virginity. The limitation outraged St Peter Damian, who replied in his treatise on divine omnipotence (A.D. 1067) that if God could preserve a mother's virginity after the birth of her son, he could surely restore that of a fallen maid who had not given birth yet.

It was in dealing with the principle of the thing that Damian reached conclusions unmatched in their refusal to shrink from absurdity. Dialecticians – as the eleventh century called rational thinkers whose stand on compelling logic threatened the Church – had asked whether God could not only make Rome disappear but could cause existing Rome to have never existed. Damian replied that if God could not change the past, he could not change the present and the future; it was no more impossible for the past not to have been than for the present not to be, and for the future not to impend. Applying dialectics to God, said Damian, would reduce him to equal impotence regarding past, present and future. It would deny an omnipotence which time and space do not limit, because in eternity God sees and does all things at once. The Eternal is changeless. His power and knowledge mean that he always can, not that he could or could not. Past and future concern us alone; what is inescapably temporal for us will appear to us also as God's past and future action. His eternal doing appears to man – who can grasp omnipotence only in temporal terms – as the faculty of undoing what has happened.

Damian chided the dialecticians for even asking if God could not only make Rome cease to exist but make it cease to have existed. The questioner, he said, forgot that the Creator of all things does not create nothing. The dialectician wants God to make nothing out of something, but God makes something out of nothing. In reality we do not find anything that is and is not, like a Rome that exists and has not existed. 'Without a doubt, however, what is not in reality is nothing. So, you blackmailer, you want God to make what does not suit him – namely, nothing,' Damian rebuked the wicked dialecticians who meant to limit omnipotence. And yet, he answered by the same dialectical means.

Damian went beyond such quibbles, however. He raised the question whether God can change the world we know, the nature of things, the ways of being and cognition, the meaning of truth as incontrovertibility. Whatever is and prevails, including the principle of contradiction, has been made by God's will. Nothing in the world is absolute. For us, at this time, in this world, it is a fact that we cannot undo what has happened, that contradictory statements about the same thing cannot both be true – but all this is due to our created nature and does not apply to God. He can change it at will. Having made all things, he can make them different. He might have created a different logic, a different natural order. What strikes us as absurd may be true for him. God is not tied to his creation, and there are no fixed laws of nature; it is only from force of habit that we call them fixed. The natural law that God made serves him like a slave and does not resist like a rebel. His will causes everything; this is why miracles keep showing in the course of things as God breaches the rules of nature. Truth depends on God's will, and so does reality. The almighty will that made the world out of nothing – against the rule of natural causality that 'nothing comes from nothing' – constantly remains the universal cause.

The import of these ideas is that we have to live in faithful submission, to give up thinking where God is concerned. Thinking will serve only as an irksome tool against outrageous talk of the dialecticians.

The original impulse under the historic garb of such ideas is philosophical. There is an insight in Damian's cipher that God-given ways of truth and cognoscibility must not be applied to God himself: the cipher of limitless power in seemingly impotent non-being will let us feel the encompassing Transcendence that makes us our free selves.

b: Damian's cipher, pointing out the abyss as our thinking fails, stands against another, gentler cipher. Any logical, timelessly valid truth binds God as well, says the other; he cannot will an arbitrary change or breach in the Creation he once willed, for he is not a tyrant. He binds himself to his will; he does not play false; he is truthful.

St Anselm maintained that if God could not undo the past this was not because he could not, but because he would not. He would not, because he wants truth to be immutable. That 'cannot' does not always denote incapacity shows in such phrases as 'he cannot lose'. Later, Aquinas cited things of which God is incapable: he cannot contravene his will and his love, and he can take no action that would be contradictory and inconceivable as such, none that would conflict with Being.

c: Comparing the two ciphers, we find that Damian's has an aggressive, destructive ring. It goes with the 'sanctity' of total withdrawal from the world, but also with a will to power over the world. Ciphers of this type let us regard incarnation as one of the arbitrary acts of God which remain not just incomprehensible but absurd, always possible only for God, not for human conception, however wide its range. No man can realize this possibility, and to admit such absurdity means to acknowledge what is inaccessible in any sense of truth that we can have as human beings. As a result, we blindly obey a thing which in fact makes of absurdity a God-given reality in the world.

The harmonizing cipher, on the other hand, confines God to an order men can understand. It sounds consoling and pacifying. It goes with a worldly power that restrains itself, limits itself by objectively valid orders, whether natural, moral, or political. Exceptions and excesses are untruths, not due to God. But to whom, then?

Damian's cipher stirs extremes, plumbs frightful depths that others cannot see, and tempts us to all kinds of destructive action.

This mystery is lost in the harmonizing cipher, which diverts us from the horrors we see in existence and tempts us to grow placid.

Both ciphers presuppose the personal God. They appeal to us, but soon they will vie with each other. Do we have a preference? As long as the one personal God is absolute, as long as he himself is not a cipher, we must make a choice between the two; but in the sight of Transcendence they move to the foreground and remain suspended, as befits a cipher.

d: Against the claim that these ciphers are more, that they really depict Transcendence itself, we hear other voices. These may come from exponents of the narrow 'enlightenment' that ignores both Transcendence and the cipher of God and views a self-explanatory world as the Absolute, or from lazy rationalists indulging their 'knowledge' of what God cannot do. But theirs is not an existential opposition. The crux is the certainty of freedom. In philosophical faith, stirred by the experiences of freedom and conscience we transcend the cipher of the personal God to touch the ground of reality – which we traditionally tend to call by the cipher of God. Philosophical faith makes us feel like traitors to our transcendent source if we betray our freedom.

We betray it if – instead of listening to the suspended, embattled ciphers and seeking the way beyond – we submit to any one, and thus to a corresponding absolute claim in the world, whether of arbitrary despotism or of perfect order. Both are totalities that wall man in instead of keeping his way open.

iii. Historic views on the primacy of thought or will in God

Does good will follow straight on right thinking, as Socrates believed – 'Man cannot knowingly do wrong' – or is the crux the will itself, good or ill, with thinking a mere tool? Does a man's freedom lie in his general thoughts or in his spontaneous volition here and now?

If we conceive the personality of God in the human image, as cognitive and volitional, the question arises: what comes first in God, volition or thought?

a: Aristotle held that God is pure thought – Being and the manifestation of Being, truth itself. This cipher, which returns to life in Christian philosophizing, regards the Ideas as the eternal thoughts of God; in other words, the truth of the general principle, the archetype, the law, of order and measure, lies in God himself. Human reason and the cognoscibility of things are the two divine traces in Creation. God cannot but will what is true and good – not because of restrictions on his omnipotence, but because of his majesty; for cognition in him takes precedence over the will.

In fact, Aristotle said that God has no will, because he has no need, no shortcoming. 'Willing' would imply some imperfection, but in God all is perfect. Thomas Aquinas also thought this way, viewing God's eternal creative will as a result of his eternal divine wisdom: in his true, all-encompassing, all-pervasive cognition God binds his will to itself.

b: Other Christian thinkers differed. Duns Scotus gave precedence to God's free will. The will knows no reasons – it wills because it will – and so we are not to ask why God wills as he will.

Contingency, the role of chance in the world, seemed to Duns Scotus not inferable from secondary causes, *causae secundae*, as the Thomists thought in line with Aristotle's theory of matter. Instead, there is contingency in the world because its first cause, God's will to create, is contingent. This first cause is all-encompassing, and nothing happens without it.

On principle, according to this view, nothing is impossible to God's omnipotence. The only limits to this *potentia absoluta* are his own being, as the absolute good, and logical impossibility. The Almighty can, for example, save a Judas already damned, though he cannot undo the past or give heavenly bliss to a stone. In his act of creation, however, he puts his *potentia absoluta* into the form of a *potentia ordinata* – that is to say, God's omnipotence takes effect in definite, God-given laws and orders.

As a rule, God acts according to his *potentia ordinata*, but it remains conceivable that his *potentia absoluta* may breach this order or set it aside altogether. In fact, God does not act arbitrarily. But Duns Scotus makes us aware of the accidental character of factuality, and at the same time he makes it less odiously absolute by showing the possibilities of divine omnipotence as against pure factuality.

c: William Occam and the Nominalists went a step farther. Testing our cognition – and only thereby the essence of things – Occam found we can prove nothing about God, neither his existence nor his essence, neither by experience nor by inference. The dogmas of the Church alone tell the believer that God is, and what he is. But these dogmas are pure facts, not necessary theses. God, by his *potentia absoluta*, might have realized other possible theses – instead of 'God became human', for instance, it might be that God became a stone, or an ass. Or Mary, just as she bore the Son, might have borne the Father or the Holy Ghost. The rational necessity of Christian revelation, which men had tried to conceive ever since St Anselm, was now radically disputed. The opposite was deemed possible: in the freedom of his omnipotence God might have bidden men to hate him, to steal, to commit adultery, and he might have forgiven sins without penance. A presently wicked act would be no sin if God commanded it to be done in his honour. It is not so now, but only because of God's will.

Occam's main purpose was to make the contents of belief factual rather than rational. He did not mean to shake men's faith in the Church but to strengthen it: we are to acknowledge God's will in obedience, not by virtue of reason.

d: The core of this idea came back later, used for other ends. What strikes us as necessary and generally valid was placed into God's will, as due to his decision. Incontrovertibility, the moral law, and virtue were called not valid as such, not absolutely, and the universality and necessity of natural laws was denied – since they were due only to God who could, or did, constantly breach them in miracles. Descartes once more taught the absolute freedom of divine choice in Creation, but he maintained that God decides definitively. He does not change or breach the laws of nature because a change of mind would not befit his essence.

Descartes put the thesis of arbitrary omnipotence to an odd critical use. He wondered whether the Creator might be an evil demon who keeps deceiving us, so we take untruth for truth. Against this, Descartes set the human being's self-certainty in thought – *'cogito ergo sum'* – which could not be deceived even by this evil demon, and on the ground of this self-certainty he meant to prove that God could not play false.

Kierkegaard in turn took such a radical view of God's omnipotent freedom from everything general and valid, everything thinkable and cognoscible, that he could speak of a 'religious suspension of ethics'. God can call on Abraham to sacrifice Isaac, and Abraham can obey because God, against all ethical tenets, demands it. God's radical incomprehensibility requires us to believe 'on the strength of absurdity'.

iv. The speculative problem of primacy

a: The question of the cause of factuality. Factuality is the limit of comprehension from general principles. The fact that things are as they are, that they happen as they do, is what we call irrational – what used to be called miraculous. In natural science, which tends to general laws, we still find factuality in the 'constants' of physics.

Factuality has been conceived as the creation out of nothing, the great miracle that made the universe a reality. The creation as the historic ground for all things limits their deduction from general principles. And the first miracle is followed by the historic ones, by the leaps we cannot deduce, by all that we have simply to admit: this is how it happened; this is how it was; this is how it is.

To put it in abstract terms, there is no deducing facts from logical generalities. The transition from the general idea to the reality in time and space defies understanding. Even Hegel, instead of facing the problem, sidesteps it in a phrase that lets the idea, the divine thought before the Creation, freely discharge itself into nature.

α: Schelling, in his basic philosophical idea, elaborated on this logically undeducible source of all things. It led him to divide philosophy into two philosophies – a negative, purely rational one that infers and constructs, while the positive one listens in the historic process of mythology and revelation for the undeducible decisions at the source and in the course of time. That process is conceived, told, and thus presently repeated, by positive philosophy.

Yet a rapid perversion came to treat historicity itself as capable of generalization, and to present it in a Gnosticism that was in fact noncommittal and yet claimed general validity. Schelling was perhaps the first modern thinker to see what remains incomprehensible to a philosophy that has to proceed in concepts, and thus in generalities; but he was also the first to fall promptly into the trap of an objectivation that he thought would take him beyond the bounds of objectivation. Instead of constantly touching these bounds in a single philosophy, he meant to enter the conceptually inaccessible region after all, with the aid of new concepts, by a new and different philosophy.

Schelling belongs to the tradition of speculative identification with the personality of God. Not content to accept the factuality of existence as God's will, this speculation kept asking about the cause of God's will. Thinking they might positively explore historicity itself, philosophers spoke in Gnostic terms of 'the nature in God that God needs to be a personality' (Schelling), and of 'the un-cause whose dark power sets the course of God's becoming' (Jacob Boehme).

β: Like many another who came in contact with Schelling, Kierkegaard was temporarily affected by that basic turn from generalization to reality. But Schelling's Gnostical objectivation annoyed him, as 'prattle'. Kierkegaard tried something altogether different: an appeal to the historic Existenz itself. He taught no general doctrine. He did not dream up a new figurative and conceptual history of myths and revelations – which would, in fact, have been general again. Trying to do the impossible, he found a way of indirect communication: unfolding thought in the figures of thinkers. He conjured with the eternal import of the moment, of decision, of repetition. Instead of a comprehensive system of concepts for all, he drew up a series of 'poetic' systems addressed, in their entirety, to the individual. Kierkegaard wanted to stay in the realm of the real, the essential, the historic, without subsuming it under any general principle. He wanted not decisiveness but decision, not historicity but the historic moment; he did not want any '-ness' or '-ity' at all. He would not repeat the perversion in which our thoughts keep withdrawing what we have only just touched – that seductive form of thinking that lets Duns Scotus turn 'here' into a 'hereness', *haecce* into *haecceitas*.

Kierkegaard gave us the idea of the limit of comprehensibility and the source of Existenz which we today – generalizing again – call 'historicity'. Kierkegaard himself did not stray into that old form of thinking; he unfolded the sense of a radically different method: of the indirect communication that springs unplanned from the seriousness of the thought movement, not compellingly valid for all, but compelling for Existenz.

γ: All this came now to prevail in the old ideas of the primacy of the divine will. We cannot give any reasons for God's will. The question what he might have done, what he ought to have done, grows absurd in view of the reality of Transcendence.

Yet the possible scope of God's will remained a question. It seemed to present two alternatives. One envisioned it either as a majestic identity of will and cognition – basically incomprehensible, up to the limit of a supra-rational but never irrational mystery – or else as so sovereign and arbitrary as to seem irrational to the human will. This second view would leave us nothing but the *sacrificium intellectus:* to be not only subject in fact, but to submit even in our thinking if we can no longer trust our reason.

Each of these ciphers, the total reason and the total unreason of God's will, may deeply touch us. Yet a philosophizing person will never take either one for the sole truth. Total reason says too much; the frightful facts of life deny it daily. Total unreason also says too much; there is no denying that reason exists in the world. Philosophizing I live by the certain faith that even if the whole is neither rational nor irrational, there should at least be reason in the world – and that I myself feel obliged to follow it without restriction.

b: Contingency in general validity. If the general principles bounded by factuality are themselves still flatly valid, we can go on to ask about factuality in their causes. In other words: does rationality rest upon irrationality? To logical thinkers the question may give a dizzy spell.

Kant raised it, but left it unanswered. He had inferred the possibility of generally valid cognition within the bounds of possible experience from the *cogito,* from the unity of this original act that governs our conception of unity, no matter what we encounter; and he had established the conditions of perception, in the forms of space and time, and the conditions of objectiveness in categories such as substance and causality. 'But,' he went on, 'for the peculiarity of our intellect that lets us achieve an *a priori* unity of apperception only by means of the categories – and only by precisely this kind and number – for that we can no more state further reasons than we can say why these are our only critical functions, or why time and space are our only forms of possible perception.'

And another example: modern logicians have made us aware of the antinomies that arise whenever we come up against infinity. This led to the question whether, in principle, pure logic is at all capable of resolving the recurring contradictions by an absolutely valid generalization. Or is the generalization purely and magnificently bound to cause its own ultimate failure, illuminating a basic phenomenon of our thinking consciousness that bears on our existential consciousness?

These problems are anticipated in the alternative question about God's being. In the end, is God thinking or will? Is his principal quality the truth that is necessary in itself, or is it the wholly irrational power of the will? Is the truth we recognize as logically compelling an absolute truth, valid even for God, or is this truth part of Creation? If it is the latter, then God made this truth by his omnipotent will – made it the way it is for us, the way it binds us as thinking creatures made in this fashion. He might as well have made it differently, and thus would not be bound by it.

There have always been two answers. Either we say that God's omnipotence does not lie in the arbitrary capacity to do everything, but in his unity, his truth, his goodness; hence its very essence precludes what cannot be because it would void that unity. Impossible, therefore, is not only what conflicts with the legality of nature and the moral law, but whatever is incompatible with Being, with incontrovertible truth. Whatever is unthinkable is impossible.

Or else we say that God's omnipotence lies in the very absence of restraint upon his arbitrary will. His incomprehensible will, for which there are no reasons, has created all that we can comprehend, including the fact that we can comprehend it. He might have created other comprehensibilities, and he can always change the one he did create – as shown by the miracles and the irrational tenets of revealed faith, by the inescapable antinomies of our thinking, and by the fact that thinking is not deducible from any general principle we understand.

No arguments for one side or the other have ever resolved this alternative. It is one duel of ciphers in which the adversary never vanished.

Equally futile, however, were the grandiose attempts to find the place of reality in reason itself – the place where, in the cipher language, God's will and God's truth are one. St Anselm thought in this direction, and so did Plotinus, whose speculative philosophy sought to unite the thinkable with the unthinkable. In this direction Hegel drafted his philosophy; he saw no difference in the dialectic process between a concept and its reality. Conceptual cognition and the cognition of reality are one, he reasoned, for what is rational is real, and what is real is rational.

Our real situation permits us only to hear all these ciphers, to take part in their struggle, and to feel the limitations of each one – especially where it may seek to be all-encompassing. We must yield to none as the absolute one; we must see that they remain ciphers.

c: Existenz and the idea of God. The cipher of God and human Existenz correspond. Existenz relates to Transcendence, can never reach it, but moves in the cipher. Man's reaction to particular ciphers influences his life, and his conception of the cipher 'God' is the image he will come to be in

One who sees in God an arbitrary despot will automatically hold himself entitled to reflect this licence. Cognition is to him a matter of miracles, and though he may have begun with a rational and moral view of this world, his way of acting in it always suggests the possibility that he may break these orders for the greater glory of God. In God's name he will do evil. Too, minds can change, can turn godless, and just as the miracles of God bring forth new things, new origins in the world, men will bring forth new facts that are not generally comprehensible, nor validly explicable. A sense of vindication by the root cause of things lets these arbitrary creators stop discussion, break off communication, and resort to violence.

On the other hand, a man may restrict that cipher of divine despotism and yet look upon Transcendence as the eternal ground of his historic Existenz. Such a man will not cease questioning himself. How does my encompassing historic ground guide my rationality? Is it so that for all my rational slips the whole of rationality derives its meaning from that historic ground? Or does my historicity fade, rather – however much I use, or abuse, the word – in a relapse into less than rationality? Does it deceptively consecrate elemental passions, the *élan vital*, the struggle for success, ambition, intoxication, if these are what seems to make me feel alive?

The road shown to me by such existential self-criticism is this:

Truly historic Existenz will not twist its thought into a vindication of real action, nor into a conquest of another's Existenz. It will, if granted this, drop anchor in the quiet certainty of Being, where God's will does not prevail arbitrarily and the very cipher of a will is unfitting. I never know and cannot know what God 'wills'.

Will meets will in defiance or submission. Not until I experience the limitations on the cipher of God's will can I be free of absolute revolt against it and yet affected by its reality in men, and by its possibility in myself.

Whatever meaning I choose in the situation of my existence must not become an absolute standard or general principle. The passionate experience of Being uplifts me to the freedom that makes me receptive for Transcendence. There I can come to feel the transcendent truth that lies hidden in the ciphers of God's will, of its irrationality, and of the doubtful existence of all created things including the sense of truth to which we have access.

There I become free for the very simple. Aware of my own original, irrational historicity, I am prepared to accept the way I am, and to carry it over into the choice of my self.

3 SPECULATIONS ON CHRIST

The apostles believed that God had become human. The distant, hidden

God who used to reveal himself in his words to the prophets was now tangibly present, revealed by his own incarnation, walking on earth as a sinless human being, dying on the cross, and rising from the grave. To believers, this act of God is historic reality.

The belief in God as man came to be the point of departure for speculations ranging from the early days to Augustine, and on to Hegel. Dogmatists developed the mystery; philosophers understood the historic event, the act of God, as the outcome of a general necessity.

Without Christ, says one such speculation, God would be distant and strange, irate and frightening rather than helpful and loving. It was to open man's way to him that God became human. The Mediator is God and man at once; man can cleave to him.

St Anselm's *Cur deus homo?* speculates on Christ as a requirement of divine justice. Man's original sin in Adam could be made up only by a corresponding sacrifice. God, in his love of man, sacrificed himself to satisfy the needs of justice and to save man.

An unusually beautiful, clear, and devout example of the great metaphysicists' speculations on Christ seems to me the one worked out by Nicholas Cusanus. The following excerpts cannot do more than suggest it.

Cusanus starts out from the infinite individualization of the universe, which is at once God's creation and his image. Every concretion is individually limited, and thus imperfect. Individual beings are greater and lesser, never the greatest or least, for the concretely greatest, as an individual, would transcend the nature of concretion.

This greatest concretion could occur only in human form, for human nature is a microcosm, carrying the whole universe within itself. As mankind concretely exists only in individuals, a real man so perfect as to reflect the perfection of the universe would be the most perfect of things, having more in common with the whole of Being than any other human. And if only one real human could attain this unity with the sublime, he would be a divine sort of man, and a human sort of God.

For faith and faith alone, this one is Jesus Christ. To believe in him is to believe also that he possessed a body to suit his most spiritual purpose – that he was not naturally begotten. Intending to show us the treasures of his glory, God revealed the eternal Word, his Son, in a way adapted to our faculties: since we can comprehend only in sensory forms similar to ours, he showed himself to us in human form.

How are we to understand that God was crucified? The voluntary and innocent death of the human Christ bespoke the extinction of all carnal desires of human nature. It means satisfaction and purification. In our 'learned ignorance' (*docta ignorantia*) we understand the sublime by the 'coincidence of opposites' (*coincidentia oppositorum*): 'The least coincides with the greatest, the deepest abasement with the highest elevation, the most disgraceful death of supreme virtue with the glory of life.'

Why did Jesus Christ have to die? 'If he had never died,' says Cusanus, 'he would have remained mortal, only without dying. He had to die, to free himself from the possibility of dying.'

How is Christ's reality true? 'Truth as it appears in time is a sign and image, as it were, of eternal truth. Thus the truth of the concrete temporal body is a shadow of the truth of the eternal body.'

Christ is an object of faith, so Cusanus does not deduce his reality and possibility from rational insight. Only the place of the possibility is conceived on the premise of faith and with its incomprehensibility expressed in the coincidence of opposites. Christ is not an intermediate being in a series; he is uniquely and simultaneously man and God, at the place where truth, as the coincidence of opposites, must seem absurd.

Cusanus consciously thinks in ciphers, signs, and images. His meanings and impulses come from dogmatic faith, but also, and no less vigorously, from philosophical speculation. His faith holds fast to what his thinking brings into the suspension of the cipher. He is one of the great instances of Christian philosophers who affect us even if we do not tread the solid soil of their faith.

The speculations of the metaphysicists – always to be understood in the entirety of their philosophical constructs, which are both historic and supra-historic – have one common feature to distinguish them from theological dogmatics.

The speculative view of the incarnation as an understandable necessity does not deny the historic reality of Christ but makes it appear as a consequence. The faith in revelation, on the other hand, regards the reality of the revelation as the historic act of God, not understandable, but to be experienced in obedience.

Speculating, we conceive a cipher as generally comprehensible; believing in revelation, we do not mean a cipher but the past and present reality of God in space and time.

There is thus an issue between speculation and the faith in revelation. Clearly drawn, it means that either the revelation will vanish as we speculate, leaving only the ambiguous cipher – or philosophical speculation will fade as we believe in revelation, leaving only the *sacrificium intellectus*, the unequivocal bow to the incomprehensible.

But the issue is rarely clear-cut, for theological thinking seeks to gloss it over. The historic reality of the eternal God is not to be abandoned, but it is also to be generally understood in what is called 'religious knowledge'.

Cipher or reality – that is the heart of the issue. To believers in revelation it is a reality that God himself, by performing a series of revelatory acts in time, is a historic phenomenon in the world of objective facts. This factual temporality of the eternal, immutable God is not, of course, recognized as generally valid, but for the faith it exists. Now the absurdities come to be insurmountable. First, any real reality is demonstrable for every intellect;

it is not a matter of faith. Secondly, God as Transcendence – 'the Eternal' – is not a 'becoming' God. He has no history.

Absurdity is one form of philosophical realization. We are methodically conscious of its meaning, then, and clearly separate it, as an element of speculative thought, from scientific knowledge. In absurdity we are playing with thoughts, and the seriousness lies in strengthened inner action, not in proclaimed truth.

Absurdity is something to be questioned – existentially, not logically. We ask what, if anything, it has to tell us. The answer comes from the individual who works on his own being.

We do not reject absurdity as such; we reject it only in conjunction with the dishonest refusal to recognize the absurdity. An absurdity perceived as such will be adopted or rejected existentially, depending on what it says.

4 TRINITY

The strangest and astonishingly durable cipher in the Christian faith is the Trinity: God is one in three persons.

The Gospel speaks of God, of the Word, *logos*, and of the Spirit, *pneuma*, but not of the Trinity as a unity of the three. The belief in the Trinity is a speculative construct that became an object of religious knowledge and thus of faith itself, an early component of the creed: 'I believe in one God . . . maker of all things visible and invisible . . . and in one Lord Jesus Christ, the only-begotten Son of God . . . and . . . in the Holy Ghost, giver of life, Who proceedeth from the Father and the Son.'

God is triune even before the Creation. As this Trinity he reveals himself in the world – first as its Creator, then as the Word that became flesh in Christ, and finally as the Spirit that enters into the disciples and all believers, unites them in truth even if they do not understand each other's human language, and is actively present in the Church.

That the faith in the triune God has stirred men to the quick and may irresistibly touch the devout even now is a historic fact. Asking about its sources or motivations, we may find three.

The first lies in the difficulties which the idea of the one God encountered in Gospel Christianity, in view of Christ and the *pneuma*. If Jesus Christ is God, what about the one God? He must be conceived so his incarnation will not spoil his unity. Moreover, when the *pneuma* is experienced as the fulfilling establishment of transcendent community, is it not God himself, then, in this living work of truth? How to conceive the one God if he exists in this third form also?

The second source is a general, endlessly variable form of our thinking, the dialectical three-step: the one, the other, the link – thesis, antithesis, synthesis. The appearance of all things, of the soul, and of the mind may be interpreted as this three-step; it lies in their nature as well as in our conception.

Dialectical speculation saw the Trinity reflected in all worldly spheres and thus conceived Creation as dialectically structured. In psychological thinking – naturally flat in comparison with existential thinking – we might say: the dialectics we experience, whether logically, mathematically, physically, mentally, or historically, are first transferred from the world to God, lending a wealth of understandable features to the triune mystery; but it is the reflection cast back from there that will let this entire empirical world be interpreted as the Trinity's image and echo.

In centuries of trinitarian debate the ways of conceiving and visualizing the dialectic relationships in the tri-personal deity received their dogmatically fixed expression. God created the world; Christ is the 'only-begotten Son', 'begotten as the Word', 'uncreated', 'with God from the beginning'; the Holy Ghost 'proceeds from' God and Christ and 'is breathed'. Trinitarian speculation is amazingly rich, both in the exegesis of God and the world and in the self-analysis of man. Its high point is Augustine's *De Trinitate*.

A third source was the urge to fill the mystery of God with the eternal inner life of three persons in the one divine nature. We already mentioned the perils of the One, the thrilling cipher that turns so easily into the meagre and distorting number; we have seen the consequences of an empty One. Can the concept of three preserve the cipher from such deterioration? Is this the way to meet the threat of an inwardly lifeless one God, of an outwardly fanatical 'abstract' monotheism? If so, the speculative construct in which one equals three must not be a matter of numbers either. The three can only be a guideline; as the thing itself it disappears in the absurdity of $3 = 1$.

The stunning edifices of trinitarian thought have risen in many styles. They are the products of vast labours, of comprehending the incomprehensible, of sublime thinking, of surrender to the mystery. The fact that the mystery would grow as fast as the speculative abundance of thinking illumination shows that the matter is one of faith and ciphers rather than of cognition.

Why, despite our best efforts to understand, has this cipher of the Trinity nothing to say to us?

The cipher purports to penetrate the being of Transcendence. The innermost life of Transcendence itself, its life before the Creation, is to become visible in the cipher of the triune God. The 'living God' – called living because he will act, will intervene, will turn to man – is supplemented by another cipher of his inner life.

The reality of believers in the trinitarian concept is impressive. They reflect on Transcendence as if it were a thing; they 'know God' so that for them, so to speak, the veil is lifted. Their penetration of Transcendence gives them a religious happiness we cannot but respect.

For us, the idea has other consequences. To put it briefly and personally: trinitarian thinking fails to guide us. It shrouds our relation to Transcendence; it is like a game in which Transcendence is unduly touched.

Our task as possible Existenz is to find our way in existence by trial and error, by asking questions and making practical decisions in concrete situations, as humans among humans. The guidance for all these experiments and ventures comes in a way we cannot determine, from a Transcendence that remains hidden as such and is heard only ambiguously, through the ciphers. If God, as the Trinity, is himself in existence and supposedly known in faith, this divine form blocks the way which the relation to Transcendence shows us. To put a glittering mystery into the centre of speculation and prayer seems futile to us, a way to miss our existential opportunities.

5 THE IDEAS OF GOD AND OF BEING

In the sense of existence, of our reality, God does not exist. The conception of 'Being', by means of which we seek to reach beyond the world, beyond the gods and God, remains without an object. Is there a connection between the ideas of God and the speculation on Being?

i. The *apeiron* of Anaximander was ageless, deathless, imperishable. *Parmenides* characterized Being as unborn and imperishable, entire in structure, unshakable, purposeless; it never was or will be, because it is wholly now and wholly one, complete, indivisible, and homogeneous. Plato, in Part Two of his *Parmenides*, raised the dialectical concept of Being to a perfection unmatched to this day. It pervades the history of philosophy. It originated in the Upanishad, in Hinduism and Buddhism, as it did in the West.

The core of this thinking is the speculation on Being and Nothingness, with Being radically set off from Nothingness and yet dialectically conceived as Nothingness. This dialectical thinking aims at an 'Above-Being' that encompasses Being and Nothingness.

The eternal, perfect, self-sufficient universal source and goal that we call Being or Nothingness is nothing only as an intellectual conception; as encompassing experience it is the true reality.

ii. What happened then, in Western Antiquity and in India, was a combination of the two origins, the idea of God and the speculation on Being: God is Being.

In India the speculative concepts became gods while the universal unity became God, and these in turn were transcended back to what was and is above all divinity. In the West, following Parmenides, Xenophanes saw Being as ever-identical, unborn, eternal, unmoved – but this One, he said, is the deity, a rational being. In Christian thinking Augustine combined Being and the personality of God for all time to come: God is the supreme Being, above, beside, and without which nothing exists. Of God we can say only that he is pure Being, sufficient unto himself. Augustine explained that when God was asked for his name – as a man's name will be Gaius, Lucius, Marcus, or whatever – he replied, 'I AM.' His name is Being. 'Go,' he told Moses, 'and say to the children of Israel: "He who is sent me to you".'

Thus the speculation on Being crystallized as a factor in the unfolding idea of God. Aristotelian motifs enriched the pattern on its way through the centuries: God is immovable and immutable, eternal, without parts or composition; he cannot fail to be, being necessary; there is no possibility in him that is not reality; his existence and essence are one; he has no antithesis within or without, i.e., no matter, and so forth.

iii. The thought of Being suggests both strengthless proximity and unattainable distance – something unreal in the world. The thought of God suggests the proximity of a strong, powerful personality as a reality in the world.

If the ideas of Being and God are combined, a tension will remain, since for our transcending speculation Being comprises the personal God and all ciphers, while the faith in God claims this Being for God himself.

The tension lies in Transcendence as manifested to us both in ciphers and beyond all ciphers. Any relaxation of this tension plunges us either into the infinite void of mere Being or into an unequivocal theistic piety that will turn image and likeness into Transcendence itself.

iv. It is a fact worth thinking about that the speculations on Being – on Being and Nothingness – have a singular charm which not only frees but fulfils us. But are they not word games that rest on linguistic equipment? Are they really ways to get to the bottom of things, not temptations to idle on the apron strings of language?

Kant's *Opus postumum* contains this note: 'God is my own thought, not a thing extant outside me. It is pointless to ask whether God "is". A *verbum personale* belongs to grammar.' This might mean: the verb 'to be' belongs to grammar. Being is not a person, nor is there a *verbum personale*; the question is what lies in my thought. To state God's being in my thought of God says nothing, because the verb 'to be' covers whatever I think, and if this unique verb 'to be' makes me think that by itself it says something, I turn a matter of grammar into a matter of fact. 'To be' has as many meanings as the language; the meaning lies in whatever statement it is used for.

Yet men do operate with the verb 'to be' as if it signified something beyond its grammatical meaning; and these operations have opened memorable paths pursued for thousands of years in the West, in India, in China – paths of fundamental meditation. Kant's line, assuming the correctness of our interpretation, would wipe out this entire speculation on Being. It would simply evaporate. What speaks against this is that for the individuals affected by the substance of that speculation it is far from voided by an exposition of the grammatical tools. Language is the means we use in existential thinking – though not yet in intellectual thinking – to make sure

of the miracle on which our own and all existence rests. The disenchantment of grammatical insight will let us restore the enchanting truth by
the reality of our thinking experience. This is not yet the miracle of
linguistic reality, but it is more: it is the miracle of our faculty of speculative
thinking.

Though tied to language, this cannot be voided by semantics, by linguistic
analysis – no more than life is voided by an analysis of the chemical and
physical processes it employs and depends upon.

We rightly use semantics to void the meaning of any philosophical
speculation in language that poses as objective cognition. There the
language would fit both substantial speculation and trifling tomfoolery,
truth as well as mischief. How can we tell them apart? There is but one way:
to experience the existential meaning of faith itself. But this experience lies
outside the area of logical and linguistic analysis – unless a new semantics
should make us methodically conscious of the language and thus turn
inevitably into linguistic speculation.

II CIPHERS OF IMMANENCE

The universe in space and history in time, both entwined as one – this is the
reality in which we find ourselves, the infinite abundance of all that
manifests itself to our senses, our thoughts, our consciousness of physical
existence. This is what we call immanence, as opposed to Transcendence.

In this realm, the line between realities cognoscible as generally valid and
experiences that are not rationally cogent – though overwhelmingly
manifest in other ways, in figures, images, or views – has been drawn only
by pure modern science. It is in immanence itself, now, that we distinguish
ciphers from the things we know, or can know.

A constant to and fro between cognition and ciphers continues, with
cognition a factor in the ciphers, and the ciphers motivating our will to
know. Yet that living relationship can be clear only if the two are no longer
confused. This is the new situation in which the ciphers of immanence have
their meaning.

Illumination of these ciphers takes an awareness of the possibilities and
limitations of scientific cognition. Each of the following chapters – on the
ciphers of nature, the spatial universe; on the ciphers of history, the course
of time; and on the ciphers of reason, of a conceivable overall world order
– will have to start with a discussion of the respective sciences.

Needless to say, our chapter arrangement denotes an emphasis for
purposes of presentation rather than a division. The three elements in the
ciphers of immanence are interwoven. Time plays a part in the natural
universe, so does space in history, and both time and space play parts in the
concept of reason.

a. Ciphers of Nature

1 MODERN NATURAL SCIENCE AND ITS LIMITS

i. The purity of modern natural science

Modern science calls for pure realization. It insists that premises and methods be known at each moment. It claims to be cogently and generally valid. It lets us make the experience that what is generally valid in a scientific sense will in fact be equally understood and acknowledged by all men who follow its observations and lines of thought. In modern science I want to know how I know what I know. I want to understand the limits and the meaning of such knowledge.

ii. Unity by mathematical treatment

'God ordered all things by measure and number.' Everything in space and time can be measured and counted, and this reality can be mathematically expressed. What distinguishes the mathematical cognition of nature is first exactness – i.e., the precision made possible only by measuring and counting – and secondly a unique methodical progress, an interaction of mathematical calculation and observation that builds up cognition step by step, *ad infinitum*. We learn that in spite of giant strides we have as yet hardly started on this road, which opens such vast opportunities.

The human mind comprehends the mathematical constructs as an ideal world detached from experience, not resting on experience in its timeless duration. We see an immense world of diverse orders and relations – but in the real cognition of nature the question is always which mathematics is valid in what fields. The mathematics required to solve some real problem may now be lacking, for instance, though some day it will perhaps be found. There is also mathematics for which we have found no real use as yet. Mathematics evolves by itself, not in view of natural reality, and becomes useful in unpredictable ways which then, in turn, will enable us to make certain discoveries about nature.

Yet though mathematics is the most effective tool of natural science, the nature it enables us to know is a limited segment of natural reality. The mathematical view of nature misses what we originally and immediately call nature, what we experience qualitatively, what we see in natural phenomena, what we live as nature. Mathematics helps us to grasp only the quantitative side and variety of nature, and will range many a qualitative aspect with the quantitative. It is confined to lifeless nature, and to the elements of life that can be viewed as lifeless. Even the lifeless sector has something qualitative and figurative which the ever-simple orders of mathematics have either failed to capture or are simply incapable of capturing.

The premise of exact natural science is that reality can be mathematically treated. Where the treatment succeeds it will yield compelling, effective cognition; where it fails we may hear that things are too complex for the present state of mathematics. But the crucial question is another one: in principle, is the whole of material occurrences in time and space entirely susceptible to mathematical treatment? Or is there a limit? The question is unanswerable, to be replaced by the challenge of our temporal way of cognition in the world: to advance *ad infinitum* without being able ever to say anything about the world as a whole.

Meanwhile, there are comprehensive possibilities of scientific cognition that do not require mathematics.

iii. Unity by modern physics

Great discoveries constitute tremendous leaps into what used to be darkness. They tempt us to think we have reached the goal in principle, even though much may remain to be done in detail.

Thus men believed that the mathematical natural science prevailing in the late nineteenth century had reached the goal, and they did so again decades later, when the quantum theory and relativity brought about a new overall picture in nuclear physics and cosmology. Matter, it seemed finally clear now, was not the mechanical motion of infinitesimal particles, not an essentially corporeal material, but a process to be expressed in mathematical equations and understood in complementary conceptions. Scientists felt they were on the way to a definitive knowledge of the natural order, a 'unified field theory' from which all the laws of nature would flow.

It was a stirring experience when the atom – so long and so firmly conceived and apparently confirmed by a mass of concrete discoveries as the ultimate elementary particle – suddenly turned out not to be that at all. The atoms showed an inner structure. They were composed of still more elementary particles, and the sequence of the atomic table could be deduced from the composition of those.

Today we look upon the elementary particles within the atom, on protons, neutrons, electrons, and so forth, as the ultimate ones. They make up the atoms, which in turn make up the molecules that form what we call matter. Today it is considered self-evident – as once with the atoms – that science knows the last particles and neither can nor need search any further.

If we tend to doubt this we cannot point to scientific results, only to the meaning of scientific research into matter: that it is the nature of science to have to proceed *ad infinitum*. Whenever I asked physicists about the chance that still smaller structures will appear, that each finite conclusion will be encompassed by a new infinity, they either replied, 'We're obviously at the end; I don't see how we could go farther,' or they would say, 'I don't know; there may be a point to the question, but scientifically it is fruitless as long as we see no rudiments of further advance.' The second answer struck me as plausible.

On the day I write these lines, I read that a new meson has been found at Stanford University. This discovery is said to lead us to a new conception of the protons, viewing them no longer as elementary particles but as structures with a high-density nucleus surrounded by a meson cloud, and to suppositions that the present elementary particles might not be the ultimate uniform parts of matter, after all. Some physicists are said to 'suppose that they may never reach a final structure of matter, but will keep discovering new substructures in the elementary particles.' The research result and the conclusions drawn from it may or may not be confirmed; the essential point is that scientists can raise the question.

But if we were now to claim that the structure of matter is infinite, that there simply are no ultimate particles, this would be as much of a presupposition as the thesis of the finite last particles. It is a philosophical insight – the Kantian one – into the meaning of science that it proceeds *ad infinitum* but must not assert the existence of either finite parts or infinite division.

Why is this insight 'philosophical'? Because it cannot be proved by scientific means. It is rational but not compelling for the intellect, and derived from another source. To assume it is a scientific attitude, because the assumption is the least prejudicial, but its positive content comes solely from the transcendental, scientifically inconclusive Kantian cognition of the phenomenality of the world and our existence.

We awaken in the world as psycho-physical creatures that are part of it. Emerging from the world as thinking Existenz, we have a different origin; neither in our freedom nor in our sense of responsibility or in our experience of eternity in love and reason can the world help us to comprehend ourselves. Yet in the phenomenal world in which we find ourselves, in time and space, our cognition advances *ad infinitum*. Incomprehensible by itself, the world as a whole can never be an object of cognition. To envision it as a whole, to make objective statements about it, is to yield to an illusion of its absolute reality – an illusion that leads to scientific assertions about the scientifically inaccessible and thus dims the purity of cognition. It confuses and beclouds our sense of Being and the awareness of our freedom.

iv. The meaning of natural unity in modern physics
It is a principle of exact natural science to envision a unified nature. In former times physics and chemistry and, within physics, the research in mechanics, optics, acoustics, magnetism, electrical theory – all would go their separate ways. The unification began with the explanation of sound as a mechanical wave motion of the air; it continued with that of heat as a mechanical motion of the molecules, and then of optic rays as an area of electrical radiation; it finally led to relating gravitation to electro-magnetic

fields. Eventually all phenomena of the lifeless world came to be based on nuclear physics. Heisenberg – whose clear and thoughtful writings I found instructive – considers a unified scientific picture of matter as already achieved in principle. The one natural science, once risen on a speculative basis, is now being developed by an empirical research that has led from inescapable initial division into partial studies to a new and scientifically founded unity.

Scientists conceive this natural unity about as follows:

The principle of the conservation of energy first brought a unity of sorts into our whole knowledge of nature. All forms of energy – mechanical, thermal, chemical, etc. – are transmutable into each other in measurable, quantitatively fixed relations, and in all these mutations the energy as such is preserved. In all its forms it has its modifications; but what energy is, and what particular ways of its appearance there are and must be, as wholly derived from each other – into that no insight has yet been gained by the great unifying view.

The modern derivations of phenomena from atomic physics have come far closer to the special qualities of matter – which is, in fact, energy. The wide-meshed network of quantitatively equivalent forms of energy has been replaced by a far tighter network of quantitative relations. Metaphorically speaking, it is as if the flow of energy were no longer being measured in a few huge river beds but traced instead, with increasingly exact techniques and a great deal of mathematical imagination, through a minutely but regularly arranged irrigation system. Yet what is flowing, what the flow contains, this remains the limit of cognition. Its diversity has been reduced to a few basic natural constants and illuminated from one side, but its essence remains in darkness. The unity of energy is not the unity of reality; it is, so to speak, the unity of a pervasive medium that qualifies reality.

We keep asking about the type of this unity.

To begin with, the gulf between atomic physics and concrete chemistry remains. In chemistry, and in some fields of physics, the procedures have not changed. So we may say, perhaps, that in analogy to water – which is found in all organisms, is essential to life, but does not itself produce life – matter is the omnipresent base essential to phenomenality; but matter itself, as the nuclear physicists know it, does not give them an adequate understanding of the phenomena in their qualities and forms.

The following may make this clearer. The concept of reality in which atomic physics comprehends the unity of nature fails to cover natural reality as a whole. It covers a specific side of this reality, a side whose universality – as Heisenberg has impressively shown – is bought at the cost of dispensing in such cognition with the abundance of natural phenomena. These remain outside the realm of explicability or of questioning, even. The one exact science covers only a unity in nature, not the unity of nature.

v. Turning premises into anticipated total cognition

Heisenberg considers 'a quantitative calculation of the qualities of matter possible wherever the mathematical complexity does not prevent it in practice'. He explains that chemists, in their concrete researches, ignore nuclear physics 'because the execution of atom-theoretical treatment would in most cases meet with unsurmountable mathematical difficulties'. We may ask why this is so. Is it that the difficulties are theoretically soluble, if not by the means available to present-day mathematics – or is the task insoluble in principle, either because it is endless or because a leap, unsurmountable by quantitative derivation, lies in the matter itself?

Lest we forget the limits of modern natural science and absolutize the result of such cognition, we have to guard against a perversion that will intrude whenever science is supposed to grasp the whole. The premises of a research that lets us see scientifically how far we can get will tempt us, notably in case of great successes, to take an unscientific view of those very premises as anticipated insights into the whole. Assumptions that are final for the time being will be mistaken for conclusive cognition – the possible mathematical treatment of all nature, for example, or the natural mechanism, or the smallest particles of matter. Methods and relative premises become the thing itself; definite cognoscibilities in undefinable horizons turn into absolute Being. This is scientifically indefensible and philosophically irresponsible.

vi. Unity of life

a: A total unity of nature would include life. Life would be a modification of the general processes that we call lifeless. It would have emerged from these processes, and increased knowledge would enable us to produce it.

Scientific study of living processes has shown that the laws of inorganic physics and chemistry apply to organisms. Organic substances – which we used to regard life alone as capable of producing – can, it turned out, be synthetically manufactured from inorganic substances. We have come to know the physical and chemical apparatus that pervades and serves the living organism.

Yet this research, however admirable its results, has always covered only the apparatus, the means of life, not life itself.

The premise of such biochemical and biophysical research is that it can proceed *ad infinitum*. But this is the proper premise only of a way to study life; it is improper to look upon it as a knowledge of life as a whole – to start with the assumption that life is nothing, in principle, but a highly complex chemico-physical process that will in due time be synthetized as a whole, from lifeless matter, as we have already obtained several organic substances from inorganic ones. It is improper to search for the specific point where a highly complex chemical substance will become an organized live substance. The term 'live substance' serves to shroud the leap to an infinite purposiveness of structure, form, and function.

Natural science enables us to build highly complex machines, but these are finite. The question is whether a living being is a finite mechanism or an endless, ever-singular realization of purposes. A building may be extraordinarily complex in the purposive production of its conditions, parts, and functions, yet this purposiveness is not endless; its very infinities are perceptible to finite human cognition. The purposiveness of a machine ends at its smallest parts. They are lifeless material. But the purposiveness of an organism does not end with the smallest parts that may compose it; it remains infinitesimally, infinitely purposive. The basic fact – however we may choose to phrase it, depending on what physical concepts we use – always remains life as such.

Hence the two ways pursued by biological science: first that fruitful chemico-physical investigation of living mechanisms in biology and biochemistry, but then the study of living phenomena which those disciplines have not even shown to us – morphological, behaviouristic (animal psychology), psychological-environmental, historic (the evolution of life as such, and of the individual organism). Dedicated biologists have discovered undreamed-of purposive forms of anatomy, of instincts, of serial development. By patient observation, by ingenious arrangement, by flashes of insight they have seen living realities that dwarf the imagination.

Attempts to fit life into the categories of lifeless matter have proved futile. Life differs fundamentally from lifelessness; our intellect and our senses, adapted to the lifeless world, will not even let us perceive life as such. To define it, therefore, and to comprehend it conceptually, we need a new perspective unlike that of chemistry and physics. To show, in this perspective, what observation can prove, to make the unseen feeling visible and thinkable – this is the achievement of the great biologists.

b: Once we understand the independence of life – an independence not to be derived from lifeless matter – we go back to asking about natural unity. If living and lifeless matter exist side by side, the lifeless is indeed a premise of the living. But life itself exists by virtue of a leap that splits nature into two parts: the immense mass of all that is lifeless and the infinitesimal world of life on the surface of our planet earth, this dust grain in the cosmos.

To save natural unity for scientific cognition, lifeless matter would either have to be able, by and from itself, to bring forth life – or else it would have to be the residue, the corpse of an originally all-encompassing life, of which a small remnant continues here on earth. Nothing speaks for the possibility of either concept.

Another abstract idea goes like this: either life has sprung up on earth at some time, from lifeless matter, or it has existed as long as lifeless matter and the germ of it dropped from space on to the cooling earth. Physical conditions make this most unlikely, so life must have originated on earth.

There is a point to such arguments, but only so long as genetic and paleontological research proceeds *ad infinitum*. They lead us astray if they are meant as speculative statements on the origin of life, on the premise that certain theses exhaust the possibilities and must not conflict with each other. What we must keep in mind here is the essence of our cognition of the world: to proceed endlessly without being able to grasp the one and the whole. Philosophically, this basic fact points beyond the world and will not let us see the absolute in a cognoscible world.

c: Life is different from the lifeless means at its disposal. It uses them to produce chemical and physical phenomena that do not otherwise occur in nature. The human scientist can produce phenomena that do not exist without life; but this does not mean he can produce life. Considering this, we ask about the unity of life.

Can any theory link up all the particular phenomena of life in one whole? Can the life of all forms be reduced to one principle? Is not each life this one whole body, this plant, this animal, this human being? Do I not know myself one with my body? What is our vital self-awareness but the consciousness of this unity?

These questions call for answers. But there is no answer that might be called scientific, none that must not be judged as a cipher, rather, by unscientific criteria. Why not? What has been said so far has proved untenable. To keep our knowledge pure, we must not confuse feelings, experiences, poetic visions or constructions with scientific biological cognition.

And yet, in principle, there is one possible answer that will clarify the meaning of our question about the unity of life: as a whole, neither the one living organism nor the one life, in all its phenomena, can become objects of science. They are true and powerful ideas nonetheless, motivating, guiding, and directing scientific cognition. In such biology, each conceived and known unity appears as a unity in life, not as the unity of life. If it grows conclusive, as an objectivation of the idea, it will no longer lend wings to an endlessly progressing science; it will freeze it, rather, in a dogmatic picture that may be impressive but is false as substantial knowledge.

vii. The whole and disjoint world
In the starry sky we really seem to see the one whole world. This is the cosmos, interrelated from closest proximity to the remotest distance, continuous in time and space. Yet easy as the word 'world' is to utter, and obvious as its existence seems, the reality as a whole becomes obscure when we want to know it distinctly.

A past form of modern science pictured the cosmos as a mechanism of masses of like matter scattered through space. It envisioned the stars as a dust cloud, a dance of coincidences subject to laws of nature, and the atoms as ultimate particles whose thrust and parry, pattern and motion, bring about whatever exists. A scientific cosmogony dealt with the origin of the solar system: the Kant-Laplace theory which has not yet been eliminated from discussion.

Then, over the past half-century, the cosmic picture came to be empirically visualized to an undreamed-of extent. Realities that seem fantastic have appeared in photographs of hundreds of thousands of spiral nebulae, each one a structure like the Milky Way in which our solar system is one among billions. Today's scientific cosmogonies refer no longer to the solar system alone but to the cosmos. Matter itself has now a history as it builds elements from elementary particles. Since the same elements occur throughout, it has been calculated from different points of departure that the world, some four or six trillion years ago, may have originated in a primal explosion that freed immense energies, formed the elements, and created the 'expanding universe' that still continues. Remnants of the liberated energy are found in the cosmic rays; having passed through the finite world of curved space, they strike our earth from all sides, evenly, extremely thinly, but with far greater energies than any other rays. Such images are more complex, more convincing, and based on more varied facts than the mythical cosmogonic images of the past, and yet they do not really objectify the world as a whole.

This shows especially in the question whether the world is finite or infinite. In Antiquity – except for a few major thinkers – and in the Christian view of the world it seemed a matter of course that it is finite. Its infinity was conceived by Cusanus as the reflection of the true infinity of God, and to Giordano Bruno it became an independent infinity, a sign of the divinity of the universe.

The question has changed fundamentally in modern physics, where it can be treated as a definite object of scientific research. The theory of relativity has shown the possibility of an unlimited but finite world in its hypothesis of 'curved space' – an unvisual reality inferred from measurements. In the dimensions to which man has access in practice, the visual Euclidian world remains the real one, though cosmic space as a whole is no longer visual; properly speaking, it is not space at all but a mathematical quantity of more than three dimensions, its reality proved or disproved by measurements that we can take in our visual Euclidian space. The question whether the world is finite or infinite has lost the pathos it had for Cusanus or Bruno. It has become an intrinsically neutral matter of objective research. Yet for this reason it no longer touches on the whole world either, but on a reality in the world, a reality concerning the distribution and motion of matter. The finite world is now a hypothesis that will be disputed, examined, and re-examined in the course of research, and finally, perhaps, discarded or kept for a time, as a step in the advancement of science. It would become visual and tangible and thus properly real only if the same star – our sun, for instance – were some day found to shine upon us from two sides, directly from nearby, and also as a minute, fast-moving starlet, perceptible only with the most powerful instruments, on the opposite side of the sky.

But even then, without the visuality of space, the question of finiteness or infinity would return in a new, different form. What is the location of this finite, unbounded world? Is it, perhaps, with all its four dimensions, part of a world of infinitely numerous dimensions? Such questions are easy to raise and unanswerable without theories to challenge observation. Yet the mere questions would preclude any absolute and definite material knowledge of the world.

The examples lead to a general question: can there be a knowledge of the world as a whole? Whatever we know, after all, refers to specific things, processes, legalities. What we call universal concerns an aspect of the world, not its total reality. All objects, however large, are objects in the world – never *the* world.

Statements about the reality of the universe cannot be empirically proven, and as mere thoughts they demonstrate their impossibility by leading to contradictory theses or antinomies. Kant has shown it: that the world is finite or infinite, that it had a beginning in time or that it had no beginning – such statements are possible only in antinomies. The world as a whole is not conceivable without contradiction. Whatever changes new cognition may necessitate in Kant's phrasing and reasoning, his basic idea will reconstitute itself.

The universe includes the world we know on earth. We draft world pictures, cosmic images, to visualize all there is – and there the result of modern science is a change that affects our entire consciousness of Being. Every past age had a cosmic image; but we have had to realize that there can be no such image that might claim to be the true and real one.

Men were committed to the medieval world order of heaven, earth, and hell; they were committed to the hierarchy of natural forms, lifeless and living, mind and soul – to this artful architecture in which everything had its place. The last physical-astronomical image pictured a world mechanism as self-understood by its legality, a world engine that ran regularly without being operated or needing repairs; and today, for a moment, we have had the picture of a universe expanding from the primal explosion, a world with a history of matter and with speculative concepts (such as Nothingness as the point of departure, or the constant recreation of matter) that are unacceptable to the scientists themselves. The modern scientific universe includes our earth and the wealth of phenomena, of life, of man; but if it is explored as matter and this is viewed as reality proper, it must include every possibility – for everything would have to originate by and from it – and this material entirety is beyond cognition. Physical science owes its very triumphs to the elimination of all such extraneous matters from its field of vision.

The consequence of modern science is a disjoint world. Cosmic images are a phenomenon of the history of the human mind, meaningful when they appeared in the world as answers to human experience, but actually never images of the world as it might be in itself. Men have argued whether the world consists of one principle or two or many (monism, dualism, pluralism) or whether its original entirety makes it comprehensible in all these possibilities at once (holism). The thinker wants to face the world entire; if he can no longer conceive it as a machine, he would still like to draft, to explain, to see through it as composed of a limited number of principles. Yet precisely this is impossible for one who has understood the essentials of our cognition of the world in the encompassing whole in which we find ourselves.

The unity of nature does not lie in a principle from which all could be derived and explained. This principle would be the one great mystery in which all previously existing mysteries would merge; in this one mystery we could comprehend the unity of nature. But this we cannot do.

Once we are as clearly, scientifically conscious of the disjoint world as of the ever-special unities, no speculation can reunify it for our cognition. Yet this only accentuates the question in what sense natural unity is possible at all, for an unrelated disjointness seems as impossible as the one knowable whole. An absolute, unrelated split would defy comprehension. Everything we comprehend is comprehended in relation to other things, and to ourselves. For us there is only one world in which everything occurs and is related to other things that occur; it is only within these relations that we find the leaps that make us speak of disjointness. The relations themselves are always sought out in the pursuit of unifying ideas. They pervade the world as a whole, but they are always unities within the world as a whole.

The truthfulness of our scientific knowledge forces us to dispense with a closed cosmic image. The philosophical significance of this, in summary, is as follows:

First, if the evolution of science – today chiefly of physics – has led to new, grandiose unifications of previously separate fields, this has always happened by clear methodical elimination. It became increasingly plain that for our cognition the world is inconclusive. The unifications have sundered it at the same time.

Second, instead of a scientifically attainable cognition of the one whole world, we find systematic unities *ad infinitum*. These unities of natural being are always specific and aiming at a total unity which the endlessness of the road makes unattainable. As Kant said, the world as a whole is not an object but an idea.

Third, the contradiction of unity and disjointness requires that in the course of cognition we should both separate its objects, by the methods of their investigation, and search for their relationships. It calls for progressive distinction and constant junction at the same time. Neither has limits; both proceed *ad infinitum*.

Fourth, a consolidation of the world in a knowable total existence by its own means would turn the world into a 'thing in itself' and void our freedom.

2 CIPHERS OF THE UNIVERSE

Conceptions, images, ideas are not voided by their failure to prove scientifically valid. Indeed, the rigour of science serves to clarify the different original meaning of the ciphers and to preserve their unrestricted scope of truth.

i. The language of nature

Every day, unconsciously or consciously, our existence is a part of nature. Seeing, hearing, living it with all our senses brings on a mood, an incalculably rich experience tied to the unique presence of this landscape, this tree, this day, this hour, this happening, this moment. When images of poetry and art speak to us – the images that form our direct personal experience and largely make it possible – they always do so in a singular, individual form in which the type is included.

The cosmic, meteorological, elemental, living phenomena of nature move us to a perception free from any purpose. Though they remain silent and do not reply, it seems to us as if they were 'speaking'. At all times, and in many ways, men have been overwhelmed by these phenomena; they felt addressed by persons – by a daemon, by natural spirits such as nymphs, satyrs, elves, or goblins, by elemental spirits of the air, of water, of fire. The experience was real enough for people to expect the personifications to show up bodily, day or night, and for some mysteriously affecting places to become sites of worship. Even today a weakened and playful bond still links our souls with places and phenomena from our personal history, and this has been so from the beginnings of humanity. Nature is not detached. As gods and demons used to appear in it and to act through it, so, now, do miraculously healing and destructive powers.

And what is the import of these natural ciphers? We love nature as a field of human communication. It brings enhancement; it conveys grandeur to our senses; it lets us rejoice in it and experience its bright expanses and dark abysses, its infinite fulfilment of existence. A solitary surrender to nature is restful because we remain tied to our fellow men. But if we flee to nature out of loneliness, having cut our ties to mankind, we shall find neither true nature nor ourselves. Losing both mankind and Transcendence, we shall delude ourselves in that supposedly pure, divine nature. What we find in it then, whatever happiness and pain, will feed on memories or on the expectation of communicative possibilities. Human communication outranks nature. We can yield to nature because we are human together.

ii. Cosmic images as ciphers

We understand our experiences of nature in the thought of its unity, of the universe. Cosmic images, impossible as scientific results, become ciphers of such unity.

I must forgo a discussion of the grandiose cosmic images – the Chinese, whose beautiful, clear, sheltering eternal order reconstitutes itself after any disturbance; the Indian, showing both the infinitely fecund and the infinitely pernicious, pleasure and pain, futility and eternal recurrence and overall senselessness; the Stoic, with its rational nature and its fair and divine universe that is the deity itself; the medieval, composed of the traditional elements but placing nature's beauty and horror in the shade of the one Creator who made this world that is going to come to an end. The variety of these world pictures is immeasurable, but a few general points about them can be made.

a: They are conceived in analogies to phenomena, corresponding to them, sympathizing with them. This can go on endlessly and can be reversed into the contrary at any time, with peculiar evidences in perception, but without criteria of truth.

b: There are underlying principles – primal forces, primal images, primal phenomena – which appear fruitful in the compilation and derivation of phenomena. These derivations are 'metamorphoses' such as the evolution from rudiments, the reconstruction of forms, the comprehension of crises and turns of events.

c: The cosmic order is the ground and model of human orders. They reflect it. Law, government, morality, and the inner order that uplifts the individual to his essence – to realize these, it helps to look at the eternal cosmic orders.

d: There are two ways of rationalization. Where it remains tied to the view and the experience of phenomena we see the cipher of the universe unfold; but where this tie dissolves, leaving abstract operations with fixed series and groupings of principles, the result is an empty activity. We can observe this endless rationalistic bustle in history, where it resembles a 'science' of intellectual toil without research, without clear premises, without criticism – a pseudo-science, from our point of view. The extraordinary satisfaction it gives the operators is understandable; they feel assured of total insight. But lingering in the background of even this odd conceptual calculating machinery we find the basic faith in the great, visual cosmic ciphers.

What passed through the history of nations and civilizations has not ceased even though its meaning changed within the whole of our thinking cognition. I am not speaking of the modern 'enlightening' faith in nature; but a word on the concepts of nature held by Goethe and Schelling may suggest our situation.

Goethe's liking for the natural philosophy of Schelling dwindled as he came to know Schelling's rash drafts of concepts without natural experience. Goethe would go only by such experience. He did not experiment in the scientific sense, to verify hypotheses by observation; he experimented to get a clear view of the pure phenomena as such. He never entered the conceptual wasteland in which Schelling lost his way. Neither man based himself on modern natural science; both sought to hold, and to develop as another way of experience, what is missed in that science.

This is not only possible but necessary, because no change will remove our existence from the world that our senses perceive, and in which our hands operate. Above and below, sky and earth – these remain. Vertigo is a momentary condition, from which we return to the ground. Euclidian space remains our space; along with all tangible phenomena it remains the cipher of nature. Science cannot void this basic phenomenon, nor call it untrue. When an educated modern man says he does not believe in antipodes, for instance, he is expressing the untouchability of our environment and the symbolic character of all its features. He does not, of course, deny that the earth is round. He does not deny that, imagined from where we stand, the antipodes appear to be standing on their heads – but we must distinguish the visual from the imagined. The roundness of the earth has always been perceptible when a ship's masts preceded her decks over the horizon; today we see it on photographs taken at high altitudes, and some day the globe will be seen as we see other planets. Travelling round it, I see by my watch and by the calendar that I win or lose a day. But all these tangibles lie in the tangibility of our environment. Only for astronauts is this partially voided by the absence of gravity in their weightless state, and that is no more a form of existence than vertigo. No imagination, no knowledge, no unusual physical condition will extinguish the tangibility of our existence. They only confuse the body's natural sense of existence – natural, because it enables us to live.

iii. Basic moods in looking at ciphers of nature

Knowledge can become an impulse. The fact – 'it is so' – can be a factor of our imagination, envisioning in ciphers what is then no longer knowable to consciousness at large but audible for Existenz. In the realm of nature, the cipher character shows in our mood as we look at nature. Here are some examples.

The One and All:

From the outset of philosophy, men have been conscious of the One and All, whether they called it world, nature, or 'all-life'. They thought they saw the one whole ordered universe in which all things have their places. They thought they knew the one universal natural legality governing the one world process.

The One and All is the cipher of quietly thinking Existenz in the whole natural universe Love, trust, the enthusiasm of soaring to an eternal Now in the cycle of recurrence – these put us into a mood of perfect shelteredness.

Good and evil creation:

If we see the world not in the cipher of eternity but in the cipher of createdness, its existence stands between Creation and the world's end. The cipher of createdness has become existentially effective in two ways.

In the first, the world, originally made good, has been darkened by the free acts of created beings. It now serves the testing of souls. It is ambivalent. As God made it, it is splendid, orderly, sustained in the continuity of all things; darkened, it is a world full of ugliness and misery, and out of joint. But not really out of joint – for the Creator himself overcomes it to help his own, those whom no horror can deflect from him, the one sure reality.

In the other cipher of the created world it is purely sinister and frightening. Discontinuity, caprice, intrusion, coincidence reign. In this world man feels exposed rather than sheltered; it seems to him not merely odd but downright evil, the function of a power bent on his destruction. The Gnostics carried this cipher of a totally hostile nature to the extreme: the maker of their world was not God but an evil demiurge seeking to catch and extinguish the sparks of souls come from elsewhere. The world's whole beauty and splendour was merely a trick whereby this wicked creator inveigled the souls into yielding to the world, and thus to him.

Finite or infinite world:

There is a strong magnetism in both ciphers. Finiteness attracts us as conclusive knowledge, infinity as an open horizon. One is a challenge to adjust, the other, to proceed *ad infinitum*. In one, on the whole, all is clear; in the other, nothing is definitively clear.

In a finite world we are at home, sheltered in a place created for man. Infinity, on the other hand, confers divine qualities on the world, whether it is the deity itself or supposed to reflect God's perfect infinity in the mere endlessness of the world.

iv. Earth and universe

Down through the ages men have thought how small must be the earth that seems so vast to us. From Sumerian times comes the myth of Etana's ride into the sky, on an eagle's back, to bring down the herb of birth: glancing down, this man sees land and sea dwindle – first the land looks like a mountain, and the sea like a river; then the land like a grove, the sea like an irrigation ditch; then the land like a hut, the sea around it like a yard; then the land like a cake, the sea like a bread-basket. At last, unable to make out either the land or the wide sea, he does not want to go on: 'Stop, so I may return to earth.'

Cicero has Scipio stand on the Milky Way in a dream, gazing on the planets, on the sun, and on the earth in the centre. It seems so tiny, with the Roman empire taking the space of a hamlet separated by the wilderness from other hamlets. And 'the universe' is the 'temple' of the god.

Dante had the same view, looking back at the globe through seven celestial spheres and seeing it 'so pitiful', this clod of earth we are so proud of, from the mountains to the sea.

Today these conceptions have become reality. Strangely, though, the real experience, compared with the greatness of the technological achievement, remains meagre. Terrestrial flight, now commonplace, does give unknown spatial sensations of height and distance, shows clouds from above and the earth's surface as a geographical map – this is strange, to be sure, and permits us to view elementary spaces of light and, flying low, impressive landscapes and previously unknown horizons, but it is no fundamentally new world experience. People who boarded a train, to get in a few hours where it had taken them days to go by horse-drawn coach, were often more afraid of this weird means of transport than people now are of the flying machine. The spatial experience merely recurs in new dimensions. What astronauts feel during weightlessness and at their sight of the globe and the stars is reported to be disappointingly trivial. They seem to be functioning technologically rather than experiencing a fundamental change in spatial consciousness and a new way of dealing with the universe.

The images surpass the reality. Etana, Cicero, Dante imagined ciphers that make us feel the smallness of our world and take the proper measure of humanity. Today the proportions have shifted. Our new, empirically well-established conceptions of cosmic dimensions reduce our 'space' flights to infinitesimality.

These flights have not taken us into cosmic space, only into the space within our solar system. Flights beyond this, into 'deep space', will be practically impossible, quite apart from the difficulties of creating artificial living conditions for years or decades of existing in space. Even if rockets should attain the speed of light – a scientific impossibility – the human life span would be too short for traversing the tiniest fraction of space. The whole of the world we live in is for ever barred to us.

But the technological achievement, which is indeed fabulous, has created an imagination as extravagant and baseless as the idea of synthetic plants and animals and men. This imagination sees no ciphers. Such unreflective thinking proves that scientific and technical strides can be made by human cogs, men whose humanity has been absorbed in the anonymous machinery of our immensely advancing technology and natural science.

A sense of declining humanity spurs our fear that the results of this grandiose technology may relatively soon destroy all life on earth unless man changes. If we really live, however, we live by the hope that the decline we feel may be deceptive, fleeting, superficial – that in surmounting this discouraging experience man will show what he is and can be.

v. Summary
We have gained a toehold outside our planet. But outside the solar system –

as by setting foot on a star – the fixed 'point of Archimedes' is beyond our reach. Outside the universe it does not exist even for our thinking. No matter how far this will take us in space, we always stay in the world.

Yet while scientific cognition and technical concepts cannot transcend the world or grasp its entirety, a speculative view can reach the universe. If scientifically we have to dispense with cosmic images, they do have their rightful place as ciphers – not of Transcendence, but of nature as a whole.

They can have various meanings.

a: If the world is conceived as rational and perfect, as by the Stoics, it is still doomed to end by fire (*ekpyrosis*) and will be reborn in eternal recurrence.

b: If the transcendent Creator becomes the only reality, the world as such is a mere transitory stage between its creation and its end.

c: If Being coincides with eternal nothingness, and the attainment of this is salvation, the world is the endless misery of illusion. It is illusory for our supposed human knowledge – which is indeed ignorance of what matters. The world is ineradicable suffering, but overcome at the same time in a proper knowledge of eternity.

Cosmic ciphers are not statements of fact. Where their peculiarly compelling evidence caused them to be treated as a total knowledge and thus, in fact, to be made tenets of faith, they became fetters. The separation of fact and cipher was our liberation.

We reply to facts – 'it is so' – by an existentially illuminating thinking in ciphers. The facts are inescapable, but the ciphers remain suspended.

Facts are investigated; ciphers tell what appears to Existenz.

The tension between facts and ciphers is confusing if the two are confused; it is liberating if they are clearly distinguished and then related to each other.

Ciphers have furnished the impulses for the scientific research that is now ndependently valid, apart from the impulses. The detailed demonstration of these origins is the concern of the history of science. The driving forces have been forms of faith, expressed in the ciphers of the *harmonia mundi* (in astrology), of the life of the elements (in alchymy), of the separate existence of body and soul (in theological anthropology), and in many other ciphers. Their meaning endures even if science eliminates them; and the sciences in turn furnish data that will aid those motivating forces in their search for ciphers of the universe. In truth, we can reject neither facts nor ciphers. We live in a world that is more than all its objects of cognition, a world that speaks as a whole through ceaselessly embattled ciphers. The battle ceases only where historical or psychological collectors and tabulators neutralize the ciphers into noncommittal random data.

A note on pseudo-philosophy

Some physicists, failing to get the philosophy they want from present philosophers, make up their own. They are entitled to it; philosophy is not the property of any profession. We may ask only what they offer us as a philosophy derived from physics.

The physicists recall the premises of their scientific approach. They find that this very recollection leads to ways of cognition, specifically when it results not only in epistemological or metaphysical speculation but allows the drafting of theories or mathematical constructions subject to proof by observation and measurement. Their philosophy also devises concepts that reconcile contradictions in actual knowledge. Such thinking has value in so far as it broadens cognition, tests the cognitive import of concepts, and clarifies connections. Yet all this is in the proper province of science. It does not require philosophy, and it is not philosophy.

Yet something quite different has also happened on the soil of modern physics. The recurrent claim of certain sciences to represent science proper, and of science itself to comprehend all cognition, has appeared in this case as a modern but vain type of thought.

What we call Positivism was correct thinking in so far as it remained scientific and concerned with the purity of science. It turns into pseudo-philosophy whenever it propounds its own rationalistic dogma. With the pathos of the scientific approach in which it wraps its theses it will set forth empty conceptual inventions – in analogy to science, but not scientifically. It will surrender the significative force of the idea, which a true scientist derives from nature itself in directly incomprehensible fashion, as systematic phenomenal connections leading he knows not where.

On the soil of modern physics, and in line with ever-recurrent examples, concepts of natural science have been used for the cognition of things that far transcend its horizons and ways of thinking – in this case, freedom and creation.

Nuclear phenomena have been found to be following merely 'statistical' patterns, which permit no causal conception. But if scientists conclude from this that here, at the bottom of matter, they have discovered freedom and shown a physical manifestation of it, we have to answer that the so-called freedom of statistics has nothing to do with the freedom we know in ourselves, though it can never be an object of our cognition. If moral statistics deals with such phenomena as crime and suicide, it does not cancel the freedom of each individual to commit or not to commit them. And if nuclear statistics marks the limit where nuclear particles cease to conform to causal thinking, it still does not introduce freedom.

There are various calculations by which scientists have placed the origin of the universe at a time about five trillion years ago. But if from this they draw conclusions on the creation as having occurred at that time, and on the divine Creator, we have to say that physics knows no creation, nor any cipher of a divine Creator. Physics does not proceed that way. It never stops questioning. It never leaps into another field of thinking. What physicists will find when extrapolation takes them to the beginning of the world is not creation but another question, even if as yet they see no way to proceed.

b. Ciphers of History

1 MODERN HISTORICAL SCIENCE AND ITS LIMITS

i. Historical science can reach neither the beginning of history nor its end· It cannot reach the beginning because it depends on the present reality of documents, eyewitness stories, monuments, or traditions; lacking these, it has no object. It cannot reach the future, for the future is not yet reality. Historical science is confined to the past. Historians cannot investigate history's origin – how it came to begin – nor its goal, and whether it has any goal. Their science stands amidst historic reality, always in the present, at a particular moment in time, open at both ends. That science itself is history, a part of its own object.

Historical science cannot be concluded, for two reasons. One is the infinity of concrete reality; every historic object remains inconclusive for our understanding. The second reason is the continuing march of history. History as a whole is inconclusive.

ii. All that happens and changes in time is not history. We speak of 'natural history', but we should not; for natural history is a process that can be known from without and inferred from facts, a process that repeats itself over long periods of time and whose inwardness, if it exists, remains inaccessible. History, on the other hand, is what occurs, what can be understood and not repeated, within man – in the medium of his endeavours, plans, and purposes, of the creations of his mind and his political structures and struggles. Natural events are historically immaterial unless related to such comprehensible topics. History is human history.

'Understanding' is the basic category in our conception of history, as 'causality' in our conception of nature. This is what makes historical science so rich, but also what limits it as a science, for understanding rises from the individual faculties in a way different from sense perception and causal cognition. Moreover, any understanding is tied to an appraisal. In this case, therefore, the scientific approach requires an insight into the limits of our understanding, and the ability to suspend judgment in understanding. This means to place ourselves in the most alien positions, to try thinking from all possible points of view, and in the course of research to give up our own will to influence events. Finally, we must distinguish between mere understandable evidence and the reality of what we understand. Historical understanding requires proof of the reality of a phenomenon, proof of the actual meaning of a communication at the time it was made; it requires a show of expression. In reality a complete, understood, conclusively evident meaning does not occur; we can only approximate it. Besides, any real meaning comprises more than will ever be covered by a specific under-standing.

A historical science that explores realities of meaning can cover only those meant or experienced by men. A meaning perceived by the historian, but not meant by anyone in the historic reality, is not scientifically explorable.

Explorable is only the significance of events to tentatively assumed goals. It is there that the efficacies and inefficacies show up in various instances, as in a study of the teleological and dysteleological elements in organisms – but with the difference that history, unlike the living body, does not appear efficacious as a whole.

iii. Historical science depends on definite methods. Its discoveries, like those of all sciences, rest on such methods. Their extraordinary development in philology, the unfoldment of categories in the basic intellectual sciences, in political science, in sociology, in economics, cannot even be suggested here. The crux is whether the method used at a time is clearly and consciously used or the process bogs down in observations, phrasings, characterizations, judgments, and narratives.

The historian wants to see and to show how things really were, and he wants to know the causality of events up to the point where they became inevitable. He can accomplish neither; but those are the goals he is striving for, *ad infinitum*.

The presentation of historic realities – events, conditions, periods, personalities – is always a work of art on a scientific basis. If successful, it is scientifically based in all its parts; but on the whole, in the choice of the theme and in the selection and arrangement of facts, it will arise only from motives which transcend science, though they must accept its limitations.

iv. All recognizable necessities, whether evident connections of meaning or causal inevitabilities, are particular. The course of history as a whole knows no necessity. 'It had to come' is not a scientific sentence.

Since the past already shows its outcome, it may fool a historian into finding his own forecast for a past situation confirmed by subsequent events. Of course, his study of the sources allows him to know some things better than the living, acting, creating contemporary who did not have access to the sources; but even so it is a self-delusion for him to assume the role of a prophet in the past.

As a scientist he has to make no valid present forecasts either. He can point out possibilities and probabilities, but the correct or incorrect know-ledge beneath any forecast is a moment of action and becomes a factor in events. Every prognosis stays in the framework of present realities and of the intellectual faculties that result from history. There always remains a horizon beyond which no one can see. No 'Greek historian could have foreseen what way of life, what kind of world, what humanly compelling consciousness of Being might spring from the biblical religion. Nor, for example, could Nietzsche's many drafts of future possibilities – partly confirmed, partly unconfirmed – anticipate the rise of the totalitarian principle in the age of technology. The great predictions, which are so surprising later, come from a perception of things that exist in rudiments and do not yet strike other contemporaries. The predictions of Kierkegaard, of de Tocqueville, of Marx are of this type. But not even Marx had an inkling of total rule.

v. To historical science, the present is already past. There is an acute tension between scientific knowledge – by definition objective and valid for every-one – and the will to influence the future. This tension lies in every historical view.

A fundamental difference of meaning divides the responsibility for scientific accuracy in historical documentation and cognition from the responsibility for historical judgment – which even as a mere view is a factor in events to come. The truthfulness of a historian depends on his distinction of these two responsibilities. If in the guise of science, 'as a historian', he actually enters the power struggle – which becomes concealed, then, and irresponsible – the result is existential untruthfulness. The great historian goes both ways, to be sure, but he will not permit them to be confused and thus remains truthful.

One motivation of historical science is the will to know so as to learn from the past, to live and to act better. True historians will suspend this motive in their work, however, for the sake of pure knowledge. They dignify their science by keeping it pure and knowing its limitations.

The bounds of history as a science form the gateway to a conception of history in ciphers.

2 CIPHERS OF HISTORY

i. Views of the overall course of history

a: Progress; evolution; eternal recurrence. History has been conceived as progress, as evolution, as eternal recurrence. All these categories have rudiments in reality. There is progress – but only in real knowledge and technology, where setbacks have so far always been made up by new advances. There is evolution, an unfoldment of forms that have a beginning and an end in history – as of Greek art until its Hellenistic decline, of Western art from the fourteenth century to its decline in the late eighteenth, of philosophical thinking from the Miletians to Aristotle, from Kant to Hegel and Schelling, from Anselm to Occam. There is also recurrence in the comparable sequences of changing conditions, as from city states to empires.

What is to the scientist a special aspect, subject to proof and of limited validity, becomes a cipher if it is applied to history as a whole. The reality of such ciphers is impossible to prove; as a matter of fact, it can be disproved. But they do express a historic sense of Being.

The idea of progress makes me feel always on the highest peak yet attained, looking with confidence into an ever-improving future. In the idea of evolution I have my place in an unfolding entirety, in which progress is a minor factor. In the idea of recurrence I expect a cyclical reiteration of all history: everything has happened before and will happen again.

b: Divine guidance Against these three ciphers stands that of a history guided by Providence. There, history is our education according to the divine plan. We obey or disobey God in what we do, and are rewarded or punished, individually or as a people. We live under the promises and threats of God.

Historiography, then, is critical reporting, distinguishing good acts from evil. (The old Chinese, on very different premises, did likewise.) It calls the present to an accounting in the future – not, as did Solon, by citing the immanent law under which evil is surely, if not always promptly, punished, but by invoking God's will.

Is the divine plan a definitive guidance? Can we count on it that, whatever guilt we may incur, the whole of history will have a happy ending? To me, Jeremiah alone seems to touch on the other possibility – that God may also extirpate all he has sown. In the biblical texts the definitive promise is dominant. We are left with a paradox: history depends on what men do – but the same history fulfils God's promise, regardless.

c: The Gnostic view. A fundamental change in the cipher occurs if history, instead of being guided by God's eternal, immutable will, is conceived in God himself, in Being as such, whose events or decisions merely find their expression, their echo, their consequences in the phenomena of this world. We call this view of history Gnostic, after one of its specific forms.

It conceives our fate as happening in supersensory reality. It is from there that the challenges come, the acts of deception, intervention, and withdrawal, of aid and annihilation. No act of ours can gainsay it; we have no freedom. We do not make history and thus do not really share in the responsibility; we can only hear, perhaps, and answer by obedience or rebellion. The answer to critical questions is that this supersensory history harbours within itself the clash of good and evil powers, leaving it up to us to take sides. A dramatic world of myths and resultant conceptual speculations – a simultaneously twisted and oblivious world alternating between grand cosmic concepts and an uncommon ugliness, with a frequent touch of servility in the dreary refrains of the initiates, and all this fed somehow by experiences of madness, though itself not mad at all – serves to compel and confirm our own ugly, agonized condition.

Such Gnostic rumination on events, with the transcendent – if we can still call it so – grown temporal, extends its incidental ciphers even to modern thinking. 'God has temporarily retired,' Strindberg said. 'God is dead,' said Nietzsche.

d: Rank. The universe is unimaginably larger than our solar system, and the latter than this dust grain, our planet Earth; the inhabited world is a paper-thin sheath of the globe; continents overbalance small countries;

populous nations outweigh the numerically weak; the great political powers absorb the little ones, and men in masses overwhelm the individual.

We are at the mercy of forces that can destroy us from the cosmos or from the interior of the earth, at the mercy of great powers, at the mercy of masses.

Whenever quantity becomes decisive, history approaches natural history. Preponderance is a factor of history proper, but not its essence. History proper is concerned with quality, which arises, is created and made conscious, on the smallest scale. Rarely will it extend to masses of men and place its stamp on the political powers. It may vanish without a trace and be forgotten, or it may endure in miniature, unnoticed, only to rise in individuals, from hidden traditions, and incalculably to exist again – always utterly unsure whether it will be allowed to live and be effective.

Jews and Greeks were very small nations. Small parts of India and China brought forth what was then transformed and misconceived into the property of great civilizations. Even Rome was a small source of the spirit of political order, the knowledge of power and law, that turned the Mediterranean world into an empire which ultimately lost the spirit of the source.

Yet wherein lies quality? Not a few historians have identified it with success. They make their science serve the victors and the powers that be, noting failure only as a foil for the victorious process – except for what the victor will later, however pervertedly, appropriate as his own.

The true historian acts differently. He sees quality in greatness as such, whether triumphant or failing. And no science knows how to tell greatness; it is something we understand originally, in ciphers, by myths and legends. Though we must evade no reality that can be scientifically explored, we still keep the ciphers of greatness in sight. We see it by scientific means, but not through the eyes of science.

Greatness is the cipher of historic immanence. Here again there is a cipher struggle, waged in communication as each Existenz points up its own view of greatness. Greatness is revealed simultaneously with the Existenz of its viewers.

Historical research is the neutral ground on which men can agree about demonstrable realities. Only an aimless historical research can pursue things at random, without recognizing an order of rank – though even then unwittingly oriented on some minor idea that represents the importance of the object under investigation.

The public communication of any historical view thrusts it into the arena of ceaseless struggles for the perception of greatness, for dignity, for nobility, for profound truth, for faith.

There, once more, the great historian seeks a truth other than the undoubtedly common accuracy of science. He wants to understand all ways of greatness, and of conceiving greatness. History, to him, is as much a history of ephemerality, of the failure, as of the lasting self-preservation of the ones who feel they own the truth; he wants forgotten greatness to be visible also. He would like to make himself the battlefield without joining the fray, to serve no party, neither victors nor vanquished, neither churches nor heretics. He will find out that this cannot be done to perfection, despite occasional magnificent achievements from Thucydides on. Try as he may, he will find himself embroiled. But self-criticism will keep him aware of his limitations. For if he could see all kinds of greatness, cast light upon them, and do absolute justice, he would have grown beyond human stature.

There can be no view of history without rank, no rank without a cipher of greatness, and no true cipher without a cipher struggle.

e: Coincidence. We see the tremendous power of coincidence in history when we measure events by human designs, or by some *ex post facto* design of their meaning. Planning – itself always part history – is exposed to coincidence in its realization. Any subsequent draft of a meaningful total history will show the coincidences that have in fact helped or hindered the meaning.

We see that some men know how to use the coincidences which others let pass unnoticed. With them, coincidence comes to make sense. It is not the coincidence which is controlling, then, but this sense that takes over for a time, to a limited extent, but in ways that astound the observer.

We see coincidences accumulate until some meaning, good or evil, will seem to connect a series of events as if they had been willed by a superhuman power. It is in view of such facts that we see the cipher of a history that is not man-made but toying with man.

A man who believes in his 'star' feels himself borne by such coincidences; one who does not feels they mark his road to ruin. The cipher of a guidance, or of powers fighting over him, strikes the man who thinks, in reviewing his life, that the meaning of the coincidences showed up only afterwards.

If history is conceived as a meaningful entirety – an operation most grandly performed by Hegel – coincidences either cease to be coincidences and become factors of the total meaning, or they are viewed as irrelevant to history and thus not worth considering. Hegel actually discards the bulk of historic reality as coincidental. Whole nations and a majority of events are said to have nothing to do with the meaning of history as the eternal presence of the spirit. They merely exist, and even makers of history go on living irrelevant lives once their work is done.

Coincidence, whether regarded as historically crucial or as historically insignificant, always gives rise to ciphers. As a beneficent factor in line with my will it becomes the object that proves my life and will to be in harmony with the course of events; as meaningless incarnate it becomes an object of outrage.

The more precious a historic memory, the greater its exposure to coincidence. A frightening tension prevails between coincidence and the eternity that speaks in history: convincingly touched by one, we seem to be flung into a sea of doubt by the other.

ii. Eschatology

Eschaton means 'the last'. In reality it means individual death and the end of anything particular. As a cipher it denotes the end of the world, of all things, and the concept of the 'end of time'. Existentially it means the change that brings man from a perishing world into a new one.

a: The empirical reality is certain, possible, or probable in space and time, on the ground of identical, communicable experience. Death is the end assured to every individual. Civilizations, languages, nations, states come to an end. Every historic particularity is sure to end. Nations perish – though not populations, which will form new structures.

That history should end with human existence transformed into a merely repetitive state – similar to animal life, but regulated, in lieu of instinct, by man's total functionalization in his omnivorous technical machinery – is a terrifying thought; considering human nature and the terms of that functionalization, we still cannot believe that it might really come to pass.

The end of mankind, along with all animal and plant life, is a real possibility, with man now capable of bringing it about.

The end of the planet, and thus of all life, in a cosmic disaster is a very remote possibility. The end of the universe lies outside our horizon.

b: Ciphers of the end of all things are, for example, the Stoic *ekpyrosis*, the holocaust that will consume this world and will be followed by the birth of a new one, or the Norse conception of a twilight of the gods followed by the dawn of another world, with other gods. Ciphers like these cast a cloud on our whole existence. They shift the weight of things. The cloud does not indicate nothingness, for beyond total perdition lies a new beginning; but the doom will recur. Those are great, historically powerful views. There is a mystery about the world we live in, something we do not and cannot know, and the ciphers speak as though this were unveiled.

c· Another meaning of eschatology comes from the individual experience of 'being changed', shedding temporal ties to enter into the consciousness of eternity. This too is always an end and a beginning, the end of temporal worldliness and the beginning of an eternity above time. The individual seems, in a way, to let go of his existence so as to be reborn as eternity. A continuous equivalent of physical death lies in this end of mere existence as the font of rebirth to a true life – which is why Plato spoke of philosophizing as 'learning to die'.

The *eschaton*, in this sense, is the present turnabout in every individual – the end, not of the world, but of the 'old Adam', the past man who is reborn, and of his past world, since a new one has, for him, come into being. 'The last' is here every moment.

d: An intertwining of virtually all these meanings occurs in Christian eschatology. In the faith of the New Testament the real end of the world is imminent as a cosmic event; impending with it, and already present in its first indications, is the kingdom of God; and the believer undergoes the change (*metanoia*) that makes him part of the new kingdom.

The cosmic process is conceived as one with the processes of salvation and human history. Christ is the turning-point of the world. The road goes from the Creation to Adam's Fall, to the deliverance by Christ, and on to the world's end on the Day of Judgment. Aligned with this image is the import of the sacrifice, of the resurrection, of the unworldly absolute ethos that ignores the world – which will soon end anyway – to anticipate eternal life as life by love alone, with all the consequences that are self-destructive in the world and irresponsible in the eyes of the world. One cannot pick out and separately stress one element such as the cosmic, the redemptive, or the ethical, without destroying the whole of this faith. It held sway in men for a short time, until impulses of adjusting to the world, of shaping and conquering the world, led to the swift transformation in which the source of the faith was lost. And yet, that source has been borne through the centuries as an enduring restlessness.

e: Critically we must remind ourselves that the images of eschatological thinking are ciphers rather than knowledge. They were turned into dogmas, and then, in reliance on an authoritative communication, they were believed and 'known' at the same time. As ciphers they evoke existential possibilities, but their perversion into tangible realities destroys our freedom.

The sense of facing the end awakens Existenz. The threat of an end in our time is based on reality and puts man into a new boundary situation: he will find the answer in his Existenz, or else he will perish.

But we can be evasive. We can conceal the end. Instead of being awakened, then, we fall prey to the course of things.

Or we are aroused, but not as possible Existenz; we are aroused only to a fear for our existence, a desire to be safe. But safety from atom bombs cannot be gained in this fashion.

Existenz awakens only when the real view of the end becomes part of the cipher of the end. Then the inner change corresponds to the eschatological picture: I will be changed and given to myself as a new man, so to speak, in my freedom.

The Christian objectivation of the change is grace, bestowed upon me in the general historic process of salvation. Today the question is whether the phenomenon of being given to myself takes a definite cipher or a physically incarnated God – or whether a free, reliable change in men will not actually come only in suspended ciphers.

Twenty centuries of Christianity, and even more of philosophy, have wrought the change only in isolated individuals. Could a reform of the biblical faith lend a broadened impact to the eschatological cipher? Or is it true, considering the whole of history, that for all the peaks of humanity it has produced, the change is ultimately futile for the course of things?

There is no guarantee. No promise can assure us. The mere intellect, observing and calculating probabilities, makes us despair. And yet – though we must not for a moment forget the realities it shows us – we cannot and need not submit to it.

iii. History as the eternal present

History has been conceived either as a passage through time that can never be repeated, or as a recurrence of the same.

In the first concept, what has happened is for ever submerged in the past; we recall it only for a while, in fragments. The present is now, irreplaceable, to be seized or missed, and the future is a realm of incalculable possibilities.

What has been is no more real than what is not yet, and the very present is not really present, but a constantly vanishing moment of physical tangibility.

In this framework man must make his unpredictable decisions, and the leaps of his experience in vision, thought, and faith. Mere existence strikes him as largely trifling, but it is in this trifling existence that his own actions show what makes him aware of its triviality.

Overlapping the vanishing moment in a flow of time is the moment that reveals something eternal. This happens in the events we call existential – in change, in decision, in the repetition of original love.

There is a cipher reflecting this existential experience; it says: what is in eternity comes to appear in history. Or, speaking of the whole of history: the eternal present and the fateful course of decision are one and the same.

In the second concept everything happens again and again, in endless cycles. The vanishing Now is eternal, because it has been and will be infinitely many times.

Both ciphers promise eternity in evanescence. The moment too is crucial in both: to feel at a time of decision that what you do now will have to be repeated in eternity is a feature of eternal recurrence. But the two ciphers speak in a different vein, if not in an antithetical one. In the one-time course we are directly at home in eternity, in recurrence only indirectly, as the cyclical concept makes time itself eternal. In the singular passage we touch eternity only on the heights of Existenz, not as mere existence; in recurrence all things are reduced to the same level of happening over and over.

Both ciphers ignore the question of beginning and end. In eternal recurrence, with each moment both a beginning and an end, the question is dropped outright. The one-time course knows a beginning and an end if we add the ciphers of the world's creation and end, both fixed in time – but neither is relevant in such speculative-visual concepts as Hegel's, for instance, with Being a cycle of cycles comprising time and history. Temporal history, then, is timeless not as eternal recurrence, but as the totality of the eternal Now with the one singular process. The encompassing whole of a Being understood in speculative dialectics absorbs everything.

iv. What do the ciphers of history mean to us?
Success in realistic planning depends on our knowledge of present realities. There a real knowledge lays the foundations of political and social science.

While we remain in the realistic area, our situation is this: we live in a world without promise or destination; we set our own goals; we preserve ourselves within our conceptions of our tasks, our ends, our happiness, our salvation. We do so always within limited horizons, constantly mistaken about facts, and guided by coincidences. We submit to a propaganda organized by all means at the disposal of special interests or self-assured power *élites*. We do not know what we really want. History is to us a tumultuous process, perhaps with certain recognizable regularities as found in meteorological phenomena or games of chance, but concretely incalculable.

If we want to know what we are doing, what we are living and acting for, we do not deal with history by knowledge alone. In the state of tumultuous process I just described there was something fatally vague about the concepts of happiness and salvation, about the final goal in all provisional goals – something that had nothing to do with knowledge but was in fact an illusion not perceived as such. This is what becomes lucid if we are conscious of ciphers. They make us aware of our real will. Let us re-examine our analysis from this angle.

a: Looking at history as progress, as evolution, or as eternal recurrence will give us the peace of a merely knowledgeable state, which anyone can acquire without having to make a free choice of his way of life. A view of history as guided by divine Providence will give us the peace of being linked with God, provided we freely choose a life that will please God. The supersensory history that has us at its mercy will give us certainty along with constant fear; this view rests on the arrogance of a superior knowledge that lifts its possessor above the crowd.

b: Our own past, the history that determines what we are and what we want, is definitive as a reality that has been, but not at all definitive for our judgment. That is to say, it determines our actions by the way in which we conceive it, judge it, accept it as a model and a challenge or reject it as reprehensible. Nothing can be justified by the mere fact of reality. We cannot change what has happened, but we can change its effects and thus, in a sense, undo it. No decision on what we can be need be accepted as final; any such decision calls for a new original acknowledgment, which we can refuse. The battles of our forebears continue in us, and the victors need not remain for ever victorious. The question faced by each new generation is what parts of history it wants to stand on, what manner of men it wants to accept as forebears. If we see through a spirit it will cease to act upon us.

In critical historiography we establish facts. We do not touch on their ambivalence. The scientific historian who communicates his discoveries keeps aloof from the partisan struggle; ideally, his readers would not even notice what the scholar loves or hates, detests or admires.

Yet though critical judgment has no scientific role to play, it is existentially decisive. It is what makes history a factor in our present life. We use scientific methods to come to this judgment, for without such means to know and understand the facts an abstract, general affirmation or negation is both cheap and blind; critical judgment can only be based on the full use of all our factual implements. We also find there is no one norm for such judgment. It is not universally valid. And yet, for Existenz it is the only way of dealing seriously with history.

The struggle of these norms will always be the present struggle of the spirits. The nations in their crises rewrite history, as it were, and so far this has almost always happened along with errors of fact. Partisanship would conceal the scientific possibilities and bury essentials in a welter of irrelevant data. And yet, with full deference to scientific truthfulness, the judgment itself can be a creative historic act. It can affect what makes life worth living for people, how they regard nobility and human dignity, what they consider their best chance in a real situation. In the mirror of history we see what we want. We get a clear view of ourselves. But the ceaseless battle of norms should be waged in communication; only thus, learning to see through the eyes of our adversary, shall we come to full clarity. Broadened minds will achieve either unanimity or a supreme effort to mould the seemingly irreconcilable into great, original views, to be imprinted on the spirits.

c: Ciphers lay out the horizons in these struggles. They orient us to possible perspectives. Their light brightens the unknown in history; their ambiguity enhances our questioning consciousness by insights that are generally valid without adding to what we know. They invigorate us for the tasks of our lives by the mere fact that a sense of our total history is sought at all. They will not leave us mired in a realistic knowledge to which history as a whole is bound to seem a pointless stumbling through the ages, an endless diversity without unity. Historical knowledge is encompassed, rather, by a seriousness that manifests itself in judgment, action, ways of life, and the space in which this happens is illumined by the glow of ciphers.

c. The Cipher of Rational Being

1 BEING AND LOGOS

Constant flux and confusion is not our only impression of things in the world. They also appear as knowable. Man finds orders in everything – in nature, in society, in himself. To this extent he sees a reign, not of chaos, but of *logos*.

Logic makes the thinker aware of himself and of his thoughts. He comes to know what he is doing. He equates the forms of his statements about things with the forms of things themselves, calling these forms categories and opening a specific field for their cognition. It is the immanence of our thinking.

The clarifications of logic and the theory of categories became reflective, planned scientific advances at a rather late date. Originally their great power rested – and has rested to this day – on a conviction that the world is pervaded and ruled by the *logos*, that the *logos* is Being, that cognition of the *logos* is tantamount to cognition of the ground and essence of all things. The *logos* of the whole, objective reason, is one of the great ciphers of immanence.

2 ASIAN VIEWS OF BEING

From the outset men have conceived universal orders, and for thousands of years a few great forms of these views, differing essentially from one another, have ruled great nations as unquestioned matters of course.

Chinese 'universism' was the knowledge of being one with the basic order of *tao* – the eternal, impervious order that will restore itself whenever it has been disturbed, and whose pursuit is the happiness and peace of man.

The Hindu experience of Being rests on the concept of endless rebirths in an inexorable cycle, the 'wheel of Samsara'. In each incarnation the soul is laden with the *karma* from its good and evil deeds in past incarnations; according to the quality of its *karma* it must pass through forms ranging from the lowest animals to gods, finding no rest save in a complete exit from the cycle, to Nirvana. In the wheel of rebirths, thinking as a way to knowledge actually conceals reality and truth; it is indeed unwitting ignorance. Only another kind of thinking, the transformation of consciousness in meditation, can attain the true knowledge that leads the soul to salvation.

3 THE LOGOS IN THE WEST

It takes a comparison with those Asian analogies – which have a grandeur of their own – to appreciate the singular Western concept of a rational world. We call the cognition of the *logos* of Being ontology, a term first used in 1656 by Clauberg, and the loftiest of its images have been conceived by Aristotle, by the Stoics, by Aquinas, Leibniz, and Hegel. All things have their place in those comprehensive pictures. The whole is arranged in steps or cycles and teeming with orders of rank, of things and values. Even God has his place.

A common feature of these forms of total knowledge is that they give meaning to Being, to existence, to my existence in the world. They all give the great, all-encompassing significance in which everything is sheltered or can find its way to salvation. And yet these Western ontologies differ extraordinarily in their methods and particulars.

Common to Aristotle and Hegel is that thought – the *nous*, the *logos* – equals Transcendence. No line divides its immanence and Transcendence; pure thought is Transcendence. As God, Transcendence has its place but is no longer transcendent, for thought brings me to it and makes me its kind, its reflection, or indeed identical with it. The resplendent order leaves no mystery. Nothing stays hidden. Truth and reality have been unveiled.

Aristotle's governing principle is a rational scale, the step-by-step advance to God, the unmoved cause of motion. Hegel's is cyclical dialectics, a movement from one cycle to the next, up to the one all-encompassing cycle. Aristotle, instead of arranging the whole in a system, a visible work, analyses things – their appearance, their essence, and their place in the graduated structure; to Hegel, a philosopher's work consists in the construction of one system. Yet Hegel's trademark remains his dialectical understanding, his penetration of the depths behind the phenomena, and his achievement of internal and external unity in each form.

Thomas Aquinas combines a rationalistic, Aristotelian-type intellectual philosophy with a Transcendence raised to the *n*th power; Hegel's dialectical penetration of all things eliminates Transcendence.

Aristotle and Aquinas exert their main influence through the Catholic Church; their work has been titled *philosophia perennis*. Hegel has had no corresponding effect in Protestant theology, only a partial one that swiftly passed. The great order that Leibniz devised has remained apart, on the whole.

4 CHARACTERIZATION OF ONTOLOGY

In immanence, our view of things lets us establish objectively how to define, to describe, and to categorize them.

The premise is that 'facts' of general validity are to be found by variously stated procedures. Those who apply them claim to get results that are scientifically compelling. They claim that the structure of the realm of Being, their very essence, is now revealed and comprehended in concepts – that there is a science of the order of Being, a scientific philosophy, called ontology when it deals with Being, and axiology when it deals with being right.

At the same time, however, what I called 'premise' belongs to the substance of this science. This premise is not an assumption to be tested; it is 'seen' as truth. It is simultaneously seen and presupposed, and it must guide our vision if we are to see the *onta*, the things that exist, and their order. Only the perspective of such seeing will yield the appropriate evidences. But the truth of the perspective depends on another criterion: on the philosophical rather than scientific significance of the various perspectives themselves.

These may be meagre, scanty, empty or momentous, rich, and stimulating – not in a literary sense but as matters of essential, properly philosophical, i.e., existential concern.

If this 'science' is not to lose itself in endless descriptions but to attain the unity of a science, it requires another premise: the systematic factual unity must have a single origin. And this unity in turn has to be seen. It means either a closing of the largest circle or the attainment of the first and highest and unsurpassable origin.

Then this ontology, which views, shows, and presents the order of Being, leads to a system of Being – a system which in the opinion of its exponents can be realized in a cogent, generally valid science. In fact, there is no realizing it at any time.

There are several ontologies. They are changeable. They seem to exclude one another and to exist in combinations. Their sole common ground is their conviction of the possible cognition of thought and Being as a whole. They believe in a 'system of Being' – an organism of Being, so to speak – and we have seen that there is no such thing for human thinking. The common ground is brittle or non-existent.

Nevertheless, in their diversity the ontologies retain the weight of ciphers. Their great forms pose a challenge. They battle over their existential import. The rational movements in them appeal to us in so far as we feel such existential motives.

5 AN AMBIGUOUS MODERN SLOGAN

In our time the concern of a 'scientific philosophy' has been posed by Husserl as a return 'to things themselves' – to original observation and to the essential insights that can be drawn from it. A literature dealing with the most varied objects has sprung up in Husserl's succession.

The slogan, 'Back to things themselves', turned into another: 'Back to the origins!' This slogan could be inspiring, but its ambiguity was philosophically fatal. As a call for original observation and visualization it is good for all the sciences and for philosophy as well; it frees them to be unbiased, to ignore prejudices – i.e., truths held to be self-evident without reflection. Yet the call cannot be philosophical until it refers to the origins of Existenz, and of the ciphers that affect Existenz. This means to talk about origins, not just to see and observe them. What I need there is not a mere contemplative knowledge, but clarity about what makes me my communicative self. In the medium of thought this clarity is obtained indirectly, by conjuring and appealing.

Contemplation has an impersonal criterion: seeing what as such is still indifferent and acquires philosophical weight only from the inner action we perform with it. Conjuring illumination, on the other hand, opens the space where self meets self, encompassed by the ciphers of Transcendence.

No observation, no image will manifest unity; it is manifested only by the realization of thought and life in a never conclusive whole.

The slogan could put an end to philosophy, could let it expire in the activities of a 'pure philosophical science'. Or it could lead to a revival of philosophy, to a resumption of contact with the eternal origins that have found so varied a voice in its history of three thousand years.

6 BREAKING THROUGH ONTOLOGY

Cognition extends as far as there is order in the world, and order can be found only in so far as things accommodate cognition. There is an optimism in cognition: the farther we get, the richer, clearer, simpler will the order be.

Our ability to find order is the premise of cognition, confirmed by each factual discovery. But a thesis that turns the premise into the result – saying, 'All things are ordered and therefore subject to cognition' – is not a compelling insight. It leaves the question whether such orders may not ultimately rest on chaos, as the most fertile fields often lie on slopes of a volcano.

We can see the chaotic other side. The human world above all, but also life at large and finally, perhaps, even the inorganic realm – these are not logically rational. They do have elements of reason. The question goes on: how much reason is there in the world, or how little? Everywhere, reason seems to come up against limits that render it impotent. As Hegel put it, 'Reality does not obey the concept' – although, astonishingly, he drew the reverse conclusion: what does not obey the *logos* is worthless and no reality; real and powerful is only what obeys the concept.

Still, it is certain that when we speak of reason we are speaking from experience. I meet reason; it works in me; there can be no doubt that it exists.

Reason, which we called the bond of all encompassing, is met in man alone. Nowhere is there reason without a human being who is himself. That reason meets reason at all is the inspiring warrant for our claim, our hope, our certainty that we should live by it.

It is a mistake to draw conclusions about reason as a whole from all the ways of reason in nature, in life, in Existenz. What men from Aristotle to Hegel have done in holding the reason of the whole to be self-evident and in charting it was an admirable achievement, unsurpassed in cogitative energy. But these attempts exist in varying forms; they contradict each other, and all of them founder on facts. Scientifically, despite their great fertility in specific views, they have on the whole turned out to be delusions.

Science has shattered the total knowledge which past philosophical systems sought to communicate. But they were not simply mistaken. They were by no means conceptual fictions either. They contain the truth of cognitive ciphers, measurable by their existential import rather than by their accurate cognition of reality. As delusions or noncommittal creations they could not have had the compelling power they once possessed as absolute truth and can possess today as a cipher language.

In the tension of order and chaos, of reason and irrationality, all the ciphers of rational immanence fail. Order is not merely order; it is an order of the never wholly ordered. Our existential experience compels us to break through any ontology that would know the whole. Yet where do we go from there?

The first answer is: we enter the realm of embattled ciphers. There, if those structures had any original substance, they remain indispensable even though their meanings change. They are no longer the absolutes they used to be; as ciphers they have lost the power of almost tangibly compelling and thus limiting our consciousness of Being. But they have not lost their voice. We need them as way stations, to take our bearings from the experience of their concrete view. We see and hear them so as to transcend them, but they cannot be transcended if they are not first brought to mind. Though we limit its field, we do not give up the *logos*. The ontologies are not discarded errors; they are lights on our path. If we do not know them, if we do not know how to deal with them, we shall unwittingly succumb to any one of their dogmatic forms. We do not reject the *logos* as the cipher of immanence; we do move it into the shade of a greater power.

The seriousness of Existenz, the refusal to be pawns to either chaos or order – the thing that makes us serious about what we do for the sake of order, whether in *logos* or ethos, in politics or law, though we do not sufficiently understand it in these phenomena – this points our way to Transcendence.

These effects of existential motivations lead to a second answer to the question where to go from the ontologies. We find in our philosophizing efforts at orientation that as we break through the ontological way of thinking we come to a basic knowledge. We take the step from ontology to periechontology.

7 ONTOLOGY AND PERIECHONTOLOGY

'Basic knowledge, is the word for a philosophical endeavour to lay a foundation for everything else. The concept has existed since Aristotle spoke of a 'first philosophy' (*prote philosophia*) – later given the ambiguous name 'metaphysics'. In recent times there has been much talk of a basic science, a science of foundations, a fundamental ontology. However the task may be posed, whatever the method of answering, the situation remains.

Basic knowledge has a twofold meaning. First, it means a basic knowledge of the varied designs of Being, the ontologies and cosmic images that go today with the great ciphers. Secondly, it means what we are speaking of: a far more modest basic knowledge founded on that tradition. This is not the cognition of any object, but the inconclusive illumination of the realms, the origins, the possibilities of that other basic knowledge in ciphers. We distinguish between an ontological and a periechontological basic knowledge.

The ontological total knowledge tells what is; our modest basic knowledge tells what we find ourselves in. The conclusive total knowledge turns into a permanently inconclusive ascertainment. Fundamental knowledge becomes a knowledge for purposes of orientation.

All we see in this periechontological basic knowledge is the most that we have so far learned about the forms of things we can experience, think, and do. We claim no substantial total knowledge. Our basic knowledge is kept open, not stabilized. Rather than the centre of Being, its standpoint seems to us the centre of our situation.

Man cannot be without a basic knowledge. If he avoids it, it will constitute itself in his consciousness anyway, only unclearly, unsteadily, and accidentally.

It is a matter of philosophical choice and depends on my inner condition whether I grant sole dominance in me to a basic knowledge that is in fact a cipher, or whether I give precedence to a basic knowledge of my situation in encompassing. Choosing the second, I live in the infinite space in which ciphers have their meanings at each time, but not an abso'ute meaning.

This basic knowledge is a framework, and not a definitive one. It contains elements of philosophical progress – not the scientific kind, but the progress that lies in the appeal which the ideas of earlier thinkers have for the thinker of later days. He does not have those ideas at his disposal, as advanced science has the insights of the past, but they can awaken, question, guide him. Far from having overcome them, he rather feels he is joining a choir of contemporaries, carriers of the life of philosophy. We could never call ourselves heirs to the thinking that has been done in history, as if we were now proprietors of that whole edifice; scientists may do that with the history of scientific insights, but not philosophers with their tradition. What we hear and adopt, or fail to hear and forget, is always our own responsibility. We do not discharge it by the work of our intellect alone, only by a way of being and living that will bring about the adoption if it has not been brought about by it.

In the basic knowledge of encompassing we move on a boundary that leads to a philosophical analogue to the advance of science. It is as if we were always summing up, so to speak, albeit in the form of mere possibilities – not gathering contents, not eclectically, not fitting the mass of thoughts into a system, but in the sense of an awareness that later generations can have about earlier ones, as though in a single contemporaneity.

8 PERIECHONTOLOGICAL BASIC KNOWLEDGE IS NOT A CIPHER

The basic knowledge of our situation is the never complete, ever-changeable consciousness that grants whatever freedom to think we can have at a time. This is both its weakness and its strength.

Its weakness is a lack of substance. It shows us nothing but the form of contents; its only content is awareness of the scope of possibilities.

The basic knowledge cannot sweep us off our feet like the ciphers. It is sober. It does not please by great views. No great, overwhelming emotions issue from it. It allows no dogma, hoists no flag, lifts no torch, beats no drum. It cannot seduce us. It throws every individual back upon himself.

Such a knowledge opens doors and lights up origins, but it does not lend a voice to historic concretions, to fulfilled truth, to Existenz or Transcendence.

To think it is an act of reason. It lets us deal seriously with ciphers without succumbing to particular ciphers. It is a product and a tool of reason.

Its strength lies in its illuminating power along man's road to himself and to Transcendence.

Being sober, it is not attractive, but neither is it seductive. The weakness of sobriety is its strength; it can be indispensable to the man who comes to himself. Its strength lies not in itself, but in the self that uses it.

The basic knowledge resembles the pure air we breathe, which we cannot see but cannot live without, and which is not a substance. Or it resembles pure light without an object in it.

Taken for a cipher, it would lose its meaning. We may, for instance, chart the modes of encompassing, however inadequately and temporarily; but as an organism of Being they would make just another ontology. Their meaning would be perverted. Such a cipher of the whole, harmonious despite all conflicts, would be misconceived as an order of Being – and it would not even have the eloquence of a cipher. In truth, while showing what ciphers can be and that they can be transcended, the basic knowledge commits us to no particular way of life and leaves us as open to order as to chaos.

III CIPHERS OF THE EXISTENTIAL SITUATION
(PHYSICAL AND MORAL EVIL)

Ciphers are weighted either on the object side, as the ones of Transcendence and immanence in our preceding chapters, or on the subject side as in the discussions that follow. We start now from boundary situations to which Existenz responds by illumination in ciphers. We might speak of ciphers in our view of death, in our views of law and love, in our understanding of sacrifice. I confine myself to the one theme of evil.

Let me repeat once again that objectivity and subjectivity are inseparable. The object of the cipher has no substance if it does not carry existential weight; as a mere fact it is an empty concept. The subject side concerns the existential origin that is illuminated in the object side; if it is nothing but subjective it becomes a matter of psychologizing.

It is only in discussion that we stress either the objective qualification of the ciphers – taking a one-sided view, we might call this a 'fact' – or their subjective origin as the situation qualifies it.

Ciphers are statements about both Transcendence and the individual who encounters it. The truth in them is never purely objective, nor ever purely subjective.

No man can see through his own religious thinking, or through another's, in the way he sees through rational thoughts about things. We may keep all ciphers and all speculative ways of speech in suspension, as man-made – and yet, speaking through this human product will be something that is more than human. There is an objectiveness in its subjectiveness, and *vice versa* If this thinking is conscious and clear – as distinguished from the incommunicable, unconscious or supra-conscious clarity of the mystical union – it refers to something that thought can only touch, not comprehend, and that casts light on thinking.

a. The Facts of Evil

There is no telling the evils in nature, in life, in man, or the evil men do to themselves and to each other. Let me cite just a few facts.

1 NATURE

The more science teaches us about the efficiency of organisms, about their unity of inner world and environment, the more marvellous it seems.

Yet this efficiency has stupefying aspects. With the accuracy of a neurosurgeon, certain insects sting the one spot of a larva's brain where it will be paralysed – not killed, but kept alive as a non-perishable food supply for later consumption.

We may be enjoying the harmony of nature by a lakeside while a ceaseless struggle of eating and being eaten goes on in the lake – and in this struggle, barring outside intervention, a balance keeps restoring itself: the eaten species are never quite finished off but will grow back in the proper quantities, to provide new nutrition. It is the cruelly efficient self-preservation of a living whole.

Nature also knows inefficient disasters. Many a splendid species or genus will die out, either no longer viable in the form in which it has evolved, or destroyed by an environmental change to which it cannot adjust. On the North Sea beaches, during the spring thaw, hundreds of thousands of seagulls and other aquatic birds run on the melting ice. Suddenly there is another cold spell. The birds freeze fast and, trying to break free, flutter themselves to death.

Man falls ill by natural processes. Organic mental illness, the approach of which some patients feel with horror, strips them of their humanity. We intern them, nurse them, treat them as humanely as possible, and if nature goes along, a large part will at least be enabled to live a free life again. Heredity works both for good and for ill.

Nature itself seems to undermine its magnificent efficiencies. Its products carry the seeds of their own destruction.

2 MAN

The pitilessness of nature obliges man to bow, unless he can master it. Not so the pitilessness of what men freely inflict upon themselves and each other.

i. Wars have always occasioned atrocities that had nothing to do with the political war aims. Most religions practised human sacrifice. The West has known witch hunts, persecution of heretics, the Inquisition. The Mongols piled the skulls of slaughtered nations into pyramids. Totalitarian states have killed millions. Under the régime that ruled in Germany from 1933 to 1945 Jewish children were torn from their mothers' arms, exposed to the agonizing fear of death, and killed only after a time of hunger and torment. An occasional delight in cruelty and a more frequent obedience in looking the other way – 'Orders are orders' – showed how men could turn into imagination-free, thoughtlessly functioning 'operators' of an extermination machinery that went from arrest to transport to the actual killing. There would be no end to a description of the horrors that fill human history and strike us as unprecedented only where we personally witnessed them or knew about them, and thus came to share the guilt.

The reality of man shows in the confusion of faith and crime. The cry 'Deus vult' set off the First Crusade, in which a self-sacrificing zeal to free the Holy Sepulchre, an ecclesiastically warranted sense of pleasing God, mingled with adventurousness and with sado-masochistic drives. The climax of the ensuing events found the Crusaders in Jerusalem, having inflicted and suffered unspeakable agonies, wading ankle-deep in blood to kneel in oddly humble prayer at the grave of Christ. (Hegel's ironic comment, 'The grave was empty', was intended to point the way to the dialectical reversal.) Has the Church, speaking ex cathedra, ever revoked this 'God wills it'? How many times have those words justified evil? They are evil, for nobody knows God's will, and the claim to know it – on whatever scale, small or large – will cause endless misery. It is the same, in effect, and equally unjustifiable when today's totalitarian powers cite 'historic necessity'. To the thought form it does not matter whether the sufferings and sacrifices are to be rewarded by a tangible bliss in the beyond or by human bliss here and now, in an earthly paradise.

ii. Our actions result from our ideas, our images, our orientations. It is how we see those – distortedly, or with their ways of truth critically distinguished – that makes out our way of life. We act on a basis of factual error or of a delusive religious 'knowledge', rarely of a critically clear knowledge of reality or the moving force of true ciphers. Thus men will fool themselves about a good world order, will plan a just society in which the state has withered away and force is unnecessary, and will seek to accomplish this by the worst terrorism and by exterminating those who are either unwilling or deemed unable to join. Whole populations such as the Albigenses were wiped out in the delusion that men could be saved only by the one Catholic truth.

What counts in the long run is the creation and dissemination of ideas and knowledge. In reality, however, this historic process seems to be more a change of delusions than a progressive comprehension of truth. Believers express themselves in religious cognition, philosophers create the concepts and the ways of thinking – but they are not the ones to move the world; the movers are those who accept or ignore or misunderstand and distort them. Those decide what will become of the ideas. The real history of human thought seems to be an unfortunate process in which great truths rise in spurts now and then, soon to be swamped again by tides of distortion.

iii. The events and conditions of human existence do not follow a thought-out human plan. Yet what man does, invents, plans, and works has consequences he neither thought nor dreamed of, consequences that are in fact incalculable. It is uncanny how these will detach themselves from man, as though persons were becoming functions of something else. The unforeseen consequences that go beyond any human will – though in retrospect there is a partly, never entirely, perceptible connection – allow us to speak of the daemonics of technology, for instance. The technological, economic, social, and political developments seem to be happening like events of nature, and yet they are always also unwitting results of the spirit in which men act. They then become premises of life for succeeding generations – and those in turn, though not under any compulsion, will freely adopt such conditions, stabilize, or change them. Thus human reality seems like a course of social events moving incalculably from crisis to crisis, from tribulation to tribulation, with no end in sight; to the intellect it finally looks hopeless. Like the products of nature, men seem to carry the seeds of their destruction from the outset. And in between lie the human joys, the moments of triumph and splendour, the greatness of men and the creations of their spirit. They make us forget the horrors. Victory determines the historic recollection. The lucky rulers of every age like to legitimize themselves by their supposed merits, by their descent, by their works – others, it appears, deserved to perish. And the failures will tend to develop the resentments that lead to a negative and hate-filled life.

World history shows its ambiguous, changing aspects: the rise of the great figures and creations; progress in knowledge and know-how, by cognition and invention; the transformation of conditions as a whole; the overpowering growth of destructiveness to a point where the swiftly approaching doom seems no longer particular but universal.

Beyond all freedom, human existence seems determined by a sombre fate that makes freedom a factor in causing what it does not want.

3 THE AMBIVALENCE OF HUMAN THINGS

Man's way leads to salvation as well as to perdition. Everything seems ambivalent if put in concepts of knowledge.

'Masses' are carriers of fancy or of truth, of malice or of exaltation.

The 'charisma' is true if based on a trust that constantly controls itself and the leader – or it is the charm of a Pied Piper, and nations, however childlike their innocence, are culpable in trailing him into the abyss.

The 'government of laws' will serve both justice and injustice.

Many of our words for basic social phenomena have either worthy or worthless connotations. 'Charismatic leader' and 'prophet' sound positive, for example; 'demagogue' and 'sect' sound negative. Sociological cognition begins with the ability to abstract from such sounds, to use the concepts for social relations or types whose ambiguity lies in their very nature. There are no value judgments implied in the sociological categories. They let us recognize typical forms of reality, at the price of draining such cognition of substance. For the substance is beyond science.

As a result we hesitate to use such words, though for different reasons. Julius Caesar was a charismatic leader, but so was Hitler. Cleon was a demagogue, but so was Pericles. We do not like to call Hitler a charismatic leader, or Pericles a demagogue; the words remind us of the high or base overtones we know from their customary usage.

The pure, critical, modest science that has relatively unequivocal results within its scope goes with philosophical insight into the ambivalence of all things human. We abuse sociological categories if we employ them for purposes of vindication. But words whose full sense exceeds that of cognitive concepts, words meant to convey substance, to enhance or demean – such words are already ciphers and implements of war.

4 THE MEASURE

A catalogue of the horrors of human reality would be as endless as one of the horrors of nature.

Yet whenever we visualize evil we do so against a yardstick, be it the beauty of nature or the good in man. The measure of human reality is that men, to be human, must join in the realm of truth.

Nature's measure is a supposition: we judge as if there could be a nature of beauty without ugliness, a life without death. The measure of the human world is another supposition: we judge as if there could be a well-made world of perfect, lasting liberty and justice, and thus a whole, true humanity.

5 THE DISTINCTION

A look at evil calls for a basic distinction between physical and moral evil. One lies in nature, the other in man. One springs from blind necessity, the other from the freedom of the seeing. By treating both alike we obscure our experience.

In man alone is nature combined with freedom. If we ask about the roots of evil in man, we confuse our judgment by failing to distinguish human nature from the effects of our freedom.

6 BASIC CONDITION AND BOUNDARY SITUATION

Tales of evil lead to what appears throughout as the fundamental situation of man. Ever since Pascal we have been speaking of la condition humaine.

Our grasp of this basic condition remains provisional. All our phrasings serve only to let us comprehend its incomprehensibility. We cannot resolve it, though we have ways to illuminate it. Let us pursue one of these to the conception of evil.

Whenever we realize something we exclude some possibilities we had before. That is what realization means: a loss of chances, a passing from the infinity of possible states into a finite real one. It gives us a place to stand on; along with the limitation, it provides a starting-point for further realization. Our basic condition is that we all face this question: can and will we hang on to the mere chance – infinite but a nullity, since it is not real – or must and will we enter into reality, which is always finite? The price we pay for this is the definitive loss of other chances. No man can realize all that he had in him.

The original reaction to this is to dread restriction. We should like to hold on to our infinite possibilities, so we balk at reality.

We look for a way out: no chance is to be lost in realization. Everything, therefore, is realized with the mental reservation that nothing will be taken up definitively. We deny, so to speak, the reality of our realization; it is to be just an experiment that can be cancelled. Life becomes a matter of trial and error. We refuse to find our identity in daring 'for ever and ever', for we feel that any limitation is a prison, and we regard as cowardice whatever might hold us in it. Adventure strikes us as the true life, the greatest joy; danger and the risk of death seem to enhance life. To preserve an infinite possibility, we spurn the ties of reality, and for the renunciation of the possibility we substitute its unreal preservation in our doom – the very waste of which becomes a way of real being.

If, on the other hand, we have the will to decide upon a finite realization, if we have the courage to identify with it, we accept the fact that we deny ourselves other chances, and that our refusal makes us guilty.

The juvenile dread of realization, the shunning of it in a succession of playful experiments – these are the initial ways of life in the basic condition. It takes the seriousness of Existenz, its quest of reality and real identity, to overcome this life, to take our chances without being able to deny the rest.

We can shed some more light on the basic condition. By excluding other possibilities in our finite realization, we violate them and incur what from their point of view is guilt. To speak in the cipher: no man can serve all gods. My failure to sacrifice to all gods and to live in line with their commandments will make me feel inadequate, but at the same time I feel my basic condition, which rules out any adequacy.

Man's basic condition is that he can never fulfil himself truly and purely, never completely, never so as to leave him content. This is where all incomprehensibility begins. The result is that we are awed by the greatness of the negation, that evil seems indeed to harbour some appealing 'truth'.

But this insight – which includes, and in a kind of honesty requires, the possibility of recognizing other powers – becomes perverted if we forget that in the real world, to preserve our existence which those powers seek to destroy, we must wage a real struggle against the strange gods and devils. It is in order to limit and ultimately to prevent this real struggle that rational beings, from their insight into the basic condition, seek by all means to achieve communication.

This involves the threat of another perversion. We should, of course, be humble in our approach to the gods to whom we do not sacrifice; we ought to respect the other, from which our own realization has removed us – but then we may yield to the dangerous pleasure of approaching all gods and devils while serving none. In this multiplicity I betray the realization in which, respecting for others what it has made impossible for me, I have become identical with myself and have thus remained faithful to one single god. I lose the existential ground under my feet. And the next step: faced with the eerie enigma of evil, I may objectify and rationalize it as an existing and therefore compulsory phenomenon. Since evil is human, it may come to seem arrogant of a responsible human being to want no part of it. So, I go in for evil and realize it myself, though not consistently.

Then I relapse into my fears at the outset of life, holding on to possibilities over realities – but now in the evil lucidity of consent. Then my knowledge of the diversity, of the varied possibilities that are narrowed in every realization and not to be realized as a whole, turns into conscious distraction in this diversity. My realization of the moment remains unserious, being accomplished with the reservation that some day I may exchange it for another. As a noncommittal, not truly realizing participant I cling to a life of indecision, where every touch is also a betrayal and infidelity becomes a principle.

A failure of humility before the seeming truth of evil shrouds the basic condition in yet another perversion. As I seek to realize a moral context of life, the good conscience of fidelity within my limitations may make me self-righteous. Proud of being right, I may scorn those not chosen to be right. In such self-certainty I lose my sense of the boundaries, and the absoluteness of a morality that has become legality makes candour and reason vanish.

The basic condition is a mode of the boundary situations – that is to say, of human situations that are immutable, unlike situations in the world. We can neither avoid nor transcend them, but their shattering impact brings us to ourselves as possible Existenz. What becomes of man in boundary situations makes out his greatness, and without considering these conditions of greatness we cannot truthfully love the nobility in it.

The inevitability of struggle, of suffering, of death, of coincidence – these are what we call boundary situations. The boundary situation in our present context is the inevitability of guilt. Man may choose to act or not to act; in either case he will be guilty.

b. The Roots of Evil

1 EVIL IS ROOTED IN MAN

Psychologists and sociologists tell us how the phenomenon of man can be analysed from his impulses and their translations, from his unconscious and his consciousness, from his disposition and his environment. This is not what I am talking about.

The point is that before all these knowable and explorable things man can feel taken by surprise and say, 'This is not I; I don't want this; I don't agree with it', or, 'This is I; in this I am myself', or, 'This I accept; I can't change it; I must make it my own'.

There we have the difference between my given existence and my free will. Moral evil does not come from nature but from free consent. In themselves, my inclinations and drives are neither good nor evil; only their free realization makes them evil or good. Evil begins with mere weakness in yielding to impulses. It grows into the will to follow my impulses in any case, without qualification. And if I go on, from instability to the autocratic will that brooks no tie or restraint, my freedom itself has dissolved in passion and turns back into a matter of psychology.

If the roots of evil lie in freedom rather than in the realm of psychological research, the question is whether philosophy can illuminate this psychologically inaccessible area. The evil in free decisions has been made perceptible, interpreted, conceived – but no concept will solve the problem of its roots for our cognition.

i. Self-will

Self-will, the first combination of freedom with the psychological drives, has been called the principle of evil.

Self-will isolates. There are no friendships among the wicked, only conditional alliances for selfish ends, with each set to pounce on the other at the first opportunity.

The self-willed rebel against law and reason. There is an analogy between their general quality and that of men of good will: the self-willed, in their sharp calculations, draw on what the intellect can know, while men of good will cleave to reason – the quality with which good will is identical. The general trait becomes a weapon to one man, a bond of union to the other.

In the absolute precedence which he accords to himself, the self-willed individual remains obscure to himself. Only in extreme cases will he see himself clearly enough to say, with Shakespeare's Richard III, 'I am determined to prove a villain'. Then, as lucid thinking combines with the blind impetus, the devil sees himself as such, and every consideration that otherwise may set unconscious limits even to self-will goes overboard. To bear this and carry it out requires a superhuman, inhuman strength of freedom in evil; the lucidity takes self-discipline in the very excess of passion, analogous to the self-control of good will. The power of disciplined, intellectually consistent, evil self-will far surpasses that of any semi-virtue; its effectiveness exposes and subjugates what only seems to be good. The self-willed defies the deity, which does not exist for him; he trusts in his own strength alone. Facing his doom, he will turn to absurd illusions or to massive superstition.

ii. Reflection

There is evil in virtue itself, because self-reflection cannot but aim at the good. To do good, I must know what is good. But once I know that my actions are good, I am already launched on what St Paul called the 'boasting' that dims or destroys virtue. A self-conscious humility amounts to pride, and he who in doing good regards himself as good has ceased to be good. One who looks upon himself as what he is has ceased to be that; he has grown self-satisfied and disparaging of others. Virtue, which no man can know and possess, becomes an aggressive moralism. Kant, therefore, differentiated between the justified pleasure in my objective act and the self-satisfaction that makes me untruthful, since I can never quite see through my ultimate motives.

'Walk in righteousness, but avoid self-righteousness,' a Chinese philosopher expressed the insight into the evil of a reflective self-affirmation of virtue. There is no teaching the smug.

iii. Kant's radical evil

Is there a will to evil as such? Kant denied it. In his view the evil principle in man is altogether different. The mere sensuality of our impulses is neither good nor evil; only the will can be good or evil. The question is in what sense we subordinate our sensual motivations to our moral ones. Which of the two mainsprings will qualify the other? Man does not mind obeying the moral law if his sensual and unlawful drives are not restricted, or not too greatly restricted. In fact, however, he ought to follow the sensual impulses only if they do not violate the moral law. This is the evil: that in fitting the mainsprings into his will he reverses the qualifying relationship. 'He makes the mainspring of self-love and its leanings a condition for complying with the moral law, whereas the latter, as the supreme condition for satisfying the former, should be fitted as sole mainspring into the general maxim of the arbitrary will.'

To rank the will to happiness, which reigns in impulses, above the absolute law that shows in reason – this is the root of evil, the tendency which Kant calls 'radical evil'.

It is not diabolical. Diabolical would be a 'malicious reason', the 'sheer ill will' that would seek the unlawful as such and 'make a mainspring of antagonism to the law itself'. But man is not a devil. It is radical evil, not devilry, that lies in every man, 'including the best'.

Where does it come from? The root of radical evil lies before and outside time; it is 'inborn' in man's temporal appearance. Yet whence the unacknowledged maxim of doing good only if it involves no great sacrifice? To Kant this is as incomprehensible as the chance of a constant restoration of the right relationship by a change in the moral way of thinking.

iv. Seclusion

We are free to be evil. I cannot be held liable for what is not in my power.

What is in my power? First and last, my own self. I can be transparent to myself, or I can seclude myself.

It seems paradoxical to ask whether man may be called purely and simply free – whether he may be required to act freely in accord with reason at every moment. But it is not enough to answer that he is either free or unfree, to be held responsible or declared irresponsible.

The secret of seclusion is that freedom may be lost by its own action. But we understand this to mean that we can regain it by an inner change – that its self-abandonment is not a natural process, no irresistible biological extinction of freedom.

Kierkegaard analysed this way of losing freedom more deeply than any before him. He showed how a desperate selfhood will want to be neither itself nor not itself, and cannot be both. I want to hide from myself and from others; I do everything to keep from revealing myself, and yet I may suddenly burst into helpless, desperate self-revelations – using these in turn as a façade for the seclusion I seek. It is the radical unwillingness to be transparent to myself that becomes the root of evil.

Telling such a man to use his freedom – a challenge which at this moment he may grasp, perhaps, but cannot really meet – may be false and unmerciful. And it is unmerciful to leave him in his isolation, to let him entangle himself more and more without noticing it. Everybody talks to him, yet at the concrete moment nobody tells him the truth, lest there be an explosion. Social conventions promote this kind of getting lost and lonely in the midst of seemingly universal intercourse.

Nothing short of loving communication can put another on the way to the change that will make him transparent to himself. As long as we fail in this sort of communication, being insufficiently transparent to ourselves and unready for the communicative venture, this source of evil will keep flowing.

2 EVIL IS ROOTED BEYOND MAN

If good and evil are rooted in man, our discussion up to this point has been appropriate. Since the dawn of history, however, men have raised entirely different questions that would stir, outrage, or bow them in resigned acceptance of the fact that they would never know.

Man feels crushed by evil without and within. Resistance helps a bit, but eventually it avails nothing. We must go beyond man to inquire into the cause of our condition.

First, whose fault is it that the world is as it is? Who or what is responsible for the existence of suffering and guilt, for this total misery?

Man is not all. He did not create himself. He is not his own source.

Is something else to blame for permitting, indeed forcing man to bear guilt? And if so, what? A supersensory being? A cosmic source? Anything God has made? Or God himself?

May man ease his own guilt, shift it, exonerate himself because he is not its ultimate source?

Secondly, while it seems right for evil deeds to beget sorrow, good deeds do not correspondingly breed good fortune. Good men do badly, evil men do well. The connection is random or accidental. The sun shines on the just and the unjust alike.

How can human existence be so unjustly directed? May I accuse the cause of things of bringing guilt upon my head? May I call it unjust?

i. The argument
There are two points of departure, and each of them directs and limits the point of the argument.

a: If there is a divine Creator of all things, he either is not all-powerful because he cannot prevent evil, or else he is not all-merciful because he permits it. If God is almighty, he is not good; if he is good, he is not almighty. Or he is not all-knowing, because in his creative act he did not foresee evil. There are two conclusions: either there is no God – for if there were one there could be no such injustice – or else the creator is not God but an evil demon.

In the Bible, man wrestles with the one personal God who is a moral God and lawgiver, a God of wrath, a loving and almighty God. The believer accuses God, the One, the supra-mundane Creator who made the world out of nothingness; he wants to understand why God makes him guilty, and why injustice dominates the world of men. The moral claim which God instilled in the human soul turns against him. As long as men do not deny his existence they will quarrel with God about God, in defiance and surrender.

b: If there is no God, however, what is there – since obviously there is not nothing? Whether it is the law of nature, matter, life, human creation, responsible will, it always leaves the same question: what kind of reality is this?

c: Only in the Bible has the line been clearly drawn. It makes other concepts seem insufficiently thought through. Even when they talk of God, and of a divine direction of the world, there is none of the high tension of the biblical struggle with God, none of the clear thinking that seeks in vain to answer the question, to unveil the mystery, to comprehend God.

ii. Ciphers of evil in history

a: India. In India, existence was felt in the context of metempsychosis. All that I am and suffer now, all my happiness and unhappiness, results from my actions *(karma)* in previous forms of existence. In my present existence I am rewarded and punished, and have the chance – by living in accordance with the law of this form of existence – to be reborn in a happier form the next time.

But where does this world come from? Among the concepts prevailing in India are these:

The world and all Being derive from an unknown primal act. The world is Maya, a cosmic dream that conceals Being and gives birth to the antitheses: pleasure and pain, rejoicing and sorrow. Both derive from Isvara, the maker, ruler, and destroyer of the world – himself part of Maya, a god in the foreground, who 'whirls about all beings as if Maya had affixed them to a wheel'. Why does this god make the world? He has no motive, being all-content, yet he would not create without knowing why; so he is playing a game – just as the Vedic Indra conjures up his foes in order to crush them.

Siva creates the world dancing and smashes all creatures in his wrath. Even Krishna, the benign world preserver and saviour, says of himself, 'I am Time, which in its course brings the world to an end, and my work here is to carry off mankind.'

As early as in the Upanishad, however, all this is perceived as Maya by the knowing, the liberated and redeemed. The knowing, in his inmost heart, is 'greater than the earth, greater than space, greater than these worlds. . . . This is the Brahma; unto him I shall enter as I depart from here'.

Buddha's word for this world-divorced Being-Nothingness – seen from the world, it is nothingness – was Nirvana.

b: China. The Shi King, the book of Chinese poems dating back to 1000 B.C., states the questions purely, in simple verse. The high heaven is infinite, but not in kindness. It sends famine and death; the mild heaven is wrathful, heedless, unsparing. The guilty pay for their misdeeds, but the guiltless topple also. Heaven shows us no mercy; is it right to crush us all?

These poets complain, but they do not really accuse, not even in their rare questions about justice. This is the way things are; to state it, to complain, to lament heartrendingly, perhaps – this, not outrage, is their attitude.

Later Chinese authors would repeat these statements of reality, these wonderments and plaints. Szu Ma Chien, a historian of the first century B.C.,[1] points to the dying of the young. A robber kills innocents daily, and yet he will live to a ripe old age; transgressors spend their entire lives in pleasure, wealth, and abundance: 'I greatly doubt whether the so-called way of heaven is just or unjust.'

This is not the historian's last word. Although, looking back sadly upon his own fate, he often speaks of the futility of candour and heroism, he does know of good men. He quotes Confucius: wealth being accidental, man had better pursue what he loves. The murkiness and squalor of the race serves to set off the pure individual. 'Similar lights reflect each other; like seeks like; human perfection does carry weight.' But then again he laments the obscurity and oblivion of the noble: 'The mountain cave-dwellers withdrawing from the world at times – how sad for such names to be buried, extinct!' Thus Szu Ma Chien justifies his historiography: he is responsible for making human beings visible in their life stories, particularly the great, perfect human beings.

Rudiments of everything the West has realized existed in the old China that was so closely akin to us: science; the path of duty regardless of certain doom; unconditional heroism; planned organization; conscious political thinking in the clash of principles. But the type of general consciousness that evolved in thousands of years came to differ increasingly from the Western one. Its basic traits can be characterized as affirmation of the world and of life in the belief in the underlying order of *tao*. Viewed on a cosmic scale, this order restores itself after any disturbance. Human nobility is harmony with the universe. In this thinking there is neither sin nor sal-

---

[1] Quoted from German translations by Chavannes and Diether von den Steinen. *Translator.*

vation, but 'complementation'. No militant dogmatic creed is laid down. There is no tragic consciousness, and no philosophical way of thought to go with it.

The consequence of complaint without accusation is to understand oneself as one with natural events. Pain becomes lucid as it is expressed without appealing to authority, without demanding, wrestling, judging.

c: Pre-Socratics. Some pre-Socratics and many later philosophers have viewed the human essence on a cosmic scale. What man experiences as law and order, what he feels in court or in himself, was conceived by these philosophers as antedating man, encompassing mankind and the world.

A line by Anaximander suggests a view of the genesis of all things: they seize their existence, thus wronging other existence, and they atone for it to one another, according to necessity and to the order of time.

The philosophical myth of Empedocles envisions the world cycles: love and strife cause the cosmos to separate and reunite over vast periods. The fate of individual things depends on their place in this process.

The Orphic idea of souls incurring a pre-temporal guilt was conceived again and again, finally by Plotinus: 'The beginning and the principle of evil for them was reckless pride, the lust of Becoming, the first Otherness, and the desire to own themselves. Thus, manifestly relishing their sovereignty, they lost the memory of their true descent. . . .'

d: Plato. Plato was the first philosopher to open his mind to the variegated tradition of speculative ciphers and to transform it with his own rich philosophical inventiveness. He would not tie himself to any of his concepts, not even while devoting his thinking energy to their systematic unfoldment, and it is inappropriate to set up one Platonic doctrine as the real, central one; his teaching is a world of suspended structures, their meanings derived from the existential power of the One they express. Hence, one who thinks along with them will be touched as Existenz, but this affection ceases wherever they are taken for fixed cognition.

Plato, seeing evil in man and the world, refused to relate it to the deity. His answer to questions about its root shows no trace of a quarrel with God; he will always say, 'God is guiltless'. But his teachings vary in line with the nature of Platonic philosophizing, and their entirety is not a system.

One of them, developed in Timaeus as 'a plausible myth', has evil, transiency, and any imperfection rooted in the world as such. Plato tells how it was made by God, the demiurge: he, the best of creators, gazed upon the eternal Ideas and formed the world in their image, as the most beautiful of created things. His unjaundiced benevolence wished all things to resemble the Ideas as much as possible. Everything was to be as good as possible; nothing was to be all bad.

Yet the benevolent cosmic architect came up against a limit: he found everything in confused, lawless motion. He brought order out of the disorder; but he could do so only 'as far as possible', since he was making the world out of a principle that was neither divine nor divinely created. Plato called this principle *chora*, empty space – a non-existence that is not nothingness, however, and later came to be identified with matter. From this material God formed the world as an artist forms his work, but an irremediable flaw was left on it by the material – a flaw that Plato called *ananke*, necessity. The world is thus composed of reason and necessity, but so that reason will govern necessity by persuading it to lead most things to a good end. This necessity is not the legality we are accustomed to connect with the term; it is the irregular and variable, the accidental, opaque basis of the world *(Statesman)*. Necessity has brought chaotic instability into the world in which only the most divine of beings, such as the stars, are constant and enduring. The world derives its beauty from its maker, and everything ugly and unjust from its material base.

Plato carried this idea further. The demiurge, he said, left the making of the world to the world soul he created; but that shifting material also has a soul, called the wicked world soul, and this is the source of evil. On the whole, however, our world is still 'the greatest and best, the most beautiful and perfect, the one and inborn world, a sensorily perceptible image of the God to whom reason alone grants us access'.

These cosmic views do not exhaust Plato's thoughts about evil. His Socratic dialogues suggest that it comes from not knowing – for no man can knowingly do evil. (This 'knowing' is not what we call intellectual knowledge but philosophical knowledge, the simultaneous practice of inner action, which makes evil evaporate.) And where does not knowing come from? Plato lays it to the soul's existence in the body. Our souls are in our bodies because of a plunge from the realm of pure spirits. The rational soul is like a team of horses, one gentle and one fractious; all confusion and disorder is due to the fractiousness of the one horse.

In the end, neither 'not knowing' nor the ties to the body could satisfy Plato. To his mind there was still something quite incomprehensible in evil, a 'pathological urge that may develop in men as a result of misdeeds not atoned for, and that will rise to plague them, now here, now there' *(Laws)*.

All Plato's interpretations, however firmly stated at the time, remain ciphers. What runs unchanged through his teachings is the untouchable deity on the one hand, and on the other the human responsibility that he states in the cipher of the souls' choice of their lots in life: 'The daemon will not cast your lot; you will choose your daemon. . . . The guilt lies with the choosers. God is guiltless' *(Republic)*.

e: Tragedy. The tragic consciousness was realized supremely by Aeschylus, Sophocles, and Euripides on the premise of the Greek myths, and by Shakespeare on the premises of Western, Graeco-Roman, Norse, and Christian traditions. It is no philosophical system; but philosophy is inherent in the ciphers which these men created for Transcendence and for human attitudes: the welcoming of existential possibilities evoked by Transcendence; the lasting question; the pride and humility of freedom; the sense of greatness and truth in failure.

The sight of such failure bares the bottom of things to the living who are aware of their own peril. They come to feel the bounds of what they are. They sense Being in the ciphers of events, of characters, of a thinking that includes philosophical motives in the way the characters and choruses think. Viewers are uplifted by the unveiled truth, by the positive and negative examples of human greatness. Their own fate is transfigured in this greatness.

Tragic reality must become conscious and effective in tragic knowledge. As the ancients said that Achilles calls for Homer, so the Greek fate called for Greek tragedy, and man's fate for the tragic ciphers.

They manifest the imperfection and imperfectibility, the brittleness of being human. There is no one true, definitive humanity. Each form of man has not only its own limits; each will die of being human, of its faults, its errors, its guilt, its ill fate.

The tragic consciousness knows no salvation by any supersensory gift of grace. The abysses in Shakespeare, his questioning experiences of human limits, are not matched by Calderon whose tragic side remains a foreground for the certainties of Christian faith. The tragic consciousness knows the deliverance of man in the stern imperviousness of the very question, placed into the realm of infinitely varied ciphers of Transcendence.

Philosophical ideas come to be elements within the encompassing pictures of tragic events, occurring not as a principle of tragic consciousness but as thoughts of particular figures – as in the exculpation of the deity. 'Whatever the gods do is never evil,' said Sophocles. 'If gods do wrong they are not gods,' said Euripides.

iii. The dualism of good and evil powers

The question of the roots of evil ceases with the assertion of two equally original powers. In Persia, Zarathustra conceived existence as the struggle of light and darkness, good and evil, Ormuzd and Ahriman. The world they pervade is their battlefield, and every individual is involved in the combat. At the devil's hands he must suffer what God cannot shield him from. He must decide whether to aid God or the devil. Not till the end of days will the evil power be crushed – again with human help – and good will triumph, the devil will sink into nothingness, and suffering will cease along with evil.

Some form of dualism always appears in the question.

In India it was resolved by the dualism of the endlessly continuing world, this endless repetition of living and dying in the cycle of rebirths, and the eternal repose of Being-Nothingness, the dreamless sleep of Nirvana.

Christianity adopted the devil, but conceived him from the very start as subject to the deity. Even so, dualism kept its power under the veil of theological simplification, because a glance at the evils of man and the world will make its cipher evident.

The cipher 'God *vs.* devil' has gone through the ages. Man is no devil. Can the devil of the cipher become flesh, as God did in Jesus Christ? We deny both of these ciphers. The devil himself can no more appear in human form than God himself. In the reality of such beliefs God has incarnated himself only once and for ever, victorious in immeasurable agony and failure, while the devil did so many times and essentially suffered defeat even in his triumphs. In the centuries between medievalism and modernity, disbelief in the devil – and in the necessity of having priests exorcize him – was sometimes considered no less heretical than disbelief in the incarnated God.

The terrified will always hear the cipher of the devil. There is no reality without an element that may be diabolically manifested, and this means that if I want to live and act in the world I have to deal with the devil. It does not mean that the world as such is diabolical, as some of the Gnostics held. Nor does it mean that I must bargain with the devil, or compromise with him. It does mean that I enter into areas where the devil will be met and that I may succumb to him whether he plagues and destroys me from without, through others, or whether he invades my soul and makes it his tool.

The brighter my consciousness, the more decisively will it exclude any unconscious bargains with the devil – but the more decisively too will the diabolical be recognized at each of its pernicious stages, down to the worst that men inflict upon each other. It will be felt in its first rudiments, forced to reveal itself, and fought.

Thus we may speak in the dualistic ciphers. They are simple, clear, and inescapable, due to the dualistic nature of our intellectual thinking. Their simplicity, compared with all our compounding, concealing, and facilitating, makes them signposts in concrete situations of man's struggle with himself. But they seem abstract, provisional, and untrue if we think of unity in the form of the one God, and of its ciphers.

iv. The personal God indicted

The unresolved tension over the roots of evil and wrong will rise to a peak if two premises are clearly kept in mind.

First, all things come from one, from the One. Every antithesis, whether dualistic or polar, is secondary.

Secondly, the One is the one personal God, the almighty, all-merciful, all-knowing fount of the moral law.

The more powerful, personal, moral, and exclusive the concept of this one God, the more impassioned the question. It goes from the human person to the divine person. Because all things have come from the personal primal being that made the world out of nothing, this primal being must answer for what exists.

One 'solution' in biblical thinking is to state the insolubility. It happens in two ways: in the thinking of Job, and in the doctrine of predestination. Both conceive the personal God as an incomprehensibly superior power they bow to. Injustice, the morally impossible, is accepted as unfathomable. Man has no question left to ask of God, and no charge to prefer.

But it is easy to say, 'There is no solution', and it is evasive simply not to know and be done with it. What this not knowing means depends on how we experience it, how the question – posed as if an answer had to be possible, had to be urged – will pierce and then reconstitute our ignorance. It keeps returning us to the thought movements that drift about our consciousness of ourselves and of God, movements whose rational clarification is idle.

Job

The facts refute the thesis that evil is the just punishment of ungodly conduct by individuals and nations. The consequences, for the state of mind of an innocently suffering man of integrity, unfold in the tale of Job and in the thoughts sprung from his relentlessly visualized experience.

Jehovah, certain of his pious servant Job, hears Satan doubt the unselfishness of Job's motives: does God not reward his piety by augmenting his house and possessions? So God permits Satan to test Job, to take away all he has, except his life. Satan does so. Job loses his children, his wealth, his health; his festering sores make men shun him, but he does not die.

Suffering does not change Job: 'The Lord gave, and the Lord hath taken away; blessed be the name of the Lord.' His wife taunts him, 'Curse God, and die!' And he replies, 'Shall we receive good at the hand of God, and shall we not receive evil?'

Three friends come to show their sympathy and to console him. Silently they sit with him for days and nights, until he speaks; then the great waves of talk surge to and fro without any real discussion. Job's theological friends advance pious theses and arguments; he perceives their falsehood, and the seeming weight of their arguments adds to his indignation. The one he really addresses, questions, upbraids, accuses in talking to the theologians is the silent Jehovah. He wants to plead his case before him but receives no answer. Finally God appears. He hurls Job back within the limits of his understanding, but forgives him while scorning the theologians; only for Job's sake are they left unpunished. Job himself begins a new, happy life, sees four new generations of his progeny, and dies 'old and full of days'. So much for the story.

The plot of the dramatic frame moves from Job's naïve, unquestioning piety to the climax of his charges against the God he seeks and cannot find, and back to his original pious assurance. Yet this has now been transformed. If the accusing reflection solved nothing, it did change Job. It kindled the glow of an Existenz that could not have come into being without that reflection.

The Book of Job is not the work of one man. The author of the old legend, the narrative frame, has been distinguished from the poet of Job's indictment in the passionately flowing dialogues, from the writer of the theoloical tract delivered by Elihu, and from the creator of the withering speech in which God points out the unfathomable grandeur of the universe – and these distinctions still leave smaller portions of peculiar beauty unaccounted for. Job's powerful emotion holds the centre, but his thoughts are not merely those of the principal poet; they reflect the thinking and writing of later-day Jews whose sole concern was what God is and does. The work is a collaboration, so to speak, based on the ancient legend, launched by the first great Jobian poet, and continued by several others. Its unity rests on the basic question to which everything relates. Solutions are set forth and passionately argued, but in the nature of the case the one solution a reader expects does not come. The following interpretative arrangement disregards the textual sequence.

a: Job laments and wants to die. 'In the days when God preserved' him, Job was rich and honoured, surrounded by a large family and helping all those he met. Now he lives in the cliffs of the valley, ostracized as a leper and shunned even by the jeering rabble. 'My bones are pierced in me in the night season; and my sinews take no rest.' Frightening dreams disturb his slumber.

He curses the day he was born; he has no hope left, no help to wait for, His strength fails, for it is not the strength of a rock. 'My breath is corrupt, my days are extinct. . . .' He wants only to die. 'I loathe it; I would not live always. . . . That it would please God to destroy me. . . .'

b: The theologians want to help with proper doctrine. Evil, they say, is God's punishment for sin. Job's children died for transgressions he did not know about, and he himself must have sinned and be suffering for that reason. The theologians cite chapter and verse: 'God will not cast away a perfect man, neither will he help the evildoers. . . . The triumphing of the wicked is short, though his excellency mount up to the heavens', for 'the snare is laid for him' and 'the heavens shall reveal his iniquity.'

What makes them so sure of this doctrine? Job's friends claim to have researched it and found it so. Later they call it handed down by 'wise men' who got it 'from their fathers'.

Reminded of a righteous man who is suffering anyway, they ask how any man can 'be justified with God? How can he be clean that is born of a woman?'

Lastly they point out that Job's troubles may not be a punishment at all. They may be a test; God may be giving him a chance to prove himself, for 'he delivereth the poor in his affliction, and openeth their ears in oppression'.

The basic truth is always the same: God is just. He cannot be perverting justice.

c: Job cites the injustice of human existence. The world refutes this doctrine. What the theologians call the troubles of the wicked are the troubles of mankind, just or unjust. Man's lot is the toil and trouble of hirelings, and his life is as fleeting as a shadow; he who goes down to the grave comes up no more. This is true of all men. But robbers prosper; they spurn God, yet they are secure. The wicked beat the timbrel and the harp; they rejoice and die at ease, yet they say to God, 'Depart from us!' Their houses are safe from fear, and none dare reproach them or exact retribution, while the luckless are laughed to scorn, and those who stumble are despised. . . .

Job's plaint becomes an indictment. He blames God for the state of the world. It is God who has wrought all this, who takes away the understanding of the aged, who increases nations and destroys them and disheartens the princes of the earth – all at random. 'Lo, mine eye hath seen all this. . . . When I remember I am afraid, and trembling taketh hold on my flesh. Wherefore do the wicked live, become old, yea, are mighty in power?'
d: Job answers the question from his own experience. His answer: It is not true that I am guilty. My conscience is clear.

The charges mount. It is plain: God has indeed perverted justice. Why? 'He taketh away, who can hinder him?' He uses force, and none can resist his power. Job feels and sees that God counts him as one of his enemies – and for no reason. This is what his whole experience looks like: God has attacked him, hurled his arrows at him, massed his troops against him. 'He hath destroyed me, and mine hope hath he removed like a tree. . . . Therefore am I troubled at his presence; when I consider, I am afraid of him.' The Almighty has broken his spirit, stunned him, ringed him with darkness. 'My face is foul with weeping.'

The indictment culminates in an outburst: 'This is one thing, therefore I said it: He destroyeth the perfect and the wicked! If the scourge slay suddenly, he will laugh at the trial of the innocent.'

The theologians imply that Job claims to be guiltless, but he never does. He speaks of the iniquities of his youth, of his transgressions – only, why will God not pardon them? To prove his veracity, he recalls that unlike Adam he never hid his sin.

But on the issue of guilt in the sense of his theological friends he will not yield. 'God forbid that I should justify you. . . . My righteousness I hold fast, and will not let it go; my heart shall not reproach me so long as I live.'
e: The theologians offer comfort by means of advice. Their comfort is the doctrine to which they cling against all evidence: that suffering and evil are distributed among men as punishment fitting their guilt. Punishment may serve to reform or to deter; either way, it is a benefit. Job, they say, has forgotten the true doctrine and so is wrongly accusing God, compounding his misery. He should not despise the chastening of the Almighty. He should turn to God and beg his counsel: 'I would seek unto God, and unto God would I commit my cause, Which doeth great things and unsearchable.' Where God wounds, his hands make whole. If Job proves faithful and permits no wrong in his

house, the friends feel sure that he can lift up his countenance, will forget all trouble and torment, and may in the end rebuild his house.

f: Job wants truth. Job is outraged by such counsels. He wants truth. 'Teach me, and I will hold my tongue; cause me to understand wherein I have erred ... but what does your arguing prove?' Honest, straight talk would help, and truth alone can comfort. 'How then comfort ye me in vain, seeing in your answers there remaineth falsehood?'

g: Job wants communication. The worst of his misery is his isolation. Friends and kinsmen have failed him; his acquaintances avoid him; his own servant no longer heeds his entreaties, and his wife is sickened by his breath.

This is the state in which he talks to the theologians: 'Have pity upon me, have pity upon me, O ye my friends; for the hand of God hath touched me. Why do ye persecute me?' He begs them to look, though they may shudder: 'Look upon me, for it is evident unto you if I lie.' He wants valid answers, he wants clarity in human discourse. 'Hear my speech,' he implores them, 'and let this be your consolations!' If they let him speak, they can mock him afterwards. He wants at least the minimum chance to communicate – if only, for once, they will listen!

h: Job will risk all for the truth and God. 'I will not refrain my mouth; I will speak in the anguish of my spirit. . . .' His misery is now secondary. He wants to win justice for one reason only: to make sure of justice itself and to let truth prevail.

He speaks to his friends, the theologians, because men are a man's only partners in conversation, but his words are aimed at God. 'Is my complaint to man?' He is addressing God, and though God does not answer, Job never doubts his existence. He will say what torments his heart. 'Let come on me what will! Wherefore do I take my flesh in my teeth, and put my life in mine hand? Though he slay me. . . .' All he wants is to place his conduct before God. This 'shall be my salvation, for an hypocrite shall not come before him'.

'Make me to know my transgression and my sin,' Job demands. 'Do not condemn me; shew me wherefore thou contendest with me!'

i: Job appeals to God against God. A trial at law between him and God? Job realizes that such a thing cannot be.

True, he did think and keeps thinking that he should answer God, that they 'should come together in judgment'. If only God would withdraw his oppressive hand and 'take his rod away' – then Job's heart would feel free to 'speak and not fear him'. But this is not the way it is. There are no legal proceedings between God and man. A man can meet only a man at the bar of justice; there is no one to arbitrate between man and God.

Job is impelled by two irreconcilable motives.

First, the God who shakes the earth, who wields lightning and thunder, who overturns mountains without their knowledge, has not only more power than man – he has all power, and man, his creature, has none. How, then, should he arraign God? As a human being, Job is in a different position.

God has ringed him with snares. 'Behold, I cry out of wrong, but I am not heard; I cry aloud, but there is no judgment.' He has no way out: 'If I justify myself, mine own mouth shall condemn me; if I say I am perfect, it shall also prove me perverse.' Job would have to beg God's mercy, as an enemy's, but even that would not help, for God does not answer. He smites Job with a tempest and multiplies his wounds without cause. 'Who hath hardened himself against him, and hath prospered?' Hence Job's incessant, consuming plaint and complaint: 'Wherefore hidest thou thy face, and holdest me for thine enemy?' Job is not God's enemy. But God is Job's.

Secondly, however, Job seeks in God the righteous judge. 'Oh that I knew where I might find him!' This is the trouble: 'He goeth by me, and I see him not; he passeth on also, but I perceive him not.'

No disappointment can extinguish Job's yearning. Over and over he passionately tries to plead his case: 'Oh that my words were now written! oh that they were graven in the rock. . . . Call thou, and I will answer; or let me speak, and answer thou me. How many are mine iniquities and sins?'

Despite the God he must now view as his merciless foe, Job remains sure of the God who will testify in his behalf. 'Behold, my witness is in heaven, and my record is on high. . . .' If he could plead his case before God he feels certain that the Almighty would uphold rather than destroy him. And this, not an act of arbitrary despotism, would be God's grace – for a righteous man would be disputing with God, and the divine judge would not torment him. 'He knoweth the way that I take; when he hath tried me, I shall come forth as gold.'

God *vs.* God – this is the situation. God, who helps truth to prevail, against God the despot who strikes fear into Job's heart.

Job wants God *and* the truth. His only thought, his sole passion, is to find no conflict between the two that seem to be in such frightful contradiction. (Throughout the Book of Job no further mention is made of the beginning of the legend – which, after all, justifies Job at the start, for Satan, not God, has caused all his troubles. Satan, not God, is the enemy Job keeps feeling. God has only permitted Satan to proceed so as to test Job.)

There is no pride in Job, no defiantly heroic self-reliance. No, he weeps, laments, cries out in horror – not from weakness, but by virtue of his moral sense. The combination of his hunger for truth and his yearning for God puts him into his contradictory moods: a will to live and a longing to die, despair and confidence, embitterment, biting irony, weariness, and the unshakable belief in the God he cannot stop questioning. And facing all this we see the monotonous, fanatical, calm but inventive religious knowledge of the theologians.

Job's basic experience is that God does not answer, that no authority, no tribunal, no umpire will hear his defence of himself and the truth against God.

It is the experience of Transcendence – supersensory, beyond reason, above Being, yet turned into a 'Thou' by the cipher of the personal God. Only by this humanization of the superhuman can man and Transcendence meet in language. On this level Transcendence becomes a Thou that man can talk to, pray to, appeal to for understanding when inconceivable evil drives him to despair.

Nowhere in the world has the urge to turn God's overwhelming omnipotence into a tangibly real Thou been stronger than among the Jews. It was they who bequeathed it to the West; it was they – epitomized in the poet of Job – whom the Thou led to the desperate insolubilities. Transcendence and man are as incomparable as the infinite and the finite, yet the divine Thou brings Transcendence into the finite realm in question and answer, to judge in finite categories such as right and wrong or good and evil, and to be judged by its actions. The insolubilities are honed to razor-sharpness in the situation of the individual crushed by calamity. He must, so to speak, split the Thou of encompassing Transcendence, appealing to God against God. Then the insolubility shatters the reality of the embodied cipher; embodiment will be transcended, but the cipher, as a possible suspended cipher, will remain.

Job in his piety can follow up his passionate outbursts of demanding truth and justice with moments of resignation, of simple pleas that God ignore him and let him alone, let him live in the dependence of being human: 'All the days of my appointed time will I wait, till my change come.' The pious man's end, then, would be: 'Thou shalt call, and I will answer thee; thou wilt have a desire to the work of thine hands.' But this, Job sees, is not God's way.

j: Job makes us feel man's ambiguous relation to God. α: With God, no man is just; man is always wrong. These theses may state God's despotism or the very opposite, his omnipotent love. The second interpretation permits a man such as Kierkegaard to experience God's love in all evil, in the way he was born, in events that plague and destroy him. In Kierkegaard's view, God is using him as an 'exception' – but man cannot know this and cannot use it in turn to justify his life and actions. His uncertainty in suffering is the will of God who performs an act of his love in making man suffer.

But the God whom the believing theologian sees, the executor of the moral world order, is not God at all. This is the point of Job's indignation, of the fierce irony with which he tells his friends, 'I know it is so of a truth; but how should man be just with God?' Arguing with God, the almighty despot, is meaningless. But the biting reply conveys at the same time what the whole Book of Job makes plain: the categories of right and wrong, of meaning and meaningless, cease where the question concerns God himself.

β: God created man. Man owes his existence to him. But this creation is ambiguous. Why did God do it – to have a creature to torment?

Job knows that he is not innocent – no man is – but the persecution to which God exposes him is out of all proportion to his guilt. You, he cries to God, count my steps and watch for me to stumble; you spy on me and repay me for sins of my youth; you circle my footprints and search for my iniquity though you know I am not wicked; if I strayed, you seal up my transgressions in a bag and never cleanse me of my guilt. No man can stand that. 'Thou destroyest the hope of man. . . .'

Water erodes a stone, and man is far less able to bear being hounded by God, tormented, toyed with, driven to and fro like a leaf, and pursued like dry stubble.

Why does God do it? 'Why hast thou set me as a mark against thee? Is it good unto thee that thou shouldest oppress?' God made man as the clay; does he wish to reduce him to dust again? 'Thine hands have made me and fashioned me together round about; yet thou dost destroy me.'

And why does it happen to man, this slight, insignificant creature whose days are troubled, who blooms like a flower and is cut down, who flees like a shadow and has no place? A fallen tree may sprout again, but man dies, and where is he? Yet despite his triviality, God sets his heart upon man and will try him, visit him day after day. 'What is man that thou shouldest magnify him?' Job cries, looking at the wretched creature.

What these laments do is to reveal the ambiguity of the relationship. They give us nothing to know about God and man, but they deny us the tranquillity of unequivocal thinking.

k: *God appears, rebuffs Job, but condemns the theologians.* Suddenly, out of the blue, God himself appears. Will he answer Job's ceaseless appeal? No. 'Where wast thou when I laid the foundations of the earth?' God asks in turn. He points to his Creation, to the power and glory of nature; he pictures the majesty of the universe and the wonders of specific phenomena. Job understands none of it. He was not present at the Creation.

Job is silenced. 'Who is this that darkeneth counsel by words without knowledge?' God demands of him. And in closing: 'Shall he that contendeth with the Almighty instruct him? . . . Wilt thou disannul my judgment?' God humbles Job, asking questions that Job cannot answer. He cites his irresistible might: 'Canst thou thunder with a voice like him?' All pleas for comprehensibility or vindication are rejected out of hand.

Job bows. 'Once I have spoken, but I will proceed no farther. . . . I know that thou canst do every thing . . . things too wonderful for me, which I knew not. . . . I have heard of thee by the hearing of the ear, but now mine eye seeth thee.'

Yet now comes the crux: God casts Job back within his bounds, for asking questions beyond the human sphere – but Job has acted truthfully, albeit presumptuously; so God does not condemn him. He does spurn the theologians, however: 'My wrath is kindled . . . for ye have not spoken of me the thing that is right, as my servant Job hath.' Job asked what no man can know, but the theologians claimed to know it. They denounced Job's love of truth as pride. While deciding against questions that are humanly unanswerable, God forgives the truthful questioner; but he condemns the untruthful theologians for asserting a knowledge that is humanly impossible. He favours Job's honesty over their dishonesty. He will spare them only at Job's prayer.

Is this scene a solution? If the faith in the tangible, thundering God were now a matter of knowledge, there would be a new dogma – a brief, flatly negative, depressing one, the very type for the theologians who have only just been disavowed.

The point is to overcome the reflections on truth and justice, not to destroy them. God, unlike the theologians, accepts these reflections on account of their veracity. But he leads Job beyond the point where thinking circles about itself and congeals – he leads him to a sphere where thinking does indeed cease, but in a luminosity that would be impossible except for the thoughts that have been overcome.

God wants truthfulness, not blind obedience. God wants freedom, not unquestioning surrender.

At the moment of epiphany, the divine presence is merely crushing, overpowering. In fact, there is no epiphany. This – as Kant put it, speaking in the cipher – is a characteristic of eternal wisdom, as helpful in what it denies as in what it grants: it wants us to be free rational creatures, not puppets or slaves.

1: *Structure, supplements, and editing of the book.* The book rests on the fact that it is Satan, not God, who torments Job. Job rightly perceives this hostile power but mistakes it for God. Of God's wager with Satan he does not know and will never hear. The myth, in which God lets Satan go ahead to test Job's piety, might seem to bring a solution right at the start, but this is not the case. The Book of Job plumbs the depths of the question what it means to be human in the world before Transcendence, and when things get that serious such a fairy-tale solution will no longer work. So it is not mentioned any more.

What the legend tells – after Job's piety was known to God from the outset, and after he then proved his veracity by wrestling with God to the point of desperation – is the tale of his new good fortune.

This ending might disappoint us. Does it not reintroduce the theory of reward and punishment, giving Job his just recompense? We can interpret it differently. Rather than as a reward, we can view the new good fortune as a consequence. For Job has never thought of it, has not reckoned with it for a moment in his manner of living. The beginning of the legend, the sense of pious submission to the divine decree, is repeated at the end. The whole rich import of the main section is not lost, but transcended. Piety was the initial simple, unreflecting, unilluminated truth, and it is the truth that Job regains at the end – not as the product of reflection, but as the language of a fundamental attitude that cannot be understood, only experienced without reason or cause, in the gift of self. Without this attitude man is left helpless. In the world he cannot find a self-reliant tranquillity that might include all men.

What occurs in this legend, as well as in the developing revolt against God in the course of seeking God, is utterly alien to the tragic consciousness. But the friendly cipher of the happy end belongs as much to Job's piety as do his extreme charges against God.

m: Consequences of the Book of Job for religious thinking. Has man ever talked to God as he talks in the Job story? Where has so much devotion to God been linked with so much rebellion? Can there be a pious rebellion?

The possibility exists only when the cipher of the personal God is first enhanced into one sole omnipotent Creator and then believed as present and tangible, even though invisible and hidden. The measure of tension between confidence and revolt, between the faith in a divine moral order and the honestly inescapable recognition of contrary realities, was bound to prove disruptive – not of piety, but of the tangibility of the cipher. For it became apparent that as the cipher of the personal God grows most power- ful, as it becomes tangible and absolute, it breaks asunder.

Its power lies in the passion it arouses on the ground of this divine tangibility – when man, the man who believes in the personal Thou of Transcendence as the final, absolute authority rather than as a cipher, lives in the hope and expectation that this Thou will personally speak to him, will hear and answer his complaints and his questions.

But the tangibility of the divine personality is bound to split on the rock of its enhancement into an absolute – for God, then, shows not one face but several irreconcilable faces.

This is the situation realized in the Book of Job. There have been two seeming solutions.

One is orthodox Judaism, the religion of the law, which regards Job's questions as solved by God's revelations. This kind of Judaism brought the book into its present form. Historically, notably since Ezra, it prevailed over the great prophetic Jewish religion; but it never exhausted the biblical faith of the Jews, who use what a pious Talmudic scholar once called to me 'the tin cans of the law' to preserve the precious content through the ages, to the end of days when God will appear and make the tin cans superfluous. Yet this end of days is an eschatological cipher; we would have to test its strength, to feel the appeal of a reality we can live by. As a principle of life in the world and a justification of the religious law it will convince denominational believers, not historic humanity.

The second solution is the orthodox Christian faith, formalized by Jews who adopted it after the execution of Jesus. There the God of wrath, who crushes man with the horrors that go on in the world, had appeared in his love, suffering all physical evil himself and blotting out all moral evil by his pure humanity. Whatever Job's charges, they could no longer be brought against a God who took all suffering upon himself. The believer was rid of God's shattering inconceivability, for the incarnated God met him as a real partner, a human Thou. The way to God was opened on a human level, as a way from man to man. But Jesus is a man who lived once, while Christ is the God whom the faithful saw in Jesus, in retrospect. With the human Jesus we can speak only as we speak with any of the dead: we listen to them and conclude, from their words and actions, what they would now tell us in reply to our questions. We do not get their real answers. Because the God who became flesh has passed away as a man – because, indeed, he can be Christ only since his passing – the new cipher 'Christ', if meant to be more than a cipher, raised new impossibilities that have confounded the most artfully framed theology for almost two thousand years.

Both solutions start out from the situation of the biblical faith. This situation is held fast to this day in both Christianity and Judaism, wherever faith survives the wrenching tension of reality, and in both cases it manifests itself in the recurrent clash between freedom and dogmatism. Freedom might win in this clash, with a return to the personal Thou as a cipher, but that would not end the struggle of ciphers. The problem of Job remains.

n: The struggle between dogmatism and freedom. This conflict goes through the Book of Job. The dialogue reflects the tension between the self-certainty of the theologians and Job's desperate search for truth.

The theologians own the pure doctrine. It rests on the wisdom of their fathers: 'For we are but of yesterday, and know nothing, because our days on earth are a shadow.' The only support is the soil of tradition, and those who uproot themselves are the wicked who forget God. The very place such a one tears himself from 'shall deny him, saying, I have not seen thee', and his 'trust shall be a spider's web. . . '. But a good man rooted in this soil will never be cast off by God.

They threaten Job: he is walking in the paths of those who forget God. He will not receive the law. He flouts the fear of God, and derides reverent prayer. 'Thine own mouth condemneth thee . . . that thou turnest thy spirit against God.'

On his own, without traditional doctrine, Job wants to understand God – what effrontery! 'Art thou the first man that was born? . . . Hast thou heard the secret of God? . . . What knowest thou that we know not?' And the worst of crimes: 'Thou hast said, My doctrine is pure. . . .'

Propound a doctrine, in fact, is precisely what Job does not do. He only makes plain that the one propounded to him cannot be true. He does refuse to bow to tradition; he wants God, not human wisdom. He is in earnest about God as the cause of all things, and thus of his own experience. His concern is not with theology but with God. That is his rebellion.

But are the theologians not saying the very thing God says at the end? They ask whether Job heard God's secret, and God asks where Job was when the earth was made. Since in the end he bows to the second challenge, why will he not bow to the first? Because the use of the words gives them two very different meanings. The theologians want to lay the ground for forcing Job to acknowledge their doctrine – and he wants no doctrine. But God, while warning Job to stay within the bounds of man, rejects the doctrine of the theologians far more radically. They mean submission to a human authority that claims to be God's truth; God means humility in the free human quest. As the theologians use it, the word that God is unfathomable sounds like a statement of dogmatic knowledge, a club to strike down any challenge to authoritative doctrine; when Job hears the same word from God, it liberates him from theological knowledge as well as from his own presumptuous claim to know. The facts refute the theological dogmatics; if Job shows signs of a new, negative dogmatics, they come from a misconception of his own will, which God relegates to its limits. To the theologians, dogmatic knowledge is primary and valid; in Job's case it is the temptation to misunderstand himself that may turn his quest into a doctrine.

His clash with the theologians resembles the clash of two incarnated roots of the human potential. To point up the sharpness of the altercation, the poet has so characterized the individuals that they seem like archetypes of what we note to this day in contending with theologians, though in feebler and less serious forms. The mutual incomprehension seems due to a sense of danger to one's own Existenz, hence the struggle is waged on both sides with a passion the poet expresses in a flood of invective. For the first time in history we hear the tone to which we have grown accustomed.

The theologians: 'Wherefore are we counted as beasts? . . . Should a man full of talk be justified? Should thy lies make men hold their peace? . . . Vain knowledge. . . . Fill his belly with the east wind. . . . Unprofitable talk. . . .'

Job: 'How long will ye vex my soul, and break me in pieces with words? . . . Miserable comforters are ye all! Shall vain words have an end? . . . Forgers of lies . . . physicians of no value. . . .' He also threatens: 'Be ye afraid of the sword!' He even curses them: 'Let mine enemy be as the wicked. . . .'

There is contemptuous indignation on both sides, but not the same kind. One is the indignation of fanaticism clinging to dogma, the other the indignation of a free faith that turns to Transcendence and demands truth. Is there a standpoint superior to both, from which we might tell which is right? None that both would acknowledge. Man must choose at his peril. In time, one might say, freedom needs its dogmatic antithesis to become aware of itself, to understand its own venture, to awaken from self-oblivion. But this would be said from the detached, unphilosophical point of view of a spectator assuming a divine position of superior knowlege. We are not serious if we are just looking on.

Job's worst experience is that his theological friends talk to him, but not with him. They talk abstractly, lovelessly, without putting themselves in his place. Again his agony makes him ironical: 'I also could speak as ye do, if your soul were in my soul's stead!' He would make up fine words and shake his head and sympathetically cluck his tongue; the very motion of his lips would assuage their grief, he tells them.

His friends, self-assured in their teachings, are pitiless, inwardly aloof from the individual and his experience of evil. Their piety is unemotional, content to believe on the basis of ancestral doctrine, without the passion of Job. They want to stay sheltered. They know they are with the mass, with the fortunate and with the fortune seekers, and they turn on Job: 'He teareth himself in his anger; shall the earth be forsaken for thee?'

Job vainly seeks an infinite consolation: to find that man, who exists with other men, is a companion of his fate before Transcendence. The other consolation – by the messages or pledges of a doctrinal authority claiming to have been divinely instituted – fails him.

He is able to hear and to speak the mighty language of ciphers. Where they are embodied, however, his passion for truth and his faith in God break through the dogmas he recognizes as man-made. He feels driven to God, not to the work of men.

And he cannot return to his identical piety of the beginning. This was true, but as yet it was not questioning; and the poet conceives a God who wants truth rather than blind obedience – a God who wants freedom and surrender, but not an unquestioning surrender to an authority or doctrine in the world.

Job's surrender to God is shown by the poet in the cipher of the great concluding scene. When the inconceivable wonders of Creation are pointed out, moving Job to resign himself, the speaker is God. What the poet has God say cannot be transformed into theology; the poetic cipher of God's humbling of Job would be meaningless as the demand of a mundane authority. What speaks in it is the faithful Job's inner action in coming to himself, constantly reborn of question and defiance. It does not end up in a new dogma of knowing that we cannot know – one rather easy to profess and apt to result in a dull, unquestioning suspension of thinking. The cipher brings the act of knowing to fulfilment, in a 'not knowing' that is encompassing, not consciously split into subject and object. But no cipher can be held fast. Whether it is an idea or an image, it can be neither known nor embodied; it remains suspended and evanescent in the movement of our temporal imagination.

The Doctrine of Predestination

Historical introduction. It was St Paul who introduced an idea that enraptures men and plunges them into despair at the same time. Borrowing several phrasings from Job, he said (Romans 9) that as unborn children, having done neither good nor evil, we are what we are by the free election of God. No human merit can alter this election; man is for ever what he is. He has no free will that might change it by good works.

What shall we say then? Is there unrighteousness with God? God forbid. For he saith to Moses, I will have mercy on whom I will have mercy, and I will have compassion on whom I will have compassion. So then it is not of him that willeth, nor of him that runneth, but of God that sheweth mercy. . . . Therefore hath he mercy on whom he will have mercy, and whom he will he hardeneth. Thou wilt say then unto me, Why doth he yet find fault? For who hath resisted his will? Nay but, O man, who art thou that repliest against God? Shall the thing formed say to him that formed it, Why hast thou made me thus? Hath not the potter power over the clay, of the same lump to make one vessel unto honour, and another unto dishonour? What if God, willing to shew his wrath, and to make his power known, endured with much long-suffering the vessels of wrath fitted to destruction: and that he might make known the riches of his glory on the vessels of mercy, which he had afore prepared unto glory, even us. . . ?

To this day, the point of these magnificent, frightening parables is stressed in Christian thinking. The unfreedom of the will, the predestination by God, has been profoundly experienced and thought through by Augustine, passionately renewed by Luther (in *De servo arbitrio*), and fully dogmatized and placed in the centre of the faith by Calvin.

The point is not the predestination of the world at large by the Creator, but the predestination of each individual human being as eternally damned or saved. What becomes of the individual does not depend on him; it is due either to the wrath of God – in which he creates as a lost soul whomever he will – or to his loving mercy, in which he creates his elect, the ones he turns to so that they may turn to him.

Salvation is 'the beyond', what comes after death. This world and our short life in it amount to nothing. The one all-pervading concern is eternity, based upon the election of grace, barred by the election of wrath.

Choice, this category of human freedom, is thus laid in the hands of God. God chooses man; man does not choose God. The chosen are the blessed. By himself, man cannot even seek God. He cannot turn to God; God must have turned to him first.

In this faith it is impossible for man to have any capacity to owe anything to himself, to have any merit. The slightest touch of human self-reliance before God, as the Pelagians conceived it against Augustine, would disturb the divine omnipotence. God alone is free.

Rationally this idea leads to contradictions. If predestination is the sole determinant there is no human freedom. In consequence, there is no human guilt either; yet the faith insists on it. Putting the same idea another way: whatever a man is, good or evil, he is by God's will, by merciful or merciless predestination – and yet he is guilty. God made a man in his wrath, denied him his grace, and now wants this man to resist the evil that he, God, created in him.

Predestination means that by God's will the bad is as necessary as the good, that one could not be without the other, that Christ would not be without Judas, that wrong and evil cannot be without God's will. Yet faith says God is just and good.

Dogmatic thinking has found immensely complex rationalistic ways either to void the contradiction or to stress it vigorously, so as to expound God's unfathomability and reinforce the demand that rational absurdities be faithfully accepted. One little instance of these unending efforts: to remove the discrepancy from God's original will, a line was drawn between his election before Adam's fall and after, in 'supralapsary' or 'infralapsary' time. The election of grace was said to take place only 'infralapsarily', in a world now corrupted by original sin. But this merely shifts the question to the place of Adam's sin, where the difficulties are the same.

Calvinism, with matchless severity, has made the dogma rationally consistent.

No moral struggle can pave man's way to eternity. I cannot wrestle with God; I am eternally predestined for the state of grace or that of wickedness. God's terrible, incomprehensible decree, his *decretum horribile*, is the source to which each individual must bow. Neither man's moral conduct nor his will to believe can change the eternal decree – it is so, and that is all there is to it. Good or evil, I experience my total dependency upon God.

Yet no one, according to Calvinist dogma, can know whether he is destined to be a vessel of divine grace or of divine wrath. I can procure only the symptoms of a state of grace by being good in my lifetime. Among these symptoms are success in my labours and well-being in the world, provided I have totally forgone any enjoyment of my success or well-being and lived an outwardly active but inwardly ascetic life. A man must exert himself to the utmost, without and within, to be able to be halfway sure of these signs of being in a state of grace – though never really sure, for the signs of wickedness may appear on his deathbed. Even in the best case the uncertainty cannot be overcome, although I am supposed to believe I am one of the chosen.

In Calvinism alone do we see this rationalized dogma become immediately vital to the whole state of life. It is no longer the pious cipher of the unfathomable, but a consistent rationalization of unfathomability. It is no longer devotion but fear that controls a life which can change nothing anyway. Harshly, mercilessly, the dogma states what had been a factor of the human condition before God since Paul and Augustine; but the ring of truth that we hear in the cipher got lost in the rationalistic perfection and dogmatization. It remains audible in the horizon of related ciphers.

Points of departure in our experience

a: I am as I am. Empirically, what I am is due to my descent, to my parents, to my natural gifts or defects, to the wealth or poverty of my mind; also to the situation in the world, to the living conditions in my particular, singular situation. This being what I am, this given state in the world, is faced with the question of my freedom: what can I change – and what must I, by another free act, accept as inevitable?

b: I am free. Am I? If I say to myself, 'I am free,' I mean that to some extent what becomes of me is my own doing; what I do with myself in the world makes me what I am. But I become in time what I am in eternity – this is the paradoxical formula for what already exists in itself, as a temporal pheno- menon, but comes to appear in time only by means of freedom. It is expressed in the maxim 'Become what you are' – if I mean by this what I eternally am and never know.

If I relate the maxim to my unfolding natural proclivities, however, I am proudly or defiantly telling myself, 'That's the way I am'. This dreadful sentence means that in view of my empirically given existence I deny being free. The supposed necessity conceals a will to reject all demands and decline any responsibility, an unwillingness to deal with myself and 'come clean' with myself and with others – in the sense that cleanness may turn into inner action and change.

c: Freedom is a gift of self. Now for the next question: if I am free, am I free by my own means? I may fail to come to myself. And what I am, I am not by my own means.

Besides, I cannot fulfil my freedom by my will alone. I can will, but I cannot will myself to will. In what I will I meet myself in love from some- where else, so to speak, and not till then do I really know me as myself.

In my freedom, in being free and in fulfilling it, I am given to myself.

d: Freedom is necessity. At the peak of freedom lies this feeling: I do not will otherwise because I cannot do otherwise. I have no choice. I come to myself in this necessity, which is myself. It is not a compulsion, external or internal; it is what I am identical with – the will in which I experience myself in my personal eternity, because in the world I shall for ever stand by it and never deny it.

The experience of necessity at the peak of freedom; the experience expressed in the paradox formula of deciding in time about what is in eternity – these experiences belong neither to empirical reality nor to objective logic. The similar phrasings are deceptive; the meanings are totally different.

To take our example: in the words 'That's the way I am', empirical existence defiantly asserts itself, as being that way.

The words of supreme freedom, 'I cannot do otherwise', do not mean the way I happen to be. They denote no natural necessity, but the necessity of the principal employing my existence – namely, my self before Transcendence.

e: The necessity of freedom is not a natural necessity. Natural necessities are objects of cognition. Their knowledge enables us to shape our dependence on nature – *natura serviendo vincitur*, as the Romans put it. We can do this by technology in the inorganic field, by cultivation in the biological field, by psychology in matters of human nature.

Knowledge itself contains elements of freedom. But if the natural necessities, those objects of endless cognition, are viewed as absolute, as reality as such, I shall come to think of myself as one with natural necessity, a mere infinitesimal wavelet in the infinite flow of time. With this total inclusion of myself I have exceeded the bounds of possible knowledge and subjected myself to a false knowledge.

The necessity of freedom is another matter. Freedom does not occur in the nature we can know – or what is called freedom, then, is not the freedom we speak of. It does not occur in man either, in so far as he becomes an object of biological and psychological cognition.

Subject to natural necessity, I depend on the world; freedom lifts me out of this dependence, but makes me feel dependent on Transcendence – an essentially incomparable experience. The difference is radical. My dependence on nature plagues or fosters my existence, engenders and destroys it, summons me, as it were, to fight it and to agree with it. My dependence on Transcendence brings me to myself, grants me my freedom, and makes me identical with myself.

f: What is freedom? The multiple meanings of freedom and necessity lead to contradictory expressions when we try to formulate their existential import.

First, freedom is the objective freedom of action as opposed to coercion by physical chains, by psychological threats or blackmail, by physical torture. Second, it is my subjective freedom to develop, to set my own course, as opposed to the constraint of given social and political facts and particular situations. Third, it is the free determination of my will as opposed to the thraldom imposed by mental illness, for example – the psychological capacity to choose, in the sense of the penal law.

We mean something fundamentally different. The freedom we mean cannot be proved as a reality in the world even though it is the part of man that changes his world and himself. It is perceptible in its effects, not in itself. Philosophically freedom can be 'made sensible', as Kant put it, but it is not an object of cognition. The difference in our use of the word 'freedom' is as vast as that between objectiveness and non-objectiveness, or between existence and Existenz. On the one hand, we use the word to conceive worldly realities, and on the other hand we use it to transcend these realities to the Existenz of self-being. A gulf divides the two uses, a change in the meaning of the category. We therefore distinguish objective categories from the 'signs' – or categories – of freedom.

Yet when we speak of this existential freedom, we can only do so meta-phorically, in words that mean our freedom in the real world. This results in constant confusions of usage. The fact that communication is impossible without objectivities makes us talk in a way that keeps confusing everything if we forget the gulf between any objective category and the thing we touch in new 'categories' beyond our categories.

Freedom needs its antithesis, the empirical necessity it strives against. If we hear that 'God alone is free, not man', we ought to answer that God's freedom makes no sense unless he is conceived in the cipher of a human person. The truth is, rather, that man alone can be free as he works his way out of bonds that endure. Absolute freedom is an absurd concept.

Yet freedom also needs to be one with necessity. Necessity, then, is no longer the category of empirical events or consistent logic; it is freedom's own perfection as a gift from Transcendence. It implies no 'must' because of anything else, no 'must' due to any psychological process; it is the 'must' of experiencing our own eternity.

Freedom is an existential experience, not an observable one.

g: *Freedom carries with it responsibility and guilt.* Where there is freedom there is responsibility, and where there is responsibility there is guilt.

The arguments used to deny guilt go as follows. In the reality we can know there is no freedom; what is done, what I do myself, is caused and should be answered for by whatever else conditions me in the world. The way I am born is due to heredity. What I have become is due to social conditions. Both particular hereditary constellations and particular circum-stances made me what I am and make me act as I do. The fault is theirs, not mine.

Along with such arguments we hear some curious ideas. Having said, for instance, that he did not ask to be born and was not asked what he wished to be born as, a man may go on to say, 'I did not want my life; I'm not responsible for it; I don't agree with it; I throw it away.' In other words, the freedom that was first denied is now reintroduced as an absolute I that was not consulted before and is now unwilling. Another may say, 'Circum-stances make me. I can't change myself, but I can change the circumstances; their improvement will yield better people.' In other words, the freedom that was denied is reintroduced as freedom to bring about social change. Similarly, the unfreedom of heredity will be viewed as surmountable by free breeding.

Inevitably, thoughts that dispose of freedom will make it reappear in thoughtless forms – and then I am responsible for what I think and do in those forms of freedom. First of all, therefore, it is essential to realize clearly that somewhere, somehow, something is up to me. Whatever is up to me to do or not to do is my responsibility and my fault.

But let us get back to unfreedom. Though free in the world, I depend for the gift of my freedom on the Transcendence that created me, brought me into existence, cast me into the world – such figures of speech are ciphers of what is meant here. If I ask whether it is by myself that I am free or unfree, I speak of freedom in a sense other than the world's. The contradiction that I am both free and unfree is insoluble if we forget that the meanings of the two concepts of freedom are not comparable.

In the world I say, 'I am free; therefore I am guilty.' In view of Transcendence I say, 'I am unfree, and yet I am guilty.' I am 'unfree' because my freedom itself, in which I come to be guilty, depends upon Transcendence.

h: Related ciphers: amor fati, *doom, Providence,* karma, *Moira.* The idea of predestination takes its place in a ring of ciphers speaking many tongues.

Amor fati, the comprehension of fate beyond fortune and misfortune, accompanies the awakening of Existenz, the transformation of life into something more than mere finite, fortune-oriented existence.

But a self-absorbed consciousness of fate without an object does not satisfy. Existenz asks why there is a fate – why this is my fate. The ciphers give varying answers.

Doom, coming we know not whence, gives and withholds, may grant breathing spells, and pounces. It is envisioned as the effect of a family curse, as the visitation of guilt on children and children's children, as an inability to escape and to avoid guilt in innocence.

Providence is guidance by a cosmic reason that has a place and a meaning for whatever happens to me. It uses fortune and misfortune for purposes of education and probation. Its certainty calms me, shelters me in a meaningful whole, justifies the *amor fati.*

The Hindu concept of *karma* rests on metempsychosis. What I am and experience now is the result of my life in previous forms of existence; what I do now is the seed of my life in future rebirths. In this present life I have no chance to better it or make it happier, but righteous living gives me the chance to be reborn on a higher plane in my next existence. I accuse no one, for I suffer the consequences of my own deeds.

The Greek Moira is the ultimate Transcendence that turns the gods into immanent beings. Conceived as the unfathomed depth of impersonal decisions about the course of divine as well as human fates, it was later rationalized into a cosmic law as opposed to chaos, into a moral world order as opposed to indifferent happenings, into necessity as against chance, justice as against despotism, the certainty of events as against their random occurrence. The gods to whom men prayed and sacrificed were subject to it; Moira itself had no cult.

i: Truth and falsehood in the idea of predestination. If the source of fate is the personal God, the course of things and of my life is not determined by a blind force, not by necessity, not by a speculatively conceived occurrence, not by an automatic mechanism, not by chance. The will of the one personal Creator causes whatever is, whatever happens. And this alone raises the questions that are both answered and left unanswered in the Book of Job and in the idea of predestination.

There is truth in these questions and in the ciphers that reply to them. 'I am nothing, God is everything' – this, in regard to the ultimate, is a true sense of Being. It is only when the cipher God is embodied, when we mean not the cipher but God as a tangible person, that the sentence comes to express submissiveness and servitude and inextinguishable fear.

It is quite another thing if piety can communicate only in ciphers without letting their real content grow tangible and objective. The word 'God's being suffices' will then, in the cipher, convey the same infinitesimality of man as the word which pious Jews bear through all evils: 'The Lord, our God, the Lord is One.'

The more the cipher is rationalized and embodied, the less truthful and the more fallible its appeal to free man.

j: When the cipher of predestination becomes repugnant. In its perfect form, with the cipher character of its conceptions voided, the dogma of predestination becomes existentially ambiguous.

α: Once the *decretum horribile* is ascribed to the personal God, the deity has vanished from this personality cipher. Nothing remains but the despotism of a tyrant. Only as long as it stays impersonal and supra-personal can the cipher move us by the veracity of its vain effort to cast light in absolute darkness.

β: The cipher shows us the abyss. We can reject it, but we cannot destroy it. The dogma, on the other hand, chills us with horror and leaves no way out but the immoderate anxiety, the restless bustle, the incapacity for thought that mark the search for symptoms of our own election. The dogma unlike the cipher, is not a dialogue but a crushing blow.

Life under such pressure can have a heroic quality. Unheard-of daring and the greatest sacrifices combine with full knowledge of the futility of any effort to be sure of being saved. As mere symptoms of election, the works and successes lose their sheen. Life rolls off in a grey dusk of the forbidden joy of living. Music, poetry, wit are called temptations; the sciences, recognized as aids to success in mastering nature, lose their true cognitive significance. The cipher of loving piety and devotion to the unfathomable is perverted into the fanatical faith of loveless rationalization.

γ: Along with humility before the terrible God, the sense of being chosen – as they are told to believe, for all its uncertainty – gives this community of the saints the pride of an aristocracy, vicious because it is always right. Acting with God, for God, through God increases my strength immensely; I have no qualms, since I do everything for the glory of God rather than for myself. With my morally unconditional attitude based on a faith in God's will, not on moral reason, I am quite capable of doing wrong as God's will. The unfathomable joins hands with the practical. What comes out of this witches' brew of humility, fatalism, activism, and fanaticism is inhumanity.

v. The cipher of the Fall

The Bible, Plato, and other philosophers of Antiquity down to Plotinus share the basic idea that evil does not come from God. Specifically biblical is the radicality of the idea: since God is one – since no dualistic pair reigns in the world, such as God and the devil – evil springs from what God made out of nothing. God created man free; freedom would not be freedom if it could not choose to side with God or against him. God wants free agreement with himself, free, clear-sighted submission rather than blind obedience.

Common to Asian and Western thought is the appearance of concepts explaining the incongruity of existence. What are the roots of the things we see and experience? The Hindu answer attributes a basic perversion to the mere fact that there is existence. The Gnostics answer that events in Being have perverted the way things are. According to Plato and Plotinus, the discrepancy of Being proper and the existing multiplicity results from what happens all the time.

The seriousness that gave rise to these conceptions is as valid now as ever. The basic wonderment at the world we find ourselves in, and at our own nature, affects not only our consciousness of Being but our way of life.

No philosophy can disregard this limit. A thinker's way of looking at enormity is the ground he stands on. However varied the philosophers' conception of the ciphers, however divergent their ways of life and forms of Existenz, they share a starting-point of experience and a goal. Here we confine ourselves to the biblical ciphers.

a: *Historic examples and interpretations.* The archetype of every man's renewed misuse of freedom is the myth of the Fall – the original free choice that determined what it now means to be human.

This original decision was made either by man himself, in the person of Adam, or by creatures who rose against God even before mankind and then seduced man in turn. God created free beings, and thus the possibility that they might rebel, might wish to be as God. It has been told in myths and reconstructed in speculative concepts how creatures of a pre-temporal world, fallen angels or demons, did something which made our own ills possible or inevitable. Thus· our freedom brought physical evil into the world, along with moral evil. The objective evil of suffering and the sub-jective freedom to do evil have a common ground. Physical and moral evil differ in essence, but one is the other's echo.

Let me cite some historic examples.

Gnosticism conceived the apostasy of angels. Self-will turned them away from God; they wished to be God themselves. One such evil spirit created the world. It is therefore entirely evil, and the spark of light in the souls – which were swept up in it – must be constantly deceived by the evil creator. To free them, the good, distant, strange God sent the Saviour who came into the world unrecognized, in his turn deceiving the wicked angels.

The Christian myth relates the course of things from the Creation through Adam's fall and the redemption by Christ to the world's end and the Last Judgment. As the son of God, Christ is as capable as the angels of divine independence, but when the devil tempts him, he, unlike the angels, chooses to obey God.

Origen knew a variant: freedom is the source of many steps among the spirits, from good angels to devils. Man is not holy enough to be an angel, not wicked enough to be a devil. But in the primal age he too misused his freedom in self-will. By way of punishment he has been cast into the body. The stuff of the body is his punishment; its coarseness marks him as one of the fallen. The good angels are made of lighter, finer stuff.

Scotus Erigena knew another variant: having turned his back on God to stand on himself, man lost his being in God's eternity. He must now exist in space and time, in definite places. Matter itself was spiritual once upon a time; it is now physical because the Fall of man broke up the unity of Being and severed all things – God and the world, spirit and matter, individual and species, man and woman.

In each of these myths the Almighty does and yet does not permit another god. The antinomy of God's omnipotence and freedom's independence of this omnipotence is the paradox that keeps recurring.

Of the interpretations of the Fall, the most impressive goes back to God's mythical word about Adam: 'The man is become as one of us, to know good and evil.' In other words, the essential human trait of being able to think and coming to know is mutiny and disobedience from the start. The faculty with which man helps himself in the world, without which he cannot exist, which makes out his strength and his greatness – this very faculty originated with his Fall.

This is the human condition: each new individual becomes aware of himself only to see curbs on his existence, snags in his path, wants he is subject to, other men he constantly depends on as he toils for his living and produces his environment.

My very first realization of the world and my activity in it leads to judgments: things should not be as they are; I should not do what I have done. In such judgments I differentiate between good and bad as regards natural events and existence, between good and evil as regards my own free acts.

The limit of this interpretation is that I need a yardstick to judge anything as bad or evil. There must be some general measure for me to judge by. These measures exist with man as such, to be sure, but as he thinks he comes to see their limitations. They are not absolute, even though inescapable for him and morally unconditional. They help him to penetrate the source, which is encompassing and more than all the helpful yardsticks.

b: Original sin and grace. The cipher of the Fall and the expulsion from Paradise shows the source of the sufferings, the needs, the challenges of our present condition. The consequences of the Fall permit us to act against misery in the world and to succeed, to improve the situation. Our own strength, our capacity for self-help, shows as we obey a divine commandment. The cipher of original sin, on the other hand, kills every hope. Original sin can be countered only by the grace of God himself.

Buddha taught that man's own strength can save him. He showed the way and set the example. He helps man to help himself.

But the doctrine of original sin gives man no way to follow. He cannot help himself; he needs divine grace. This is not obtained by thought and insight, however, but by faith – a faith which in turn is granted only by grace and enables us to make its redeeming experience. It takes faith itself to realize the totally lost state from which the redemption by faith delivers us.

When we talk of original sin, of grace, of justification or reconciliation, we must know that these concepts presuppose a special view of the basic human condition. What everyone can understand from experience and reflection is here transcended. Even to see the condition is an act of faith, for it is incomprehensible to anyone save a believer in the revelation. The whole is a closed circle of faith: Grace lets the believer know himself for a sinner and simultaneously offers to save him, to reconcile him with God.

A person outside the circle cannot help seeing deceptive materializations in the objects of this faith. The total guilt that appears with human Existenz turns into substantial original sin; the cipher of immortality becomes the resurrection of the flesh at the Last Judgment; the man Jesus – a prophetic figure unrivalled in its revolutionary illumination of the vastness of evil, the depth of love, the radicality of the change required – turns into Christ, the real incarnation of God. But even one who cannot join this circle of faith can feel its ciphers move him to critical self-reflection.

α: The accusing voice – 'You are what you freely became; you did what you did; you can atone, but not eradicate' – is bound to make us shudder. The self-accordant voice – 'I love and am for ever identical with myself in love' – can lend us wings. There I hate myself; here I love myself.

A man is not self-righteous if he asks of himself what he is capable of doing. He is self-righteous if he thinks that he, by himself, can change himself so as to bring forth love and virtue.

As a whole, the cipher of original sin is not acceptable to us because it lays exclusive stress on the expectation of grace, backed by a promise under ecclesiastic warrant. But the cipher does ring with the truth of the essentially human demand for an inner change, and of man's feeling to have himself as a gift he knows not whence, or how.

The cipher of original sin needs rounding out with the cipher of innate nobility. This too is unacceptable as a total cipher, because it would place everything in my strength and minimize culpability. Yet this cipher rings with the truth of the demand to heed my intrinsic potential, to be what I become as I change.

Both ciphers may lead astray. To expect grace from the true faith alone makes for moral passivity; it may let us stay 'valiant' in sin, being sure of grace. To expect virtue from my inborn nobility may cause moral confusion, the perversion of thinking that a thing is good because I do it. It can let me be pleased with myself, since the way I am is noble in any event.

β: The idea of original sin appeals as a cipher of the 'out-of-jointness' we find as soon as we awaken to ourselves. In dealing with himself, man comes to feel snagged from the outset. He recognizes his failure, yet he will be subject to it time and time again. As Existenz he must struggle between the bog he always finds in himself and the freedom that puts it up to him to pull himself out by his bootstraps and to change. The cipher humbles him when he would be proud of himself.

But the cipher leads him astray if he seeks shelter in grace, saying, 'That's the way I am', and crying, 'Grace! Grace!' For there is no real grace to be experienced as a factual intervention from without. There is nothing to be expected from objectifying a salvation process imparted from without. The cipher rings true only in so far as it encourages freedom and spurs us to do our best. If it helps us to relax in 'grace' it becomes pernicious. Individual guilt, the only tangible one, is then made light of so as to find tranquillity in the intangible total guilt – for if I live as a total sinner in the cipher's sense I tend to beg the question of my specific guilt here and now. Instead of purifying myself, I depend on 'justification by faith'. Instead of justifying my existence by my actions, I pride myself, wrapped in humility before God, on the achievement of my faith in admitting my total guilt as an original sinner. I am reconciled with God, and for the trifles of my individual worldly guilt no man may judge me.

Despite all this deceptiveness there may perhaps be some truth in the cipher of a possible 'reconciliation' with God. It has power to lift me up in desperate guilt feelings, to bring me out of a total breakdown simply because, amidst annihilating finality, I have still another chance.

γ: The cipher has something unfitting when it voids realities.

To be truthful, we must insist on recognizing the full extent of evil, of misery, of want. To be truthful, we must not expect to be freed from guilt otherwise than by atonement and a posture in this world that can be trusted.

Forgiveness is a matter between human beings. It is that most wonderful act of human communication in which wrong is recognized on both sides, however different its kind and measure. Born of love, whose clear-sighted honesty will not permit us to overlook anything, forgiveness makes for new, loving communication. Ineradicable consequences of guilt will remain, but the guilt is no longer absolute; it has been brought into the unity, the union, that awakens us by communicative good will. To let God forgive us otherwise than by the forgiveness of men would be to flee from mankind and from ourselves to God – it would be godless. Nor is it given to the living to forgive the living in behalf of the dead who can no longer do so. Those who crave such forgiveness can only do themselves what they hear in the cipher of hope for an eternal, temporally inaccessible forgiveness of the dead.

A reconciliation by faith in the objective process of salvation – by the belief that the sacrificial death and resurrection of Christ has redeemed me – is philosophically incomprehensible if meant as the 'justification by faith alone' of St Paul and Luther. Failing utterly to understand, we can only marvel at the fact that men can speak in that vein. Not even as a cipher can I find any approach to such 'justification'. How can it be meritorious to believe in something laid down in a creed, in statements about an objective occurrence? Where the reality of revelation loses even the voice of a possible cipher, we sense a disturbing limit.

This disquiet is not removable by such an existential levelling of the reconciliation concept as forms the basis and conclusion of Hegel's philosophy. His is a reconciliation conceived and carried out in the conception; everything negative is included in it but viewed as overcome. Hegel knows too much, and that impairs his credibility. A reconciliation so fully known and seen through is no reconciliation.

Quite different is the trust I cannot justify and do not know. It seems bound to fail when men lapse into incurable mental illness, for instance – when the 'immortal' soul created 'in God's image' is destroyed alive, on earth, by nature. Must it not fail when human freedom leads to acts such as the murder of six million Jews in our time, or when we now face the possibility of mankind's self-immolation? Astonishingly, though, this trust can always restore itself.

Trust in what? In whom? There language fails. The very word 'trust' says too much. The hidden God and this unjustifiable trust belong together – not to be attained by any knowledge, not to be confessed in any creed.

vi. Waiving the guilt question?
The question of guilt concerns human beings. To dispense with it generally would amount to saying that what man is and does is not due to him but to a necessity of nature. It would mean that thought and decision are mere natural phenomena, rudimentary in the animal kingdom and fully developed in man.

'I was born the way I am,' said a defendant in a North German courtroom some forty years ago. 'I could not help acting as I did; I was compelled by my nature. So I cannot be justly convicted.'

The judge replied, 'I am compelled by the nature of the judicial process to apply the law. I can no more help convicting you than you could help acting.' What the judge meant to say was 'Both of us talk nonsense. You and I are free human beings. As you are responsible for your action, I am responsible for mine – which is to perform the duty of my office.'

We cannot evade the question of man's guilt; but it is another matter to shift it to the root of Being, to a Transcendence conceived as residing there in analogy to a human person.

The cipher of the personal God tremendously intensifies this aspect of the question. Rebellious man thinks as if he were on his own. He is utterly powerless, yet even in total failure he will assume a position of spiritual superiority over the amoral, irrational, and incommunicative side of God.

If Transcendence were a personality – instead of personality being one of its ciphers in our human language – there could indeed be no justifying it. To get around this, man seeks other ciphers that will let him comprehend his suffering and guilt as necessities, obviating the question of the guilt of Transcendence.

But in order to feel any existential effect after dropping his charges against Transcendence, he must first have felt that rebelliousness and heard its expression in ciphers. Otherwise the quashed indictment seems simply innocuous. The seriousness will be gone, along with the enormity.

The ciphers we turn to now may appeal to some and incense others. They deal with two questions. First, what is evil? What necessity drags it up from the bottom ground of things? And then, what becomes of it? What is its meaning in the world?

a: The nature and the origin of evil. We made a distinction between physical evil in the world and the moral evil men do. Both can be experienced.

But the nature of all evil has been speculatively conceived as resulting from the metaphysical character of things as they are. Let us look at these conceptions.

α: All entities are limited by dint of their particular being. That things are finite means they are unfinished; their completeness is a particular one, excluding other things. The way they are is flawed, compared with universality. All finite things are potentially perfect, actually imperfect.

β: All entities are antithetical. The fact that everything positive is tied to a negative, that Being itself is tied to nothingness, makes for success and suffering, for good and evil. They are the necessary forms in which that basic fact appears.

Plato showed that even nothingness has a way of being – because there is no being without non-being – and that antithesis is for us the foundation of all being, including ours. In mythical ciphers the antitheses appear as two fundamental powers, in the physical world as light and darkness, in society as the constructive and the destructive, in action as good and evil, in cosmic imagery as God's heavenly kingdom and the devil's infernal realm. They reach all the way into the forms of life, pitting eagle, lion, lamb, useful animals, and wholesome plants against snakes, toads, spiders, vermin, poisonous plants. It is an endlessly ramified dualistic view of two primal forces.

In the world, the negative is a condition of the positive. Evil is a condition of good. In the cipher language: what comes from God in the world cannot avoid the devil.

γ: Foremost among the antitheses is that of Being and nothingness. Evil is conceived as the non-entity among entities. And an odd thing happens to it in this category of non-being: it is not destroyed, but it is made to disappear.

Origen interpreted the Apostle's word that before God the wicked are 'as nothing' to mean that nothing evil is known to God. God is ignorant of evil – not because his total knowledge cannot grasp it, but because it is unworthy of his knowledge. In this sense, Origen thought, God is not omniscient: he does not know sin, and the sinner does not know God. 'I know you not,' Christ said; 'depart from me, all ye workers of iniquity.' Evil is without the divine presence. God pervades the world; he dwells in his creation, but not in evil. Similarly, Dionysius Pseudo-Areopagite wrote that as the sun emits light, God emits good, illumining first the spirits and then every kind of created thing down to matter. Evil is simply 'the omission of good' – mere non-being, not a part of Being.

b: The point of suffering and evil. Whenever evil is viewed as not really being, the views of its effects tend to become ambiguous. We are told that the guiding hand of a higher power makes this thing, which merely seems to be, accomplish good ends, that as non-being it serves Being. This thesis – beginning with Plato, elaborated by the Stoics, richly revived by Plotinus, and then received into Christian thinking – answers the question about the point of evil. Though not considered an independent power, it will not give up the fight, and the result, in a world full of both good and evil, was described by Plato as 'an incessant struggle calling for all but superhuman vigilance'.

The philosophers show us the good effects of evil in principle, not for specific cases. Their basic idea is that God guides all things. Plato began by holding that everything good is due to *thea moira*, a divine dispensation – as the philosopher may conceive the ideal state, but it will not become a reality until, somewhere in the infinity of time, *thea moira* brings it about. 'God's dispensation alone gives virtue to whomever it is granted.' The creative madness of a poet also is God-given; universal guidance turns evil into good. Calamity is not all calamitous. It has good consequences.

Suffering is education, says Plato; it keeps men from indolence and laxness. Suffering is probative, say the Stoics; it will show a good man that it really does not affect him. Suffering is punishment, and punishment is good both in itself and as a deterrent, says Plato. And when the equal suffering of the just and the unjust compels an admission that it does not follow from wrongdoing, the Stoics and Spinoza tell us that wrongdoing carries its own punishment in itself.

Do we find moral evil also explained as a means to the good? We do. Evil works in the passions, and Plato says no great thing, good or evil, was ever done without passion. So says Hegel. Jesus inclined to sinners. Aquinas wrote that the wicked too can work miracles, and Pascal found evil that may take as much greatness of soul as does the good. Passion is ambivalent; it can glow in the light of reason or plunge into darkness. It becomes possible to ask whether the productive depths of the mind are tied to evil, whether absurdity is an inevitable root of faith, whether blindness is a premise of creative action.

In the end we are asked to look at 'the whole' in judging evil. 'The preserver of the universe calculates all for the good of the whole, so that each individual part will do and suffer its due share,' says Plato. 'The whole does not exist for your sake, but you exist for the sake of the whole.' Also, man is the gods' property and their plaything. God moves souls as on a chessboard.

c: The reality of evil. However it may be conceived as an actual non-entity – as finite, as matter, as sensuality, as a mere shadow, as disharmony resolving itself in harmony – against all this, the serious Existenz insists that evil is real. It is not just a limit; it is destructive negation. What can destroy must be something. Nothingness, which is not, cannot destroy; as it destroys, it exists. Evil is no absence of being. It has being.

A limit, a non-being, is not a force in reality. Conceived as non-being, evil would be overcome from the start. For all the mischief it does, it would really be harmless. Yet evil is a powerful, perhaps an overpowering force in a destructive struggle. This evil is a will. A detached, self-sustained will directed against the rational course of things – this is the adversary as such, a hatred that feeds on itself, not love's passing shadow.

The question is not resolved by demonstrating in conceptual ciphers that evil has no real being, that it derives from finiteness, from the antitheses, from non-being. If those conceptions express the nature of things, why, then, are things of such a nature as to involve evil? If the guilt question ceases beyond good and evil, what is responsible for the existence of entities involving good and evil? If evil has no real being, what lies behind its apparent being?

The conceptual interpretations fail to explain the basic condition of Existenz. Something in me makes decisions; I know I am responsible, so in some sense I must be free; I become guilty. What or who is responsible for my being free in the sense that I can – that indeed I must – become guilty? This is no longer a question about the concept of the way I am. It is a question about the real root of freedom.

d: Beyond good and evil. Evil and good would vanish if we could transcend to the ground of Being. Only because this exceeds our capacity does evil remain the antithesis of good. Only from a standpoint 'beyond good and evil' would we be able to say that there is no evil and no good either, that where we stand there are no more antitheses, that all of them have been resolved in the inconceivable – which in our temporal condition cannot even be mentioned except in antitheses.

For us, evil exists in the phenomenality of time. We delude ourselves if we attempt, however feebly, to think from the standpoint of supra-personal Transcendence. The most we can try is to think toward such a standpoint.

c. Observation and Practice

Ciphers of the root of evil are not matters of fact; they are ideas that clarify or produce a state of mind in the thinker. We do not think of them with the neutrality we feel toward factual hypotheses.

The ciphers appeal in archetypical forms to each Existenz. They show particular ways of the individual potential. By our way of conceiving them we share the responsibility for ourselves.

The subtlest conceptual elaboration of ciphers may be significant if the thinker is not playing an intellectual game but understands what he is doing. He is doing three things:

1 He experiences an 'inner condition', a 'basic mood', a 'sense of life'. Such words do not have one unequivocal meaning, and no clear statement fits what they convey. It is not a subject of psychology. The inner condition does not show as such; it shows in the objectivations that are performed in it. It has been described in a variety of terms: original experience – what I am in all modes of encompassing – the encompassing that is myself – possible Existenz – privity to Creation – *pneuma* – inspiration. If present, it appears in the stirring of my soul as the ciphers reflect on it.
2 The thinker engages in inner action. Combined with his thinking, this will give him a support or stimulate a guidance that keeps firming up, though it will always be fluid.
3 The thinker acts in existential relations. This means that Existenz communicates with Existenz – the mundane meaning that encompasses all purposes.

1 SERIOUSNESS AND UNSERIOUSNESS

i. Like scientific cognition, a philosophical treatise is useful, perhaps, as an analysis of facts and description of phenomena, but it is not essential. It becomes essential only together with the real Existenz it serves.

The same is true of ciphers. If we let them pass in historic review, in factual order, we are compiling data. We can be neutrals setting forth what has been. But an adoption as our language, related to present Existenz, is something else again.

The difference between the moral judgment I pass as an observer and a moral decision in my life is the same as that between objectively reviewed ciphers and the reality of Existenz on which they have an impact. Observation matters only in connection with the will of real Existenz to be illuminated.

ii. As human beings, says one objection to the ciphers, we want to possess the Absolute. We want to circumscribe Transcendence in time, to have and to hold it in a definite form. What good to us are ciphers that are not solidified to support our thoughts and actions? They do not give us what we want and need. – This speaker wants what is impossible for human beings and seeks an escape in the delusions of corporeality.

Another objection asks: are definite ciphers such as the dualism of God and the devil, or the indictment of the personal God, not limiting in themselves? – They are not limiting if we remain aware that they are ciphers. The objective forms required by our consciousness fit them to serve our temporal Existenz. They illuminate the supersensory space of its environment. They will not permit us the laxity of taking things in our stride and letting ourselves go. They refuse us any definitive pacification in time. They demand an inner struggle. They forbid us to harden and armour-plate our hearts, and they make us fight evil in earnest, in ourselves.

iii. There is an antithesis that goes through the history of thinking. One man seems to think evil out of existence: at bottom, he feels, all there is must be all right. The other insists on the originality of evil; he feels it has its own absolute reality from an inconceivable source. A majority thinks in between: somehow, of course, there is evil; but then again, maybe there really isn't.

If evil loses its weight in such harmonizing ideas, the indecisiveness will carry over into systematic thinking. It comes to be no more than a thinking away and talking away of facts as well as of the existential earnest.

Men will look for a way out of the seriousness of evil, and of good. The remaining, unquestioning levity of life as a matter of course appears so beautiful. The very efforts of cognition may become means to this flight from seriousness.

iv. We have no way of knowing definitely what evil is, where it comes from, and how it might be overcome. We want the comfort of definitive answers – to the physical evil that may strike us and others at any time; to the moral evil that we do, that burdens us with the guilt we should like to be rid of. And failing to get this comfort, we want to plunge into desperation, as in the cipher of the Last Judgment or the opinion that mankind is totally doomed, or in the triumphant statement of Goethe's Mephistopheles that 'whatever is deserves to perish' – it would be better if there were nothing.

v. By 'beyond good and evil' we do not mean a surrender of man in the world to the savage forces of his natural being. We rather mean the place, so to speak, where serious humanity ultimately originates. This place lies beyond all ciphers. Thinking stops there. No sound of language can be heard from there.

Any way, to any goal, that lights up for freedom is overshadowed at the same time by nothingness. This experience leads to the deep seriousness of Existenz that will put its full strength into its activities without permitting itself to feel arrogantly absolute.

He who takes this way in philosophizing risks losing his balance in the world. For the sobering awareness of Transcendence 'beyond good and evil' may turn the total levity that will take nothing seriously any more, degenerating from Existenz into nonsense. In the delusion of having found the way out of the world, men may lose themselves in eccentricity. In the world they become buffoons or maniacs or criminals – all in the belief of having reached ultimate truth.

2 THE SIGNIFICANCE OF RATIONAL CONSISTENCY

i. Consistency and inconsistency

There are only three entirely consistent interpretations of evil: the Hindu *karma*, Zoroastrian dualism, and Calvin's doctrine of predestination. Their consistency is made compelling by their rigour. One who believes in such knowledge will not live laxly, will not be making things easy for himself, though his basic mood will be quite different in the three cases.

The flaw in these consistent constructions is that each one rests on a premise – the first on metempsychosis, the second on the two primal powers, the third on the 'horrible decree' of God. Each of these three basic ideas is incomprehensible. Clearly envisioned, lifted out of their matter-of-course acceptance, and thought through, they come to look rather dubious. They can stand only as unquestioned tenets, or as the objects of a stubborn will to believe.

The premise itself is in each case a narrowed-down incomprehensibility that seems comprehended because it has been made specific. In fact, it is a *fiat* that cuts off all questions by demanding submission.

On the premise given each time, the ideas have a satisfying logical consistency. But since they put man into a straitjacket of substantially baseless logic, the consistency becomes unbearable to Existenz. For all its logical disguise, the absolute *fiat* becomes existentially untrue.

This logical consistency on far from evident premises has two consequences. The first is a fanatical religious knowledge, accompanied by an odd and most uncomfortable religious practice. Secondly, Existenz is made comfortable by the thoughtless finality of a rational structure erected with much intellectual toil.

Opposed to both these consequences is the true humanity that understands itself as a way, a possibility that cannot be fulfilled in time. On this way, inconsistencies and contradictions help us to shed the straitjackets of religious knowledge. If the premises are absurd, the method permits a temporary liberation until the premises themselves will be transformed from dogmas into ciphers. It pits a deeper truth against the rationally unequivocal conclusions drawn from existentially untenable beliefs. The manifest truth of not knowing breaches the dogmas of faith; the solvent power of their own rational consequences brings them into the suspension of ciphers. For a free Existenz it is this metamorphosis that makes the dogmas part of the rich, evanescent language of Transcendence.

ii. A rational statement of despair: Ivan Karamazov's 'rebellion'
Dostoevsky[1] created the man who looks at the world, voices his outrage to the last extreme of rational consistency, but fails to put it into practice, unable to take the consequences in reality.

'If I am to love a man,' Ivan Karamazov tells his brother Alyosha, the believing Christian, 'he must be hidden, for as soon as he shows his face, love is gone.' One can love a stranger, perhaps, but not one's neighbour. No man can know what I suffer, nor will one readily admit another's suffering.

'I like to collect certain facts, and I even copy anecdotes of a certain sort rom newspapers and books,' Ivan says and cites an example: 'A trembling mother with her baby in her arms, a circle of invading Turks around her. They pet the baby, laugh to make it laugh; the baby laughs. At that moment a Turk points a pistol four inches from the baby's face. The baby laughs, holds out its little hands to the pistol, and the Turk pulls the trigger in the baby's face and blows out its brains. Artistic, wasn't it?'

He sums up his observations: 'The world stands on absurdities, and perhaps nothing would have come to pass in it without them. We know what we know! I understand nothing; I don't want to understand anything now. I want to stick to the facts.'

The crucial point is this: all that Ivan's 'poor, earthly Euclidian understanding' can tell him is that suffering exists and no one is guilty. Above all, the children are innocent. People talk of eternal harmony – but, Ivan asks, 'if all must suffer to pay for eternal harmony, what have children to do with it? Tell me that, please. . . . I renounce the higher harmony altogether; it's not worth the tears of one tortured child. And if the sufferings of children go to swell the sum of suffering which was necessary to pay for truth, then I protest that the truth is not worth such a price. I don't want harmony. From love for humanity I don't want it'.

Ivan wants justice. 'And not justice in some remote infinite time and space, but here on earth. Justice that I can see myself. Surely I haven't suffered simply that I, my crimes and my sufferings may manure the soil of future harmony for somebody else.'

He asks if there is anyone in the world who could forgive, who would have the right to forgive – and even in view of horrors such as the slaughter of children the believing Alyosha points to Christ, who can forgive everything because he gave his innocent blood for all.

---

[1] *The Brothers Karamazov*, quotations from The New American Library edition – *Translator*.

But Ivan finds God neither a disturbing question nor a sheltering reality. He has long decided to stop wondering whether man made God or God made man. For Ivan, nothing is certain but facts, logical conclusions, and a scale of justice he can understand.

The result of his view of the real world is that he cannot agree to be part of it, to live in it: 'I must have justice, or I will destroy myself.' God? He says he accepts God simply, without reservations. 'It's not that I don't accept God; it's the world created by him I don't accept. Let me make myself plain. I believe like a child that the whole insulting comedy of human contradictions will vanish like a mirage, and that at the cosmic finale, at the moment of eternal harmony, something so precious will happen and appear that it will suffice for all hearts. Well, all that may come to pass, but I don't accept it. I won't accept it. It isn't God I don't accept, Alyosha; only I most respectfully return my ticket to him.'

'That's rebellion,' murmurs Alyosha.

As a matter of fact, Ivan does not commit suicide. He does not take the consequence of his rebellious theory: 'I want to live.' He does say, 'While there is still time, I hurry to take my own measures' – seeming to hold on to the alternative of justice or self-destruction, but putting off the execution into the future.

Why? 'Till I am thirty, I know that my youth will triumph over everything – every disillusionment, every disgust with life. I've asked myself many times whether there is in the world any despair that could overcome this frantic thirst for life.' The reason is 'the strength to endure everything – the strength of the Karamazov meanness'.

But Ivan's thirst for life has another strange aspect: 'I go on living in spite of logic. Though I may not believe in the order of the universe, yet I love the sticky little leaves as they open in the spring. I love the blue sky. I love some people.' These are the beauties appreciated, according to psychiatric observations, even by people classified under the diagnosis of moral insanity.

Love life more than the meaning of life? asks Ivan. Certainly, replies Alyosha. Life must be loved before logic – definitely before logic: 'It's only then one can understand the meaning. . . .' The crux, both brothers agree, is Alyosha's 'before logic'. What comes before logic? If one knew, one would have the whole truth. Ivan says, 'Karamazov meanness'. Alyosha says, 'Christ'.

In Ivan, Dostoevsky shows us logical consistency and its pre-logical failure. The rebel who repudiates the world is a mere spectator; his thesis does not hold in practice. For Ivan judges but does not act. Later on, when his inaction contributes to his father's murder, he cannot bear it and goes out of his mind. The Karamazov meanness and its maxim, 'All is permitted', founder on conscience, which convicts him on grounds of passivity.

Let truth be recognized – this is the great principle in Ivan's rebellion. But on this principle the rebellion itself must be questioned about its truth.

We are moved by Ivan's arguments and by his ruthless veracity. We know the experience of asking ourselves: who is mad, the world or I – or both of us? We know situations that are hopeless, or at least overwhelmingly threatening up to the point where every way out seems blocked. We know the compulsion to lie that seems to permeate existence and makes us lie with the rest. We take part in the uprising against the lie that the world is all right – against what Schopenhauer called the 'villainous optimism' that will not admit facts. We sneer with Voltaire at the 'best of all possible worlds'.

Hardly anybody who wants truth will be protected from this train of thoughts, and from the inner condition it expresses. The about-face may come suddenly in adolescence and may require lifelong repetition. Do we really believe what has been said in outrage, even assuming all the facts to be true? We hear a false note in the rationality; we sense untruthfulness in the rebellion that insists so loudly, passionately, on its truth. In our own mood of yielding to it we feel something that is not really ourselves. The test is not logic alone; it is our own Existenz that intrinsically calls for truth.

This test presupposes a philosophical insight: truth is required of all statements – whether factual accounts, logical conclusions, or professions of faith – as well as of all actions; yet the whole truth will never be had in any stated form. To test each statement, we need distance. In the testing, even though we use all available rational means, the decisive criterion is one that is not rational but determines our relation to ourselves. It keeps us true to ourselves. Kant calls it sincerity.

3 SINCERITY

i. Kant on intellect and conscience

'A person,, Kant wrote, 'cannot always answer for the truth of what he says, for he may be mistaken; but he can and must answer for the truthfulness of his statements – for of that he is directly conscious.' The essential difference is this: when I compare my statement with its object, I am testing it with my intellect; but when I compare it with myself as subject, with what I believe or really mean, I am testing it with my conscience. 'If one declares a belief without as much as a glance inside oneself, to see whether one is in fact conscious of holding it to be true, one is lying.' For one is stating something other than what one is conscious of. This lie is 'the most preposterous if it takes place before God, who knows the human heart'. It is the most iniquitous, because it undermines sincerity, the foundation of all moral purpose. It is the 'deeply hidden dishonesty with which man knows how to falsify even his inner statements to his own heart'.

ii. Can conscience err?

There are two answers to the question. If my conscience makes a judgment

I may be mistaken about the substance of it, and thus mistaken in my judgment that I am factually right. But, says Kant, 'in the consciousness whether I actually believe to be right I simply cannot be mistaken'. There 'an erring conscience is nonsense. If there were such a thing, one could never be certain of having done right, because even the court of last resort might be mistaken'. This is simple. But in the simplicity lies the immense difficulty.

In time, since the assurance of conscience does not exclude a mistake about the substance of the matter, there is no way to finish the examination of the question. We call this continuing examination conscientiousness. In the matter itself it never comes to an end. As Kant put it, formal conscientiousness lies in truthful thinking, material conscientiousness in 'taking care never to dare anything at the risk of its being wrong'.

In this simple and beautiful solution I have first to be assured by my unerring conscience, and then to be interminably careful and conscientious. This does not suffice, however.

iii. Observation and action

The first question we must address to the solution based on the Kantian sincerity is this: Existenz has to decide in time. It cannot go on indefinitely with its careful examination. Time is compelling; Existenz cannot wait. Its duty, of course, is to know what can be known, to weigh the facts and the arguments carefully, to hear the ciphers speak from the encompassing. But it must act before concluding an inquiry that will always want to be continued. Kant bids us never to let material assurance move us to dare anything at the risk of its being wrong; but does this demand fit in with the situation of human Existenz in time?

No knowledge ever covers the given realities; generally there are arguments and counter-arguments *ad infinitum*. But Existenz must always decide at some moment. It must anticipate what may perhaps not be manifest until the end of time to infinite cognition.

Existenz must dare – though in the act of decision, at the very moment of resolve, it still keeps listening to what goes on.

Even so, it knows that it is free and responsible. The mere fact of acting will necessarily put it in danger of doing wrong, perhaps irremediable wrong. Yet if it fails to act, if it allows things to happen, it shares the responsibility for what happens. In each case it must accept the risk of guilt.

How are we to understand Goethe's strange line that 'the actor is always unscrupulous; only the spectator has a conscience'? Probably so that the acting Existenz, obliged to realize things now, in time, cuts the knot, so to speak, while the spectator pretends that there is endless time for inquiry, and that in principle one might gain a definitive insight into the right course. The cheap conscience of a judging observer, which Goethe speaks of, is something other than the unconditional conscience of the man who acts – who knows and acts in a tension that is insoluble, and who can be convinced but never certain of knowing what is right. The clearer its conscience, therefore, the more modestly will Existenz claim to be certain. For conviction – without which, existentially, I cannot take a step – is not certainty.

The mere observer who will weigh *ad infinitum*, as if time did not exist, is existentially unserious. Possible Existenz knows resolution, and thus the risk of guilt. It realizes its ideas. It takes practical action. This is why Dante leaves the indecisive, the lukewarm who were neither good nor evil, in limbo: they are far from paradise and not even worthy of hell. They are nowhere. Even the vigour of evil may be better than the dispassionate ambiguity of endless reflection. Sinners may reform, but an indiscriminate unseriousness is all but hopeless.

iv. Can I know that I believe?

The second question to be asked of those Kantian sentences comes up as follows. Sincerity is truthfulness with myself, and Kant finds its mainstay in a final, undeceiving and undeceivable authority within myself. But is this authority absolutely sure of itself? Can and must this too remain constantly subject to testing? It would have to be its own examiner. There is no other authority in the world we might appeal to.

Let us now ask about sincerity or truthfulness in professions of faith. Kant views the possibility of a sincere statement as beyond doubt. But the question is this: once a true believer sincerely examines himself, can he still claim to believe in one possible statement or another? Is it not true to say, rather: If I am sincere I do not know whether I believe? In real life, what I believe is being done, confirmed, and understood beforehand, and even so it remains beyond the range of absolute statements.

It is with faith as it is with action: the inner test, the final judgment, remains for ever *en route*, interminable in time. Believing or acting, I have to make my decision at the moment without ever ceasing to examine it.

v. Sincerity about rebellion and harmony

Let us return once more to our attitude in view of evil. We have seen rebellion, and we have seen the idea of a total harmony. But does rebellion not involve insincerity if it makes itself absolute? And is it not insincere to reject rebellion if the truth in its language is overlooked? Is the idea of harmony not insincere if it conceals realities? And is it not insincere to reject harmony if the harmony found in the world is set at naught?

It has proved impossible to solve the question of evil in a way that would be both logically consistent and borne out by all the facts. Every construction of Being in a cipher of entirety will fail as it claims to comprehend this entirety. All that remains is to comprehend the incomprehensibility.

There is the mysterious teleology of life in the world, the beauty and glory of things, and at the same time there is the dysteleology, the ugliness, the loathsomeness, the horror.

There is reason in the world too, and the possibility of human Existenz, and at the same time there is unreason and the deterioration of Existenz.

There is human greatness, visible in the heroes, thinkers, poets, and saints of the world, and at the same time human pettiness and meanness.

Not knowing the world as a whole, we have no right to judge it. We are in it; we make our way in it with the rest; we reach beyond it. Unable to overlook it as a whole, we must go wrong in judging the whole.

To agree with the world is as insincere as to disagree with it.

vi. The endless movement of basic historic attitudes

Infinite motion marks the great, basic historic attitudes – the Chinese lamentation without accusation, the Greek tragedies and those of Shakespeare, Job's failure in wrestling with God. These are interminable thought movements, steps on the way, factors of ascertainment rather than truth itself in the completed form of thought structures or poetic figures. The Chinese plaint does not round itself out in cognition. Shakespearean tragedy points beyond all he ever wrote. The Book of Job is resultless.

Section Two: Beyond All Ciphers

Among the biblical ciphers is the commandment of God: 'Thou shalt not make unto thee any image or likeness.' We can never comply with it, but the insight into its truth remains.

The eternal, the indestructible, the immutable, the source, the encompassing of all encompassing – this can be neither visualized nor grasped in thought. In the sense of our objective knowledge this cause of all being, our own included, is nothing. When we cover it with categories such as being, cause, origin, eternity, indestructibility, or nothingness, when we call it by these categorial ciphers, we have missed it already.

And yet it is not an indifferent limit that is thus missed in all thinking. It is not something which no eye or thought can reach, and which therefore does not concern us. It concerns us so much that no other source of light will make all being, ours included, transparent.

Transcendence – which is not a cipher but something we relate to in the cipher language, something unthinkable which we must think all the same – is as much Being as Nothingness.

If it remains real for us where thinking ends, where nothing is known, where there is no hint of any form or language, then we ourselves have changed. But in the end, as well as from the beginning, we shall have changed in one of two ways: either so as to realize the meaning of life as a way to Transcendence by our actions in the world, as Existenz in the realm of ambiguous ciphers – or so as to step out of the world and directly beyond all ciphers. The first happens by an illumination of consciousness that will always leave the essence hidden; the second is supposed to happen by a transformation of consciousness into a meditative ascent to Transcendence.

To speak of something that vanishes as you speak is paradoxical. Existenz, not only our intellect, is the premise of really hearing and entering into the magnificent phenomena of thinking that exemplify the paradox in history. We are about to discuss these existential experiences of thinking the unthinkable, to develop them from the nature of this kind of thinking, to cite historic examples. What we meet in them may seem odd and alien or self-evident and close. It may look like a parlour game with the void or like a springboard to fulfilment.

We reflect upon these ever-failing thoughts. They seem to flutter round an unreached hub of light or toward the infinite distance of Transcendence.

Thought is asked to venture into empty space with nothing to hold on to, no ground to stand on. Eventually the very air for breathing seems gone. But method, discipline, and guidance from the uncomprehended goal may turn this fluttering into flight.

If these thoughts do not reach any goal as thoughts, in the sense of mundane knowledge, they still leave us with an irreplaceable thinking experience. We sense what they bring about, or may bring about, in ourselves.

1 WE CANNOT KNOW GOD AND WE CANNOT HELP CONCEIVING HIM

Gaunilo, a monk arguing against St Anselm's proof of God, said that man could have no conception of the highest and greatest: I do not know what God is, nor can I infer it from a possibly related concept of the highest and greatest, for this is just as far beyond my conception or misconception. Against Gaunilo, Anselm pointed to God's actual presence in the human soul, and to Creation as a means to an analogous view of the Creator.

Assuming a belief in God, the denial of any rational cognition of his existence points to revelation.

Gaunilo's renunciation of thought leaves a vacuum. So does the corresponding method – later developed by Occam, for one – of using the authority of revelation to beat down reason. Against that, we follow Anselm and other great philosophers if we proceed on the premise that there is an answer to the question whether the gulf between man and Transcendence can be bridged in cogitative forms.

The answer is this: even though the absolute Transcendence which those thinkers meant by the cipher God does not permit itself to be known objectively, our insight into the impossibility of its cognition entitles us to try to justify the meaning of its ciphers – thus subjecting the form of these ciphers to the criteria of philosophical truth.

i. The abyss between the finite and the infinite
If I say, 'God is the infinite', I think of God in a concept that makes him both unthinkable and unimaginable. Imagination is finite; we cannot imagine what lies beyond all finite things.

Between the infinite and the finite, an old adage says, there is no relation. Attempts to reach God's infinity as infinity are bound to fail. Yet the fact that they are futile does not invalidate the attempts made, for instance, by way of *a* mathematical infinity, *b* infinite possibility, or *c* the infinity of the world.

a: Concepts of the infinite have brought it within the range of mathematical operations. But beyond every infinite that mathematics can define lies the undefinable infinite – and this alone is the infinity of God. For all the depth of its thinking, for all the operational techniques it has discovered, mathematics cannot wholly master the infinite which has been called its basic problem.

An actual infinity will always be beyond conception, for any conceivable infinity will be transcended again by the infinite momentum. The task of infinite advance cannot be terminated by any final attainment of an absolute infinity.

b: If infinity is not conceived as complete but as infinite possibility, the infinity of God would seem to lie in infinite capacity, in inexhaustible genesis and change and creative power.

The grandeur of this conception is deceptive if it is to cover Transcendence. It reverses an Aristotelian concept, of the infinite potential of matter, into the infinite potential of God; but Transcendence cannot be anything but actual infinity, the inconceivable coincidence of infinite reality and infinite potential. The eternal completeness of absolute Transcendence encompasses the infinite Becoming of this world; it encompasses Creation, and the infinite possibility of cosmic creations; it encompasses also the quaint cipher of God in a process of becoming.

c: The infinity of the world, though we can neither experience nor conceive it as an actuality, seems thinkable as an infinite possibility. Everything real is finite. Whatever we find as an object, whether the number of grains of sand on the beach or that of the stars or even that of the atoms – however large a number may be, it is finite. It may be impossible to write down except by means of mathematical symbols; it may be practically infinite because no man could count it in a lifetime of counting – it is still finite. And if, in the world, we think of an infinity of possible phenomena in infinite time, this indefinite thought states only a refusal to foreclose the future. It comprehends no reality. To give the name God to the possibility of infinite

Becoming in the universe means to shrink God into a cosmic idea deprived of Transcendence.

If, on the other hand, the world's infinity is conceived as an actual one, we run into contradictions – into the Kantian antinomies, variants of which will reconstitute themselves in any state of scientific cognition. They arise from the fact that we never have the world as a whole for an object, that all we can do is to explore *ad infinitum* in the world.

To state the infinity of Transcendence in definite categories means to shroud it in mathematical speculation, in the infinite potential of a becoming God, or in the contradictory idea of an actually infinite world.

Yet this very fact, that any definite idea of infinity employed to grasp the infinite Transcendence will fail, is a way for us to become more clearly aware of it. When our thinking wants to make sure of Transcendence, its own existential impulses keep it from straying into dead ends. The ideas which are true in the particular but false on the whole are not null and void because we must overcome them to illuminate what would remain pointless and unconscious otherwise.

ii. Negative theology

Transcendence defies conception not only as infinity but in any category. If we call it God, the rule is the same as for the finite and the infinite: there is no relation between God and man, between God and the world as conceivable objects, even though we say that human Existenz relates to Transcendence.

It has been held that even without such relation there is an analogy – a kind of relation – between God and the world because God created the world. We can try to interpret Being as a likeness, an image, an analogy; we can see the abundance of God reflected in the world's abundance. Although the mathematical infinities and the concepts of the world as actually or potentially infinite are not the infinity of God, the endless world has been viewed as an image of divine infinity by Cusanus, and endless time as an image of eternity by Plato.

And yet God and th e world, and God and man, remain incomparable Any thought that makes God an object will put God himself out of our mind. However he may be discussed, the impropriety of such discussion will strike any pious thinker. Still, such thinkers will not simply throw out all ideas of God; they will preserve them in the knowledge that they cannot know. This very knowledge becomes a kind of idea of God, in what we call negative theology.

Augustine, the great Christian thinker, conceived it in principle. 'Everything can be said of God, and nothing is properly said of God.' Thus the most general statement will be the most nearly true: God is the supreme Being, the Being above, besides, and without which there is nothing. That God is Being says both everything and nothing, because it remains quite indefinite. 'God is ineffable; what he is not is easier said than what he is . . . Whatever you understand is not God.'

To Augustine, therefore, self-abrogation came to be the form in which to say things about God. If God is to be conceived, he must be conceived in categories, because we can think only in categories – but since no category applies to God, the categorial aspect of this conception must, paradoxically, be rescinded at once. 'If we can,' says Augustine, 'we know God as good without the quality of goodness, as great without quantity, as a creator not wanting for a creation, as enthroned above all things without a place, as wholly omnipresent without localization, as eternal without time, as the maker of changeable things without any change in himself.'

Aquinas, the great systematizer who adopted and developed all possible ideas of God, also went in for this negative theology. Infinitely much, he wrote, can be said of God, for as the source of every created thing he has something of each; but then again, nothing can be said of him because of the disparity between creation and creator. Everything positive that might be said of God must be negated again: he is not a body, not matter, not a living being, nor is he a spirit or a person. He has a life that is no life, and a wrath that is no wrath; his love and mercy are neither love nor mercy. Hence the to and fro of affirmative and negative statements.

In particular, in God, the categorial generality is indistinguishable from the reality it covers. In him *essentia*, the general being, and *existentia*, the singular reality, are one and inseparable, nor does one precede the other. God is neither genus nor species, neither general nor individual – he is all in one. He is *deitas* and *deus*. He is individual not as distinct from others; he is the one individual that has nothing besides itself, and thus no longer truly individual.

We can speak of God in any way we wish and are still bound to miss the indefinable which all definitions fit in negation only. As Aquinas put it, 'What God himself is stays for ever hidden. And this is the highest knowledge we can have of him in this life: to know that God is above all we think of him.'

iii. Cusanus and the coincidence of opposites

a: Cusanus starts out thinking along the lines of negative theology, holding that the unfoldment of thoughts and images has no more to do with the ineffable deity than the finite has with the infinite. If the idea is to unfold God himself rather than an image, this is idolatry – for it is idolatrous to give the image what is due to truth alone. So, the negative statements are indispensable. No affirmative statement about God will fit him; only the negative ones can be true. Without them God would be revered as a creature.

Cusanus, however, is not content with this. In the very process of thinking he finds a way to transcend it. Our finite thinking is tied to antitheses; asked to think what is above all antitheses, it founders on the antitheses – but if this foundering is carried out methodically, it will touch Transcendence. There is one principle Cusanus never tires of thinking through: since God is beyond all antitheses, everything antithetical must coincide in God. Negative theology, the negation of all finite statements about God, merely drops the thought; but an insight into the nature of human thinking, and into its objects as split into antitheses, will lift our thinking to God in the forms of the unthinkable, the *coincidentia oppositorum*.

The principle is simple: God is what he is and has no opposites. Being infinite and boundless, he is the unity of opposites, the affirmation and negation of all. He is everything, and at the same time nothing of anything. No definition can make him 'something' – which would mean to make him particular and limited. Cusanus carried this principle through all the categories we use in speaking of God.

b: For example: if we look for God by asking whether he is or is not, we shall not find him. 'The best answer to the question of God's being, therefore, is that he neither is nor is not . . . yet even this remains a supposition, since the precise answer is beyond our intellect and our reason.'

Unity is opposed to diversity. This unity is not God's; the unity of God would have to be one not to be opposed by any diversity. Although unity may be a better word for God than diversity, it remains infinitely far removed from the truly fitting word.

God is all, without any 'otherness' *(alteritas)*; he is the '*non aliud*'. Unity in things of the world is tied to otherness, hence they are finite; God is that absolute unity without otherness. He is the 'non-otherness' not opposed to otherness – nor to nothingness, since this too is preceded and defined by him. He who precedes the possibility of becoming cannot become other than he is. And whatever we may wish to make him out as, God is not – for this, unlike God, can turn into something else.

Nor is there in God an antithesis between reality and possibility. Both are one in him, the *possest*. He is what he can be, free from the possibility of becoming other than he is. Everything can change, but not God.

He is the greatest and the least. He must be the greatest, for he encompasses everything, and the least, for he is in everything.

As for God's infinity, it does not face finiteness as the other – for then it would be finite also. 'Thou art, O God, thine own end, for thou art what thou hast. Thou art not limited by another end, but by thyself.' Thus he is not the mere absence of an end in endlessness, but its completion. He is the complete infinity that includes everything finite instead of confronting it.

c: If the truth of statements about God lies in stating the coincidence of opposites, the price of discussing God is always to say the unthinkable, in the sense of intellectual thinking.

But Cusanus says that this negation of all definitions in negative theology, this failure of definition in the *coincidentia oppositorum*, is just what will give the human mind the 'most precise assurance' of the absolute unity of the infinite God.

d: This 'thinking toward' God gives the categories a peculiar quality for human reason: where God is concerned, the mind can raise no question without presupposing what it asks. To ask whether there is unity presupposes its being; to ask what it is, its nature; to ask why, its cause; to ask to what end, the end of everything. The invariable premise of all doubtful questions must be the greatest certainty.

To every possible question about God, therefore, we must reply first of all that it is improper – for it presumes that only one of its alternatives could be borne out. In God's case this does not apply.

e: Cusanus confines his thinking to the rich, yet magnificently simple unfoldment of his one basic idea. He does not ruminate about absolute Transcendence; he dispenses with the rich imagery of the speculative mystics, who would like to settle there. The condition of his images is not to violate the distance between man and God, not to sneak in any mediations or intermediate links, not to attempt a cognition of the deity itself except by the clear-cut thinking of the unthinkable.

Purely, soberly, simply, Cusanus thinks his way through the world under a speculative empyrean. He does not polemicize against the mystical union that would remove him from the world, but he is factually unready for it. Nor is he ready to think himself into God's nature as if one might set foot there, as if the gulf between the finite and the infinite might be vaulted directly. There is but one possibility of an indirect leap: formal transcending in the pure concepts that rescind their definitions in the *coincidentia oppositorum.*

Cusanus thinks in a direction where nothing is conceivable, definable, imaginable any more, in the direction of that which really is – and which is nothing as well.

iv. The transcending ideas and Existenz

Let us take another brief historic look at the pattern. We see the polytheistic faith in many gods in the world. We see the monotheistic faith in one God facing the world he made. And we see the concept of an impersonal cause above the world, above the gods, above the one God – the Being that is nothingness, that is both and neither.

The sequence of transcending the idea of God and then reidentifying God with the goal of transcending took similar forms everywhere. The contents differ greatly, but we recognize the structure of subordinating gods, and God.

The Babylonians knew an order of stars above the gods. The Chinese *tao* was superior to all Being. In India, the Bhagavad Gita shows the impersonal One that precedes all divinity and manifests itself in personal aspects; to Shankara, the Brahman – the point outside, the absolute Transcendence –

was the source of Maya, the magic delusion of existence that includes the world, the gods, and Isvara, the one God and Creator of the world.

In the form of superiority, the Hindu Brahman and Nirvana are comparable to Plato's *agathon* and 'beyond Being', and to the One of Plotinus.

From such comparisons – if for a moment we permit ourselves this barbarous juxtaposition of forms irrespective of content – we see that the mere form of transcending and subordinating signifies virtually nothing. If we take similar forms of concepts for the essence, the result will be an empty game of endlessly varying distinctions and combinations. The point is which distinctions let us understand original decisions to put those ideas into existential practice, and thus to make them a language.

If asked, for instance, whether Transcendence can simultaneously coincide with God and the Being-Nothingness of the impersonal, suprapersonal cause, we have to say that such a combination of ways of thinking means nothing unless it serves as a language for original Existenz. And then it is no longer to be understood as a combination.

The idea of God and the speculation on Being meet in the thinking of negative theology, of the *coincidentia oppositorum*, of all other ways of formal transcending; but their common feature is always the same: that there can be no categories of Transcendence. Categories are classifications of thought in the world. To break through them, by thinking them in such unthinkable forms as coincidence of opposites, contradictoriness, circle, tautology, can be a way of transcending, a way whose import lies not in the thought – which is indeed bound to fail – but in the existential effect. The goal of all these thoughts is the true insight of knowing in not knowing. They reject all definitions of Transcendence, from the most general categories such as identity, likeness, being, something, to conceptions of personality and life. None of this can apply to Transcendence, which lies beyond all finite phenomenality. Not even freedom – a property of Existenz in the world, and meaningless elsewhere – can appertain to it. This is why no concept of Transcendence can help failing: they always lead us to state something. We say, 'the One', or we say, 'the utterly Other' – and each statement brings us back to a category, to making Transcendence rational and finite.

v. Like alone knows like

This ancient maxim, known as 'the *homoion* theorem', means that the object of our cognition must at the same time be present within ourselves. We already are what we know, or we become like it. We know only what we are, or what we can be.

a: The meaning of the theorem. Taken literally, it is absurd. After all, what we know is exactly what we are not, what exists without our participation. Yet this applies only in so far as we pit subject and object against each other as two separates. The theorem might have a different meaning: it might mean that in all the modes of encompassing which confront subject and object in the dichotomy they are simultaneously tied to each other. They are not two that meet; they are poles resulting from a split, and what has been split is primary as encompassing. Then the subject is qualified by the object, and the object by the subject, and neither can be by itself. They are not alike, as two objects that we compare; likeness here can only mean the way they are linked by their original unity. This unity means that the sense of truth will be lost if one, the subject or the object, parts with the other. In other words, the known object is inseparable from the knowing person.

The truth of the objectivity that appears in each mode of encompassing depends on the presence of the corresponding subjectivity. It is only in the split that the whole will be understood from the objects as they become phenomenal. Hence the *homoion* theorem changes its meaning according to the mode of encompassing: there must be a subject and an object in consciousness at large, life and environment in existence, Existenz and Transcendence in the reality of myself.

b: The mode of encompassing. In the encompassing of scientific knowledge we have the borderline case that the subject is mere consciousness at large, the point of a correct and generally valid knowledge of objects. This 'subject at large' that thinks identically everywhere shows in reality, in real subjects, immense differences in the scope, the clarity, the purity of knowledge; but it does exist wherever men think, and it illuminates the subject side of each mode of encompassing. What we are as existence living in an environment, as creative mind, as resolute Existenz, shows up in this thinking, which goes beyond science. It shows in the changes wrought in the thinker by the thinking of the thought, and in the thought by the thinker. What he knows affects his state of being, and this in turn lends substance and truth to a thought that would be merely 'accurate' otherwise. The encompassing itself is not objectified on either side of the dichotomy.

This other encompassing is also present in the cognition of consciousness at large, determining not its accuracy but its concerns – its choice of objects, for instance. The will to know for the sake of knowing, the original scientific curiosity, is itself a state of Existenz.

The meaning of ciphers and speculations on Being lies solely in their existential importance. They can only be true in conjunction with the thinker: how he loves and chooses, acts and reacts will show their truth. As I can judge nothing empirically without sense perception, I can have no perception of Being without possible Existenz.

c: The other judgment in science and in cipher thinking. There ensues a judgment other than that of scientific results. When we think speculatively and in ciphers, it is a perversion to seek factual decisions on matters that can be settled only in the reality of the Existenz that makes them communicable and comprehensible in those objectivities.

Linked with the interest in ciphers, therefore, is an interest in the Existenz that thinks them, in the singular historic form of their appearance – a form they cannot exchange for generally thinkable didactics without a loss to themselves. We look for criteria of truth that are not merely logical. As we test empirical statements by observation and logic, we want to sense the truth of philosophical statements in the Existenz that made them. We may note how far it is from intellectual virtuosity to serious involvement, or from knowing doctrines by heart to taking them to heart, or from a thinking that is not really original to one that is always at the same time inner action, or from facile, sympathetic reproductive talk to genuine, original adoption with our own being.

This judgment is primarily a self-judgment, because the experience of how the ideas turn out in me exists only in my own self. Reflecting, I judge their effect and acknowledge or reject the moods and feelings they evoke in me. I X-ray them, so to speak, and either make them my own or tolerate or fight them.

d: *The* homoion *theorem in mysticism.* The theorem states a basic truth. In the subject-object split, subject and object relate to each other in a way that makes each, so to speak, the other's mirror. Thus we may ask with Kant about the 'identity' of the subjective forms of thought and the objective forms of things (of categories and ontal structures) or about the 'identity' of the biological forms of existence and environment, or about the 'identity' of Existenz and Transcendence. There is no real identity in any of these cases, but there is an indissoluble interrelation all the way down to their encompassing ground.

For us, in time, the mirror images remain divided. The relation of Existenz and Transcendence especially – objectified as a language in the realm of the ciphers – exists as faith, not as likeness. Now a question arises: does it make a difference in the meaning of the homoion theorem, in the meaning of 'likeness', whether the 'knowing' occurs in ciphers or beyond all ciphers?

Mystics have expressed the idea of nullifying the subject-object split altogether. They have reported experiences of the kind: object and I alike are extinguished in the encompassing fullness of the deity. Existenz and Transcendence, I and God, become one. To know God means to become God.

'I am as big as God, and he is small like me; I am not without him, nor without me is he,' said Angelus Silesius (1624–77). And: 'So I must fathom me in God, and God in me – and come like him, a God in God, to be.'

On such paths the thinking consciousness of temporal self-being cannot follow. It cannot bridge the chasm between man and God, between Existenz and Transcendence, although all philosophical thinking moves in the direction and under the guidance of Transcendence. The astounding words uttered by the mystics of all civilizations mean a union of God and the ego in which both ego and God have disappeared. The human being living in a world, as himself, does not exist any longer. In the mystical union there can be no more talk of God, nor of man – both have become inaccessible in a private realm.

Even so, what mystics have been thinking beyond all ciphers, what they have said in the world about their incommunicable meditative experiences, carries tremendous weight with us. We turn now, not to the practice, but to a few mundanely comprehensible ideas of some historic figures.

2 EXAMPLES OF A RADICAL TRANSCENDING OF ALL CIPHERS

Negative theology seems like a gentle shadow, which in the West, in fact, merely sets off the light of the beautiful cipher world. In Asia, on the other hand, that world has been consistently transcended not just in vigorous thought but in the ensuing way of life, and to depths hardly paralleled elsewhere. How much of this we understand is doubtful, but it can surely leave a singular impression and make us more sensitive to our Western rudiments. We ought to understand that striking paradox of a language to end language.[1]

Wherever they have occurred, there is a marvellous power in those attempts to pass not only beyond reality but beyond all ciphers, to reach the unthinkable, unspeakable ground that bears us and encompasses all encompassing. While any such attempt must be made in a form we can think, this is neither its purpose nor the thinker's intention. It is what makes that thinking so strangely ambivalent – either, as to the intellect that wants objective knowledge, an unintelligible gibberish signifying nothing, or else a revelation of the unsaid and ineffable by the transparence of those rationally senseless ideas.

The ideas touch us in so far as we hear in them a historic person in the reality of its meditative way of life. Since only faint perceptions of such personalities, if any, have come down to us, their necessarily highly abstract thoughts may seem tenuous. Yet in this very abstractness they can be more moving than any others. As we adopt them they probably are no longer what their extraction implied.

BORO BUDDOR

The mighty edifice of Boro Buddor in Java combines images, symbols, spatial arrangements, and the pilgrim's movements in that space into a thrilling visualization of Buddhist thought beyond all ciphers.

A terraced pyramid rises under the sky, in wide open country. On its lower levels rows upon rows of bas-reliefs keep the worldly forms of life before the pilgrim's eyes. Ascending higher, up archways and stairs, he passes statues of Buddha in meaningful poses. At the top all images cease.

[1] Cf. the chapters on Buddha in Karl Jaspers, *The Great Philosophers*, V. I, and the chapter on Nagarjuna, ibid., V. II.

Cupolas and geometrical forms remain until the last cupola points at the empty sky, with which the wayfarer is left alone.

Everything is symbolic. The happy images of the rich world below are seen in narrow corridors whose picture-strewn outer walls block off the view of the landscape. Above, however, the blue void already appears.

Not until the topmost of the angular terraces does the pictorial abundance diminish. The narrow space widens as the outer wall drops down to an imageless, cupola-topped balustrade, baring the formless vault of heaven to one side of the way – for the upper square ambits are already removed from the form-filled world of the senses. Their bas-relief chronicle deals with the coming Buddha Maitrenya whose radiance has not yet been seen by any physical eye, only in inner visions.

Finally, on the upper circular terrace, all forms of pictorial representation and ornamental continuity have disappeared. Seventy-two small cupolas of stone lattice-work ring a central pedestal on which a large closed cupola crowns the edifice. Like a forest of Nirvana symbols they rise into the pure heavenly void, their tops reduced to pure stereometric forms of a mathematical nature.

But the latticed cupolas do not yet signify the perfect state beyond all images. For each one holds a Buddha figure, its shape almost concealed from the eye by the stone filigree, but still visible. They symbolize a higher, formless vision, the forecourt of Nirvana. Towering above them at the end is the one massive closed cupola that also harbours the Buddha figure, but withholds it from view.

Heinrich Zimmer[1] has interpreted the meaning of the ascent: the pilgrim's inner image is first developed by way of unfoldment, then by melting down what has been unfolded. The evolution of the ciphers ends with the transcending of all ciphers.

Buddha himself must vanish as a cipher. On the lower walls he was in plain sight, in niches; in the latticed cupolas he began to withdraw; in the massive central cupola he is invisible. The symbolized forms of inner vision were followed by images of the transition stage, the cessation of all forms, and finally by the sign of transported being. This is the way: from the regions of form-filled inner vision to eternal Nirvana.

The sculptural-architectonic representation is a parable of the road to the unrepresentable. The goal is the pure void of eternity, sundered in human consciousness into the I and the objective world. Through the world of the senses, the world of figures and visions, of the pleasure and pain-filled diversity of life, the road climbs through the realm of formless vision, and on to Nirvana that has no beginning. The chains of the ignorance that hides the pilgrim's own being from him drop off in rings and stay behind; he can see them beneath him as the terraces he has passed.

[1] *Kunstform und Yoga*, Berlin, 1926.

The symbolism of the Buddha image runs through all the steps of the building. The pictured legends show Buddha involved in human lives and bonds of nature. In the niches he is alone, no longer entangled in existence, but still plainly visible. In the latticed cupolas he passes out of sight, and on the summit the eye can no longer reach him.

No word about the planners and the architects of this marvellously powerful work has come down to us, no document to witness their intentions. The vast ruins have been preserved, weather-beaten and dilapidated, thanks only to the durability of stone. The builders did not care one way or the other. Their minds were not on the future, on permanence and mementoes, but on the eternity of Nirvana. They did not think historically of posterity, but unhistorically of worldlessness. For his exegesis, Zimmer had to draw on Indian Buddhist texts, but those can enlighten us neither about the infinite pictorial detail nor about the meanings of the individual terraces and stairs and archways. Only the whole seems clear.

The following ought to be kept in mind as we try to form a conception of this Buddhist transcending of all ciphers.

The Buddhist ascent is not accomplished as a speculative transcending in pure thought; it comes from specific meditative exercises, from a transformation of the state of consciousness. The meditator segregates himself in the world. Upon his return to communicability he will understand himself as the essence of the ineffable, eternal Being-Nothingness which in Nirvana sheds all deceptive individuality, all the deceptive objectivity of worldly ignorance.

By taking up and then discarding all ciphers – i.e., all meanings – the meditator does not reach a standpoint for his future activities in the world. He has left the world. He drops back into it, but henceforth he will experience it only as an indifferent course of existence. It no longer means anything, except for cryptic signs that may hint at ways to the disappearance of both world and meanings.

It is a mistake to believe that what we are talking of might be achieved by pure speculation, in general consciousness. The point is the real experience, to be gained only in years of performing the meditative exercises and living apart from the world. We tend to overlook the fact that this experience basis is essential – just as the Jesuits cannot be understood without the formative power of their *exercitia spiritualia*.

But the question is whether the speculative ideas of Buddhism do have a significance for us. We take them for communicable ideas in the world of general consciousness, detaching them from their roots in meditation, which transforms consciousness. We lack the specific experiences of those men, experiences to which we have no access; but we think the thoughts which their liberating operation makes transcendent – and as such we find them irreplaceable. We come to feel addressed, not by a curiosity, but by something of concern to us. The great difference from the original Buddhist world is that we use their ideas to come to ourselves before Transcendence, while the Buddhist seeks to lose all sense of self entirely.

Let us try to visualize the state of the perfect Buddhist. The past and future Buddhas are called the 'universally kind'. They are the all-merciful and non-objective love, the phenomenon of him who dwells already in Nirvana. To represent them in gestures and realize them in a life that has become indifferent otherwise – this is what remains to be done in the world by one who knows its indiscriminate emptiness. The Buddhist does not impose his knowledge and his way of life on anyone; Buddhists alone have never waged religious war. He disdains no one, does not flare up, shows compassion and pity without the suffering of pity. The entire being of the world, its happiness and its evil, the worldly ways of the rebirths up to the glories of paradise that still entice men and keep them from reaching Nirvana – all this he can 'let go', in the calm of complete emptiness. He helps by showing the way to Nirvana, by teaching and factual example, not by demands. The unwilling are welcome to everything worldly; the Buddhist will not intervene either by force or by resistance. Liberated from the world, he knows neither emotions nor fixed purposes, neither pride nor resentment, neither desire nor want, and least of all the daily piques and peeves of men. Death finds him indifferent. He does not fear it; he does not long for it either.

There is little doubt that now and then this human-superhuman state has been achieved; the texts we read would not exist without such a basis. But the price of this complete deliverance from the world is the relinquishment of all its meaning, of any way of possible fulfilment in the world. The price is not only to transcend but to give up the cipher nature of our own experience and way of life – it is simply the loss of all ciphers.

MASTER ECKHART

Master Eckhart interprets in the concepts of Christian theology. He gives us Western air to breathe; neither his points of departure nor his formulas are Buddhist. And yet he moves on the same boundary, looks for the same goal that is attainable only by transcending everything, all ciphers and God as well.

1 Eckhart distinguishes between *deus* and *deitas*, God and Godhead. 'Godhead and God are as different as heaven and earth. God too comes to be and passes away.'

God comes to be by 'flowing out' of the Godhead – an act that simultaneously brings the triune God, the world, and time into existence. By this outflowing, in the 'simple Now of eternity', that which did not happen happened – 'not in time, but with time'. God, the Trinity, and the world are coeternal: 'At one and the same instant did God, by becoming, by begetting the Son as an equally eternal, altogether equal God, create the world also.' God's outflowing from the Godhead is altogether different from his acts of begetting the Son, breathing the Spirit, or creating the world. It is the source of all these.

3 And yet, to Eckhart, God and the Godhead are identical as well. Then the distinction becomes intra-divine: in eternity God performed only one act, which made him God. Before that – not temporally, that is, but before time – he is the Godhead, inactive and ineffective, impersonal and worldless. The distinction takes Eckhart beyond God. It is expressed in many of his formulas:

The Godhead is being, not action. It took God to create all things, to become the whole world's Father. God exists only since the creature exists; he not only created it, it also created him. Thus one may say, I am a cause of God's being, but the Godhead is its own cause. Before the Godhead, creator and creature lie in the same sphere.

4 How does thought make sure of the Godhead? By voiding everything thinkable, every distinction, every definition.

'Equality', for instance, cannot be said of the Godhead. 'Where there is equality there is no unity, for equal is privative of unity; and where there is unity there is no equality, for equals remain distinct and multiple. Where things are equal they cannot be one.'

And: 'In unity the Father never knew of a Son, nor the Son of a Father; for there is neither Son nor Father nor Holy Spirit.' There can be no equality until there is distinction. And where there is distinction there is not the unity that lies beyond definition and beyond the category of unity.

The Godhead is unthinkable because thinking requires definitions of the undefinable. Being, God, Creator – these are already conceived in categories that do not fit the Godhead. We have to transcend all definitions, including the idea of God.

In thinking, we think of 'beingness' (*essentia*) and of Being (*esse, existentia*). We put them side by side: they are two; and we think of one in the other: they are one. Yet the Godhead can be grasped neither in its distinction nor in its unity.

5 With God we are linked only as his creatures in the realm of our existence. Yet man is free to penetrate where he was once and will be again – where indeed he always is – not with God, but with the Godhead. Through God, man can find his way to what God was before he became by setting out on his work of creation.

We humans have both: our inmost, which is one with the Godhead, and the creatural side that God brought into existence by becoming himself. Thus it is only in the Godhead, not in God, that we find peace. We come to rest when the createdness, the doing and becoming, dies in us – when we are no longer *en route*, when we turn to nothing, when we 'un-become' Then we no longer need to know of God and the three divine persons who are still in the sphere of being something, in otherness and multiplicity. We are blessed only where there is not God the Creator but the Godhead in its oneness and nothingness – where through all being we find the identity of God and Godhead, and the equal past and possibly future identity of our own tiny sparks of souls with the Godhead – the place where God was not yet a person, as I was not yet this I.

'God originates only where all creatures address him. While I was abiding in the fount of the Godhead, no one asked me what I was doing or whither was bound. . . . Yet when I flowed out, all creatures said, God. . . . Thus all creatures speak of God. Why not of the Godhead? Whatever is in the Godhead is One, and this is unspeakable.'

And: 'When I enter into the fount of the Godhead, no one asks me whence I come or where I have been. Nor does one miss me, for there even God un-becomes.' From 'created light' we shall be changed to the 'uncreated radiance' of the divine being, and 'shall be what he is'. It is 'nobler' to 'break through' to the Godhead than to 'flow out' of it; yet this breaking through means to experience what I am – uncreated, eternally, as this 'spark of a soul'.

The soul, in Eckhart's thinking, will not become equal to the Godhead – for the oneness of the tiny spark and the Godhead extinguishes 'God' and 'equal' and 'become'. The caesura between the world and Transcendence is not between the world and God any more; both belong to the Being that originates when God and the world come to exist at once, a single realm in which things, men, and God are inseparable. The caesura lies between this whole realm of Being and the Godhead.

There is the gulf: between what we are as God's creatures and what we are without God, before God, in the depth of the Godhead, as the spark, the uncreated we belong to.

3 THE QUESTION OF THE FIRST CAUSE: WHY ANYTHING? WHY NOT NOTHING?

i. Kant

In discussing the futile proofs of God, specifically the one that posits a primal being as 'necessary', Kant showed that our intellect cannot 'find either a concept of absolute necessity, or an absolute necessity of any concept'. We not only experience this incapacity, however, but a matter of such import to our reason will not let us rest. 'The absolute necessity,' Kant went on, 'which is so indispensable to us as ultimately underlying all things, is the true abyss for human reason. Even eternity, however awfully and majestically a Haller may picture it, leaves far less dizzying an imprint on our mind; for it only measures the duration of things but does not carry them. It is an inescapable thought, but an unbearable one as well, that what we imagine as supreme among all possible beings should say to itself, as it were: "I am from eternity to eternity; besides myself there is nothing but what I willed to be – yet whence am I?" Here everything sinks beneath us; the most perfect as well as the least hang in an unsettled balance before mere speculative reason, which can make either one vanish without the slightest hindrance and at no cost to itself.'

Kant furnished no answer. He saw that in the context of his philosophy there can be none. He refused to answer, realizing that he would have to resort to a deceptive way of thinking.

Yet this way, which we call speculative thinking, is not an accidental error that we might correct. It lies in the nature of our reason, along with the deception it entails. We see through it, but we go right on with it. We make the experiences it brings, though we are not deceived any more.

To raise the question, and thus take the speculative way, is an 'awful' experience. We cannot escape the thought, but neither can we bear it. It dizzies us.

Yet this happens only in a kind of thinking which 'at no cost to itself' can, by a mere thought, make all things vanish. It is so cheap because it involves no cognition. Speculative thinking operates with objects that are no objects.

Cognitive thinking, on the other hand, is either consummated in empirical reality or it runs against that transcendent reality which dawns upon us solely in our freedom.

The biblical answer to the question 'Why anything?' would be, 'Because God created the world.' So, Kant attributes the thought to the supreme being that wrought this creation, making it visually plain that wherever we shift the question, it will reappear. It is inescapable for our thinking.

ii. Leibniz

Leibniz came to the question from his principle that nothing happens without sufficient reason. He answered it as follows: in the sequence of accidental things, of bodies and of conceptions in the souls, we can go back as far as we please without advancing a step, since the same question, 'Whence and Why?' will always arise again. Therefore, the sufficient reason that makes other reasons unnecessary must lie outside the sequence. It must be the reason for the whole sequence – a necessary being that bears its *raison d'être* within itself.

The question thus served Leibniz only to repeat one of the ancient proofs of God. It never occurred to him that the Creator might raise it about his own existence.

And with his answer leading to the proof of God, Leibniz could promptly raise and answer the second question: why this rather than something else? Because, he said, it follows from God's perfection that in creating the world he chose the best possible plan to achieve a maximum of diversity with a maximum of order – that is to say, to bring forth the real world as the best of all possible worlds.

iii. Schelling

Schelling took up what Kant had said, and after praising Kant's 'profound sense of the Being that comes ahead of all thought', went on: 'If we want any kind of entity outside thought, we must begin with a Being absolutely independent of all thought, a Being we cannot get ahead of with any concept, a Being we are not free to think about as about finite being.' This is the great difference: in thought we can indeed get ahead of all finite being, because we can anticipate it *a priori*, in the categories. We can get ahead of it, moreover, because we conceive it as possible – and the concept of its possibility makes it conceivable that it might as well not be. But we cannot get ahead of infinite real Being. We cannot conceive it as possible. Nor is it possible to think that it might not be.

iv. A comparison of Kant, Leibniz, and Schelling
Leibniz raised the question incidentally, for the purpose of repeating an old proof of God in a new form, and answered it.

Kant also raised the question by the way, as a dizzying, fictitious one addressed by the Creator to himself. He did not answer it, because to enter this level of questioning is a self-deception – albeit an ever-recurrent one due to man's metaphysical makeup, one that can be seen through but not eliminated – about the possibilities of human cognition.

Schelling, in what amounts to a denial of Kantian thought, raised the question to a pivotal point of philosophizing. Unlike Kant, he did not stop at the limit. Schelling undertakes to tell us why there is something rather than nothing – for instance: the fully valid answer is not 'something'; it is 'all', or God. All is what is squarely incapable of not being, as nothingness is squarely incapable of being. The opposite of nothing, therefore, can only be all – not something, which is only relatively opposed to nothing. A thing is not absolutely incapable of not being; it is incapable of not being only in so far as it is with, and related to, other things. It is a mixture of real and unreal, an intermediate entity.[1]

The philosophical meanings of question and answer are entirely different in the three cases, similar conceptualities notwithstanding. Leibniz demonstrates a simple cogitative operational technique; Kant's clear and profound thinking produces vertigo at the brink of the abyss; Schelling assures us of eternal affirmation.

All three men have this in common, however: they are concerned with a philosophical idea. Though the question is couched in concepts, there is a moment – the moment of sudden understanding – when they are not operating with concepts, when their seeming conduct of such operations takes them in fact to the outer limits of cognition. What they think at those limits is what they are basically sure of, but their certainties differ in kind. Leibniz, sure of God, conceives his necessity; Kant, in his state of vertigo,

[1] Martin Heidegger has taken up Schelling's question, discussed it in a new manner, and further enhanced it into 'the basic question of metaphysics'. I hope to be able to deal with this on some other occasion.

points the way to the basic assurance of freedom and what rests upon it; Schelling, originally baffled, opens the door to a penetration of the deity so that we may know its nature and its life.

v. A pattern based on philosophical history

A good answer to the question 'Why is anything?' would be another question: what does 'is' mean here? Some historic pointers may suggest a pattern of the ideas of being.

Parmenides: What is being? It is, and it cannot not be. Nothingness is not, and has no way of being.

Plato: But non-being does have a way of being, because all becoming is, and yet it is not. Being is either pure Being, eternal and immaculate, or it is the being of becoming – being and non-being at once, not truly Being, though it has a part in it. The relation of pure Being to the things that are (of the *on* to the *onta*) is further conceived as that of the one to the many, or of Being to appearance.

Aristotle: Being is not unequivocal. It is not simply what is. It has many connotations. But it is not a generic concept under which various concepts of being might be subsumed as species. It is that which 'analogously' lies in all the things that are, because they are beings.

In the end, what we find as we get to the bottom of being cannot be defined as Being. Plato called it 'beyond Being', *epekeina tes ousias*. Plotinus defined it as that which cannot be grasped without going beyond Being – for beyond the intelligible world of all thinkable things lies the Above-Being, the One, and beyond the physical things lies the non-being of matter, and both, though utterly incomprehensible, are principles of all being. Being is not primary; we understand it from Above-Being and non-being. Plotinus assigned no categories to the One and to matter, since both are beyond conception, and thus beyond expression. We touch the One in the dialectics of transcending thought, and experience it in the rare states of ecstasy we may perhaps be granted; we touch matter in thoughtlessness and sightlessness, the way we gaze into the dark of night, and experience it in everything confusing, shackling, bad, and evil.

To Plotinus, Above-Being and non-being are the two poles, and between them lies all there is. Both poles might be called 'Nothingness', but one as lying above all thinkable things, the other as lying beneath them. We drop the distinction if we go back to the simple antithesis of Being and Nothingness. This antithesis is voided by the mystical experience, which we cannot think; any attempt to conceive it will founder on paradoxes that point to the basic experience withheld from all thinking.

vi. The dialectics of Being-Nothingness

The question 'Why not Nothingness?' rests on the assumption of an alternative. It assumes that there has to be either Being or Nothingness; the fact is that there is Being; the question asks why. But the alternative disappears in the Being-Nothingness speculation that led Hegel to conclude that pure Being is Nothingness. This is no longer a matter of alternatives, but of dialectics.

Pure Being, we are told, is the abstraction from everything finite and definite – but where there is nothing finite any more, and nothing definite, there is nothingness.

If Being is conceived as distinct from Nothingness, our question 'Why anything, why not nothing?' would thus point to Being and to nothingness at once. As our thinking cannot separate the two, we fail in the attempt to affirm or to deny one against the other.

This speculative dialectics can unify: it can show that in nothingness there is essential Being, that Nothingness itself comes to be fulfilled as true Being. Or the effect can be negative, when the main experience in Being comes to be that there is not nothing.

These ways of thinking reinforce ontology and nihilism; they support doctrines of Being and doctrines of Nothingness. Together with the dialectics, ambiguities appear at every step. A thought will turn and show its own perversion. For dialectics is both: a fruitful and illuminating movement and the mirage of a specific sophistry.

The magically attractive dialectics of Being and Nothingness harbours truth and delusion, reality and sorcery.

vii The philosophical state in which we raise the question
The question of Being is not the same when God, in the Kantian fiction, asks himself, 'Whence am I?' or when we ask why there is a world, or when I ask myself why I am, and whether I might just as well not be. The first is the question in the world of ciphers, conceived as addressed by a personal primal being, God, to himself. In the second case a thinking, self-conscious creature, man, inquires about the unknown being of the world. The third is the question which a thinking Existenz – that which I am – asks of my possible self.

Question and answer are guidelines to produce or clarify an inner condition.

No research, no cogent train of thought, can answer the question. It is empty, along with its answers, in the realm of knowledge. To the intellect it may be a joke, something to laugh about. If any answers are given to it, they are ciphers, not insights, and their multiplicity adds to the question.

Yet there can be no real answer until the question is put in earnest – that is to say, until I am affected by the personal experience I make in this thinking. It may be Kant's dizzy spell in view of the rational abyss, or the 'ever-negative spirit' of Goethe's Mephistopheles – 'Whatever is deserves to perish; I'd rather nothing came to be' – or the affirmative stand on existence, on Leibniz's 'best of all possible worlds', the 'eternal Yes' of Schelling.

The thought always seems to express some kind of certainty of Being – not a logically reasoned one, however, but a pre-logical, vital, existential one. It need not be thus.

We usually attach no great importance to experiences of the insane, but they can tell us things of philosophical significance that may be deeply moving to the physician in charge. There are conditions that we call pathological, conditions known and recognized as such by certain criteria, in which the patient will say, perhaps, 'I am not – nothing is – I just live as an extra, and I have to live this non-life through all eternity!'

There also are mental states not recognizable as pathological that lack a sense of Being – not to the vital, sensory, physical, material extent of those others, but in the sense of essentiality. 'I'm nothing,' such a person may say, 'and neither is anything else. It's all totally futile and completely irrelevant Thus the question may be answered in a mood of equating the reign of chance with Nothingness: there is Being, but it amounts to nothing.

Here, instead of certainties, we have uncertainties of Being. Mere arguments cannot cope with them. People who live without faith, and thus without meaning, need to be awakened by philosophical thought and a corresponding way of life; they need a destiny. It is idle to try to enforce the basic certainty, to expect to conquer the contradictory states of the human mind by thinking alone, whether rational or philosophically speculative.

At the point where it becomes clear that we exist, that there is a world, that we are possible Existenz, this consciousness itself is an instant revelation of the roots of Being. To ask, 'Why not nothing?' makes us not only dizzy but acutely aware of Being, and thus historically sure to accept ourselves as Existenz. 'There is not nothing,' man will say to himself. 'What is should show. It ought to be plain.' And the man who awakens in reflection will tell himself, 'I cannot have come into this existence in vain, for nothing.'

It is important to note that this revelation is not the same in all men, nor in all states of mind and situations of an individual – so important that if a philosophy forgets this, its sense of truth must fail at a crucial point. We do not have a psychological problem to describe and interpret here. We are dealing with the existential problem of communication.

The basic state of Existenz depends in part on whether and how that question of the first cause is experienced.

The question about Being, if asked everywhere in this form, would be differently answered. Being might be the one God or the Brahman, Nirvana or *tao*, the One of Plotinus, Spinoza's one substance. Or it might be nothingness, the desert, the void, chaos. The phenomena in which Being has been conceived at particular times are historic; but at all times it is man, in all his ways of encompassing, who serves at the present stage of this manifold revelation – in existence, in consciousness at large, in his possible Existenz, in the mind, in reason.

4 THE OTHER KIND OF THINKING

i. The ciphers of Maya and ignorance

Let us once more regard the world and our knowledge in a cipher that has been most strongly felt in India: everything is illusory. Knowledge – in the world, about things, in purposive action – is really ignorance, the veil of Maya. And what to our shrouded existence seems like nothingness is truth and plenty.

In this cipher any cognition, especially the scientific one of our times, is a cognition of mirages, itself a mirage, caught in the circle of mirages. Rational, objective clarity merely thickens the veil. Held against a true knowledge of Being, this tremendous knowledge of ours is in fact a single sham knowledge, an 'un-knowledge' (*avidya*).

What is the source of this veil, this reality of our existence that is not real being? A primal delusion? Did a historic event darken the light that was? Was a deceptive world created by an act of magic? If any answer is forthcoming, it comes in ciphers in which the very point at issue – the transcending of all ciphers – fades from sight.

An insight into the state of our world and our knowledge takes another kind of thinking, one that will tear the veil. If the sham comes from a reversal, this would reverse the original reversal that plunged us into darkness.

Yet this whole view of a 'world history of Being', of our being, as a mirage caused by an incomprehensible fall and maintained by ignorance – this view itself is unhistorically conceived. Both the reversal and the reversal of the reversal happen all the time, not at some time. At each moment there is apostasy from the realm of truth, and at each moment we return to it.

We return by another kind of thinking – whether by the meditative transformation of consciousness or by the speculative thinking which our intellect performs but cannot fathom.

i. Cues to the other kind of thinking

It can only be hinted at, but to have felt it is to experience a strong, soundless magnetism. The other kind of thinking silences us, at first, but it will not let us keep silent. For we want clarity about ourselves and the silence, even though it returns after each clarification.

I think of the realm 'beyond all ciphers' – but in fact, at that very moment it no longer exists. The cost of thinking it is its evaporation in the act of thinking.

The thinking in which it evaporates is the objective kind – thinking in views and images, in definable concepts, in ciphers.

Is there another kind? It would have to be a thinking that voids itself. It would break down thoughts and objects, reduce them to nothing – but so as to bring to the thinker's mind what is intrinsic and essential and by itself, not for anything else, not for us as an object of thought. And these very words, 'intrinsic' and 'essential' and 'by itself' and 'beyond Being', already say too much.

For these and all traditional metaphysical terms are statements and designations, and thus parts of the veil. Whatever breaks the silence clears the air, but it also disturbs it. Put into words, the silence loses its depth. In the end, therefore, Asian philosophers would use this whole kind of thinking only to destroy itself – a self-liquidating thought process they never tired of repeating.

What such a process brings forth in the thinker, what it makes accessible to him, what it reveals in the returning silence – all that does not arise from the self-liquidation of thought. This only clears the space. It pursues our objective thoughts into the last nook and cranny in which they would take refuge and from which they want to reappear – for in the end we should probably like to triumph by grasping 'the essence' in that other thinking. But then we would be betraying it, and what we wanted to know would be more deeply hidden. Time and again we should like to have it – to name it, at least – but at that instant of dragging it back into the thinkable realm we have lost it again.

In Asian philosophizing, therefore, this thinking serves only as a safeguard and preparation. Carried to the point of total failure by sublime dialectical means, it is not a way of fulfilment – fulfilment, there, comes as a transformation of consciousness achieved by way of meditation. To the Asians this is the beginning and the end of conceptual speculation, of the 'new thinking' as opposed to intellectual thought. Lifelong meditative exercises are the way to the truth that reduces all objective knowledge to mere ignorance.

The Asians call this truth emptiness. And even for our consciousness, without that transformation, the goal we seek is emptied in transcending beyond all ciphers, because our invariably objective thinking cannot reach it. Cleansed of all objectivity, it strikes us as nothingness. Can we cast anchor where there is no bottom to touch, no hold to grab? Our thinking consciousness, which wants substantial knowledge, obviously cannot; and no other consciousness is known to us, since we neither perform nor believe in those meditative transformations.

But could it be that this 'nothingness which is Being' might cast new light on our existence in processes of thought – that without submerging ourselves in meditation we might find our freedom in the world, and our freedom in the cipher language, fulfilled beyond the bounds of world and cipher? The answer to this question comes from existential experience, both active and passive. It shows in ways of dealing with our real cognition, of moving in the cipher language, of consciously experiencing our condition in the world, of seeing standards arise all round without knowing whence, and sensing a guidance without knowing how.

This reality is served by the other kind of thinking, by the philosophical speculation in which we meet the Asians. This is the thinking that voids itself. From our intellectual point of view it no longer seems like thinking. It does not arrive at cognitions; it is another kind of meditation, one that does not transform the state of consciousness. Its evolution in thousands of years has been as rich as that of music, but access to it is more difficult. He who gains it will make experiences that are unique in thinking. They may seem less potent, feebler, fainter than the massive ones of the meditative exercises and techniques, but this appearance is deceptive. It is precisely its lack of technical psychological effects that gives the speculative experience its pure existential impact.

Such thinking may vex us. Then it will often, unjustly, be felt as pointless travail, or else – sometimes justly – as an unserious delusive concept-shuffling. But where it kindles a spark it can be thrilling. It takes a participant where thought itself will put a stop to thought, where the guidance takes over after thought has made us free. It is the kind of thinking which at the peak of abstraction ceases to be abstract, because in shedding objectiveness it becomes existential.

iii. Again: why transcend ciphers and categories?
Let me repeat once more: any cipher delimits. It makes conceivable and figurative in thought and imagination. Whatever I think confronts me and my other thoughts.

Any cipher I think falls under categories. They may be as comprehensive as being, nothingness, substance, meaning, etc., but they remain categories. If a thought is conceivable it is already narrowed down. Definition is limitation.

Beyond all ciphers and categories lies Transcendence – and again, as a designation this word 'Transcendence' is already inappropriate. It denotes a passage beyond all objects and all ciphers. What it means, however, is not the step, not the act of passing, but the destination to which the passing takes us – and precisely that defies expression. Therefore, no statement about it is either true or false; it is a passage, a step, in speculative thought – as 'God is Being' or 'God is Nothingness', for instance.

To us as humans, as sensory rational creatures, transcending does not mean to renounce ciphers and categories. It means not to be trapped in them, to let them help us get beyond them even though we promptly fall back into them.

'I know nothing of God,' wrote Ludwig Curtius, a great modern humanist; 'I cannot even say that he exists, and yet I constantly feel sheltered in him.'

iv. Self-cancelling metaphysics
Metaphysics may be said to void itself.

The first step after its unfoldment as objective technical metaphysics is the demolition job that Kant performed on it, to preserve its cipher character:

the demonstration of the inevitable unintentional and unrecognized contradictions, of the endless, sterile disputes, of the typical logical paths of those aberrations, and of the lack of existential commitment in such knowledge.

The second step, which follows on the realization of the ciphers and their struggle, is to transcend them, to get beyond all ciphers, as men have done for thousands of years.

We are not losing the cipher world as we transcend it, but we are stopped from settling in it as absolute.

The thought of this transcending can dissolve ciphers, but it cannot produce them. Or, it will produce them only to dissolve them, with the dissolving game looking like truth itself.

Buddha and the Buddhists were the first to think this self-cancellation of metaphysics radically and explicitly. We note the ambivalence at once, for this kind of thinking cannot be at home in the real world, nor in any conceived one. It is 'at home' in vanishing and letting vanish. In temporal existence this self-dissolution of the cipher metaphysics leads to nothingness.

v. Existenz wants to live in the world

But temporal existence exists. Totally dissolved, man can no longer want anything in the world; he can no longer do or build anything; he no longer knows anything but indifference, licence, absurdity. To us, this is so far from acceptable as the last word that the mere possibility it expresses evokes opposition from our existential energies.

For we are not mere playthings of chance, not just a prey of nature. We are not in the world in vain. A timeless 'eternal kingdom' is a cipher, but one that speaks only in the world. It is not another world that I might escape to; it is present in this world. If I base my life upon a future kingdom, on the 'other-worldliness' that awaits me elsewhere, on the resurrection of the flesh that will enable me to live there permanently – if I turn these ciphers into tangibles of a reality, the world will cease to be a serious matter and eternity itself will disappear. Unless I realize, in the world, what eternity can show me here, I am nothing. If I miss the world, I lose eternity as well. True, the eternal is the measure of our worldly being, but I must not give up what it measures. What is eternal – as the paradox expression goes – what I am in eternity, is settled in the world, in time.

We of the West, self-educated in the traditions of Antiquity and of the Bible, will transcend all ciphers and still feel the challenge of our given existence: to realize ourselves as Existenz in the sight of Transcendence.

5 SPECULATION ON BEING

i. No cognition; no progress; no theory

Speculation on Being has no object, and to that extent it has no substance.

Formally it is carried out in evanescent abstractions. Since we can maintain those only for instants, however, they will turn either into the wealth of images and metaphors that puts an end to all conceptual definition, or into conceptualities that we take for facts and use to satisfy our need for objectivity. Such thinking seesaws between emptiness and objectivity. Instead of achieving the impossible – a cognition of Being – we come to speak to Being, as it were, or to have Being speak to us. The very failure of thought becomes an impulse. The silence speaks.

In such thinking there is no historic progress either, though it can be broadened and enriched. There will always be new forms of thinking the same: the vortex in the thought, vertigo in the thinker, and then, so to speak, the order of vortex and vertigo.

Speculative thinking drafts no theories in the scientific sense, which might then be confirmed, improved, or replaced by new and more accurate ones. But it does give us the vast hoard of speculative circumlocution in philosophical history.

ii. What is 'mysticism'?

By mysticism we mean, first of all, two antithetical experiences. We mean visions, which are understood to come to us from a supersensory realm, and we mean the mystical union, that incommunicable state in which there is no more distinction between myself and the object – the state in which I, the object, and other objects all blend into one. But the word is used in yet another sense. We find it applied to the speculation on Being, to dialectica movements that bring Being to our mind by thinking, in bright consciousness, and with all objectiveness gone.

The three ways of mysticism fight each other. The pure thought of Being spurns the visionary and ecstatic fantasies; its 'holy' soberness rejects the mystical union as a mere experience. In disciplined, methodically performed thinking we keep aloof from exercises that would transform our consciousness in meditative stages.

But the three stay related. In dialectical speculation we interpret the mystical union and take our metaphors from the contents of visions. Visionaries and practitioners of the union, on their part, feel the urge to understand themselves in speculative thinking.

iii. What the speculation needs

Speculation on Being is expressed in rational statements. It can be brought to methodological awareness. It is pure – but by itself it is empty. It may touch us, but it cannot presently fulfil us. Its unchanging rationality makes it monotonous.

To prove its true quality, the speculation needs something to supplement it, or else there must be a previous state of fulfilment in which the speculation itself is but a function.

The supplement may consist of experiences, states of consciousness, visions – and then, from the viewpoint of serious philosophy, we frequently have magic and delusion, self-gratification and self-destruction.

If the supplement is Existenz, however, the speculation will provide the broad scope of Being to shelter it in the faithful, unconditional performance of its historic tasks.

While the rational movements as such may seem like an inconsequential intellectual game leading to mere non-being, their existential effect can be altogether different. By the failure of thought they can change our basic condition. They can serve to tie all critical cognitions and all our actions in the world to the bounds of their meaning.

iv. Speculation on Being and the existential state of life

We differentiate the speculation on Being by its way of influencing Existenz in existence. It may be hypostatized and chosen to fulfil this life, at the cost of missing out on existential reality and eventually losing the speculation's own truth. It may be tolerated as an interval and become one odd thinking experience among others. And it may, once carried out, remain the lasting background of our existential consciousness, the factor that brings measure and limit to the fore and makes the orders of rank essential.

v. Illumination of not knowing

In the speculation on Being we illuminate the boundary where knowing ends. We find out how invisible, how unthinkable, how inexpressible Being is, and thus we tear the shroud of ignorance that keeps us unaware of that boundary.

Logically, the state of not knowing is our conquest of the duality of subject and object in thought. From thinking one thing and the other, we move by way of unfolded conceptuality to the conceptless, imageless, spaceless, timeless vanishing point of everything, the object, and the I.

In the Western world this fulfilment of not knowing is the encompassing *raison d'être* of the figures and constructions of great poetry and philosophy. It makes them meaningful within their limitations. Shakespeare and Kant offer indirect, uniquely quiet examples. If that limit is unfelt and unconceived, if its light fails, poetry will become photographic or fantastical, and thinking – even in such men of genius as Fichte and Hegel – will as a whole relapse into a narrow pseudo-knowledge, no matter how grand, and no matter what important points, true knowledge, and effective speculation it may contain.

6 PERVERSIONS OF THE SPECULATION

i. The lure of new objectiveness and visuality

It is only as a boundary process that Existenz can void the cipher world by breaking through to Transcendence. In temporal existence the boundary cannot be crossed. In fact, both as existence and as Existenz, the thinker will remain in the struggle of powers.

With our thinking tied to tangibility and objectiveness, we cannot overcome the urge to take what we sense at the limit and to convert it into the conceivable forms within the limit. This perverts the meaning of the breakthrough.

That from the dissolution of the ciphers we must always take the step back and return to the ciphers is another matter. This step is necessary in existence and not a perversion, if only the thinker knows what he is doing, and if the unperverted breakthrough lights his way and backs him up.

ii. Endless progression and false fulfilment

If transcending becomes independent, an end in itself, we have lost it. First, the unending 'onward' that is necessary as against any fixation becomes pointless as an enigmatic 'just once more' – as if the final step, the last, crucial question, had so far been missed. Secondly, then, there will be a false fulfilment by the very ciphers that no longer have a place here – ciphers of some act or omission, for instance, of a withdrawing and hiding on the part of Transcendence, or of its opening doors to itself. In Gnostic thinking, both European and Asian, such cases are numerous. Eternal Being-Nothingness may now have a history, for example, permitting apostasy and evil, sending liberators and redeemers – there may even be talk of a God whose historic becoming is mirrored in the epochs of human history. Gods, we hear, are born and die. 'Being' does this; it is the power that casts the lot in this weird world process. Such thinking will show up now in formal dilutions, now in fanciful structures, in concrete interpretative views of the factual history of mankind – mostly as one huge process of apostasy. It is a seductive thinking, whether due to the mystery or, on the contrary, to a fabulous exhibitionism, or to the fascinating to and fro between them. It has a tradition of thousands of years behind it, with appearances shifting according to the views, the knowledge, the conceptualities of any period. Schelling, in the framework of German philosophical idealism, raised it to a new peak, and Klages seems to me to have produced the last of these Gnostic philosophies, drawn from an original historic vision but modern in spirit.

iii. The intrinsicality of the existential import

'Facts' may be guidelines in the speculation on Being, but they are not its substance. The truth lies in what encompasses the relation of thought to thinker, not in the trivia of flat facts. True speculative thought is inner action. Being is illuminated as I undergo a change; it speaks in the way the change happens. But thinking has this import only in motion, not in didactics. What the play of thoughts assures to Existenz will long have reached it from another source, not from insight alone – but it is clarified only by insight, and not without it.

7 THE WILL TO READ CIPHERS IS THE WILL OF EXISTENZ IN THE WORLD

Existenz finds itself in the world. It wants to learn what is. It wants to experience it, by itself, in the world.

The unthinkable Being before the ciphers – the Being that lacks whatever lends reality and objectivity in the world, the Being that from the world's point of view is nothing – will not allow any cipher to become absolute. In this sense it keeps even the cipher of the personal God from turning absolute. But it does not destroy the ciphers, nor does it destroy that of the one personal God.

i. The void

Transcending beyond all ciphers – not just beyond the world, but beyond the reality of our Existenz in existence – takes us to the great void, to the 'All' that is nothingness, to the fullness that stays unrevealed.

If this endeavour seems to succeed for an instant, I and the object, space and time, everything disappears in the pure light that does not shine on anything. The feeling takes our temporal and finite breath away. And from this superhuman, unconscious or super-conscious state we return to the ciphers.

ii. Life in the world goes on

For one who has reached this plane above the world for an instant, existence in the world goes on just the same. How can it? There have been men who left the world, who went into forests and deserts, dying there unless people who revered them as saints would bring them food and they took it.

If a man who had this worldless experience remains in the world, he will appear ambiguous. How can we tell the superhuman from the fraudulent? To others, such renunciation of all for the sake of One makes a man either a mysterious figure they believe in or a magician they see through. The road to the highest goal becomes a worldly business.

The road to the quintessential nothingness leads out of the world. It permits no shred of further interest in the world. But as factual existence goes on, as our senses, our perceptions, our thoughts continue, an extreme of tension is required for this road; nothing else will lead to real repose. Otherwise, instead of sensing the cipher of eternal nothingness, of the absolute void, the thinker will get into a state far from this experience, a state of conceptual contemplation, of a speculation that has become a pseudo-philosophical game.

It is curious to see how unattainable truth can be touched, so to speak, and how this touch can turn so completely into deception and self-deception.

iii. The existential will to the world

From this superhuman temptation, finite man returns to the world. He will now find it irradiated, but speaking in ciphers. The will to realization in the world is the will to hear the ciphers. What we do and accomplish in freedom derives its meaning from the glow of ciphers. Life in the world is linked with that ultimate origin only by a readiness for existential action in the world – which is the reception and production of ciphers. Ciphers come to be real in language, and realities come to be ciphers.

Existenz refuses to escape from the world, but its existence in the world turns into a reading of its own historic, individual ciphers. It returns to the world, knowing that in temporal existence what it seeks is unattainable except by its own realization in the world, in time, in hearing ciphers.

Instead of evaporating in the abstraction of the negative One, instead of emptying the world in the mystical union, the fulfilled presence of Transcendence reconstitutes itself for Existenz, audible in the ciphers.

iv. Abstract speculation and superstitious embodiment

In our situation as finite humans we seek both the liberating, untouched, transcendent One and the infinite language of finiteness.

The One is present for us in the individual existential reality that is not transferable, does not become common property, and feels it is a mirror of the unique One that nobody knows or has. We lose this chance if we take something in the world for an absolute One, permitting it to enchain us.

The infinite language of finiteness comes to us from the immense world of the real and conceivable. We move among finite things, encompassed by the infinite Being-Nothingness of an Above-Being we cannot even think. If this encompassing is muted, things become opaque and impervious for us and we lapse into indifferent endlessness.

Rationally we may seem obliged to choose between an evaporating abstract speculation and embodied superstition. But it only seems that way. In our philosophizing we reject both alternatives, lest the true reality be lost as Existenz makes its way through temporal existence – a way substantially illuminated by the ciphers, and formally assured and justified in thought by the basic knowledge.

8 THE LIBERATION OF MAN

i. The stages

The liberation of man proceeds from dark, savage forces to personal gods from gods beyond good and evil to moral gods, from the gods to the one God, and on to the ultimate freedom of recognizing the one personal God as a cipher. We may call this last liberation the ascent from God to the Godhead, from the ciphers to what makes them speak. It is our liberation from the hobbles with which our own conceptions and thoughts prevent us from reaching the truth that halts all thinking.

ii. The consequences

This last liberation has essential consequences.

I stop claiming that the cipher of the God I follow as mine must be God to all men.

I stop appropriating God, so to speak, for my existence and my interests, my way of life and my substantial beliefs. I stop clothing my worldly struggles in the garb of a struggle of God against the godless, the enemies of God, as if God were fighting with me against others, and I for God.

I stop taking God for reason – which is my human reason. I stop relying on something that appears to my human desire to be the highest, the purest, the best.

iii. The perpetual chain

The roads to liberation are open, and have always been open. But there is no end to them, nor any permanent place of rest. We are granted insight and reflection – above all, we are granted action, the decisive fulfilment of the moment – but then we have to go on, and 'the rest is silence'.

The moments vanish, but there are moments that harbour as well as transcend both past and future and reflect perfection in the present. Such a moment is the supreme gift, whether granted to an individual or between two people or in an inspired community.

But that moment will turn from freedom into a chain if I fix it objectively, if I know it is absolutely, generally valid and make it my firm support and my claim on others. If I keep it a profound historic memory, its recollection will encourage me for ever. The great moment speaks out of each individual life, and our task is always to live in the present, to lose ourselves neither to the past nor to the future. If the two do not enhance the present, they corrupt it.

Part Six. Liberation and freedom now

The story of man is the story of his freedom. Wherever freedom has grown, wherever it speaks to us even from the distant past, we recognize ourselves in the companions of our fate, creatures akin to us, in the same human condition. We know that we belong to one great community, which is the community of freedom.

Only in the ties of free community can we fully realize our inner freedom. The more freedom surrounds us, the greater is our own; the more we feel at the mercy of the dark forces in men and in each one of us, the weaker will be our sense of freedom. It is then that we confuse liberty and licence, that we tend to violence and try to find our inner and outer security in commanding and obeying, in ruling and being ruled. Instead of becoming our free selves in communication with other selves, we are caught helplessly in the web of existence and strive to unite in unfree forms alone.

Liberation is the road from the dark bonds hostile to freedom – bonds we cannot throw off even if we know them – to the freedom of lucid ties. Absolute freedom is a self-contradictory concept.

The very road of liberation is a hazard to freedom. For it is ambiguous: it may be a mere negative liberation from something, as well as an original, positive freedom. Mere liberation leaves us at a loss, apt to slide back into unfreedom. It will succeed only if it serves to realize a freedom sprung from an original source.

a. On the Way to Inner Freedom

Two factors of liberation have been at work in bright consciousness since the beginnings of philosophy as well as in modern times.

The first is the change from embodiment to the cipher, and finally to the boundary of doing without all ciphers in fulfilled silence. From embodiment to speechlessness – this is the path we must tread over and over.

The second factor is the reflective change from naïve, matter-of-course immediacy to a universal methodological consciousness, an awareness of what we are doing. This is the way that brings everything we think and do into suspension and links it with the encompassing unknown.

1 FROM EMBODIMENT TO THE CIPHER

To sum up once more:

Ciphers are the language of transcendent reality, not Transcendence itself. They are not universally valid but can be interpreted in many ways. They do not speak to our intellect; we hear them only as possible Existenz.

Historical accounts turn them into a mass of fantasies arranged from various external points of view; but the accounts serve philosophical reflection, and in this we can prepare or recollect ourselves by inner action with the accounts in mind. It is only at each unique moment, when Existenz originally ascertains and decides, that the ciphers can exert their true illuminating force.

Modern scientific cognition constantly increases our store of knowledge and skills. To the uncritical intellect these successes suggest that what it can know and make is all there is. To the intellect, Existenz and Transcendence are non-existent, nonentities of which intoxicated philosophers will talk in unintelligible conceptual constructions.

When the uncritical intellect applies its mundane knowledge and proficiency to the world as a whole, it is fashioning a supposedly scientific world image. The result is the world's disenchantment by scientific superstition.

There is no such thing as a scientific world image, as science itself has now made perfectly clear to us for the first time. The past world images that ruled the thinking of whole ages were marvellous ciphers. Their appeal continues to this day. But the so-called modern world image – based on the Cartesian way of thinking, the upshot of a pseudo-scientific philosophy – is not a cipher for Existenz; it is a mechanical and dynamic instrumentality for the intellect.

The world that exists for science, the whole world that can never be a scientific object, is disjoint for cognition. No matter what ideas of unity may govern our exploration, our infinitely advancing penetration of it – in the scientific approach we live without a world image. Existentially, the cipher language with its many interpretations places all possible world images at our disposal.

If a theologian, unable to tell science from scientific superstition, comes to regard a modern world image as irreversible, it may occur to him to remove the difficulties for modern man by 'de-mythologizing' the biblical faith.[1] He thus expects to save what is left after de-mythologization: a belief in the salvation process 'witnessed' in the New Testament. His de-mythologization remains incomplete, since an arbitrary act of his faith declares the process of salvation to be not a myth; but altogether it would remove the entire world of myths – that is to say, the realm of ciphers. It would deprive Existenz of the language of Transcendence in all its richness and diversity of meanings.

What we are called upon to do, rather, in our situation of critical scientific thinking on the one hand and of scientific superstition on the other, is to

---

[1] Cf. Karl Jaspers, *Rudolf Bultmann, Die Frage der Entmythologisierung*, Munich, 1954.

translate all tangible myths into the cipher language of Transcendence. Once that is done, pure Transcendence, unsullied by any false realization in finite space and time, comes to be the silent, overpowering encompassing that brings us to ourselves. It is not an illusion, then, to hear the cipher language, but a hearing of transcendent reality in many languages that press upon each other. The cipher world – if we speak once more in the cipher of powers – is an arena of spiritual struggle, a meeting-ground of human beings who become themselves and communicate in movements manifested in ciphers.

We are finite rational creatures tied to our senses. Truthfulness compels us to give up the tangible possession of transcendent reality and to content ourselves with its ambiguous cipher language. But we must preserve the weight of that reality in the ciphers, for on their experience depends the illumination of the meaning and the goal of our life. We are more serious about it when our seriousness is no longer tied to embodiment, when it can no longer turn into a fallacious certainty of our senses. Man's highest possibilities are opened to him by the renunciation which his truthfulness exacts.

2 FROM IMMEDIACY TO UNIVERSAL METHODOLOGICAL CONSCIOUSNESS

i. Detachment

In conception and thought, in production and vision, in action, omission and surrender, in all this we want to know at the same time what we are thus doing and experiencing.

In science we call this critical apperception 'methodological'. In philosophy, the thinking penetration of all that we are and do and can be, we use the same term in an encompassing sense.

Methodological apperception detaches us from whatever we think, do, and are. But it is only if at the same time we stay completely involved that this detachment will make us not only liberated but free; it is only then that it will purify and enhance the activity from which it detaches us. We are not really identical with ourselves until we have attained this truthfulness about ourselves and our doings.

What man thinks without knowing how can flower as an invention of the mind, but it is bound to turn unnoticeably ambiguous, existentially weighty or weightless, true or false. What he does unconsciously may be great and admirable in its immediacy, but its fame can lead on to paths both good and evil.

It is only in reflecting upon our thoughts and our thinking actions, in clarifying what it means if the things we hear and say are true, that we become philosophically truthful. We come to be free, then, from things taken for granted, free from 'firm statements' and peremptory thinking in *fiats*, free from the compulsion of logical constructions of whose premises we are still unaware. We are liberated from all definite categories, from the fetters of language and from those of our own thoughts. We submit to no thought beyond the discoverable limits of its meaning.

ii. Plato

Plato is the earliest philosopher whose study gives us the methodological consciousness of philosophizing. He awoke from the somnolence of prematurely assuming matters of course that had numbed the pre-Socratics, for all the grandeur of their speculative visions – as Kant later awoke from the fatal dogmatic somnolence in which the post-Cartesians took metaphysics and modern natural science to be one and the same.

When Plato construed the world in his *Timaeus*, in the forms of things and in the way they came to be, he knew he was not engaged in scientific cognition but was telling 'plausible tales', *eikotes mythoi*.

When he designed his state in *The Republic*, he knew he was not drafting a programme for the organization of a proper state. What he drew, rather, was an image of the eternal idea of the state – an image visible to the philosopher, not an absolutely binding state form. The one binding part of it is the thought he put in the centre of his treatise: that there can be no true state unless philosophers are kings, or kings are philosophers. A true state cannot arise from a programme or from a realization of such 'utopian' designs, as they came to be called later. The method is not the organization of a state but the education of philosophers; they are the ones who, unfettered by any law, image, or draft, will then find the right course from a vision of the idea. Accordingly, when he was called to Syracuse, Plato did not begin with a programme to reform the state. He began with the education of its ruler, Dionysius, teaching him mathematics as a way to the visualization of the idea, and thus to the capability of directing the state.

The methodological consciousness that we can have today is subject to further conditions unknown to Plato.

The first of these is the modern, universal scientific approach. What to the Greeks was scattered has now been fused in the idea of an open universe of science. The task has come to be the clear conception and cognitive realization of the meaning and the limits of this approach.

The second condition is the progress, uninterrupted since the seventeenth century, of natural and historical research. The question of true reality has become basic.

The third condition is the systematic employment of science for technical ends, raising the critical methodological question of what can and cannot be 'made'.

iii. Modern philosophers and Kant

The question of method has played a dominant role since the seventeenth century, since Bacon and Descartes and Leibniz. The search, then, was for a method that would permit the cognition and production of anything, for a sovereign, absolute method. The previously prevailing logical thought, which would always limp after things, was to be exchanged for a creative method.

That search, however, was by no means the origin of the methodological consciousness that is now possible. Instead of liberating a thinker, opening his mind to possibilities, it forced him into the method that was viewed as absolute. The diversity of methods was lost sight of, as was the special meaning of each method, its definite premises and limited validity and applicability to an invariably particular cognition.

It took Kant to achieve the liberation that enables us to know what we are doing in each mental act. His questions – What can I know? What should I do? What may I hope for? What is man? – are not answered on the identical level of one method, nor are they raised from one and the same motive. But all of them do belong to the one encompassing reason in the Kantian sense, to the reason whose specific forms extend all the way to the 'judgment of taste'. When we know, act, or feel, it does not satisfy our freedom just to do all this; in the course of each mental act we want to know what happens in it, and what it means. Thinking, the philosopher in the artist brings truth to his creation. His authority is not the rationalistic reflection of an opinionated intellect; it is reason whose constant self-criticism tests and transforms the work, measuring it by yardsticks that originate in the creative mind's transcendent guidance.

v. Present methodological consciousness

a: *Concepts of truth.* We can clarify the different truth concepts in their originality and in their interrelation in the ways of encompassing. We discussed this in Part Three of this book, about the basic knowledge.

The meanings of whatever we say, do, or experience are subject to illumination by this basic knowledge. It liberates us and leaves matters in their proper place within their manifold objectiveness. It limits the object-iveness and ultimately voids it in the Encompassing of all encompassing. It reinforces the responsibility of truthfulness to the truth.

b: *Methods of transcending.* Methodological consciousness shows us three way to the philosophical possibility of transcending: the formal transcending of speculation, the illumination of existential relations to Transcendence, and the reading of ciphers.

The three ways are intertwined in the reality of Existenz, and separated in methodological interpretation. They indicate ways of thinking and bringing to mind, ways we can take to experience the preparation of the leap that occurs in Existenz alone. Our thoughts proceed from the leap, and toward it; the leap itself lies only in the act of thinking that is also a way of life, and in the way of life that is also thinking. What no philosophical word, no detached thesis, no literary work can do will come to pass in the historic ingularity of Existenz. The 'other wing'[1] must beat, to add its lifting power to the lame, onesided stroke of mere philosophizing.

c: The limit of methodological consciousness. Methodological consciousness works through the rationally analysing intellect. Could it be, then, that intellectual methodological thought ranks above original thought, as a critical authority? This is a question about the point of self-reflective philosophical thinking.

Thinking is hobbled by unreflective identification with itself, liberated by detachment from itself. But our intellect, which seeks to clarify methods – except those of science proper – in generally valid fashion, cannot help us understand what happens in the kind of thinking that proceeds intellectually but is more than intellectual when we speculate, illuminate Existenz, or read the ciphers. The judge would be less than what he judges without understanding it. Actually, it is not so. The detachment is not the work of the intellect; it makes use of the intellect, exactly as does speculative thinking. The methodological detachment is an act of philosophizing, not of a mere rationality that deems itself superior.

The limit of methodological consciousness is reached when we can no longer objectify the essentials and determine them under criteria of that consciousness. Essential is Transcendence as such; so is Existenz in its singularity of each moment; so is the unity of individual and general self-being.

d: Philosophical polemics. Can we illuminate, criticize, attack, and vindicate what is not objectively determinable? Here we are asking about the possibility of philosophical discussion, communication, and polemics – a polemics basically unlike scientific polemics, in which discussion will finally lead to agreement because of the generally cogent nature of the thing discussed.

The premise of philosophical polemics is the will to communicate even when we can no longer seek unanimity, when all we can strive for is increased mutual illumination. The idea is that we are linked by bonds not to be reached in the area of present discussion, and the consequence is that rejection will be experienced only along with better mutual understanding. It goes even further, to a solidarity transcending whatever excludes a union now, in the power struggle – a solidarity that we keep feeling and will feel more and more if the struggle is properly waged – the solidarity of common citizenship in this world of embattled spiritual powers.

What does an angry refusal to talk signify? It means either the limitation and impotence of finite being or a rupture of communication in principle, on the grounds of a truth that would, on principle, deny all other truth. The untruth of such a rupture of communication is the premise of meaningful philosophizing, of philosophical faith.

---

[1] See p. 317 on the 'two wings' of philosophizing – *Translator*.

e: The refusal of methodological consciousness. This rupture refuses the unlimited expansion of methodological consciousness that might regain communicable ground even in the most acute conflicts.

Disparagement of methodological consciousness is one way to kill the last chance of communication. It is false to spurn 'talking about it' as keeping aloof, moving outside the only area that matters. In fact, a methodological reflection 'about it' makes sense only to one who is, or was, or would like to be, 'in it'. Otherwise it will indeed be random talk about things not known from involvement, things known only from objectivations in words that are understood as words, then, not as what they mean. This is a kind of methodological non-cognition.

Too, if methodology is understood or used as machinery for the manufacture of cognitions, it may be right to belittle it as a procedure for mechanizing even thought and crippling insight. But to shrug off this constant requisite of truth leads to an untruthfulness that can always be resolved in methodological detachment only.

v. What has and has not changed since Plato

The modern expansions of our knowledge of methods have not altered the principle that was alive in Plato, of liberation by methodological consciousness. They have only enabled us to go about it more purely, more inexorably.

We can adopt what for thousands of years has happened in thinking and appeared in ciphers. The struggle of the powers that have worked on human history goes on. The dead are still with us.

If, to be truthful, we are required not just to repeat but to transform what we adopt – to become ourselves in its adoption – the premise of this requirement is methodological consciousness.

b. Liberation as a Factor in Our Present Ills

What are the consequences of renouncing embodied Transcendence and reflecting in methodical detachment? Can Existenz still have faith? Are we lost because we no longer 'believe' in tangible realizations? Does this liberation lead to nothingness rather than to freedom? Is the result a helpless longing for blind submission to no matter what?

1 RENUNCIATION OF EMBODIMENT

As a result of this renunciation we may no longer be in earnest about the transcendent cipher language either. Ciphers may cease to illuminate the realm of Existenz. Whether the sensory forms made us feel secure or anxious, liberation from them may stop us from relating freely to Transcendence; the reality of Transcendence may be lost along with its corporeality. The disenchantment of the cognoscible world may tend to turn the world at large into the sum of what we can know and make.

2 DEFLATION BY METHODOLOGICAL CONSCIOUSNESS

The demand for universal methodological clarity may have other consequences. As we detach ourselves from our own thinking, as it grows transparent, substantial thinking may cease to be self-understood. Our methodological consciousness may disengage us and leave us with a life of talk about things, about thinking, about methods, with a life of constant appraisals. The truthfulness of reflective detachment may cause permanent vertigo. Reflections may consume our substance. Liberation from the chains of thought may void all our freedom of substantial thinking. Methodological consciousness may estrange our thoughts and actions from themselves.

3 THE SENSE OF POWER AND IMPOTENCE

Today, both the situation of the mind and that of existence seem to imply an inevitable liberation. We cannot escape from the knowledge derived from science, nor from the conditions in existence which science and technology continue to transform at an alarmingly increasing pace. The intellectual effects of our modern liberation coincide with the impact the technological age has on our existence.

The result is an unprecedented sense of power on the one hand, and on the other, the most crushing sense of impotence ever experienced by men.

Let us look first at the sense of power. Many of us think we are about to master nature and will soon know what is still unknown. Today we conquer space; eventually we may abolish death. In the end man will be making man, designing and producing the perfect human.

Politically, the totalitarians seem to regard their possible power as limitless. The goal has not yet been reached; today we see only unheard-of shifts of power. The drives of the blind multitude and every kind of rebellion are channelled into the realm of modern total rule that will enslave them all. The rulers themselves are enslaved by the despotic power they turn into reality, a power that surpasses any yet seen in history and enables them to aspire to global dominion. One man will rule the earth and shape the planet to his will.

Finally, an unprecedented sense of dominion has grown in the mind of man. We know the facts of history as no age knew them. We understand realities and meanings in a horizon that has never been so vast. In the elation of universal understanding we see everything that has been great at any time, and everything can come to be newly present.

A related sense of power appears under totalitarian forms of rule: it is now up to us whether things that have been will remain in effect or be annihilated. Something monstrous has become possible: we can manipulate the recollection of history. The mind, used as a tool, attacks its own past. It can wipe it out; it can consign it to oblivion. Cast and recast at will, the image of the past can be imposed upon men.

Corresponding to this unheard-of sense of power is an equally intensified feeling of impotence. When all is said and done, we are as much as ever at the mercy of nature; we only seem to have conquered it, and our safeguards only serve to show how unsafe we are. The daily accidents of the technological world take more lives than wars of the past, as if the human hecatombs once offered in some religions were now exacted ten times over by technology. Men can now destroy mankind and corrupt it, but they cannot breed higher forms of it. Nor can death be abolished.

Feelings of impotence also respond to the immense reality of political power. Blind submission leads to a total dependence extending to every corner of a man's home and soul. To rise against it is to court destruction. Obeying, men lose their sense of free personal responsibility.

The spirit of our times may seem like the last moment of dwindling human greatness. It may seem like the terminal point of creative activity, while the potential of technical production grows apace, irresistibly. Furthermore, it may seem like the last possible moment for understanding the past. However ample our external information on creations, works, and deeds, the past will soon be forgotten because the extinction of our faculties of understanding will prevent us from perceiving it any longer. Our own creative germs will wither in the meagreness of our new environment.

Power has come to denote the annihilating impotence of all.

4 REBELLIOUSNESS

A symptom of the pervasive evil and our unclear consciousness of it is the rebelliousness that characterizes our time.

From adolescence on we have been living in an inner revolt against bourgeois standards – against mendacious conventionality, against a hypocrisy that covered up everything and showed us nothing great or venerable, against an education whose smug inaction, timid silence, and cheap negativism seemed superficial and devoid of substance. We wanted truth. But we found out that we did not know the truth. It took the most intense self-critical efforts to find even the way of truthfulness.

We found the revolt in Nietzsche, with grandiose, bewildering power; we found it in Marx, whose will to social justice became a fanatical injustice; we found it in Dostoevsky, in ideas and figures that transcend all psychology into the existential and metaphysical, into extremes of revelation; we found it as an existentially irrelevant, psychologically straying and thus pernicious exposure of the soul by Freud. We found the revolt in Kierkegaard's way of thinking, of questioning the inaccessible, and in his seeming achievement of the impossible in indirect communication.

All these were phenomena of the mind, ultimate manifestations of the depth of rebellion – a depth so indefinite it seemed to point to the very origin of man.

Added to this, today, were the factual threats to humanity. The peoples of the earth have risen against Europe – first in Russia, using and abusing the ideas of Marx, and then in most non-Western lands. And if total negativism wishes to destroy mankind it now has the atom bomb at its disposal.

Every kind of revolt began with a truth – hence their apparent confluence against seemingly obvious enemies: the lie, injustice, the whole men-dacious life. As it happened, however, the spirit of all these revolts would drown in turn in the confusions of the time, and in mendacities more banal than any others. The question of truth or falsehood would abdicate in favour of brute force.

What took over in the rebels' state of mind was simply the lust of being against', of destruction as such, of smashing traditions, orders, measures; it was aggressiveness in itself, the brazen avowal of vulgarism in word and deed. The delight of the 'we' in joint unsubstantiality caused the illiberal intolerance of a No born of nothing. Everything is to become nothing, except for this No itself.

When revolt becomes a principle of life, when men mistake it for real truth and freedom, they sink into a state without Existenz, a life without principle. Rebelliousness becomes a habit. In such an atmosphere the ice-cold manipulators of violence seize power by terrorism. They use the formerly free emotional rebelliousness as they need it, as a new means provoked by themselves, and they prohibit it wherever it makes trouble.

5 WHAT NOW?

We stand at the brink of the abyss, both in the mind and in existence. The question is, What now?

i. Can we withstand the nihilistic revolt within and around us? And if we entrust ourselves to overall conservatism, to traditional contents of faith, orders, and masses, are we not going to fall back into the hypocrisies and conventions we rejected, into the false tranquillity, into the life amid stage-props and spectres that cut us off from reality once before?

Can the revolt not be turned into a force of reason? This would enable us to live truthfully, undeceived by the props of either rebellion or traditional convention. On this open road we would neither lapse into negativistic despair nor take refuge in an absolute order.

The exceptional breakthroughs we see in such men as Kierkegaard or Ni etzsche – not cheap noisemakers but existential witnesses whose experience is our illumination – those were the great instances of self-sacrifice. They did not show us the way; they are not models we can emulate. They are the irreplaceable individuals who keep questioning us to the limit, disturbing us, liberating us.

We want to be liberal in listening to all, and simultaneously resolute in any concrete struggle. We want unlimited communication. In our affirmation of these impulses we are beset by those great exceptions, lest we grow complacent. There also remain the disturbing ciphers of Transcendence, which it would be untruthful not to hear. To withstand them, we heed other ciphers – though in the cipher world we never have the final Absolute otherwise than as a fleeting assurance in the encompassing beyond all ciphers.

Where rebellion is overcome, then, and ceases, we lose the truth of reality; where rebellion becomes absolute, reality will perish. In time, to remain both true and able to live, we must keep the dialectics open.

The ciphers show the tension between rebel and conservative as a ceaseless struggle of both. A cipher of their union, of dialectical harmony, would be deceptive.

To transcend the ciphers, to glance beyond all ciphers at the realm we cannot reach, and then, encompassed by that source of the cipher language to hear the ciphers and to keep hearing them in their struggles and ambiguities – this is the condition of our freedom.

This freedom is our chance to go our way in the world, and to have peace in failure.

i. Are we lost because we now believe in ciphers rather than in tangible realizations? Will all thinking faith be extinguished as a result? Faith can take new forms. What we give up is not faith but its forms and contents, and those are valid for ever.

If today's radical liberation can destroy freedom itself, if an existential vacuum ensues, the question is, rather, how to replenish it so that we come to be ourselves. If the cognoscible world's disenchantment seems to extinguish all faith, the question is, rather, the new form of faith itself. No one can tell how it will look as it spreads among men.

We can see two possibilities. Either the way goes from liberation, through the nihilism produced by scientific superstition and technological dominance, to the total evil of rationalistically governed unfreedom, or liberation will lead man from his ever-present origin to free, creative self-being.

At first, only individuals can show in their way of thinking and living what the utmost clarity, on the premise of our knowledge and skills, will let a man do if he is absolutely truthful. There is no predicting it. But as we live now and once only, no man can wait. Philosophy, although *en route*, must always be at the goal too. Its significance does not lie in the work of thought, but in practice and the way of thinking.

iii. For the course of things today it matters less than ever what an individual can do or a few are granted. That all men learn to read and write, that they communicate and can know about each other by the means of our technological age, enables them all, not just a tiny minority, to share in what the best of them are thinking, seeing, doing. The greatest works of the past, of arts and letters, are now as generally accessible as the achievements of the present.

Today, therefore, what the individual mind can accomplish and the individual Existenz can realize is not enough. Their being and doing lays the ground for what is to become of man, but only if it affects the masses and does not only exist in the mutual recognition of a few friends. Every individual lives among the billions who populate the earth, and each of those is an individual. The future depends on whatever will find an echo, whatever will be taken up and realized on a broad scale. For the first time in history, the democratic way – Kant called it the republican one – is the one way to provide for human chances. Individual and political freedom promote each other.

If the totalitarian world destroys political liberty, if it subjects man's inner freedom to unprecedented pressures, the future depends on whether political liberty as the condition of all freedom in the world will unfold elsewhere, whether it will then be realized in men, and finally in all men, by the power of conviction – without violence, which would run counter to its nature. The question whether or not liberation leads to freedom is being settled now, in the world that is politically free.

It cannot be adequately answered by the conception of a historico-sociological process, nor by a supposed knowledge of the way men are. The last and only answer will come from the decision of individual human beings. How man, as an individual and in community, will freely shape his freedom remains up to him.

Everyone proves only to himself what can and cannot be. The proof is born and strengthened in communication. The reality of men who are themselves serves, so to speak, to guarantee the chance.

c.· *What is Man?*

Those who deny that liberation might bring human freedom point to human reality.

An overwhelming majority, if not indeed all men, they tell us, are really helpless and unhappy in a freedom that makes them responsible for themselves. Obedience alone gives them peace; the presumption of personal freedom leads to perdition. The individual – so the argument goes – is incapable of freedom, nor are nations capable of political liberty. It is always their road to a new, more cruel bondage.

In fact, the answers to the situation of today, to the boundary situations encountered at any time, to the basic condition in which man finds himself – all these answers spring from his conception of his humanity.

Do we know what man is? Whatever we think we know is an element of what becomes of man. The human image is a factor in the realization of the human essence. How, as what, man imagines himself is not just an acceptance of given facts, but his own responsibility.

He can succumb to his general anthropological, psychological, sociological knowledge of himself, and yet he is always more than he can know about himself. He can succumb to a knowledge of his history; but he is a creature that encompasses history, a creature whose history links him with eternity.

He can see himself consisting of nothing more than ciphers of his origin and his resultant sense of being. But a great many such ciphers appeal to him, and yet they are merely the language of his potential.

And he can see himself as his own challenge, as the free gift of his self, a creature in which all that may become of him, thanks to Transcendence, lies still hidden. In this view no image of himself will be absolute any more; all of them will become elements of his imageless course through the world, related to imageless Transcendence.

1 MAN AS A RESEARCH OBJECT

We speak of physical, psychological, medical, and social anthropology. What we are is to be discovered and fitted into a knowledge of ourselves as creatures that occur in the world among other creatures.

In psychological research man has been a psycho-physical entity with drives and innate conceptions, with expressive phenomena and ways of self-representation. He has been consciousness and the unconscious. He has been the perceiving creature that subjects its outward perceptions to processes of thought and feeling and then works outward again, in will and action. He has been the object of various methods of observing his empirical occurrence in healthy and diseased states.

Sociologically he has been the *homo faber*, the *homo laborans*, the *homo oeconomicus*, the *homo politicus*, and so forth.

Such research, guided by these and many other conceptions, deals with the infinite diversity of human phenomena. Yet there is a limit to it: we cannot really explore man as himself. For all the ways it may take, science never comes close to the human self.

For man is not merely an object in the world, along with others. Instead, he comprises all objects that come to be present in him. 'The soul is all, so to speak,' said Aristotle.

Man is always more than we conceive as the known human being, and at the same time he is something basically different.

There is a premise to each human image, a kind of framework that will be filled out, then, by our conceptions, observations, and investigations. For instance, we look upon man as a psycho-physical creature moved by psychological necessity to form conceptions and thoughts. The premise, in that case, is the causality of the psycho-physical process. Or we regard him as a product of the evolution of the world, of life in particular; the premise, then, is the universe that generates it all. We may see the social creature in man, the particle required for the existence of community; our premise is the history of human community, and the individual is its product. Or we may see the thinking creature. The premise, then, is that man's essence is not just to exist but to know.

Made absolute, these premises always restrict the human image. But if the premises are understood as such, each of the images has a relative meaning.

Against all these premises – each possibly valid as a particular perspective – stands another: man is related to Transcendence. He is 'the creature in the sight of God'. This view, as tangible in atheism as in religious history, may look like a history of illusions to be explained by psychology and overcome by cognition; but though the supposed illusion can be eliminated in each special form, the whole is irremovable. There is a place of the Absolute, we might say, a place which man, even if he wished to, cannot help filling, as it were, with his conceptions. But the issue is more than a place: it is the reality of Transcendence. Man, every individual human being, is free by virtue of his relation to Transcendence. It is the source of the decisions by which man – instead of suffering his history as a natural process – helps to shape it without knowing how or to what end.

2 MAN AS A HISTORIC OBJECT

i. The empirical picture of history

The historical sciences have amassed an immense knowledge. Scores of centuries that used to be inaccessible have been brought within our range of vision by excavations and other discoveries. Today we know primitive man from bones that have been found; we know prehistoric man from the artifacts he left us without remaining audible in language; we know historic man from linguistic documents that testify to him in places as varied as Mesopotamia, Egypt, India, China. We see the man of the axillary period, from 800 to 200 B.C., simultaneously laying the ground for things to come in China, India, Persia, Palestine, and Greece.[1] We see technology conquer the world from Europe, from the seventeenth century on, and we see the modern global unity of communications, the start of a world history of united mankind – united either with or against each other, or jointly bent on suicide.

Compared with the time spans of the history of earth and then of life on earth, this framework covers an infinitesimal period, with documented

---

[1] Cf. Karl Jaspers, *The Origin and Goal of History*.

history in turn constituting a minute fraction of the preceding history of human existence.

Developed with the cogent knowledge of the modern scientific approach in mind, our historical sciences dispense with theses that do not invite new real, empirical findings. They can be pursued *ad infinitum* in an under-standing interpretation of facts, with each interpretative step calling again for empirical documentation and methodical awareness of meanings and limits. The tiny segment of time that they deal with is open at both ends – to an immense past that has been, and to a future of immeasurable possibilities – and the pictured framework must always remain a provisional one of diverse aspects.

ii. Unchanging man under changing conditions

Is historic man always the same? Does he only appear differently under different conditions of existence, or is it indeed a different human essence that shows in the spirit of various ages and civilizations? Is the individual subordinate to history, determined by history alone, or is he above history, part of another world throughout his history? Who is this creature who knows all about dependence on the times, including his own dependence on his time – and who thus seems to stand outside history, after all?

Man himself, without having planned it, has brought forth all the vastly different conditions of his existence and situations of his mind. Once he has done that, he is at their mercy and must see how he can conceive, shape, and master them as an individual with his fellow men, in groups and orders. In the origin of his potential he is changeless, and by his way of tackling the new situations he decides what they will make of him.

Man has not become different in the thousands of years we know about, for we deal with men of every period as if they were our contemporaries. This is the premise of historical understanding. If we were not as men have always been, we would have to treat human history like natural history in which we know morphological changes from without, for instance, but do not understand them from within. The changelessness of being human lies in a contemporaneity that runs through the millennia. They not only preceded us – they still have something to tell us.

The theory of changes in man refers to his historic appearance. The theory of man's unchanging essence refers to the one comprehensive possibility of being human, which no appearance can satisfy.

The differences in appearance subject us to history; the unity of our essence makes us independent. Amid the swirling tides of history this unity anchors us in history's own unhistoric ground.

What decides our sense of humanity is whether in all dreadful strangeness we still feel akin to all men.

iii. The radical break today

No one doubts any more that our time marks a break in history deeper than any past one. Notable in rudiments since the French Revolution, the feeling has kept growing stronger. As if to accentuate the turning-point, the possibility of mankind's self-destruction arises now for the first time.

I should like to stress another new basic fact, a point of departure for any and all things to come. The men who rose to clear insight and to a way of life in keeping with it have always been only a few, a small minority drawn from an upper class that was numerically very small itself. The masses had no chance of participation. We know little about their thinking, their reactions, their dominant conceptions; their voice does not reach us directly, only indirectly through what we hear from the few. We have to infer what was going on inside the many. Not until the eighteenth century do we have more direct views on a large scale, but all the way down to our time these are inadequate in comparison with our views of the ruling classes and of individuals known in their existence, in their lives and works. It was like a discovery when inquiries among workingmen began to be taken at the start of this century. Even today the task of getting information on the existence and the thinking of the many in all groups is far from solved.

The crucial change is that all men now learn to read and write. The means of the technological world give everyone access to everything, to all thoughts, to all information. Events on the globe, if they become public anywhere, can be known everywhere. Furthermore, all men can share in the great human tradition. The great works of poetry and philosophy are available in inexpensive editions. We cannot tell what will come out of that; at the outset we note that the general state of mind is confused, passive, distracted. But the chance for a rise to humanity, once the prerogative of a very few, is an extraordinary one, especially if we develop the educational methods to disseminate the proper understanding and mental discipline.

The initial change in our time is not the development of a new state of mind by the present reception and adoption of a previous spirit; it is a decline of the general level, combined with the external technical process of enabling all to rise. Once again a liberation is not tantamount to freedom. At first, in fact, it seems to speed freedom's fall.

General freedom now depends on its inner growth in the masses after their liberation. No other road remains open, and this one will lead either to freedom by way of democracy, where all learn how to be free and responsible, or it will lead to the slavery that results from an abuse of freedom by citizens as well as politicians. Then it may pass through the stages of irresponsible one-party oligarchy and public mendacity, to end in such total enslavement as has never existed, because there have never been the technological means to bring it about.

iv. The supra-historic contemporaneity
This is the new basic experience in being human. What has been is now past

only in concrete appearance; its voice, its challenge, can be with us at any time. History comes to concern the living, who live with centuries as if they were a single moment. Yet this moment still makes its appearance now, in our time, and links us all only by its singular presence at each time; its substance lies in the original eternity.

If we look at the history of myths and revelations, at the history of philosophy and its speculations, at the ethos of ways of life, we learn how people of the past found their way in existence, how they lived, despaired, found their salvation. Then we, as the same kind of human beings, will see first what we have in common with them, and only afterwards the story of their errors and illusions and curiosities, which in essence have never differed much from ours. However striking our progress in knowledge and skills, at the crucial point we know no more than people of the distant past. Under different conditions of existence, in a different situation of the mind, we stand beside them, facing the same questions.

3 MAN CONCEIVED IN CIPHERS

No human image as a reality in the world can be conclusive. For the reality of our existence among other mundane existences does not exhaust the free human self.

We may venture a strange proposition: man, as Existenz, is just as incomprehensible as Transcendence. For without a relation to Transcendence there is no Existenz. Man's way to experience Transcendence in ciphers is his way to experience his own ground. Like Transcendence, Existenz lies before and outside the world, so to speak, and what man is can therefore, like Transcendence, be expressed in ciphers. Like any ciphers, those of humanity are not the reality of which they speak in many forms, subject to many interpretations. They turn false when they appear as knowledge.

There is, however, something unique about ciphers of humanity. They speak to us about us; what they speak of is the same thing as they speak to. We might, after all, be expected to know nothing better than what we are, what we can find out at any moment, both from without and from within – but the contrary is the case. One might say there is nothing of which we know less than what human beings like ourselves really are. As a result, these ciphers are revelations – though none can ever fully express our humanity, the object they speak to as well as about.

If we want to group such ciphers, we may differentiate between those of man's place among living creatures, those of the total history of mankind, and those of the non-empirical cause of being human.

i. Ciphers of man's place among living creatures

The world image of medieval Christianity, completed in thought by Aquinas and in poetic vision by Dante, gave man a place in the graduated scale of creatures. He stood between animal and angel. He had his temporal existence in the world, and his future eternal one either in heaven above or down in hell.

In a Hindu view the scale of living things consists of plants, of animals, of the different castes of men – the concept of a uniform humanity is lost – and of demons and finally gods. A creature can pass through them all; I may be reborn as a worm or as a god. This levelling means the extinction of humanity, its reduction to a mere transitional stage in which the creature must bear, suffer, enjoy whatever is unalterable in this particular form of life. Man no longer bears the stamp of a distinguished being.

ii. Ciphers of human history as a whole

The endless facts do not help us to know the whole, neither the substance of specific ages and civilizations nor that of man's substantial course in time. And yet, though for ever inaccessible empirically, the total history of mankind has been imagined over and over, from the oldest historical myths to the Christian schedule of events from Creation to Judgment, and down to the modern views of Hegel, Schelling, and recently Spengler.

Here we must distinguish between ideas on the course of history that are set forth as hypotheses and can in principle – as Kant still thought – be tested by experience, and the historico-philosophical ideas which are in principle not subject to empirical proof. These are in the nature of ciphers. In the philosophies of history the two types keep intermingling, though in the line that goes back to Democritus the emphasis may be on the empirically conceived hypothesis of a causally comprehensible process, while the substantially conceived and irresistible total process is stressed in the line originating with Hesiod.

Our own historical consciousness is split: on the one hand we have real knowledge and the history that can, in principle, be known; on the other hand we have the ciphers of history. To get out of the existential confusion of our state of mind, we must constantly strive afresh for purity in real knowledge and clarity in hearing ciphers.

To the concept of a substantial total process, all the historic phenomena that we observe are testimonies, symptoms, or elements of that process. The process alone controls everything, and what we call freedom is but an element of this entirety, which is the Absolute. History is seen as the way of God, or as God himself. It is the supreme authority to which man must submit because he is subject to it already.

Against this entire philosophy of a meaningful total history stands another thesis. Goethe touched upon it, irked by the absurdities he saw in history, and Schopenhauer stated the metaphysical principle: history does not make sense.

A third world of thought has now arisen in modern times – a world that in planning and making all things, including history as a whole, means to supplant historic ciphers with scientific know-how, the cipher as such with total knowledge. This way of thinking was first put into practice during the French Revolution, when men sought to destroy all historic foundations and to start afresh, really building the political existence of mankind, constructing the future from plans laid by human reason. Then, on the basis of Hegel's philosophy, Lassalle and Marx definitively conceived this political attitude and found new ways to reconnect it with the history that had been overcome. History was now managed to shape the world in line with known necessities, just as natural science is used for technological purposes. Once, in the cipher, history was in the hands of God; now this God was the knowing human being. Man, we heard, knows the necessity – which he is – and acts upon it. Whatever stands in the way will perish by itself, or it will be crushed by the power that knows the necessity. Historically, the practical application of this kind of thinking has demonstrated that all it can do is destroy – but that thus far, despite it, there will be a comeback from another source, of something not envisioned by the planners, makers, and enthusiasts of compulsion.

To the free, the cipher used to speak in suspense. The loss of the ciphers corresponds to that of freedom, the total lack of ciphers in the thinking of 'know-how', to total unfreedom.

But what can the cipher of history still mean? If cognition cannot tell us all about where things are heading, the question still remains.

The only limits to factual contingency, to senseless chance in the course of events, are particular necessities and connections of specific meaning. This applies to political action as to everything else we do.

As human beings we are not isolated individuals. We are received into a human world that strikes us as making sense, a world we constantly seek to re-fashion so that it will make sense. We cannot do this unless we encounter a sense in which community encompasses all individuality; losing that, we feel bound to lose ourselves. But as each concretely felt sense is encompassed again by senselessness and a new possible sense, all the way to the 'sense' of all human history, we cannot avoid hearing ciphers of this entirety as if it were the ground under our feet.

The following are examples of such ciphers.

One: in time, history is inconclusive. There is no completing it; it can be cut short and terminated only by violence.

Two: human history is the history of freedom.

Three: history is due to the original disparity of the forces that motivate men. These forces work on each other in the medium of communication and are related to the One that gave birth to mankind – the One which science vainly seeks in biology, in language, in comprehensible meanings.

Four: the One is transcendent. It is origin and challenge at once.

Five: history is directly tied to Transcendence at all times. Its future direction lies always wholly in the present, across time; it is supra-historic historicity.

These five phrasings are merely abstract suggestions of the area in which the concrete ciphers of history are existentially examined and adopted, each in its own way.

iii. Ciphers of the cause of humanity

Let us take two concepts out of many: that of Prometheus, and that of the Fall of man.

Prometheus[1]

a: The myth. Gods and men are of the same stock, distinguished only as mortals and immortals. No god has created men; along with the gods, they have existed from the beginning.

Not until the age of the theogonic process did the gods become what they are. The turning-point, the origin of the present state of gods and men, was the moment when Zeus came to power. As Uranus, eons ago, was overthrown by his son Cronus, Cronus was now ousted by his son Zeus. The Titans, progeny of Uranus, were crushed by Zeus, who then ordered the world, assigned a place to all things in existence, and fashioned the new law. And mankind, that most wretched and pitiable of all races, was to be exterminated.

But one of the Titans, Prometheus – whose name means 'Forethought' – held a unique position. When the other Titans ignored his warnings, he had gone over to the side of Zeus and become his adviser on the new world order, agreeing with him on all points but one. Prometheus did not see the human race as Zeus did. Like Zeus, he recognized their misery, but he loved the poor wretches for their potential.

Prometheus alone dared oppose Zeus. The decision struck at the heart of the new divine kingdom: should humans, those originally wretched, helpless beings, live or become extinct? Prometheus wanted them to live; he wanted it so much that he gave them the means to help themselves. Through him, they gained an independence in the world that Zeus had not planned for. They could not be wiped out any more, could not all be hurled into the maw of Hades. The act of Prometheus was an original revolt of supreme significance.

What did he give men? Fire, first of all, stealing it past Zeus' eye in a glimmering fennel stalk. But fire was just the beginning: he would teach men thousandfold art *(techne)* in every sense of the word. Previously they 'dwelt in hollowed holes, in sunless depths of caverns'; now they learned how to build houses and practise carpentry. Prometheus yoked the ox to pull the plough and relieve man's body of that burden; he harnessed the horse to a chariot for man; he built the first ship. He showed men ''neath the

[1] Aeschylus, *Prometheus Bound*; quotations from the Harvard Classics translation by E. H. Plumptre.

earth the hidden boons, bronze, iron, silver, gold'. He taught them how to ward off sickness by drugs. Not knowing the signs of the seasons, they had lived in disorder, without regularity, until Prometheus showed them 'the risings of the stars, and settings hard to recognize'. He taught them numbers, 'chief device of all', and writing, 'Memory's handmaid, and mother of the Muses'. He 'gave them many modes of prophecy'. In short: 'All arts of mortals from Prometheus spring.'

A great deal more had happened than the use of fire and the many arts. Prometheus had enlightened the human mind. Men used to be dull-witted dreamers: 'Though seeing, all in vain they saw, and hearing, heard not rightly.' In other words, they could not observe. 'Like forms of phantom-dreams they muddled all at random.' Now they grew conscious and came to be masters of their minds.

And to enable them to live the life they faced with such great and yet limited powers, he 'made them cease from contemplating death' and gave them 'blind hope' instead.

b: Interpretive discussion. α: Man owes Prometheus his existence, the fact that he is not vegetating like an animal but helping himself. But this is the size of his debt: the faculty of mastering nature, shaping his environment, setting out on rational undertakings. Prometheus did not give him the order of the state, morality, the law, the salvation of his soul. He did not give him peace of mind, religion, or philosophy. He created the 'Promethean' side of man – which was not yet what man himself could come to be on that basis.

β: In the myth Prometheus defies Zeus, who unmercifully sends him further torments. But revolt and punishment have their own history.

At first there are no bounds to Prometheus' defiance. 'Yea, willing, willingly I sinned,' he says; to help men, he gladly brought his suffering upon himself. 'All the gods I hate. . . . My care for Zeus is nought, and less than nought. . . .'

He asks nobody's help and complains only to the great realities of nature, which precedes the Olympians:

> *Thou firmament of God, and swift-winged winds,*
> *Ye springs of rivers, and of ocean waves*
> *That smile innumerous! Mother of us all,*
> *O Earth, and Sun's all-seeing eye, behold,*
> *I pray, what I a god from gods endure!*

And the last word:

> *O Mother venerable!*
> *O Aether! rolling round*
> *The common light of all,*
> *See'st thou what wrongs I bear?*

Two invincible powers of the titanic god set this apart from any human defiance. First: 'What can I fear whose fate is not to die?' Zeus will never be able to kill him. And second: 'All too clearly I foresee the things that come.' He will drink the cup of agony 'to the dregs, till from his wrath the mind of Zeus shall rest'. He has 'seen two great rulers driven' from power over the world; the one now reigning also will be overthrown unless he makes peace with him, Prometheus – the only one who can show Zeus the way to escape from that 'quickest, basest fall'.

The question is whether Prometheus is right in his defiance.

The chorus tells him that, not fearing Zeus, he has loved men too much. They could not help him even if they would, for

> *Never shall counsels vain*
> *Of mortal men break through*
> *The harmony of Zeus.*

In fact, men do not even establish a cult of the titanic god, to show their gratitude. Oceanus, the chorus of ocean nymphs, and Hermes, therefore, all advise him with more or less vehemence or gentle sympathy to temper his defiance. He refuses. He will rather suffer the worst that Zeus can do to him: 'Nought finds me unprepared.'

Yet now the origin of the turn in this mythical drama: Zeus and Prometheus both are right and wrong at once. There is *hubris* not only in Prometheus's defiance, but in the power of Zeus. He has caused the terrible suffering of Io, driven madly through the world, and in his unbridled vengeance on Prometheus he mistakes his own limits. For Zeus himself is subject to another power: 'Not even he can 'scape the thing decreed.' Moira, necessity, is stronger.

The myth sees three powers: Zeus, Prometheus, and necessity. Zeus has power to inflict the most frightful agonies on Prometheus, but not to kill him. He had the power to destroy mankind, but he has lost it since Prometheus gave men their independent faculties: thought, technology, self-help.

The mythical drama leads to a reconciliation of Zeus and Prometheus which must have been shown in the lost conclusion of the trilogy – 'Prometheus Unbound'. Prometheus acknowledges Zeus, and Zeus stops abusing him. Both gods have changed, and the crux is that humanity, which the revolt of Prometheus made possible, is not reversed. It has become part of the world order.

γ: Prometheus became guilty by philanthropy, by doing good to man. What makes man human – the knowledge and skills he can develop without limits – is connected with guilt.

There is defiance in the origin of humanity, as wrought by Prometheus Human self-help reflects the defiance of Prometheus, his constant spiting of the divine order. From the start there is something defiant in man's thinking and in his *techne*.

The mythical cipher illuminates the mystery that manifests itself in questioning man's sense of being. Once it has struck him, he will no longer live in the plain, beautiful, unquestioned sense of existence; he will be buffeted by impact after impact until his very existence becomes a question.

For man himself to stage the revolt against God seems so monstrous in the mythical cipher that the blame is placed upon the titanic god who endows man against God's will. '*Nemo contra deum nisi deus ipse*' – a line that Goethe quotes from a source I have been unable to locate – may say, perhaps, what was visualized in the cipher of Prometheus.

It shows us the abyss in being human. It shows the majesty, the power, the forming, acting heroism, the dignity of man – but human experience and questioning make all human greatness 'questionable'.

Still, once arisen, the question ought to be kept on the human heights on which it grew. Nowhere else can it be adequately understood, so the answer, in suffering, will not sound either resentful or timid.

δ: Among the reinterpretations of the myth and the mutations of its mood is a reversal of the basic idea: man was not wretched but happy, once upon a time, and the Promethean way plunged him into all his troubles. Horace, in the first of his Odes, describes the man who set out on that way: threefold armour girded the breast of the fearless one who first entrusted a frail craft to the savage sea. Death did not frighten him as he looked dry-eyed at towering waves, at cliffs and sea monsters. God had carefully parted land and sea, but wicked man launches ships on the waters he ought not to touch. Brazenly set for all suffering, he heads for forbidden realms. Brazenly, by fraud, Prometheus brought him fire; Daedalus donned wings and took to the air; Hercules broke into the nether world. Nothing will faze mortals. In our folly we mount assaults against heaven, and our crimes force Zeus to hurl his bolts of wrath.

Horace was still thinking of the Promethean evil on the high level of the Greek myth. The level declines in the interpolated verses about the glory of a one-time, sinfully abandoned humanity: death, it says here, which the old law of nature kept far off and coming slowly, is now accelerated. Modern thought, dulled to the myth, sinks even lower in its rage against technology: as early as 1852 a philologist remarked that Prometheus did not relieve human wretchedness, since 'every invention, from fire to the railroad and the power loom, makes nature serve us only so as to add to our sins and ailments'.

The Fall

God created man in his own image, male and female. He blessed them and gave them the garden of Eden. In the garden stood the tree of the knowledge of good and evil, and God forbade them to eat the fruit of this tree, 'Ye shall not eat of it, lest ye die!' But the serpent beguiled them: 'Ye shall not surely die: for God doth know that in the day ye eat thereof, then your eyes shall be opened, and ye shall be as gods, knowing good and evil.' They ate the apple, and when God came they hid themselves. God cursed the serpent and doomed man to the fate of his life: 'In the sweat of thy face shalt thou eat bread, till thou return unto the ground; for out of it wast thou taken: for dust thou art, and unto dust shalt thou return.'

The other motif of the myth is the creation of man and woman. In Genesis 1, 27, man is created male and female, but in 2, 22, Eve is made out of Adam's rib. The meaning is the same in both cases: to be human is to be not alone but with each other, to be in communication. In the one version, however, man is originally created in two sexes, and the two meet on the same level of self-being; in the other, Adam is created first and Eve just as an afterthought: 'It is not good that the man should be alone; I will make him an help meet for him.' Such help meet for man can be no animal, only the woman as flesh of his flesh. She was thus not made on the same level, but after the man and in order to help him. Her inhuman subjection continued with her picture as more susceptible to seduction, and more capable of it, and finally with the aggravation of her punishment: not only the pangs of childbirth are imposed on her, but instead of helping the male she is to serve him: 'And he shall rule over thee!' All of this dims the great, pure cipher of being human, the word that 'God created man in his own image, in the image of God created he him'.

Man, created as an immortal being, must now die. 'The man is become as one of us, to know good and evil,' said God. And so, 'lest he put forth his hand, and take also of the tree of life, and eat, and live for ever', God drove him and his wife out of the garden of Eden and set cherubim with a flaming sword to guard the way to the tree of life.

Man's origin, according to the cipher of the Fall, was no common crime, no theft or fraud such as Prometheus perpetrated in the Greek cipher. It was his disobedient seizure of his own chances, laid in him by his creation in the image of God. Now he can know, but at the price of mortality. The earth is his, for activities beyond measure, but at the price of endless, consuming toil. This ambiguity of human existence, this restive will to know as a premise of human greatness, allows the cipher to be interpreted either way – as the disconsolate sense of evil in longing for the lost paradise, or as enthusiasm for the great challenge.

'Add deeds to thy knowledge,' the angel says at the end of Milton's *Paradise Lost* – 'add love,

> . . . *the soul*
> *Of all the rest: then wilt thou not be loth*
> *To leave this Paradise, but shalt possess*
> *A Paradise within thee, happier far.*

With this encouragement Adam and Eve leave the sheltering garden.

> *The world was all before them, where to choose*
> *Their place of rest, and Providence their guide.*
> *They, hand in hand, with wandering steps and slow*
> *Through Eden took their solitary way.*

4 MAN AS HIS OWN CHALLENGE

Being human, we ask about man. The answers change with new conditions of existence; the question would cease only if human selfhood were submerged in mere existence.

Where do we come from? What is the present meaning and goal of our life as individuals, as nations, as mankind? What are our possibilities and limitations? What is our essence? What is our place in the world? What is our task of the moment?

These questions were all but forgotten in the tranquillity of the cultured, conventional, bourgeois Christian world that spoiled its own freedom and lost touch with its origin. It remained forgotten even among the restless, those who were sensing things but never in earnest, and thus for ever barren. People were content with matter-of-course activity and with the unserious *Weltschmerz* typified by Schopenhauer. Or else the question of man was pushed aside: 'Let's not think; it doesn't lead anywhere.' But we cannot silence the question. It is back today, more urgently than ever.

i. Man has become aware of the state of freedom
Has modern liberation led to freedom? So far it has not. It has created the possibility, but not the reality.

In fact, the most radical liberation we know of, the one in our own era, seems rather likely to wipe out the freedom of man. What was freedom before this liberation? This we should like to know – to sense a chance to recover an unreflective freedom still dreaming its truth, so to speak, and to recover it more purely after our liberation.

Is it enough for individuals to be free if the nations cannot follow, if they will never be able to follow? It is not only not enough; it will be less and less possible. For the old, fairly loose forms of despotism never could suppress an individual's will to be inwardly free, because he retained some elbow room. The age of technology can complete the suppression of inner freedom.

It all depends on the awakening of freedom by the free. An individual can be free only in so far as there are free men around him. To those who doubt this, who think men cannot be free at all, we say that once we take the road of freedom, once we experience Transcendence and ourselves, we can no longer regard this road as impossible. The venture of its possibility is our life; to refuse it means to suffocate the individuals who have made Western history. They constitute its peaks, and their deeds, their creations and insights, bear witness to the human potential.

The extinction of freedom would mean the extinction of faith as well. Only together can they remain real. If the present situation should result in the self-destruction of freedom, human history would seem irrevocably at an end. That this cannot happen while men live is a matter of faith, not of knowledge.

It is an abstract notion already devoid of faith that after hundreds or thousands of years in the desert there might be a new beginning, another history of freedom such as the one that started sixty centuries ago. But what an immense difference! That former evolution began on the ground of mythical thinking and of the wealth of language, the two warrants of an immemorial human substance – which on that other hypothesis would have been used up in history. After the present ruin it would have to begin on the ground of an unfreedom without substance, on the ground of the labour apparatus of the technological age, of the rationalized, controlled work and leisure of the unfree who do not know what to do with themselves; it would have to begin on the ground of a mass production and mass consumption pattern that devours men and nature. The new history would have to spring from an unfreedom utterly unlike the one that led to the first. It would be an unfreedom that pinions man like a steel brace and turns his very soul into such a brace, while the Promethean age had roused him from a slumber of fulfilled unfreedom. After the present ruin men would have to start out from the unfreedom of unhistoric rationality; the first time they started out from the unfreedom of immemorial history.

ii. Man's way to truth is struggle
Instead of enjoying complete truth, we human beings are embattled on the way to truth.

To be alive in all the modes of encompassing that we are, we need the passions of our existence; but they constantly lead us astray. To have relative clarity and accuracy, we need the intellect of consciousness at large; but this perverts our sense of truth by its pursuit of an accurate absolute truth. The magic of the mind is vital to the domain of our imagination; it allows us to hear the language of phenomena, but it lures us into a world of aesthetic make-believe. And the unconditionality to which historic Existenz always owes a glimmer of the exceptional tends to bewilderment, to failure in the world, to disappearance.

Whether the struggle is for existence, waged by cunning and force, or the contention of reasoned debate in consciousness at large; whether figments of our imagination compete for rank and effect in the realm of the mind or Existenz wrestles lovingly with other Existenz for common selfhood – at all times there will be struggle.

These vast struggles are man's way to truth. Each success is confined to the moment and will soon become a starting-point of new struggles – for in time the road can never end. Whatever rest we are given is but a breathing spell to gather new strength.

iii. Man, constantly aiming at entirety, does not become entire
No man is everything. No truth realized in a human being is the one whole truth.

In self-reflection we seek clarity about the source and the point of our life. But the achievement of full clarity takes more than being sure of our concrete historic decision.

We can dispense with no element of the modes of encompassing that we are. Each is essential. None may turn into an absolute that would stand on itself alone.

Yet the whole is not a real organism of harmonious unity. We can conceive it as such a unit only if we shut our eyes to other factualities and possibilities.

If there is no unified entirety, however, there is still the search for it, which we call reason; and there is the magnetic attraction of the One, which is Transcendence. Reason, as the encompassing bond in constant motion, meets the one Transcendence in its inconceivable tranquillity – both non-objective, both beyond the subject–object split.

iv. Our knowledge of man shows insoluble discrepancies
We experience the natural necessities of our existence, which we can know, and the powers of our freedom, which we cannot know. We feel the urge to immerse ourselves in the world, and the urge to detach ourselves from the world to reach the ground of our freedom. We see the historicity of our Existenz, without which we could not be, and we find ourselves above history and tending to remove it from our human essence.

The paradox part of being human shows in the fatal shifts that occur on the road to freedom:

Liberation from the embodiment of Transcendence may make us utterly unserious;

from the freedom of suspended ciphers we may turn to bottomless nihilism;

our freedom of knowledge may become the unfreedom of scientific superstition;

individual accomplishments may, in others, be translated and transformed into the opposites of their reality and intention;

the freedom of technological inventiveness may result in enslavement by the mechanics of mass production;

political liberation may become the external and internal unfreedom of total rule.

All these perversions are by no means inescapable. The task of the free is to show they can master the unfreedoms of their own making.

What remains is the question without which the venture of freedom would be no venture at all: is man's way like a self-consuming flame? Must his soaring ascent lead to the eventual suicide of human existence?

Man is more than, and fundamentally different from, any living creature and more than all his knowledge of himself as an object of anthropology, psychology, or sociology. Man as such is not a peculiarly successful kind of animal, with special traits and a predestined course of life that will be identically repeated through generation after generation. In the sense of mere life he is an extremely brittle creature. But he is destined for his supreme task of daring to be free, and this is why he can assume no definitive, merely repetitive form. From failure to failure he makes his way through the world, uplifted by hope, but without knowing whither.

v. Human destiny

This old phrase means both the lot that is cast for man and the task he faces. Our sense of destiny moves in the polarity between predetermination and the challenge of free choice.

Predetermination leads to the necessities to which man is subjected. It leads to cognoscible natural being, to history, to the divine will, or to what we conceive as cosmic order or the order of Being. In each of these cases man becomes a puppet – of the laws of nature or of history, of the predestination of God or of fate, whether called Moira, cosmic reason, or Providence. Man can only obey, submit, get in step with a movement that proceeds without him, or he can revolt and thus nullify himself entirely.

The challenge, on the other hand, means that man has a hand in deciding what will become of him, and of whatever else lies in his sphere of action. The concrete task can become clear to him as the Goethean 'challenge of the day', but never definitively. He sets himself to his task in the world on the ground of his faith, among men of other faiths, who set themselves to other tasks.

Yet man, free man, knows that he does not owe his freedom to himself. He is aware of an origin which – as distinct from being prey to necessity – he expressed in the cipher of 'necessity'. This 'necessity' is neither lawful nor arbitrary. It is more than the category of necessity, used here only as a cipher in which to touch upon an incomprehensible destiny.

5 THE FUTURE OF MAN IN A MODERN PERSPECTIVE

i. The question of the end

Today the feeling spreads that we have reached the turning-point – not of a historic period like many past ones, but of history as a whole.

Our increasing knowledge of history merely moves its beginnings farther away from us, without making them more accessible; but the future no longer confronts us as heretofore, as the continuation of the same kind of existence. It now stands before us as a set of the most extraordinary possibilities – limited, however, by the threat of total destruction.

Is human history, then, a curious short interval in the immeasurable history of the earth and of life? Is it a magnificent but futile process of freedom, infinitely precious in itself, a chain of high creative moments, but basically self-destructive just the same? Has history gone wrong from the outset, and is that why in the end this apostasy from the chance of freedom will cease simultaneously with the existence of man?

ii. How do we live with history?

There has never been so much historical knowledge as in our time, nor so much opportunity for the mass of people to inform themselves. Whatever men have thought and done – provided they made it public and the texts were preserved – is intelligible to us. We can rescue it from oblivion and make it effective. We see the historic diversity of views on man and the world in which each period meant to understand itself.

Modern man's mental equipment includes every possibility that history offers. He has the chance of an unheard-of sovereignty. Having at his disposal all the past views men would take of themselves, he can easily come to a free, true knowledge of himself.

But once again the liberation is ambiguous. It can happen in dealing with history that we let all things be true, sit back to enjoy them without struggle, and seek the one whole truth for mankind and for every individual by adding up the contents. This is an existential impossibility. The so-called cultural synthesis is either a noncommittal aesthetic notion or just a common cultural technique, or it is an empty, abstract, levelling generalization, satisfied with skimming the surface.

If we deal existentially with history, the struggles continue. The mirror of history intensifies them in our own consciousness, and at the same time it makes us aware of the new, for which there is no mirror. The challenge we come to feel on the material and mental premises of today is to establish the eternal Existenz in a new form of appearance.

iii. Can modern man regain solid ground?

More and more people, torn from their traditional historic moorings, make the painful experience of losing the ground under their feet. They turn into shiftless wanderers, at home nowhere and everywhere as chance pulls them hither and yon. Rootlessness comes to seem natural to them. The émigré existence becomes typical.

History tied human life to roles in which the individual existed, with which he identified. The man of today plays many roles and is identified with none. Granting that the historic roles had long been eroded and were eventually consumed by the overwhelming relativity, the fact remains that it is now the very condition of man's existence to give up his identification with any role. Is this a tremendous liberation or radical ruin?

Since man cannot be himself without historic fulfilment, without a continuous phenomenality of his essence, the question of the future is how the individual in our general bustle and drift can regain such fulfilment in his personal community.

iv. The futility of inquiries into the future

There is no way of knowing the future. Neither the observation of political, social, and economic events nor a philosophical reflection on what ought to be can show us what will happen.

Great religious forces have claimed to know the future, but the real future always proved very different. The primitive Christians' belief in the imminence of the world's end, of the Last Judgment and the kingdom of heaven, was refuted by the unforeseen Church with its practical politics and its combination of such incompatibles as the biblical Christ and the reality of civilization. The historic construction of Marx was refuted by the reality of totalitarianism. In these cases, as in others, the 'faith' of later days will not admit its perversion. It will either fail to see it or shrug it off.

The plans that men make on the basis of their knowledge, and the ways they choose, out of the maze of possibilities, to follow at a particular time – this is what determines the future.

Not to see realities, not to include them among the bases of decision, means to end up in a void. Not to experience and recognize freedom of choice as a decisive factor means to be enslaved by supposed realities.

What is reality? This is the great question that cannot be definitively answered – which makes the future not merely uncertain but always quite surprising to those who experience it with the expectations of a traditional knowledge.

v. The change in man

In a situation in which man seems stripped of everything, about to surrender his freedom, entangled in total evil and in his own guilt, the cry has always gone up that he ought to change. We hear it from Plato; we hear it in all phases of the biblical experience, down to the New Testament call to penance (*metanoeite*).

In modern times Kierkegaard asked for a change in man regardless of the world, solely for the sake of individual salvation. Marx envisioned a change in the world, from capitalism to communism, as the necessary course of history, and its cognition as a simultaneous call on every individual to promote it. Kierkegaard's change would not affect the future of the human world; he thought only of the individual soul and of eternity. Marx's change is a supposedly known objective process, a dialectical about-face. He ignored the individual and his importance; to him there were no individuals, only 'exponents'.

In philosophizing we do not know the future. But we do know the change in the individual – the change in many individuals who meet in communication.

We realize that we are the world's only scene of the manifestation of truth and reality. This feeling brings us to the existential experience of a prehistoric and, so to speak, pre-cosmic origin. The ultimate, then, is neither the universe nor history; it is what Existenz perceives in that experience. For all man's dependency on existence, an incomprehensible trust in something before any world lifts him above his existence, because as Existenz he feels sheltered elsewhere. That we can know of everything that exists and does not know itself is a preliminary step to this superiority; but to demonstrate it is the sole responsibility of our freedom.

In its attainment lies the change. It can occur now as ever, but today it can affect the course of things more profoundly than ever. A new way for man to be changed under the conditions of our time – this is the one great possibility.

It means to make our way out of our confinement in forms of objective natural and historical knowledge, and out of our confinement in a subjectivity of each claiming his right as the way he is, as the opinion he holds. It means to get over making absolutes of ciphers, which can never be Transcendence.

Liberation by the constant renewal of this change is no longer a mere liberation from something. It is the original freedom we live by.

The outcome of this possible change in man is unpredictable. It is not enough to meet all present and impending horrors with the soothing assertion that man is naturally free, that his essence cannot change, and that freedom, therefore, will always restore itself. Even pretending to know as much is adverse to freedom, for a trusting pseudo-knowledge of its indestructibility may paralyse the unknowable energies that freedom derives from Transcendence. In such pseudo-knowledge we give up our own freedom so as to depend on that of others.

It is when we feel changed that we become truly human. Today, in the present situation, any chance of rescue springs from such a change. It is the one possibility that includes everything else.

Instead of being hoodwinked by an optimistic or pessimistic pseudo-knowledge of the future we come to be conscious of our responsibility. This responsibility confronts us in everyday life, in our impulses and emotions and in our personal conduct, in our dealings with people, in being close or distant, in liking and disliking, in all the major and minor decisions that bear not on ourselves alone but on the course of things. As we think of man, as we let the ciphers affect us, as we judge them, as we use them to take our ultimate bearings – in all this we perform free acts for which we are responsible.

d. Can Philosophy Help?

1 PHILOSOPHY WANTS TRUTH AND POINTS BEYOND ITSELF

That liberation alone does not make us free is obvious. When we note this phenomenon we are still at a loss what to do about it. It does not give clear directives and does not let the intellect 'know how' to handle it.

The intellect, therefore – whether of 'atheists' or of believers in revelation – would much rather say that philosophy brought us the troubles of liberation but no freedom, that it liberates man but fails to fulfil his freedom.

The first reply to this is that philosophy wants truth.

It cannot preach, can show us nothing solid, nothing absolute, no reality that would support us in the world. It remains in suspended ciphers.

If we want to be honest, there is no prophetic philosophy any more – none that might possess and teach its knowledge by rational insight as the one exclusive truth.

What philosophy wants first and last is truth, and as no man has the truth, it wants us to demand truthfulness.

Philosophy stakes its all on the truth, without foreknowledge. Hence its ever-reiterated, ever re-initiated question: what is truth?

Philosophy realizes that there is no right way to arrange the world. There is no one absolute truth for all. Man is and remains *en route*.

Philosophizing, we believe that all roads will lead in the right direction if we are truthful, but that all is lost if we are not. Only a life that pursues truth without restrictions can have meaning. This pursuit takes thought-fulness and calm along with a passion for truth, for an uncritical truth fanatic has already perverted his passion and will lose it in short order.

Truth seems indifferent to what we call happiness, indifferent to our desires. Truth may appear to us as a radiant, inspiring goddess and may wear a petrifying Gorgon's mask.

Truthfulness takes courage. Philosophy teaches us not to shut our eyes to extremity. It calls for steadfastness in vision.

The second answer is that every vital philosophical thought points beyond itself to a transcendent reality. This alone fulfils the point of philosophizing and accomplishes what no meaningful statement can cover.

Philosophizing has two wings, so to speak. One is moved by the energies of communicable thought and general doctrine, while the other, by means of such thought, beats in the individual Existenz. To make us soar, both wings must beat together.

Reflection grants us clarity for things we realize only in our way of life.

Philosophy takes us where each individual receives himself – as a gift, not of philosophy, but of Transcendence – and decides by his Existenz.

Once having drunk from the fount of philosophy and tasted truth, we can never again do without it. Its insight can help even when I fail myself, for it still lets me know what is possible. Having taught me patience and humility, it keeps calling on me to act, to prepare myself in thought, and to remember.

2 NO VISIBLE WAY OUT

If ours seems a time of general decay disguised by technological advance, by the huge rise in living standards and in military power; if no more great ciphers are either effective or forthcoming; if the light of Transcendence fades in the existential darkness of 'enlightened' intellectual knowledge; if existence is partly tyrannized, partly emptied, and entirely levelled; if the course of events leads to universal fraudulence, to mendacity, or at least to obliviousness; if the terrors of destruction hang over us in atom bombs and total rule, and the several models of totalitarianism may clash and cause a nuclear holocaust between them even after a surrender of the free world; if all signs suggest that to avoid total destruction, we may choose a life that would no longer be worth living and fail to avert the final extinction of organic life anyway – if these are our prospects, what hope remains?

Can philosophy help? Is this situation not too much for man? Instead of helping, will philosophical clarity not further overtax him?

Let me reply in another set of 'ifs'. If the voice of suspended ciphers is to give man the pure and serious experience once produced by an embodied Transcendence; if the detached philosophical questions that test his truthfulness are only to bring him closer to the substance of true reality; if the actual course of events gives him and mankind a choice: either to leave a lifeless globe behind, as a grain of dust in the cosmos, or to become truly human in a community of fate with others who can live right and ward off that end – if this is too much for him, he is being overtaxed by real and intellectual circumstances he brought on himself, unwittingly and unwillingly, by his own thoughts and actions.

3 OVERTAXING MAN

Can man hope to cope with this situation?

Whoever philosophizes will believe that he can. He will believe that while it cannot be certain, it must be possible for man eventually to perform the tasks imposed upon him, through himself, by an inexorable fate.

Excessive demands may crush us. But they may also stimulate all energies of Existenz and reason; they may lift us out of levity and triviality. Philosophy has always sparked the revolutions in the way of thinking, and it is doing so now.

4 PRESENT EXISTENCE, SUICIDE, AND THE DIGNITY OF INDIGNITY

Philosophizing points to the present, rests upon it, fulfils it.

Only in the present is man given to himself. This is why we love the present, why we are thankful to be alive, to be living now and at no other time.

The moment – as distinct from the vanishing Now, which always only flows past – is our only presence of eternity.

We hear the simple, incomprehensible voice of the present in the medieval verse I quoted at the beginning of this book:

> *I come I know not whence,*
> *I am I know not who,*
> *I die I know not when,*
> *I go I know not where,*
> *I wonder why I am of good cheer.*

When good cheer is more than the beautiful *joie de vivre* of an evanescent vitality – when it is the certainty of our eternal origin – it remains the possible fulfilment of the present and will be possible as long as we exist.

But again it would be false to regard this as plain, definitive truth, valid for all and real in everybody. In philosophizing we see the Other in man. We look at extremity, but we do not overlook it.

There is dignity in the fact that man, and man alone, can take his own life – that his resolve to do so can be clearly conscious, undimmed by emotion, true to himself.

All tyrannies, all churches, all powers wielded by some men over others and claiming to extend to the others' souls – all these have execrated suicide because it attests the freedom of the individual, of man as such. He can foil oppression and destructive suffering. Once I am ready to kill myself I am free.

The suicide has crossed the boundary. We go on asking, but at last we halt in awe and silence.

Beside the dignity of being able to die by one's own hand, if need be, stands the dignity that man retains in the worst humiliation and the most frightful suffering. I am referring to Jesus – the man, not the cipher of Christ. This 'undignified' dignity demonstrates what human beings really are and can be. It shows us how untruthful we are if we believe that our Existenz is unconditional – if we take it for the one true humanity, and our dignity for the only dignity. The question what man is and can be deepens with our insight. Jesus revealed the dubiousness of all laws and orders; he showed the power of love; he proved his utter freedom from the world by dying not under a cloak of stoicism but truthfully suffering the long-drawn agonies of a slow execution such as men have perpetrated on their fellows for thousands of years to this day, in many ways and in innumerable cases.

5 FREEDOM BY PHILOSOPHY

The theses that state the liberation by philosophy are negations. Far from destroying Existenz, however, they broaden its scope. Philosophy's supreme knowledge is that it does not know. This is not our initial ignorance, for which we should substitute knowledge; it is the not knowing that consummates all our knowledge, that becomes apparent only at the very bounds of knowledge.

If philosophy is a liberating force in its negations, the truth of this liberation will make it the way to consummate freedom.

Philosophy is every individual's way to live up to his responsibility to truth, and not to dodge it by confessing a creed. Knowing, questioning, he testifies by his judgment and his way of life in communication. The form of confession is untrue as such, because it shrouds the real task of man and avoids his real situation.

We pervert philosophical thinking if we want contemplative cognition to give us what we can realize only in action, within and without. The real philosophical thought is inner action. Even if it lapses into a mere thought of something it can always be recovered.

But inner action alone does not bring about freedom either. We realize freedom only by communicating all the ways and stages of its possibility.

Philosophical doctrine can clarify and suggest. It can illuminate our horizons and there, by thinking in ciphers, give us room beyond what we can know. This is simply a liberation from chains of obtuseness, error, and deceptive unconsciousness. Whether an individual will consummate his freedom is always up to himself, to the self-being he is given.

6 DOUBTS OF THE INDEPENDENCE OF PHILOSOPHY

We who take our stand on what we meet in philosophizing seem to rely on a nonentity. We hear that freedom can come only from religion, from the revelation that is the truth. We find ourselves attacked as villains or pitied as poor, lost souls devoid of grace. A modern Catholic humanist of philosophical bent and a resigned disposition can liken philosophy to 'a vine sprouting on the soil of an old oak, religion; grown into a tree, it entangles and strangles the oak but will die with it' (Ludwig Curtius, *Torso*).

We deny this. Philosophy faces religion and revelation, but on its own ground. It would not die if the faith in revelation should die. It is older. It exists at all times. In the sense of ascertaining the absolute, of illuminating man and making him serious, of allying freedom with Transcendence – in this broad sense philosophy may be called religion. It has – confusingly, to my mind – been called philosophical religion or religious philosophy. It is religion's kin, not its enemy. But it is by no means a secularized religion. It is its own source, along with humanity's.

It does not help as the faith in revelation promises and claims to help. If the gift of self and the direct relation to Transcendence enables man to help himself, philosophy comes to his aid with a world of truthful thinking.

Part Seven. Common ground?

Churches are organizations of religious tradition. What happens in them, what and how they preach, how they develop their thinking and their symbols, how they perform their rites – to the Western world all this is of vital importance. It might provide truthful and serious individuals with the foundation of a great community. Rallying round the cult, the faithful and the clergy and the theologians might testify to their Existenz in the presence of eternity.

What will become of the churches may decide the Western fate. If all things ecclesiastic become stage-props of life, if they level off into conventions, habits, matters of mere outward repetition, their strength wanes even if most people keep up their church membership. If untruthfulness grows at the same time, the ground is prepared for all evil. Hence the great concern about the vigour and veracity of ecclesiastic faith.

Philosophy, unlike the faith in revelation, is unorganized, dispersed in individuals, without the powerful backing of a church, a state, a party, an organized mass movement. What philosophers think is considered 'private'. They may claim to belong to the *philosophia perennis*, but their claim goes unrecognized.

No power in the world entitles us to philosophize. We have to do it on our own, responsible to an authority that we establish for ourselves and find in four thousand years of philosophizing.

When we discuss possibilities in the churches we must know that what we say is deemed wholly unwarranted. But we are concerned with the serious things that occur, or fail to occur, in or through the churches; so it is only natural for our thoughts to turn in that direction. For there the determinant factors of future humanity can be made to prevail.

Perhaps we can glimpse areas of opportunity and for a moment see farther than the usual acquiescence in the *status quo* permits. Perhaps our thinking can even be helpful to individuals who feel originally stirred and look to the church for clarity. Perhaps we can encourage a life that is unaware of the *pneuma* goading it lightwards. Perhaps we can furnish concepts indispensable to such thinking. Perhaps we can now confirm premonitions of things to come, of chances already budding.

I am convinced that in its present jeopardy the substance of the biblical faith will undergo so radical a change of language, preaching, and living practice that to the captives of traditional forms it may look like the end of ecclesiastic religion. The churches will not remain convincing unless they accomplish this transformation in the deepest biblical earnest, unless that earnest melts the shells of their dogmas and institutions and finds in them a contemporary voice.

The very brittleness I think I see in modern Protestant theology seems to me to offer a chance. The brittleness, together with the Protestant principle of religious freedom, might let new forms arise precisely where Christianity is now weakest, both ecclesiastically and as a practical faith.

What I say is mere thought without action. It is the churches that would have to do all this – and thus, at the same time, to think it better than I can. Only in practice, by common realization, can pastors, preachers, practising communicants accomplish what philosophers try to conceive.

How oddly disproportionate it is for an individual to write about such things! How infinitesimal his thinking looks against the overwhelming sweep of history and its spiritual forces! His thoughts may range far and plumb deep, but the experience makes him humble. Here and there, perhaps, he may hope to brighten a glimmer of light or cause some old, forgotten truth to be remembered.

It has always been awkward for philosophers to try to mind the theologians' business and to tell them what to do – as if philosophy, the philosophical faith, were the court of last resort for all faith. All I mean to do is to raise questions, to show possibilities, to look for patterns, to recall to memory.

Individual believers in revelation can be close to individuals who philosophize. Their judgments and their ways of life can coincide in fact; they may be alienated only by the tone of their statements of faith; by different orders of rank, by exclusiveness, by hidden ruptures of communication. On both sides, a believer will hear the ciphers with the seriousness that is the truly human trait, the true vinculum. If we believe, whether philosophically or in revelation, we would not like to quarrel but to communicate.

a. How the Two Faiths See Each Other

1 A PHILOSOPHIZING VIEW OF FAITH IN REVELATION

In our historical outline we distinguished between prophets, who proclaimed what God told them; churches and priests, who declared texts to be inspired and claimed to interpret them correctly; and apostles, who testified that God, in Christ, had appeared on earth.

All three ways of revelation require an additional authority in the world, to decide which prophets were genuine, which texts are inspired, whose apostolic testimony counts. The believer must heed this authority; he has nothing else to hold on to. We quoted Augustine's magnificently unequivocal line, 'I would not believe the Gospel if the authority of the Catholic Church did not prompt me as well.'

If this authority is not believed, however, the select status of the Scriptures in literature has an end, and they are just like other exalted writings. What has been a matter of course for two thousand years – how short a time! – cannot alter this. That writings were selected as canonical is a historic fact, then, of explorable origin and with parallels in China and India. In fact, the canonization of these writings changes their rank only for believers in revelation, not for the rest of mankind.

Their contents, however, are by no means null and void for one who cannot believe in the revelation. Only his relationship to them is different. It is a free relationship. Prophets, apostles, and inspiration are now phenomena of the entrance of truth into the world. We conceive these ways of appearance in ciphers – 'prophet', 'inspiration', and 'apostle' – with two consequences.

First, the cipher can find an echo in the individual's understanding of himself. The sense of being an instrument, for example, of thinking and acting in line with the demands of an encompassing Transcendence whose servant I cannot know but can and do feel myself to be – this may become a cipher that makes humble. It can only be true as man's claim upon himself, not as the vindication of a claim on others. For it is by my words, my actions, and my insights, not by regarding myself as an instrument, that I must prove whether the cipher can be true, and what it implies.

Second, nothing that is claimed to be revelation or proclaimed, as by a prophet or apostle, can be valid as such. A cipher is a possibility, not a reality. Whatever claims to be sacred and absolute and vested with unconditional authority is subject to criticism. What the prophet says, what comes into the world by inspiration, what the apostle witnesses – all that has to be tested by the possible Existenz of every individual.

This is not, as theologians would have us believe, a criticism of God, a foolish human attempt to tell God what he can or cannot do. It is criticism of the mundane authorities that claim to be empowered to speak in God's name. Humans, no matter what their office or creed, remain humans, and to us who cannot believe in revelation they seem to be demanding falsely, as obedience to God, what would be obedience to their positions, to their church, to human handiwork.

We are not judging God but the demands of men. Statistically, what appears in the faith in revelation is God's Word for only a minority of mankind; in fact, it is God's Word for only a second minority within the first. For us it is a world of ciphers, not of divine realities – a suspended language of Transcendence, not a real act of God – a challenge to interpret possible meanings, not a demand for obedience.

We do not speak against God, but against human claims to speak for God. We must state what we hold to be true – negatively, first: there is no direct reality of God in the world. That is to say, there is no God who speaks in the world, through a representative authority, about such things as office, word, or sacrament, and whom we are to obey by obeying those offices. Positively we say: God made us for the freedom and reason in which we receive ourselves. In both, we are responsible to an authority found in ourselves, an authority that is infinitely more than ourselves but speaks only indirectly. We agree with Kant's interpretation that divine wisdom is no less admirable in what it denies us than in what it grants us, for if God appeared to us in his majesty, we would become obedient puppets and cease being the free creatures he willed us to be.

Applying the standard of the hidden God, we find that the God who shows himself in the reality of revelation cannot be God for us. This is no denial of God as against faith in God; it is the hidden God as against the revealed one. It is the philosophical consciousness of transcendent reality opposing the material reality of revelation.

2 HOW THE FAITH IN REVELATION VIEWS PHILOSOPHICAL FAITH

i. The charge

To one who believes in revelation, a philosophical faith cannot be faith in God. I quote from one of the most tolerant of theologians: 'It is indeed only either here or there that God is rightly understood, and from the standpoint of Christian belief a humanistic deism must be called an error and a delusion – in so far as it is meant to be faith in God' (Bultmann, *Studium generale*, Vol. 1). This example – without a trace of the arrogance we find now and then in theologians – may serve to show that it lies in the nature of the faith in revelation to make even such a man think in this fashion.

The result is the constantly repeated charge that thinking of Transcendence is a merely speculative experience, pale, abstract, impotent in meditation, and unreal, being aimed at unreality. We hear that to the believer in revelation God is personal, facing man as the Thou he can communicate with in prayer, person to person (while philosophical faith knows the personality of God only as a cipher of the source of personality, a source that is infinitely more than personality and not to be defined in this form). We are told that the revealed God helps in the world, that he intervenes effectively, causes the good things I wish for, and assures me that what looks to me like evil is for the best, after all. I experience his grace in his acts, which I inwardly feel to be real (while in philosophical faith I conceive Providence as a cipher whose implication in specific historic events strikes me as rationally absurd and clearly refutable – though as a cipher, stripped of knowability and realization, it illuminates the mystery that burdens us). To a believer in revelation everything begins with the revelatory act of God: it is not we who seek God. The believer applies this thesis to concrete actions and events (while in philosophical faith such a thesis applies only on the whole, to the gift of human selfhood in a world that is apparent or transitional rather than ultimate). The God of the faithful is

said to be concrete and near, the living God of the Bible, while the philosophical Godhead is abstract and far, a mere conception.

ii. The answer

We reply that the nearby God is indispensable to finite beings but exists in
ciphers only. These are naturally manifold, and as a result the nearby God
will come to be polytheistic. Surreptitiously this happens even in the faith
in revelation, which dogmatically preserves the one God: if this one God is
near, he will imperceptibly appear to the believer in one specific form at a
time, while the One remains the distant God whose very Oneness is a cipher.

If the ciphers turn into God's concrete reality, they will soon be many
gods, untrue, and objects of superstition. Only as ciphers, as historic voices
of the distant God, can they stay potentially true.

It is precisely as a mere conception that the distant God expands the scope
of our freedom. His conception liberates us from concrete, superstitiously
fixed gods and revelations; it liberates us from all exclusivities, all fanati-
cisms, all acts of violence that lie hidden in the faith in a God who shows
himself in time and space.

If in philosophical faith we deny ourselves the exclusionary revelation, if
we translate it and its contents into ciphers, this is partly due, of course, to
an enlightenment that tells us what we do and do not know as we proceed.
But the main reason is that in philosophical faith we feel the reality of the
hidden Transcendence. Measured by the corresponding idea of God, as
found on the peaks of the Bible and in philosophy, the thesis of his incarnation would, if philosophy allowed us to use the language of believers in
revelation, seem blasphemous – as it would have seemed to the human
Jesus, as far as we know about him.

We feel the reality of God most strongly where no concretion, no human
propinquity, shrouds it – where we are quite serious about the biblical ban
on any image or likeness, about the warning that our thoughts are not the
thoughts of God – and where these words hold good for a believing Existenz
even at the limits of failure. For as Existenz I read the suspended and
ambiguous ciphers, but I do not make myself an image of God.

EXCURSUS

Recently I came across a passage by Karl Barth (Dogmatik III, 4, pp. 549ff. 2nd
edition, 1957)[1]. My name is not mentioned, but I must assume that in part,
at least, my writings are referred to, since there is no group that employs
the expressions and phrasings cited below. I am italicizing the segments of
Barth's passage and inserting between them a few remarks of mine.

[1] By kind permission of T. & T. Clark, Edinburgh, publishers of the authorized translation of Church Dogmatics by Karl Barth, the excerpts in this excursus are quoted in my
translation – Translator.

'The term "God", after all, is far too often used only to cover the bounds of all human understanding of self and the world. Far too often when a man says "God" he means by this cipher a mere something: that so-called "Transcendence" – empty, barren, and at bottom profoundly dull – which then, rather than as the true Opposite, the wholly and truthfully Other, the genuine Without and Beyond, will be much better interpreted as an illusionary reflection of human freedom, as its projection into a non-objective void.'

The bounds of knowledge can be shown by compelling cognition. This is not easy to achieve, and most men do not yet honestly seek it either; that the 'term' God was used to cover these bounds had not yet occurred to me. The agnostics of Positivism are indifferent toward a limit which to them means nothing but clarity about what can and cannot be known. Such clarity may have effects other than indifference, however. It may plunge us into despair – because an ever-limited, never conclusive knowledge seems pointless – or it may invite a new reflection. It may serve us as a springboard, so to speak, with the landing place not determined by cogent knowledge.

Since Barth does not inclose the word 'cipher' in quotation marks, he too might seem to be taking 'the term "God" ' to be a cipher – but this conjecture can hardly be correct. In any case, the main charge levelled at my writings is that by the cipher I mean something empty and barren. This cannot be argued. It looks that way to Barth, but not to me.

It is true, however, that while the cipher is an 'opposite', Transcendence is not. For as an opposite – whether as an object of conceivability or as embodiment for our senses – it would indeed disappear to the thinking in which I live. It would be entirely concealed by such objectivities, without which it strikes Barth as profoundly dull. To me the ciphers are suspended, to be questioned over and over; but in this suspension they are a language of the transcendent reality that meets the reality of Existenz. They are not extinguished in unequivocal submission to unequivocal acts of revelation.

In philosophical thinking, the idea of an opposite as the 'truthfully Other, the genuine Without and Beyond', seems like a blasphemy of Transcendence.

In his interpretation of Transcendence 'as an illusionary reflection of human freedom, as its projection into a non-objective void', Karl Barth employs a traditional psychological jargon, a 'psychology' that serves for purposes of defamation, not for real cognition.

'It is of the essence of this "Transcendence" that it confronts man with no definite will, performs no definite works, finds no definite words, and has not even a definite power and authority.'

This is indeed true in the sense of revelation as Barth understands it, but such statements wrongly deprive ciphers of their meaning. How the suspended ciphers may serve as an irreplaceable, true, and effective language is the responsibility of Existenz at crucial moments. Yet this language, in our human situation, always involves the risk of escaping from the challenge into the comfortable confessional faith of a fixed revelation.

'*It cannot really bind him, or really loose him. It can neither justify nor satisfy him. It can give his life neither a clear meaning nor a distinct purpose.*'

This is true, provided man's desire for assuring, sheltering restriction will not let him realize his great original potential of serious experience *en route*, on his own responsibility, in commitment and freedom – and provided also that he wants justification (which he is neither in need of nor entitled to) or satisfaction (which he may well be granted only at the cost of illusions), and that he desires a distinct purpose in life (which man is always given only in particular, not on the whole).

'*Instead, anyone daring to advance such claims for it will be quickly and quite rightly squelched by its high priests and prophets with the advice that definite statements about it, attributions of form, personality, or faculties of speech and action, let alone of definite words and deeds, can at most be "mythologizing" and thus had best be omitted.*'

High priests and prophets? Oh, what epithets we are accorded here! I can see no humour in them, only theological self-assurance sneering at philosophy. As for the question itself, it concerns the point of the statements, not their omission. The lasting antinomy for man as a finite, sensory, rational creature is this: he shall not make himself an image or likeness of God, and yet he cannot help doing so as soon as his mind turns to Transcendence. There is no escaping the antinomy. It shows in the very first word – God, Transcendence. If we say 'God', the word contains essentially what moves us; if we say 'Transcendence', it contains essentially what thinking clarifies. When I say, God is a cipher of Transcendence, I mean a definite, personal, acting, speaking form of God; when I talk of ciphers of God, I identify God with Transcendence. The changing usage ceases to be logically irritating when we keep the point of all such talk in mind: the task in our human situation is not to omit forbidden statements, but to give up the fixation – which is really, radically forbidden – and thus to achieve mobility in forbidden areas.

In the struggle of ciphers we ourselves take wing. The realm of ciphers is vast and not to be invented; it has grown since time immemorial in the relationship of Existenz and Transcendence. It is far from uniform, due to the diversity of powers in quest of a voice, and yet it is subject to the idea and reality of the One. Unless we move in this realm, unless it affects us, we become obtuse; but the cipher realm itself is exposed to obfuscations and perversions.

In Barth's use of the phrase 'at most', in letting us say 'quite rightly' that talk in this realm can 'at most' be mythologizing, lies a demand for another, non-mythologizing kind of talk. Yet for all the distinctions that have been made in religious history, between myth and revelation and between types of myths, the one radical difference between the cipher language and empirical reality remains. I myself have spoken out against the de-mythologizers, but in calling for the other kind of talk one will involuntarily assert the physical reality of the divine. In philosophizing, this mode of reality will lose us both the deity and our freedom.

' *"Transcendence" can indeed mean nothing else, nothing more definite, than that behind, above, and ahead of the human act lies something open, some abyss which man – sage or fool, pardoned or condemned, salvation-bound or perdition-bound – is destined ever and ever again to plunge himself into.'*

This seems a not unwitty burlesque of the philosophical way of thinking. I assume that the words used by Barth convey different meanings to him and to us; but deeply concealed in the burlesque lies still a glimmer of the disquiet of one who has come to take life seriously. Karl Barth will, for instance, pronounce judgments on past history. Having excellently described a fifteenth-century Japanese sect whose positions, in part, curiously resemble Protestantism, he ends by saying that, after all, they still remain poor, lost heathens. The judgment implied in his characterization of the concept of Transcendence is scarcely hidden: to Barth, I presume, men who hold that concept are not sages, not pardoned, not salvation-bound, but fools, poor, condemned souls headed for perdition. What great men, what luminaries on our human way this verdict would cover!

'*And the slightly arid commandment of tolerance, i.e., of shunning all "absolutizing" – in fact, refraining from all positive statements on its possible contents or directives – seems to be the one comparatively sure thing to be derived from a contemplation of this spectre.'*

On the soil of faith in revelation, it would appear, no understanding of the 'slightly arid commandment of tolerance' can grow. It is truly not arid.

In politics it is the basis of rights and duties that we, today, are infinitely grateful to live by. It is the most magnificent human victory over the inhuman faith in ecclesiastic dogmas which marked the time of the religious wars. It still inspires us to think historically of the period of the Reformation and its consequences, that witches' sabbath into which the struggle in the realm of ciphers turned, and to hear the men whose valour and whose sacrifices blazed the trail of tolerance in those days.

Inwardly, however, tolerance is the essential expression of the will to communicate. There the mere toleration that has a point and is attainable in politics would be an insult; the essence of this tolerance lies in receptiveness, in concern, in acknowledgment. It could be 'arid' only on the premise that the theologically interpreted faith in revelation alone is not arid. Tolerance does not spring from the contemplation of a spectre.

And why this 'spectre'? By spectre we mean a bodily apparition that is unreal – a phenomenon that has no substance and is thus intangible, although materially present. It is a thing that is nothing, but will frighten and deceive us anyway. The charge of talking in spectres seems to me, therefore, more applicable to the proponents of an embodied God than to those who view any embodiment – excepting only the kind that we finite, sensory, rational creatures hear as ciphers – as dimming the purity of God. But where we do end up if on the crucial existential issue we berate each other as spiritualists? I know I misconceive a truthful faith in revelation if I accuse it of dealing with a spectre of God; perhaps a theological believer in revelation is no less baffled by our way of thinking, by our experience and our way of life. Yet this must not be the last word.

I have quoted Karl Barth in order to document the thinking of today's best-known, most highly respected Protestant theologian. What he really seems to be saying is that philosophy is a superfluous nuisance. It would lead to the conclusion that men who philosophize should not be engaged in serious communication but in casual polemics, if need be – carried on with an amiably aloof but sometimes rather acid humour.

b. A Change in the Appearance of Biblical Religion?

Can the biblical faith in revelation change its appearance? Can such a change mean that it will regain its original earnest? Can its steadily weakening vigour be revived?

The weakness may be denied – and with some justification, since we cannot possibly know what an individual believes deep in his heart, in suffering and dying. We see only his conduct, his decisions, his judgments, his actions in the world.

In every country of Europe we have seen resistance fighters and the courage with which they met death. Their decision to fight was made freely, not in obedience to any mundane authority. We read the words that tell us how they saw themselves. In every class or group not only Christians but liberals, socialists, sceptics, and men who thought of themselves as communists demonstrated the same self-sacrificing courage, the same calm in the face of death, the same strength of faith, the same sense of true freedom in acting under an illumined compulsion.

The way in which people state their understanding of themselves may be inadequate to their experience and their actions. Entirely different tenets of faith were expressed by the resistance fighters, and nobody knows the reality. It is only when we look at the individuals themselves, when we hear the tone, the utterly simple as well as the strangely complex ways of thinking, judgments, and reasonings, that the documents strike us as credible and fitting.

Nor can anyone else know how the biblical believers in the resistance came to be in earnest. Jews and Christians both died as witnesses to their faith in revelation. That contemporaries of ours have proved a serious faith of high rank, and that the biblical faith did not outrank others, is certain.

But this seriousness, which can be the property of all men regardless of their historic and spiritual background, is not the point of our question now. We mean the special world of the biblical faith, the continuity of a tradition that allows men to share in the seriousness of their forebears.

Can the biblical faith be reformed from its own roots, to the kind of earnest that lies not in confessing a creed but in the state of the soul, in action, in factual decisions? One of these decisions may be a 'martyr's' confession in extreme peril – but not the riskless, tranquillizing general confession that is felt to be meritorious and is often noxiously aggressive.

Can the *pneuma* regain the status of a power jointly felt as a present source – a power so moving in its brightness, measure, and thoughtfulness that the individual feels as one with the encompassing that links him with the rest of the community, like an influx of the fullness of Being?

It is not the substance of the biblical faith that needs transforming, but its appearance in religious statements. We need such statements, of course, to make the substance communicable; but where the statement is detached from the substance the original believer will no longer recognize his faith. Ways of conception, phrasings of thought, and ciphers which on other premises used to fit the historic situation are no longer fitting today. To preserve the substance, we do not need any progress in it; we need a change in its garb.

1 DEALING WITH THE BIBLE

There is such a thing as theological expertness. It lies, first, in the huge body of dogmatic work done over thousands of years, and secondly, in the historical knowledge of the Scriptures that was introduced by Spinoza and further developed from the eighteenth century on. It may seem frivolous of a 'layman' to take the floor in this expert world.

But what has happened and is still happening here concerns all of us. Except in things we realize ourselves, therefore, we need not defer to an esoteric, would-be dictatorial theological science. Since the essentials are simple, the point is not to miss them and not to drown them in a mass of irrelevant knowledge.

i. Deposit and canon

The Bible is the deposit of a thousand years of religious, mythical, historic, and existential experience. Its texts, differing immensely in their literary form, were culled in the course of that time from a much more voluminous literature; finally, the process was concluded and the whole declared canonical. This canonical character has since prevailed through the centuries. As the expression of historic ties it can no longer be removed from the Bible, no more than from the corresponding Hindu and Chinese writings.

Still, historically the selection of the Old and New Testament canon from the then extant and now only partly preserved writings is an incidental result. It is not vital to the adoption of the contents. The motifs of this historic process are manifold and hard to disentangle, but they are a matter of historical rather than factual interest.

ii. Exegesis

Like any text, the Bible takes understanding. This is conveyed in exegesis. But the text itself already conveys understanding; it refers to an underlying basic text, so to speak, which the spoken and written one is already interpreting. Where is the line between basic and interpretive text, and between the interpretive text and our own interpretation?

Theologians have made a distinction between the substance of revelation – which comes from God and is eternally the same – and our exegesis, which is accomplished by theological effort and cannot claim absolute truth for its interpretations in time. These are called subject to change.

Yet where is the thing itself, the revelation, and where does exegesis begin? After all, there is no sentence in the Bible that is not exegesis. At the very least, it is translation into human language, into human ways of thought. We never have the thing itself, except in exegesis. Pure, uninterpreted, it is beyond us.

This view is opposed, first, by Luther: 'Das Wort sie sollen lassen stahn' – the Word should be allowed to stand. But Luther himself made distinctions in the Bible; he rejects the whole Epistle of St James, for instance. Who can tell the Word that ought to be allowed to stand from the one that is to be questioned or even rejected?

Opposed, moreover, is any formulated creed. But what is a creed if not exegesis? This speculative-dogmatic interpretation with the aid of Gnostic and philosophical thinking begins in the New Testament itself – a compendium of writings containing multiple interpretative theologies that defy reduction to any common denominator.

I repeat: for us, the object of exegesis exists in the exegesis only. Whatever text we come across is either interpretation or reinterpretation; nor will a historical analysis of the New Testament discover any revelation that has not been interpreted already. And these interpretations grow and unfold, take many directions, and receive very different accents.

If thus the unity, the substance, the immutable part of the divine revelation actually does not exist as itself in any sentence, preachment, or theology; if all this remains a cipher language; if the will, the words, the very acts of God are interpretations in ciphers as soon as they are put into words – could there not be an eventual meeting of philosophical and theological interpretation, both of which draw upon each other from the outset anyway?

iii. Historical study and adoption

A thinking concern with the Bible and what it talks about means bringing to mind what was seen, felt, and thought in it, from the marvellous old tales and the historic accounts of the prophets to the pious songs and down to lines of a dogmatic nature.

An exegesis that is existentially concerned, not just historically observing, lifts the interpreter's weight above random historic facts. Being in earnest, it is vigorous, essential, and consequential in practice.

Essential interpretation is adoption and rejection at once.

Study gives us the information, the conceptions, the ideas that form the basis of historical knowledge. Historical understanding is a means to the pure visualization of the documentary material, to a detached view of what concerns us and what does not.

Yet adoption is more than historical understanding. Adoption means to turn the embattled ciphers into the voice of a reality, a voice that touches us if we are existentially receptive. We reject it if we feel it is an unreal voice, or that of an alien force, or a lure of darkness, untruthfulness, and evil. Adoption is a matter for the individual, for each unique, irreplaceable Existenz that has found its own serious language in the Bible.

We study texts in their historic context, but the truth we hear is timeless. Historical research brings us to the existential meaning – the more so if the factually historic elements, the realities and intended meanings, help us to assimilate the unhistoric and supra-historic one that defies general conception and adequate visualization in any general thought. The supra-historic is the eternal that knows no progress as it appears, reappears, and renews itself in time beyond measure.

We have to guard against considering this never-muted voice of eternity as speaking definitive truth now, in the language of our time. Though we can never survey our phenomenality, we know that as phenomena we are historic even in our concepts and our ways of thinking, even if we base ourselves on a great cogitative tradition that we cannot do enough to make our own.

Thus, though we have the insight to resist fixed dogmas and creeds, we are aware of something lasting, something that keeps speaking through all change but is not definitive in any speech, something eternally present in every phenomenon and absolute in none.

Historical research as such does not lead to faith. It shows us the phenomena of faith, lucidly, but from outside, as it were. Yet it imparts a knowledge in which faith can illuminate itself.

The point of a historical cognition of the Bible is not to destroy it critically by exposure and relativization. It is to help us bring to mind, truly and with historical accuracy, religious experiences that have no real meaning for us until we react to them in adoption or rejection.

We owe it to the extraordinarily thorough work of theological historians that we can know the phenomena, the transformations, the heterogeneous motivations of faith. If the historic facts are honestly uncovered we find the ground without which there can be no truthful faith.

Yet if we look for the New Testament revelation itself, for its beginning and its source, we cannot find it in such historical studies. Where is the source? In Jesus as a historic figure? In the faith of the apostles? What we find historically is not revelation yet: it is the reality of Jesus, who lived and was executed. And what follows is not revelation any more; it already interprets the revelation.

Primarily, for our common thought, this story exists not as historical knowledge but as adoption, constantly repeated and constantly new. We feel and affirm it as the ground of what we are. Historical knowledge may destroy this historic fulfilment by making everything relative, or it may enhance it by a sense of present eternity.

iv. The biblical battleground

What happens in the free adoption of the Bible is the awakening and enhancement of variously derived impulses. It bears out martial blood-lust and long-suffering non-resistance, the ideas of nationalism and of mankind, polytheism and monotheism, sacerdotalism and the prophetic religion. We hear about knowing God and knowing the law, about love and about justice. Pure Transcendence speaks, and the immanence of an incarnated God is preached; there is fanaticism, and there is free renunciation; we meet God as a warrant of mundane ends and as the pure, unpurposive cipher of faith. We find denials of the world next to its affirmation, mystic darkness next to luminous faith, apocalyptic visions of history next to the eternal present, the transfiguration of low passions next to the purity of life, the joys of nature next to asceticism.

The Bible is as rich as life. It does not document one faith; it is an arena in which possibilities of faith vie with each other for the depth of the divine.

v. Biblical contradictions and religious unity

The Bible is full of contradictions, a meeting-ground of irreconcilable spiritual forces, views of life, and ways of life. It is with this book of books as with life itself: to share in its truth, one must move in its contradictions. They alone cast light upon the truth.

These contradictions have always challenged human thought to overcome them exegetically – by attributing several meanings to a line, for instance – in compromises and combinations. While searching for a harmonious unity of faith, men would assert it prematurely and design it rationally in theologies. Christian dogmatics turned the God-Man, Christ, into the central unit; all things were not only related to him but violently misconceived in the process, and this faith in Christ was itself not unified but torn in dogmatic schisms. Neither historically nor conceptually can we fix upon a centre of biblical thought and experience. Therein lies part of the Bible's vast, life-giving power.

Nor is there a historically determinable unity of the particular Christian faith of the New Testament within the Bible. We know that men believed in such a unity, and that in canonizing the selected writings they laid down the object of their belief along with the contradictions it contained; but in fact we see the unity only in the Church, in its unifying will and reality. The Church became the centre of crystallization. Its decisions brought Gnostic thought, Stoic ethics, and Greek speculation together to permeate the biblical substance.

In the course of time this unifying will prevailed, albeit with recurrent splits and schisms. But does it really evince religious unity and its one exclusive truth? It does not. The sociological possibility of ecclesiastic unification may be one of the most durable phenomena on earth, but in the process the original faith was made dependent on the ecclesiastic faith, on a belief in the church as the mystical body of Christ. The original faith was transformed or forgotten. And truth does not lie primarily in the socio-logical realities of the Church, or in the belief in it; it lies in the diversity of ciphers read by each originally different Existenz.

vi. The bisection of the Bible into Jewish and Christian parts
This bisection – taking what is Christian from the Old Testament and rejecting the rest, and critically eliminating after-effects of Judaism from the New Testament – is an outrageous act of Christian orthodoxy. Sober scholars have been induced to operate with ideal-typical entireties of Judaism and Christianity, not in ways that would cast a specific, limited light on earlier phenomena from subsequent points of view, but so as to construe two mutually exclusive religious forces by simply denying the Jewishness of the best Jewish heritage. This act of spiritual violence not only prevents free adoption and frankness in dealing with the Bible; it effects a prejudiced division that is both factually and historically untrue. Jews wrote the New Testament as well as the Old. The faith of both grew out of Jewry; all the contradictory possibilities arose within the religious struggle of the Jewish soul. Jesus was a Jew. All the apostles were Jews. The establishment of synagogue and church is a secondary historic phenomenon; for the impact of the truth of faith – whether called philosophical or theological – it carries no weight beyond that of mundane institutions claiming to wield a sacred power. Their guidance leads swiftly astray; the believing life of men families, communities, on the other hand, is an immediate reality, and to be linked with it, or born in it, is a gift of fate. Dealing with the Bible does not mean belonging to a church. All it means is taking part freely, individually, in adoptive interpretation.

vii. The Protestant principle
A return to the source, past all the traditional forms, is not a Protestant creed, but it is the principle of Protestantism. Protestants find this source in the texts of the Bible. There, amidst changing traditions, they see the broad,

lasting ground. But this ground too exists only as men understand it in their time.

To the Protestant principle, a premise of original understanding and adoption of the faith is the learned familiarity with the texts, their study, their historical knowledge. This is why we read the Bible with scholarly annotations – not so as to be content with the knowledge and understanding they convey, but in the hope of truly gaining the historic ground on which the texts themselves will come to have an unhistoric, immaterial meaning. The authority lies not in the word but in the 'spirit', which in the Bible speaks only to kindred spirits. It is interpretative adoption, not learned knowledge or any kind of insight that awakens us to the present reality of original faith.

viii. Scriptural evidence

There is a distinction in the interpretation and adoption of the Bible. Theology knows 'scriptural evidence', philosophy does not. Both of them interpret, but in philosophical interpretation the Bible is not, as a matter of principle, superior to other texts.

In practice, one who acknowledges 'scriptural evidence' reserves the right of correct interpretation to himself, whether on his own authority, like Luther, or by the catholic authority of a church. Other interpretations are deemed false. But experience teaches us that there is no end to such theological disputes; the real issue is who is empowered to make the correct interpretation. The self-certainty of a reformer claiming this authority disturbs his environment – provided it will listen – while the silent power of ecclesiastical authority brings peace. To follow the combat method of scriptural evidence is as irksome to clear-eyed believers in revelation as to people who philosophize, for this battleground shows what lies hidden in such a dogmatically 'proving' kind of faith: the persecution of heretics, Luther's 'firm statements', a barren striving for religious knowledge, and specious attempts to reconcile the contradictions in the Bible.

The historic consequence of these contradictions has been the ability of men to cite Scripture to support antithetical ways of faith, almost all ways of life, and practically any concrete decision. The Bible justifies so much that we tend to call it contradictory in everything. Nor is this surprising in a collection of writings that originated over a period of a thousand years.

One who rejects scriptural evidence – because a procedure that will let you prove everything proves actually nothing, and because in the area of faith any 'proof' is absurd – acknowledges for himself what he can make his own. He will grant the reality of another man's faith and will never make statements of absolute self-assurance. To him, essential decision lies in the choices of life, in the continuity of Existenz in phenomenal existence, not in acts of confession and tenets of a creed. In the Bible he finds the ground of both such freedom and such earnestness.

Authority does not lie in the word, not in the text, not in the Bible, but in the encompassing that is at once subjective and objective in original adoption, in free association with the Bible.

Can we hear the revelation? We can always hear its substance in human language – but not that it is revelation.

Revelation has to be distinguished from the faith in it. If the revelation were real, it would be unconditional; if God himself speaks, there is no authority that might impose conditions on his word. Nothing would remain but obedience. But the faith in revelation is a human reality and subject to conditions.

To receive tenets of the biblical faith into the philosophical experience of Transcendence, we must divest them of the form of revelations. Can the biblical faith be adopted at all, in philosophizing?

The philosophical believer may well agree with the lines aimed at him by a modern theologian:

What commandment of science or other obligation requires a critical thinker to limit his pursuit of truth by confining the ways of cognition and 'illumination' of Existenz to philosophy, poetry, and all kinds of doctrinal wisdom, excluding the unique possibility that has been gnosiologically distinguished as 'revelation'? What reason, what cognitive stringency bids a philosopher learn from documents of philosophical history, of world literature, mysticism, and oriental religions, and forbids him to learn from the biblical tradition – notably since there he will find an incomparable stress laid on the central problems of Existenz? The business of a free and open mind is not to set arbitrary limits on the possibilities of the logos, *but to stay open to hear the Word, whatever its order and origin* (Heinrich Barth, *Theologische Zeitschrift*, Vol. 9, 1953).

We would add only this: to stay open does not mean to hear and obey. It means to hear in the sense of listening with all that one has in one – but it need not be the hearing that means to hear God reveal himself. No man can justify hearing a revelation as revelation. In the framework of gnosiological clarification it is absolutely unjustifiable, for it can only justify itself. It does not belong in the line of possible ways to experience truth. Gnosiologically it is not distinguished but absent; it does not occur in the field of gnosiological clarification. What begins where revelation is heard as revelation is something else entirely.

Yet this other thing is not 'forbidden'. We are forbidden only to justify it by any kind of *logos*, or to turn it into generally valid cognition. If we attempt to do that we violate the point of revelation – which is that grace alone enables us to hear it – and at the same time we obscure the possibility of the *logos*. For in truthful philosophical thinking we do not mean to deny its due to the incomprehensible, to the a-logical, anti-logical, and enormous.

It may happen that as we adopt the Bible we do not come to believe in revelation. An open philosophy demands that the thinker should not let this failure make him smug. On the other hand, we cannot admit in true openness that the revelation must be heard as revelation.

Not hearing the revelation as such, we cannot submit to the believers. But neither can we submit to the false enlighteners who would take their stand on nothing but science. When those chide philosophy as a secularized theology, a theology in disguise, we answer that philosophy is older than the biblical revelation, that it is existentially more original, being accessible to all humans as humans, and that it is fully capable of hearing and adopting truth in the Bible as well.

2 SOME MAIN POINTS OF POSSIBLE CHANGE

No one can tell what tenets of faith will influence men in the future. Their true prediction would already be their realization. The individual can express only the way of thinking of his own faith, as I try to do in this book. The chance of a serious common religious life seems to me to depend on giving up three things. I discuss these renunciations with people in mind who were born in our time, people who live with the knowledge and with the realities and unprecedented experience of our time.

i. Jesus, to many believers, is no longer the God-Man, Christ
a: Let me sum up once again how Christianity came into being as a form of the biblical faith.

Jews, in their experience of God, laid the foundation. Their Bible is our Bible. After Jesus was executed, Jews who believed in him as the Christ added an appendix, the New Testament, which also contains the traditional story of the man.

Jesus, along with his original preaching, is a perceptible historic reality. Its limits are as uncertain as those of any such reality, and up to a point it is accessible to historical research and its methods. Yet in these materials, to one who can see and react, Jesus emerges as a unique, unmistakable, transcendent reality whose subjective certainty goes beyond any objective, rational proof.

Equally certain, however, by virtue of historical analysis, are several negatives.

First, Jesus did not proclaim himself Christ, the Messiah.

Second, Jesus did not establish himself as a sacrament. It was the apostles who made a rite of his last supper.

Third, Jesus did not found a Church – for his life and preaching rested on the premise of an imminent end of the world, before the passing of his own generation. The Church developed slowly, beginning with the apostolic community and the establishment of congregations. Jesus was not its founder. The Church had to do with Jesus in so far as he was believed in as the Christ, a belief that appeared only after his execution.

Smouldering within the churches was a fire which time and again burst through their incrustations and mundane adjustments. Although the churches base themselves on Jesus, they conceal what he makes manifest: the question of man's fate and man's potential. It was the Existenz of this man, Jesus, that raised the question at an unmatched depth, out of his link with God. Question and answer both lay in the realization of a human being capable of saying what he saw, what he believed, what he demanded, lived, and suffered.

The measure which this man in his sincerity applied to all things was the true humanity in the kingdom of God. Knowing himself directly before the end of the world, he was a harbinger of the reality of that kingdom.

He was the last of the Jewish prophets, closely tied to them. The national idea, the idea of the law, the organization of priests and rites – all these faded away for him, and theologies became a matter of indifference.

The Jews, those unending victims of lovelessness and injustice, persecuted, tortured, slain over and over, and yet saving remnants time and again in league with God, on the sole strength of their faith – the Jews, this miracle of history, produced in Jesus their great, representative human figure, a figure that stands for man's fate and the Jewish fate in one.

As a man, Jesus is a cipher of being human. It says that a man who lives and thinks as he did, a man who is true without any restriction, must die at the hands of men, because human reality is too untruthful to bear him.
b: As this cipher is adopted, however, its interpretation proceeds.

The cipher of a true human being's failure turns into the ancient one of divine self-sacrifice. Jesus comes to be the Son of God, the Christ, and finally God himself who in his love saves man from sinful perdition by sacrificing himself in human form.

Next, the cipher becomes a model. Man will attain his eternal salvation by sacrificing himself, or being sacrificed, like Jesus Christ. The sense of imitating an act of God grants peace in active martyrdom, and in passively suffering the worst.

The imitation will be evaded by any individual who wants to work and to build in the world. Yet there is help for him too: without sacrificing himself or being sacrificed, he will be saved by the faith that God, in Christ, was crucified as a substitute for him. The belief in this divine self-sacrifice fully justifies him. A startling twist: I do not make the sacrifice; God made it for me. He has freed me from the worst, and in such faith he lets me live in peace.

It takes no more than a glance at the human Jesus to disavow this evolution of the cipher.
c: One thing is vital to the future of the biblical faith: to make the human Jesus and his faith prevail. As the Christ cipher threatens to become absolute, our full strength can go into that effort only if we dispense with Christ as one of the Bible's particular religious conformations.

But the imitation of Jesus is not man's only task either, nor is one who declines it dependent on 'justification by faith alone'. It is plain that we and the faithful of all churches not only fail to heed the Sermon on the Mount but admit – if we are as honest as Jesus bade us be – that we do not want to heed it. This unwillingness rests on our positive will to love, to work, to plant, to build in the world. The way we choose is the way through the world. Not being granted another way to eternity than Existenz in the phenomenal world, we are required only to be unreservedly truthful toward the unworldly alternative: not to confuse it, not to go halfway down that other road, but to respect those who take it, as did Francis of Assisi and many another.

We are to take our bearings from Jesus, moreover, to become as truthful as we can, for our worldly reality exacts an inevitable price. Taking our bearings from Jesus makes us clearer about what we do and want. The cipher of his humanity shows us how to discover our fundamental limits and shortcomings. The urge of martyrdom, in whichever form, does not deliver us, nor does any justification save the one by good will, by sincerity, by the firm resolve to be truthful, and above all by the power of love in which we are given to ourselves.

d: What roles the human Jesus and the divine Christ play in the biblical faith is a particular question, not to be settled in general. We do not come to God by way of Christ alone, as taught by the apostles; a man comes to God without believing in Christ, and we are 'Christians' without believing in Christ as the incarnated God. What are Christians? The name must be seen historically. A complex situation caused the biblical faith to be dressed up in the name Christianity, under which it became the fundament of the West. Today it seems both historically and factually proper to call the Christian religion also by the broader name of 'biblical'. Though ancient, the historic name 'Christian religion' is restrictive and thus misleading. The texts it rests on, the texts it holds sacred, make it the biblical religion.

The greatest merit of the men who founded the Church during the first centuries may well be that they impressed the Bible in its entirety, both the Old Testament and the New, upon Western faith and thought and interpretation. The attempts to eliminate the biblical religion – to reject the Old Testament altogether and to delete various writings now included in the New – were defeated then, but to this day there is scattered applause and sympathy for these efforts to get a supposedly pure Christianity. Whoever is in earnest about the biblical faith in God will be shocked and alarmed by the phenomenon, a poisonous product of motivations ranging from comfortable liberalism and abstract asceticism to the racist mania.

ii. Revelation turns into a cipher

Could it be, we ask as we philosophize, that not just the content of a revelation but the very reality which believers claim for it may become a

cipher? As far as our insight goes, we shall never come across a real revelation unless we quit philosophizing. But is there no hope of comprehending
it – this reality which exists for the faithful – as a cipher? To us it would
seem that either the revelation is a reality, bound to exist in itself and not in
need of signs, or it is not a reality and the believer finds signs for it. For him
too the reality would not exist in itself, then, but in signs and ciphers.
Moreover, he would not speak of it in the general sense of the word 'reality',
but as a cipher.

What does it mean for revelation to become a cipher? Can a cipher of
Transcendence carry weight by being physically felt as a reality in the world,
yet known to be no such reality?

Take Moses on Mount Sinai, for instance. The power of the words in
which the event is described in detail makes us feel that the Commandments
are more than legal precepts that might be amended. We ask: whence this
unique power of the absolute moral demand, far beyond its general
phrasing? An answer to the question lies in the cipher of a real act of God.

Children will receive such ciphers with deep feeling, like fairy tales where
the question of reality or unreality does not yet clearly arise, and their
impact on the adult is not lost even when they unequivocally cease to be
realities for him. Tales of an act of God, of a divine event, of a man who is
more than human, will endure as ciphers. Their reality is voided, and yet,
as ciphers they retain a voice.

Do such concepts mean a weakening of revelation? They certainly change
its meaning; as a cipher it is no longer what the believer in revelation meant
it to be. In any case, the theologian would be distinguished from the
philosopher by the potency of his unfoldment of the cipher.

The paradox seems inescapable: the contents of revelations would
become more pure, more true, if their reality were discarded. The reality as
such would turn into a cipher of the presence of God, lending an extraordinary weight to the contents.

If revelation as such could be made a cipher, the faith in it would undergo
a metamorphosis. This may have happened at all times; for the general
consciousness of our time it seems necessary. Dogmas, sacraments, rituals
would be melted down, so to speak – not destroyed, but given other forms
of conscious realization. With those as media, the biblical faith would once
more derive an inspiring, salient, credible appearance from its full earnest,
not merely in ritual, meditative satisfactions, not in the shelter of a church,
and surely no more in conventional activities. Under the conditions of our
time, of its new knowledge and its new world situation, the metamorphosis
would occur in line with the nature of things. Not the substance, but the
appearance in consciousness would change. Philosophy and theology
would be on the road to reunification.

Such goals are more easily set than achieved. They are not matters of
planning. Philosophizing will let us hold only vague hopes of the kind,

paired with an awareness that the revelation whose embodiment is only a cipher for us may for many a confessional believer hold greater secrets than are dreamt of in our philosophy.

Viewed as a cipher, revelation would no longer be raised above the rest of the cipher world. It would be the cipher that allows man's boundless yearning for the real presence of God to be satisfied for an instant, so to speak – but only so as to thrust him back at once into the hard, great, free state he was created in, and in which God remains inexorably hidden.

I hear the argument that no theologian can join us in transforming revelation into a cipher – that if one did, he would be destroying the fundament of his belief and of his thinking. My answer is that it may well be impossible for the theologians holding forth today, many of whom are brilliant historical scholars but theological epigones. They cling to their beliefs without continuing to feel the *pneuma*. But the transformation may not exceed the capacities of modern men who refuse to yield either to dogmas they doubt or to the conventional enlightened nihilism, men who view the ciphers from their real present situation.

To us who philosophize, the theologians' refusal to join in the transformation seems like an involuntary and unconscious act of violence. Although we feel certain of this – which makes the situation so disturbing for us – we must take care not to proclaim our feeling as the truth. This would be giving tit for tat to the believers in revelation who charge us with obduracy; but we, being not so sure that our thinking represents all men, wish to respect even what strikes us as recalcitrance. To ourselves we cannot help saying that this rejection of a transformation into ciphers goes not only against philosophical reason but against the very idea of God, and against the chances of free Existenz. In philosophizing we forsake embodiment because we have to, because we want what has stirred a believer at all times, from the beginning and without embodiment. We want to convey the philosophical way of thinking to modern men and nations, to be able to convey it so that they will not just succumb to rationalism and emotionalism but will grasp the meanings of ciphers and open themselves to Transcendence by thinking of God, with all that this change would entail.

Cannot philosophy and theology meet, after all, across the gulf between their senses of reality? Can they not meet in these interpretations of original philosophizing and revealed faith?

The premise would be for both sides to be clear about what they mean by real acts and words of God, and for the power of faith to stand up clearly, honestly, without internal or external violence.

It is surely false for the faith in revelation to fly in the face of cogent or possible knowledge. It is equally false for any total knowledge to be asserted as rationally definitive.

Philosophical faith and faith in revelation might meet in a sense of standing together in the unfathomable course of things – one canopied, so to speak, by revealed tangibles, and the other absorbed in the consummation of not knowing, as Plato, Cusanus, and Kant conceived it across every difference between them.

The two ways of faith might be linked in every individual's feeling that he can become himself in what we inadequately call 'sense', or 'salvation', or that which is neither temporal nor timeless but eternal.

This, whether as revelation or as not knowing, is what makes us restless, and thus earnest, in time.

Questioned, it will not answer and its very silence seems to be questioning us; we tremble at questions that no intellect, no creed, no cipher is fit to answer – questions only answered by the seriousness of Existenz as it lives a life inseparable from ciphers and tangibles in which the real silence of Transcendence is never sufficiently, never adequately captured.

Today this seriousness would have to be shown and proven in our sinking world that makes it so hard for men to find themselves, because transcendent reality seems less and less audible in the din of our vast performance bustle and in the emptiness of our leisure.

iii. Dogmatic religious truth ceases to be exclusive

By exclusiveness we mean the claim to be, or to state, the one absolute truth for all men. It lies in a Bible verse that does not come from Jesus: 'I am the way, the truth, and the life: no man cometh unto the Father, but by me.' It lies in the maxim, *Extra ecclesiam nulla salus* – outside the Church there can be no salvation.

Whenever faith – whether faith in revelation or philosophical faith gone astray – has claimed exclusive truth, the results have been discord and life-or-death struggles.

It is up to the believers in revelation, by forsaking the thought of exclusiveness, to sheathe the sword – literally in times past, and now metaphorically. Another word that may have been falsely ascribed to Jesus – that he had not come to bring peace on earth, but division – does not apply any more. Not till the poison of exclusive claims is removed can the biblical faith come to be communicative, peaceful, and truly in earnest about its pure realization.

Removing the poison consciously takes a simple yet momentous insight: that exact, generally valid truth is relative, dependent on premises and methods of cognition but compelling for every intellect, while existential truth is historic, absolute in each man's life but not to be stated as valid for and all others.

Exclusiveness must fall so that the appearance of faith may come to be true to its essence – so that the struggle of ciphers may be pure, tolerant, candid, and free from the constant admixture of worldly concerns.

Without its massive concreteness the unique revelation would also cease to be historically exclusive. The one and only comprehensive historicity of all that we know and are does not rest on revelation; it rests on our common humanity, which includes all kinds of ciphers of revelations differing in their historic background.

3 THE POSSIBLE TRANSFORMATION OF PROTESTANT CHURCHES

i. Discrepancies at the root of being human
Man dares and sacrifices, but without knowing to what ultimate end. He seeks to shape his world, but something ruinous strikes back at him out of the world he has shaped. He calms down in fleeting intervals of peace, and this self-delusion aggravates the coming evil.

If he will be honest, to make the delusion disappear, he finds that honesty is but a way, not truth itself. His honesty involves the appearance of truth in inconclusive dialectics.

The contradictions in reality are insoluble. There is no way out of them, and the ultimate reason why this is so lies beyond our comprehension.

ii. Tensions peculiar to the biblical religion
in the West, the biblical religion is the prime example of the way to make our basic condition conscious and to receive it into the human state of mind.

This religion – whose historic peaks, such as Jeremiah, the poet of Job, or Jesus, make it appear like a mountain range of human truthfulness and insight – constantly fluctuates between apostasy and reconcilement.

Its ciphers, lapsing into tangibility, made an absolute reality out of realities of existence. For instance, the 'covenant' of God with the chosen people engendered the militant nationalism so strongly, enthusiastically, self-sacrificingly, and mercilessly expressed in the Song of Deborah.

Or God's moral demand became a passionately heeded mass of external regulations.

Or the existential knowledge of the limits of man and the world led to the expectation of an imminent physical end of the world.

Or Jesus, the man, turned into Christ, the God.

Since the high demands of the faith could not be met in practice, there emerged a virtual aristocracy, a segregated class of men determined to meet those demands at any cost. In Judaism there were those learned in the law, and there were those who complied meticulously with every last letter of the law. To the rest, to the unlearned, to the people, the law was inaccessible, but the scholars themselves could not really satisfy it either.

In Christianity there are the monks, whose life consists of doing what is beyond the people. There are pure souls among them. But there have been others whose monastic asceticism would turn from scorn of the world into an ecclesiastic will to subjugate this world to God – meaning to their own faith, to themselves – by resorting to the coercion of conscience and to world conquest.

We take these phenomena for aberrations, but they do have a peculiar grandeur. Not so another recreant phenomenon that goes through all ages: the practical adaptation of the absolute divine command to the social and political realities of the time, and to the average psychology. The unfulfillable is made fulfillable, at the expense of truth. In efforts that compel our admiration as intellectual accomplishments, ecclesiastic thinking has vainly sought to compromise and void the fundamental discrepancies – to systematize the basic antinomies, to bring them into a convincing harmony, to comprehend the encompassing in the human world as its own ecclesiastic embodiment, and to stabilize it as authority.

Since the Christianity of the Gospel had nothing to do with the world, it could not adjust to mundane 'civilization' without constant contradictions and reversals. The hypocrisy was exacted by the basic situation: only in untruthful forms could this religion hold its own in the world. This untruthfulness – grown to dimensions unmatched in the world, perhaps – is one of the reasons why Asians despise the Christian West.

The antinomies at the root of biblical religion lead both to greatness and to perdition. They lead to the supreme creative tension of the will to truth that can never be satisfied, that seeks to understand even the lie and to adopt it, so to speak, in translucence; and at the same time they lead to abysmal mendacity. Nowhere in the world has the struggle for truth risen from such a pitiless demand for truth, a demand that will give us no peace and is only increased by the enormity of the apparent untruthfulness.

How to get over this hypocrisy? How to make truth speak without it? The biblical religion has had its revolutionary and reformatory side from the beginning. There has been rebellion in it since the Hebrew prophets. This is what makes the biblical religions unique: the passionate struggle between the God-given demand for truth and the rank untruthfulness constantly sprouting in their own realm. The truth lies in the rebellions, but so does the discrepancy that reappears in them instantly, in new forms.

Accordingly, a recurrent return to the source marks the history of the biblical religion – in the prophets, in Jesus, later in the recurrent necessity to found new monastic orders. The schisms resulted in part from such revolutionary change. If the establishment did not manage somehow to absorb the movement, it was destroyed, or it vanished, or the schism produced sects, first, and then new churches. The last great event of this type was the Protestant Reformation.

iii. Protestantism

It was the last great attempt to break through from untruthfulness to the source. Unintentionally, at first, it split the Western Church, and then caused further splits among the Protestant schismatics. Even today the ecumenical organization of Protestant churches shows this characteristic picture: all agree in saying nay to Rome, but among themselves all say the same nay to each other. What they mean by the faith is mutually exclusive –

a fact scarcely disguised by sitting down together and talking past each other. From Catholic sources we hear that the Protestant principle must in the end lead to a denial of God's incarnation in Jesus Christ. I think this is true, and therefore I think it is this very Catholic religious principle whose perpetuation keeps Protestantism everywhere imprisoned in Catholicism. How do I arrive at this view?

To Catholics, their Holy Church is the mystical body of Christ, his divine presence. I have repeatedly quoted Augustine's illuminating line that he would not have believed the Gospel unless prompted by the authority of the present Catholic Church – in the Church this applies in full earnest. The Protestant churches, by abolishing the sacrament of holy orders, have put an end to this kind of divine presence, and if embodiment thus disappears in fact, if it lies only in the past and remains only as a word, the character of this God-Manhood has changed completely. From a daily experience in church and in its visible phenomena it has become a thing that happened once upon a time. Kierkegaard substituted a simultaneousness of the one-time event – that God became human and existed, on the cross and as the Risen – for the simultaneousness of the concrete Church; but if the point is a perceptible object of faith, that way seems violent and artificial. To a faithful Catholic the Church is present first, as the body of Christ. It is the Church that testifies to the past in which God became human, to the past in which he established this church with its sacramental powers, its authority, its keys to the heavenly kingdom. Holy Church is concrete. Protestantism has only the word, the past revelation, the essence – poor and stunted in comparison with the Catholic one. With the sacrament of holy orders discarded, the Church is no longer holy, and its profanation must eventually make Christ's own God-Manhood unworthy of belief.

Yet the essence could only be stunted because Protestants misread its revolutionary character. They clung to an inwardly disparate Catholicism and blocked the breakthrough that was their principle. Protestantism must be completed in earnest, or else it will sink into the trivial and dishonest mimicry of a Catholicism it can never equal.

The transformations we hope for may appear like nothing but surrenders. Our critical negations may seem to affect the substance of the faith: Jesus without Christ? Faith without a creed? A cult without divine magic? Meditation without prayers for finite happiness? Relating to Transcendence by means of ciphers, without having it? Is not all this a yielding without any gain?

Yet what is the substance? It is nothing we can 'have', nothing an authority in the world might offer us, nothing that could be incarnated in a Church. We can come to the substance by a metamorphosis, a change in every individual. It takes an earnest that we can make conscious in thought but cannot realize by thought. He who has it, originally, has judged the aberrations from the start. The substance of faith alone can give meaning to judgment and renunciation.

How could this earnestness invade the forms of ecclesiastic community? Without such community it would be extinguished. In the long run, community is its premise; man as a mere individual, without community, is an exception, frightening to himself. The community, whether it be called church or synagogue, is the inevitable form for handing down the substance of faith and morals.

But is it also tied to rites and liturgies, to dogma and creed? That it is not so tied is the Protestant principle, the one thing that entitles Protestantism to confront the Catholic Church on its own. To Protestants the Church means something other than to Catholics. It means a community of institutions and forms in which the faith is preached, but which as such are not holy.

c. The Situation After Kierkegaard

1 KIERKEGAARD'S FIGHT AGAINST THE CHURCH

Kierkegaard took the Christianity of the Gospel seriously. God became human – the consequences are inexorable. Kierkegaard made it possible for a thinking individual to believe on the strength of absurdity. He developed an impressive set of concepts that has since governed modern Protestant thought, at least in so far as it terms itself dialectics. From the outset, he saw the tremendous difference between Gospel Christianity and the reality of ecclesiastic Christianity, between Christianity and Christendom. One year before his death, finally, he launched the most radical assault on the church that our time has seen – for the justification of this onslaught came from the heart of Christianity itself. The existing Christian Church, said Kierkegaard, is a falsification and betrayal of Christianity.

This fight was not a late aberration of his, but the outcome of an irresistibly maturing insight. It resulted from the poetic construction of Christianity he had derived from theological dialectics and communicated mainly under the pseudonyms of 'Climacus' and 'Anticlimacus'. Hardly ever has an entrance into the public arena been so slowly, so thoughtfully, so hesitantly prepared for as was this step of Kierkegaard's. Once his mind was made up, however, he followed through with matchless vehemence, in supreme consciousness, in line with the situation and with the historic moment.

Kierkegaard unmasked the reality of our time: all men call themselves Christians, but Christianity itself has ceased to exist. A 'Christian' world has to be shown that it is anything but Christian, that it is a fraud. 'Not one of us, myself included, represents the Christianity of the New Testament in full personal earnest. . . .'

I need not reiterate his pitiless exposure of ecclesiastic realities. To

Kierkegaard, the Christian minister of today, every pastor or theologian, is an unchristian and thus essentially mendacious figure. Confirmation, Christian marriage, Christian family life, Christian education – all of them are lies, measured by the demands of the Gospel.

But now for the strange, crucial, really modern part: Kierkegaard is not fighting here as a Christian, for Christianity, but as a human being, for veracity. 'Quite simply: I want honesty. I am neither clemency nor rigour – I am human honesty.'

If men want 'to rise honestly, unreservedly, frankly, straightforwardly against Christianity, if they will say to God, "We cannot, we will not bow to this power" – but mark well: if they do it honestly, unreservedly, frankly, straightforwardly – all right, strange as it may seem, I will go along. For I want honesty. And wherever there is honesty I can go along'.

Despite the risks he took in fact, Kierkegaard stoutly denied any intention of martyrdom for Christianity. 'I will dare for honesty. I am not saying I dare for Christianity. . . . I would be victimized, not on behalf of Christianity, but as one who wanted honesty.'

In this task he felt sure of himself. 'With me is the Almighty; and he knows best how to strike so that the laughter that is used in fear and trembling will be felt as a scourge – this is what I am employed for.'

Christianity – there Kierkegaard agreed with Nietzsche – calls for radical truthfulness. 'But of course, since Christianity is spirit, the soberness of the spirit and the honesty of eternity, nothing will strike its detective eyes as more suspicious than fantastic quantities: Christian states, Christian countries, a Christian people, and – how odd! – a Christian world.' Hidden in all this, Kierkegaard saw 'a monstrous crime, continued from generation to generation. . . . The point is to shed light on this Christian crime that has been going on for centuries, this astute attempt to cozen God out of Christianity, piece by piece, with the end result that Christianity is the exact opposite of what it is in the New Testament'.

Along with Kierkegaard's words and actions we have his views of himself, beginning in his youth and strangely compelling for us.

'I am only a poet,' he said about his magnificent drafts of the state of human Existenz, up to his construction of Christianity. But in the fight against the Church he declared, 'I am not a reformer, nor a profound speculative mind, a seer, a prophet – no, I am a man with an unusually well-defined gift for detective work. . . . I am not a Christian. And unfortunately I can make it plain that the others are not either – even less than I.'

How did he see his work, consummated in the fight against the Church? 'In the eighteen hundred years of Christendom there is nothing to match my task,' he said. 'For thus far everything extraordinary has worked in the direction of expanding Christianity; and my task aims at putting a stop to a mendacious expansion. . . .'

'The only counterpart is Socrates. . . . You noble simpleton of Antiquity!

The only man I admiringly acknowledge as a thinker . . . mankind's only martyr of thought, equally great as a character and as a thinker.'

Shall we ask Kierkegaard, the battler against the Church, what is to be done? What can be done? What are his demands? He never made suggestions for Church reform; he called for nothing but honesty. But in the course of the battle he raised his demands as far as the repudiation of dishonesty was concerned. At first he only wanted the Church to admit that it does not stand for the Christianity of the Gospel, that it is an abatement, an adjustment, so that divine guidance might decide on its acceptability. Later he came to view such an admission as futile. The established Church of Denmark seemed to him so utterly un-Christian it would have to disappear. The state should stop paying the clergy. At the end – in his 'cry at midnight,' *This Must Be Said, So Let It Be Said Now* – he was no longer addressing himself to the church but to every individual: 'If you cease to take part . . . in public worship as it is today . . . you will be constantly relieved of one guilt, and of a heavy one. You will no longer take part in playing God for a fool.'

2 CRITICAL REMARKS

i. Kierkegaard's thesis of Gospel Christianity applies to main features of the New Testament but not to the whole, and certainly not to the whole Bible. As everywhere in the Bible, there are contradictions in the New Testament. I cannot agree with Kierkegaard when he proclaims one feature – the incarnation of God – as the essence of the whole. I cannot agree when he rejects historical research about the New Testament, thus shutting his eyes to whatever does not tally with his poetic construction of the faith.

I cannot admit his contention that this Gospel Christianity is Christianity as such, the biblical faith as such. But Kierkegaard's clear demonstration does confront everyone with the decision whether or not he will and can believe in this as the Christian essence. There is no getting round this decision. There is no half-way, no middle way. If one really believes in the God-Man, the way that Kierkegaard laid out is all but unavoidable.

Rejection for myself is not rejection in itself, however. Should Kierkegaard have hit upon a possible truth? If so, then only for one who will take the consequences.

ii. Having made my choice, I may express my opinion that the way shown by Kierkegaard under the pseudonyms of Climacus and Anticlimacus – the way to a faith on the strength of absurdity, by an ingenious and seductively conceived categorial edifice and a construction of following Christ in the unequivocal sense of total world denial – would lead us astray. Logically, this way also ends in the total denial of the church that marked the end of Kierkegaard's fight and life.

It only seems as though his dialectical theology might be separated from his fight against the Church.

Long before that fight, when Kierkegaard was still thinking that he himself might enter the ministry, his honesty drove him to his merciless dialectic-poetic construction of the Christian faith as a faith on the strength of absurdity. The construction has a fascinating speculative power even though it rejects all traditional speculation as a false effort to achieve comprehensibility. It is a dexterous but not dishonest way to save the embodied God-Man.

And he proposed only later, in the fight against the Church, to make it as mercilessly plain that Church and Christendom are perverting the Gospel into one great unwitting lie.

But in both cases, in his dialectical theology and in the fight against the Church, Kierkegaard's truth is his honesty. The yardstick which the Church itself seems to maintain in its tie to the New Testament serves to show up its mendacity and that of Christendom. Kierkegaard wants them to admit it.

If he were right, it would mean the end of Christianity in the world. If the Christian faith is what he construed it to be, probably no one can believe it any more – and Kierkegaard, though passionately eager to believe, never claimed to be doing so in person.

Attempts have been made to utilize some of his concepts for a modern theology that will satisfy contemporary Christian unbelievers, and to discard his fight against the Church as unserviceable. The Protestant theologians who tried this appear in fact, by the existential contradiction at the root of their own thinking, to have compounded the plain evidence of Christianity's end. For it is impossible to utilize Kierkegaard's conceptual-dialectical thinking as a language suitable for people of our time. This new theological language – made up of a dash of science, a dash of philosophy, a dash of theology, and a dash of literature – is not Kierkegaard's any more. It would admit his dialectics and deny the struggle that is an integral part of his thinking. In truth, one cannot theologize Kierkegaard and affirm the Church.

I myself have tried hypothetically to understand Christianity along Kierkegaard's lines, but I cannot help finding this concept of the faith unbelievable – or something, at least, of which there is not a rudiment in my own experience of belief. If this concept – Climacus calls it a 'poetic impertinence' – is now offered to me as Christian by theologians, I have to doubt such theology. Could it be useful, perhaps, as a theology for moderns who cannot really believe any more? Are they crawling into a hole prepared by Kierkegaard, so as by a complicated method to hold on to the faith they want in a world spoiled by false enlightenment and social conventions? Is it the artificiality of it that causes them to make militant noises from that hiding-place, which Kierkegaard did not at all intend to be one? Do they mean thus to force such a faith, in keeping with our age in which nothing exists unless it makes noise? But if such questions can be put at all, they can be directed to the aspect of an impersonal, general public phenomenon only, not to the faith of any individual. We cannot see through what a person truly believes.

I repeat: a Christian faith that uses Kierkegaard's theological construct to comprehend itself as incomprehensible, as necessarily absurd – thus justifying itself, so to speak, in a modern world – would be as apt to mean the end of this Christianity and this church as would Kierkegaard's exposure of ecclesiasticism.

iii. All this is not to be taken lightly. A man like Kierkegaard who actually staked his life, who lived and created with an all but miraculous and at the start unquestionably spontaneous consistency, gifted with extraordinary powers of imagination and thought, with the faculty of experiencing all human possibilities in himself and reconstructing them as a poet – such a man cannot be dismissed.

In his lifetime Kierkegaard was given a wide berth. Whoever tangled with him, whether freethinker or bishop, received a blow that sent him scurrying for the shelter of silence.

His death promptly set off the two great camouflages of the event that was Kierkegaard.

At the funeral, a man with Kierkegaard's last writings in his hand disrupted the ecclesiastic ceremony to make a propaganda speech for a revolutionary mass movement – the first of many attempts to claim Kierkegaard for freethinking and political anti-clericalism, trends with which he had nothing to do whatsoever.

The other camouflage began in writings by Bishop Martensen, Denmark's long-time leading churchman, an eminent philosophical and theological scholar and a deadly enemy of Kierkegaard who had brilliantly taken his measure. We have extensive critical discussions of Kierkegaard's work and person from Martensen's pen.

In the mild, just tone and with the superior wisdom of a prince of the Church he de-fanged and decomposed the man he survived by decades, anticipating all the shrewd arguments we hear repeated against Kierkegaard to this day. To one who knows Kierkegaard, reading Martensen will give the oddest feeling. Kierkegaard confronts us with the 'Either-Or'. He brings clarity; he compels us to choose – not in thought, but in the reality of life, as Existenz – and even if our decision goes against his poetic conception of Christianity it will be lucid only through him, thanks to him. There is no comfort in it. But Martensen, writing with superior calm, described this dangerous business as if it were a sickly aberration deserving of pity and forbearance. His was a belated revenge on the dead man; secretly the victorious prince of the Church was terrified by the other who had stripped his whole ecclesiastic existence bare and pilloried it in all its untruthfulness. He gulped down his terror and wove the threads of his philosophically learned language around Kierkegaard's ideas, making them unrecognizable.

iv. It cannot be our task to conquer Kierkegaard. For one who understands him this is impossible. Kierkegaard is not a position but a way of thinking, and as such inevitable, infinite, and inconclusive. We are to listen to him – not so as to follow him, except in his will to be honest, but to hear what is imperishable in the thinker of the 'existential human condition'.

3 AFTER KIERKEGAARD, CAN ONE STILL HONESTLY TAKE THE CLOTH?

i. The import of Kierkegaard's fight

Kierkegaard's writings against the church strike me as the most important to have appeared on the church question in our time. They make all the attacks of enlightened liberals and Marxist atheists seem flat. Kierkegaard alone is in the earnest that befits Christianity. Every theologian, everyone who does not wish to dodge the question of his own Christianity, will have to study these works. Is it still possible in our time to be 'Christian' as a matter of course? The man who no longer regards himself as traditionally Christian, but as living in the biblical faith, will find in Kierkegaard the radical Christianity that remains unforgettable.

One who accepts Kierkegaard's views of Gospel Christianity and of following Christ – and there can be no doubt that in the New Testament these loom large – can no longer be a minister of the Church and of the Christianity it preaches. Kierkegaard's fight seems to bar men from honestly taking the cloth.

Even without accepting the premises whose consequences forced him to break with the Church, the traditional views of Church, ministry, and form of faith can be maintained after Kierkegaard only by men who shield themselves from thought – in other words, who are not serious. It is likely, due to the phenomenon of Kierkegaard and his thinking, that if the biblical faith keeps working in the world it can do so only in a renewal of which Kierkegaard is both the target and the cause.

Kierkegaard helps not so much to this faith as to purer, more conscious distinctions. Those who do not share his view of Gospel Christianity will come the more lucidly to the idea of a radical reformation of the faith itself. I would imagine this on Protestant soil.

ii. Protestantism and Catholicism

Looked upon with historical objectivity, the Catholic Church as a religion has far better prospects. Consider its unified, world-wide papal leadership, the methods of Catholic ecclesiastic thought, and the life-pervading sanctification of existence, both in everyday life and at great moments; add the present glory of a thousand years of art, the multitude of religious activities, the impressive power of priests and religious, spiritually rooted celibates whose existence the faith consumes; top it off with Catholic piety, based on the Church but far from its violence and political cunning, and even spreading a touch of philosophy among the populace – compared with all this, Protestantism seems poor.

Yet Protestantism, whatever may be held against it, has one virtue that outweighs all flaws. It is the principle of its birth: the chance of breaking through every religious phenomenon to a new original realization. In Catholic eyes, Protestantism is purely negative. It gives up tenet after tenet, ending in what must seem to a Catholic the total disappearance of all religious essentials – the God-Man, the Resurrection, the personal God, the sacraments – and it pulverizes itself by endless internal schisms. Many phenomena are seen correctly in this Catholic perspective, but it completely ignores the true, substantial reason why a Protestant will be in earnest: his principle makes the faith a personal responsibility of the individual. His protesting is the outside of a biblical faith for ever searching for its source, for ever rediscovering itself. He will protest against his own structures if they linger in Catholicism or lapse into imitating what they can never equal.

iii. Ministry and immediacy

According to the Protestant principle the individual stands directly before God, without an intermediary; hence the 'general ministry'. Freedom of conscience is inviolate.

Where this principle reigns, everything depends on the individual, on the state of his faith, on his responsibility and realization.

Not only the Bible but the biblical faith must be newly, freely taken up by each generation, by each newly commencing human existence.

The pastor addresses the individual in the congregation. In concrete situations of life and in political events he lends a voice to moral obligations and to ciphers. Instead of deducing from dogmas what is to be done, he awakens each individual power of judgment and conscience from its source, by the light of the Bible.

Unlike the Catholic priest, the Protestant pastor is no official functioning as the impersonal conveyor of grace (*ex opere operato*). He is an individual personality, depended on to realize his faith for the orientation of others. He is an equal among equals, a shepherd of souls and a thinker of unshakable honesty.

The Protestant principle seems to ask the impossible. It demands too much of human beings, of the members of the congregation and of their pastors.

Indeed, we seldom see the principle realized substantially, and never completely. It is a great idea – not an ideal, which would be utopian if conceived as a reality.

Wherever liberty turns into licence, freedom of conscience into self-will, biblical faith into random toying with ciphers, the Protestant principle has been lost.

From the outset – since we tend so much to all this – the principle has been so often denied in practice.

Yet whenever we are tempted to say that weak, misguided mankind needs the authority of God and the coercive power it confers on God's deputy in the world, we must remember that every authority and every power is wielded by men over men. Claiming God for oneself is always a dreadful confusion; it has nothing to do with faith if critics of the Church are judged as blasphemers of God.

Here we must make a distinction. What is necessary for the existence of politically organized community life – and therefore regulated, however imperfectly, under a government of laws – is not the world of faith and morals. Faith and morals, to be real and true, must run the risks of uncurbed freedom.

v. The Protestant pastor today

I return to our question: how is it possible nowadays, after Kierkegaard's elucidations, to enter the Protestant ministry?

The first requirement is faith, be it philosophical or faith in revelation. This can be neither willed nor shown nor confessed.

Equally imperative is truthfulness. The admission that Kierkegaard called for will not suffice, and general statements of guilt and inadequacy are as meaningless. Truthfulness depends above all on insight and admission in each concrete case, concerning specific actions or omissions, utterances or silences.

With faith and truthfulness it is not impossible to grave such simple challenges as the Ten Commandments and the attitude of the Lord's Prayer deeply into the daily lives of men, lest they become lax and lukewarm.

In the distraction of worldly life the pastor keeps us in sight of eternal things. He guards and illuminates the sphere in which they speak and shine in ciphers. He sees to it that individuals remain at home in the sphere where such language is spoken.

The pastor must speak of these things so that they will be believable. He will succeed only if he himself is believable. Otherwise he cannot make the Bible heard in earnest.

Having heard it so, the faithful can also have contact with an opponent who is in earnest – the contact that is required to come under the encompassing sway of Transcendence.

The pastor's life and work should be steeped in tradition. He should feel linked with the individuals of his congregation in a fellowship of fate before the deity; he should not feel above them.

At the same time he must be ready to provide authority for the weak, to sustain them with a firm word, to 'requite' the gifts of each stage and manner of being human without losing the premise: the inner equality of all. And this puts him in a quandary.

It is an easy one to evade lovelessly, pleading honesty – that is to say, to presume complete freedom in one who cannot be free as yet, to force freedom on the man who wants a guiding hand. It is easier still to presume to authority, to grant peace of mind by assurances of which no man is really capable, and to demand obedience.

It is hard to see the size of the task and to pursue it nonetheless, neither shutting your eyes to it and lapsing into frivolity nor letting yourself be crushed by the demands. But there is no other way to keep the ministry from becoming dishonesty, the preaching from turning to play-acting, the work from becoming a fraud.

It is hard to have to admit your constant inadequacy. The ministry requires its practitioner to cope with this situation.

What it takes may dishearten him. He can gain confidence only to the extent to which he feels on the way of cleansing himself of self-will, subordinating material concerns to inviolable conditions, being ready to sacrifice, leaving behind all aestheticism and all vanity. The Protestant minister has no impersonal *character indelebilis*. What counts is he, not his office. What weight he carries lies in his personal veracity, in his ethos, in the strength of his faith.

v. Minister and Church

The Church is the mundane organization in which the faithful as ociate, aided by their pastor. This association maintains the basic state of faith. A failure of the Church throws the individual back upon himself and his neighbour, to live solely in philosophical faith – which must as such remain without the organization employed by great human communities to consolidate themselves. In philosophical faith, the individual can find himself only in the socially unorganized tradition of the great philosophers.

Men can enter the adytum without ecclesiastic guide-rails, but the churches are, in a sense, its visibly open doors. If an individual enters without wanting to leave the world to which he owes his factual existence, he must not refuse to live today in the world as it is, in this world we were born into, and to whose infinite transformations we have access. His stand on the Church, however it may be, will then be a positive one in the Protestant sense of taking part in its transformation from an ever newly comprehended source.

One who dares enter the ministry because he believes in his vocation shows a purpose much to be desired in the common interest. He ignores our current public values. It depends on these ministers, not on the theologians, what will become of the Church. The schools of divinity impart knowledge, but they do not create faith; they are tools for pastoral use. The pastors alone set the trend of ecclesiastic reality; it is not a product of Church organization or dogmatic and historical knowledge.

Today it has been made easy for us to look down on churches and pastors, to size them up as one more profession that will protect its collective interests and draw good pay for fostering a conventional, theologized Christianity – a profession as respectable as any other, though with the enormous, both depressing and inspiring claim of not having to do, like the others, with finite ends. It is easy to dismiss the churches without having anything else to offer, to think that the human world in its worldliness might be left to its own devices and that man's relation to Transcendence, with the ethos founded on this origin, would come by itself.

Since the churches do have this great task, however, a total failure on their part makes them rather dangerous. Then it might be better if they vanished, as Kierkegaard said at the end. What they are now keeping up may be only a huge deception, worse then being face to face with nothingness. The sight of nothingness might give rise to reflection, and this in turn to faith – which in the West would spring once more, wholly transformed, from the biblical soil.

These are abstract discussions, mere circumscriptions of the tasks that men will find and can take up today if they seriously enter the ministry. Such discussions can induce reflection, but they cannot tell us what ought to be done.

4 CREEDS AND BIBLICAL RELIGION

'Christianity' is a historical concept, not a confessional one. As a reality it is unclearly defined, comprising a great diversity of embattled, mutually exclusive creeds that have poured astounding energies into the establishment of their 'doctrines of differentiation'.

I prefer to speak of the 'biblical religion', or the 'biblical faith'. Against this term it has been argued that there is no biblical faith, that people can only be of the Jewish, Catholic, Protestant, Lutheran, Calvinist, Anglican, or Islamic faith. I take the contrary view expressed by Cusanus: *Una religio in rituum varietate.* The historic guise of the creeds has power and meaning for those who were born in them; it is not without significance for their historicity; but neither is it the form in which to acknowledge the absolute truth they claim. What matters is the 'invisible Church'. The weight, the truth, the worth of the visible churches depends on their share in the invisible one which no man can claim exclusively for himself alone.

Though the denominations are the diverse historic forms of the biblical faith, the identity of its one living content remains undefinable. It cannot be reduced to one denominator. A believer in God feels the weight of transcendent Being so heavily he can dare say, 'God alone matters.' But this faith speaks in the infinite abundance of ciphers throughout the Bible. The creeds are more than creeds; potentially, each of them is the whole biblical faith. Although historically it seems indispensable, the biblical faith in each creed – even in the Catholic one – will shatter it at the same time. Genuine believers hold hands across all creeds.

The Protestant principle of liberation in the biblical faith has not been realized. It has been covered up, rather, by the establishment of many new 'Catholicisms' featuring ecclesiastic claims, dogmas, liturgies, and titles. The true, historically effective upsurge of Protestantism lay in its unconditionally serious way of living in the faith, as in the Calvinist 'asceticism in the world', for instance, and this has been – although it need not be – linked with a fanatical dogmatism.

From a historical point of view I can conceive all the concrete 'Christianities' as phenomena within the undefinable comprehensive Christianity that cannot be construed as a whole, an ideal type. Adopted in suspense, these historically specific forms can serve my orientation.

The Protestant principle includes: participation in the biblical religion in its historic denominational guises; incessant return to the source; a communicative union of believers across all creeds; a liberal view of the historic guises; the living struggle in the cipher language; probation in practical life.

d. Can the Two Faiths Meet?

Unless there can be communication between the two origins of faith, theology and philosophy will remain separate and mutually exclusive.

The original Greek unity of religion and philosophy did not end when individual thinkers began to live by the fount they had caused to flow. It was only in the West, and not until about the thirteenth century, that the unity was unintentionally but decisively broken – on the one hand by the ecclesiastic claims of the right to control thought itself, and on the other by the powerful and truthful Existenz of individuals prepared to answer for themselves. Our goal today cannot be reunification, nor can it be an authoritarian direction by one side, or by a power superior to both. All that we might aim at is to regain the once unquestioned unity as a conscious unity of disparates, of communicating poles that keep not only attracting but rejecting each other.

1 THE DIVISIONS

Let us recall what divides the faith in revelation from philosophical faith.

The two are divided by the origin to which they trace themselves – either to revelation, or to the gift of individual selfhood in the medium of reason, a gift illuminated by participation in the philosophical tradition.

They are divided by the manner of worship. On one side it takes the form of a common liturgy, implying the sacramentally envisioned certainty of salvation; on the other side it takes the form of philosophical reflection.

They are divided by the sense in which they speak of Transcendence. This, to the believer in revelation, is the Other that comes from without and is guaranteed by its mundane embodiment in holy churches, objects, acts, persons, and canonical writings. The philosophical believer knows no general, objective certainty in the world; he must depend on his inmost inwardness for Transcendence to be – or not to be – felt as a reality.

2 CONJURING IN CIPHERS AND HOMILETIC PROCLAMATION

Preaching in church and conjuring Transcendence in philosophy refer to the same thing. The difference is that conjuration is a free, critical movement in ciphers, while a sermon is bound to proclaim the revelation. The authority for the first springs solely from the personal responsibility of an individual who can be himself; the authority for the second is granted by the Church and conferred along with ecclesiastic office.

The philosophical believer cannot preach – he has nothing to proclaim. He is properly barred from the pulpit. One must be ordained to have the right to preach in church.

For the controversy between theology and philosophy to disappear, the things proclaimed in church would have to shed their character of revealed realities, dogmas, and creeds – in other words, their proclamation would have to become a conjuration of ciphers. Today such a metamorphosis appears utopian in all churches, and perhaps it would indeed cancel what no church can be without: the historic authority itself as an element of faith. The question is whether the cipher language might not intensify rather than weaken the seriousness of Existenz, whether the bolstering force of authority could not as well be maintained by a historic cipher as by a claim of general validity for all men. It would be up to the free individual, then, how to experience historic authority and sermon when the rationally undefinable unity of authority and suspense is realized in the minister's Existenz.

Will the churches accomplish this transformation from within? It may be their only way to ally themselves with the hidden forces of truth in the modern masses. The stern language of reality, the strength of love, and the guidance of reason would help them to rouse the practical seriousness that might move the world in view of its present peril. They would liberate the individual Existenz, whose faith can 'move mountains'. They would not permit the world to fall asleep, but would let the truth spur freedom to realize justice and peace.

Today, outside the churches, this seriousness is found only in the personal freedom of the individual. However potent for him, it is doomed to ineffectiveness in the great community of all. Its appearance in the world goes with the wind; philosophical faith does not yet emerge as a visible, strong, public phenomenon. It stays hidden away, thus far, in personal communication.

A determining factor in the course of events is still how the forces of faith are shaped by the churches and by their dogmatics. If these fail – as they may now seem to be doing – the world will plunge into scientific super-stition, and thus into general unbelief and unfreedom. Philosophy should do its level best to bring reason into the religious thinking of the churches, so that it may become believable for the informed masses – so every individual may find his human self in accord with that thinking, and may draw on it for the impulses to his decisions and his way of life.

Why worry about philosophical conjuration and theological procla-mation? Because the ciphers may speak to us but may keep silent as well, leaving us to a horror of the void without and within us. Because some ciphers may grow overpowering, obscuring all others. Above all, because only the cipher struggle shows the depths where Existenz relates to Transcendence, and where we can find the guidance for our life.

3 THE DIFFERENT SENSE OF FREEDOM AND AUTHORITY

I start with an extreme interpretation. All existence and each Existenz is hazardous; are the hazards greater, perhaps, on the way of philosophizing than on the way of faith in revelation? Yes, replies Dostoevsky's Grand Inquisitor, for men cannot be free. Jesus, who once brought freedom, reappears and is arrested by the Inquisitor who argues that men, these poor, self-destructive victims of passion and licence, cannot help themselves. Men need leading strings. To subject them to total rule, to liberate them from their freedom, from responsibility, from doubt, from thought, is the only possible way to bring them happiness.

There is a general point to this principle of subjection as a premise of human happiness. Whether the dogmatic form has been assumed by faith in revelation or by an ideology such as Marxism makes no difference, from this point of view; Marx also would be arrested if he appeared today in Russia or China. The point is that only the slaves must believe in the truth, not the masters. The self-denying masters rule in the name of God or of necessity, natural or historic.

Wherever this kind of rule should really aim at universal happiness – except for the knowing rulers, who must do without faith and happiness – it would inevitably fall far short of its goal. The supposition that such rule is necessary for human nature tacitly entitles tyrants to rule for themselves. But under such rule there can be no human happiness, nor any lasting order of existence, nor any free step of faith along man's way.

The decisive rebuttal to the Grand Inquisitor's theory is the fact that the rulers themselves are always human, members of the very species that is supposed to need slavery because it cannot be free.

The demand that a rule in the world be obeyed as the rule of God, or of history, is not made by God or by history. It is made by men. As rulers, these men need not believe either in God or in history, or they may forget their belief in practice. They will judge any reality by its usefulness for the acquisition, expansion, and consolidation of their power, or by the dangers it may present to their power. They will couch the applications or their judgment in terms of a party line or an infallible ecclesiastic decision. Many, in fact, believe in the total authority they cite as having been conferred upon them, a belief enhanced by the assurance of belonging to the powers that be, or will be. The enormous growth of the Church once Constantine had made Christianity the state religion is as characteristic as the fact that almost all men turn into Communists – in Germany, into Nazis – at the moment of totalitarian victory. The demands of an exclusive faith that is assured of power make a horrifying set of facts; at certain times in history they will sweep folly, cowardice, injustice, and licence into a riptide that inundates everything. Despair at self-inflicted intellectual and political anarchy causes the plunge into blind, total obedience, which is the mortal enemy of man. Along with the totalitarian order – if it succeeds, and the technology of our time makes its success seem possible – that obedience kills the chances of freedom, truth, and justice.

In fact, whatever we do depends on what we expect of men – and that means of ourselves. He who despairs of man despairs of himself. To despise mankind is to despise oneself.

If we do not fall into such despair and contempt, we live by what the Greeks called the deceptive gift from Pandora's box: by hope.

Hope will not deceive us only if we test it by insight into realities, if it conceals nothing, if it permits no utopianism. Only broad consciousness lets us be clear in our minds about where we stand, what we want to live and work and die for. The true hope shows in our way of life, in the choices we make in concrete situations.

Furthermore, hope will not deceive us only if we do not mistake it for certainty, not even for probability – if we dare live by it, rather, because such a life can be worthy of us and can have a transcendent foundation.

The greatest hope in historico-political conduct and thought is that man might be free.

For the thought of freedom to give rise to hope, however, we must know and clearly keep in mind that freedom can mean many things. We must always recognize the misconceptions of freedom. We must realize the interdependence of freedom and authority.

What role does the faith in revelation play in freedom? Is the claim of mundane authority – and thus, in fact, of power, coercion, and violence – an integral part of that faith? It certainly is not, even though force has undoubtedly been often used in behalf of the faith in revelation. In times when political power degenerated into either anarchy or despotism, when no way out was in sight, the relatively best method to give the spirit its due may have been the attempt to regulate the use of political force on a basis of faith in the revelations of the Bible – for through this Holy Scripture even the organization of religious violence remained imbued with contents that would spawn freedom, time and time again. If such contents are lacking, as in the writings of Marx and Engels, the sense of obedience to faith will be misinterpreted as obedience to science; terrorism, and then the organized coercion that works under the threat of terrorism, will rest on scientific superstition rather than on the beliefs of men who feel the transcendent origin of their freedom and thus can be really free.

There is no need to reject faith in revelation because its exponents have long used it as a tool of political power, and are in part still using it so today. That faith as such is non-political. It includes the chance of human freedom.

There does remain a very different distinction between faith in revelation and philosophical faith, and that lies in their ways of hope. Hope on the ground of revealed promises, for instance, or of the reality of Christ as revealed in the Resurrection, differs radically from hope on the ground of the truth shown by philosophical reason.

4 IS MUTUAL REJECTION AN INHERENT NECESSITY?

i. The proper level of the question
'No one who is religious comes to philosophy,' Schopenhauer wrote; 'he does not need it. No one who really philosophizes is religious; he walks without leading strings, dangerously, but in freedom.' He also called religion 'metaphysics for the people'. Conversely, we hear from Protestant theologians that philosophy is not to be taken seriously, that it is superfluous and really a nuisance. In such positions the opponent is despised. They are extremes of mutual rejection.

Then there is the ambiguous line, 'If I believed, I would not be philosophizing.' Does that mean it were better if I could believe? Or does it mean it is a good thing I am philosophizing instead of lapsing into faith, which is unphilosophical by nature? Or is it just to be an outside observation to the effect that faith and philosophy do not mix? In no sense can I make that line my own.

Escape routes are frequently found, weakening both revelation and reason. One may comply with all ecclesiastic ordinances, take part in sacraments, and still reserve one's philosophical freedom in a tacit scepticism that ties everything into everything else. But in this manner one may well fool oneself too – a believer in revelation, about having maintained the freedom he keeps, and a supposedly free philosopher, about the strings that lead him.

The matter is too serious for this entire level of rejecting each other in coexistence and uniting without taking a stand. The stark, ill-starred alternative conceived in philosophical or theological fanaticism is no more unconvincing than are the conciliatory compromises of sceptics or friendly enemies.

We repeat our questions:

If revelation is true for a believer, if it really exists for him, is he at all capable of acknowledging another truth of equal rank, meeting it on the same level? Is this not impossible to a man for whom God speaks?

And is the philosophical believer not bound to conclude that a divine revelation is impossible, and therefore to reject it in principle as illusory?

What are the common premises of mutual recognition? The fact that the bulk of mankind fails to follow him would have to bring the believer in revelation to the conclusion that what is absolute to him, as revealed by God himself, may not be binding on all men. He may preach his faith but must not expect others to accept it.

The philosophical believer, on the other hand, would have to admit that the faith he finds strange may be a truth derived from another source, even though he cannot understand it. If he loses the sense of its limitations, his thinking faculty will tend to drive him to the supposed insight that revelation is absolutely impossible because it is not possible for him. He must resist this temptation.

To both, there is something irresistible about their own premises. It takes the full critical energy of reason to see the limitations and to keep them firmly in mind while remaining unconditional.

ii. Self-doubt

One sign that this may be possible is the fact that contempt, on both sides, may turn into feelings of deficiency. How beautiful it would be to believe that God is present in the world and will help me concretely! But, says the man who philosophizes, I cannot believe that; I just have a kind of nostalgic longing for it. How beautiful it would be to have the philosopher's capacity for original thinking and thus to find peace in Transcendence! But, says the believer in revelation, I fail in this kind of thinking, and at certain limits I forbid it to myself, lest it disturb the faith I live by. Clearly, the individual human being can feel the possibility of both ways of faith in himself.

The experience of self-doubt is unknown only to the thoughtless 'enlighteners' and positivists, to those who live in the obtuse self-certainty of conventions, whether ecclesiastic or non-ecclesiastic.

Self-doubt assails the believer in revelation when the painful cogency of philosophizing will not let him really believe any more in the revealed concretions – not in the divine promises, not in God's incarnation, not in Christ's resurrection, not in the Church as the mystical body of Christ, not in the sacraments. His doubts are conquered by the real presence of God – felt and impressed upon him ever since he first awoke to consciousness – in divine service, in prayer, in the sacred ecclesiastic phenomena he meets each day. God himself seems to be conquering the doubts.

The philosophical believer is no less familiar with self-doubt. It is infinitely hard to live in uncertainty before a hidden Transcendence, to bear the assaults of defaulting selfhood, of failing love, of empty unbelief. What a deliverance it would be if God were to show himself then, to give me complete assurance and to take me by the hand! How magnetic are the attractions of embodiment in divine service, of sanctified life, of knowing that the universe, the landscape, my environment, and all human doings are permeated with a Church-confirmed holiness! Honesty compels me to step aside in awe, to renounce all this rather than to enjoy it aesthetically. But the spell is so strong, it can be recognized as doubt and conquered only by the absolute veracity that Transcendence commands.

The conquest of their doubts is what makes both sides recognize each other's faith, if they are honest.

If the believer in revelation has overcome his doubts by a clear view of the revelation that is real for him, if he has found peace of mind in its truth, the consequence will be a deep, wide-open humanity. For he will not expect of others, as an act of will, what he has received as a gift of divine grace. He will no longer charge them with wicked obduracy. He will no longer ask all men to believe the same. But if he conquered his doubts by doing violence to himself, by a dishonest will to believe, the result – no telling where or when – will be violence against others. The will to believe, the readiness for 'implicit faith' and blind obedience to a concrete 'Holy Church', is tantamount to violence. Thereafter, life becomes seclusion, and one who secludes himself is unwittingly coercing his inmost being. He does not want to keep thinking and asking questions; he has rolled an immovable, all but untouchable boulder into his path; the 'entirely Other' cuts off human communication. No man to whom it suffices to be open to God in his own sense, who will find therein his deepest satisfaction, can remain unconditionally open for human communication. The conquest of doubt seems to remove him from the hazard of Existenz among men.

If a philosophical believer has overcome his self-doubt by the presence of reason, the bond of all ways of encompassing, he will be affected rather than passively tolerant in leaning toward any real, serious believer in revelation. But if his doubts were conquered by a violent intellectual rationalism, the result will be intellectual violence in all things. Intolerant disdain in the guise of indifferent tolerance is inhuman; it is apathy toward human seriousness. It is the very untruthfulness that will submerge reason in the rationalistic intellect.

The crucial question for mutual communication remains whether or not there can be mutual recognition. When a believer in revelation meets someone who, in his sense, is an infidel – can he, even though pained by the other's graceless state, respect him and his way without reservations? When the philosophical believer meets a believer in revelation, can he, even though pained by his failure to find a companion on man's impervious way, show the same respect and be constantly ready to hear the other's experience and to join him in all human tasks in the world?

Can the two co-operate in existence without dishonesty or mental reservations?

Originally different ways of life, and of the faith that goes with them, are indeed mutually exclusive: they cannot be realized in the same human being. But they do not exclude each other if they meet in different human beings. Each Existenz is historic; each can be in earnest about loving the other; each can know that between him and the other runs an encompassing bond.

Index

Abelard, Peter 23f
Above-Being (definition) 166 273
Abraham 143 157
Achilles 218
Adam 2 162 192f 233 239f 308f
Aeschylus 123 217 305n
Ahriman 218
Albigenses 46 206
Ambrose, St 110
ananke 217
Anaximander 166 216
Anselm, St 9 23f 26f 55 154 156 160 162
 188 256
apeiron 166
Aphrodite 129
Apollo 129
Aquinas, St Thomas, and Thomism
 9 24–27 42 45 146 154 156 197f 245f
 259 302
Archimedes 184
Aristotle 23ff 75 110 143 147 155f 167
 188 197f 200f 257 273 298
Artemis 129
Astronauts 181 183
Athena 129
Augustine, St 5 9 23f 26ff 42 44 55 115
 122f 162 165ff 232f 258f 322 345

Baal 96
Bacon of Verulam, Francis 289
Barrabas 146
Barth, Heinrich 336
Barth, Karl 108ff 113 147 325–329
Bede, the Venerable 4
Berengarius of Tours 24
Beyond Being (definition) 273
Bhagavad Gita 261
Boehme, Jacob 119 158
Bonaventure, St 23
Brahma 215
Brahman 216f 275
Bruno, Giordano 43 46 176

Buddha, Buddhism 8 35 41 101 166
 215 241 165–268 279
Bultmann, Rudolf 287n 324

Caesar 207
Calderon de la Barca, Pedro 127 218
Calvin, John, and Calvinism 20 46
 232f 238 249 355f
causa sui 115
Charisma 207
Chavannes 215n
Cicero 86 182f
Clauberg 197
Cleon 207
coincidentia oppositorum 162f 259–262
complexio oppositorum 42
Confucius, Confucianism 17 41 123
 215
Constantine the Great 41 44 47 359
Cronus 305
Crusades 46 205
Curtius, Ludwig 278 320
Cusanus (Nicholas of Cusa) 9 26f 55
 162f 176 258ff 342 355

Daedalus 308
Damiani, St Petrus 153ff
Dante 67 72 123 127 183 254 302
Deborah, song of 343
decretum horribile 233 238 249
Democritus 303
De-mythologizing 287 327
Descartes, René, and Cartesianism 3
 157 287 289
Devil 149 209 211f 218f 239 244; Satan
 (Book of Job) 220 224 227; Mephisto-
 pheles (Goethe) 248 274
Dionysius Pseudo-Areopagite 245
Dionysius of Syracuse 289
Dionysus 129
docta ignorantia 162